Introduction to
Comparative
Politics

Political System
Performance in
Three Worlds

John D. Nagle

Introduction to
Comparative
Politics

Political System
Performance in
Three Worlds

Second Edition

Nelson-Hall
Chicago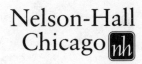

Project Editor: Dorothy Anderson
Designer: Claudia von Hendricks
Illustrator: Cynthia Schultz
Cover Designers: Claudia von Hendricks, Richard Meade
Typesetter: The Typesetters
Manufacturer: BookCrafters

Cover illustration: T.D. Burton, "Oriental Decision," watercolor, 7″ × 10″, 1981.

EXCERPT FROM Harry Magdoff and Paul M. Sweezy, "Notes on the Multinational Corporation," in K. T. Fann and Donald Hodges, eds., *Readings in U.S. Imperialism* (Boston: Porter Sargent, 1971), p. 109, and excerpt from Susanne Bodenheimer, "Dependency and Imperialism. The Roots of Latin American Underdevelopment," in K. T. Fann and Donald Hodges, eds., *Readings in U.S. Imperialism* (Boston: Porter Sargent, 1971), p. 163, reprinted by permission of the publisher.

LIBRARY OF CONGRESS CATALOGING-IN-PUBLICATION DATA

Nagle, John D. (John David)
    Introduction to comparative politics.

    Bibliography: p.
    Includes index.
    1. Comparative government.   I. Title.
JF51.N34   1989   320.3   88-19671
ISBN 0-8304-1194-1

Manufactured in the United States of America

10   9   8   7   6   5   4   3   2

Contents

Chapter 1

An Introduction to Comparative Politics Texts

COMPARATIVE POLITICS IS A BROAD FIELD, so any single text, no matter how well turned out, can only begin to elaborate an approach to the comparative study of political systems and illustrate that approach with a limited amount of detail, example, or data. This means that extra effort must be made to select those issues and areas that are most important in terms of a given view of comparative politics and to drop or sharply curtail coverage of perhaps interesting but substantively marginal or secondary information. It is this information-selection process that makes this text different from other introductory texts or readers in comparative politics. It is worth spending some time and space outlining these differences at the outset.

AN OVERVIEW OF COMPARATIVE POLITICS TEXTBOOKS

First, there are aspects of comparative politics with which this book does not deal but which other introductory texts spend much space outlining. Thirty years ago most comparative texts went into great detail about institutional, constitutional, and other configurational differences among the political systems considered most important (very often those of the United States, Britain, France, and the Soviet Union). While some texts still use this traditional approach, it began to come under criticism in the 1950s for focusing too much on the formal institutions of government and too little on the deviations from constitutional provisions, the roles of semipublic and private groupings (parties, unions, citizen coalitions, business and professional associations), and in general the variety of informal ways in which governments are run or influenced. A good introduction to foreign governments (a more appropriate title for the institutional approach) would quickly have to amend its description of structural differences among the governments covered to note that the real stuff of politics does not necessarily follow prescribed lines.

Probably the breaking point for the traditional approach to comparative politics came with the granting of independence to the former colonies of the Western powers. By the mid-1960s, comparative politics could no longer

1

ignore the politics of the Third World governments on the grounds that they were not formally sovereign states. Indeed, the great majority of governments are non-Western and noncommunist Third World regimes. It became quickly apparent that the formal institutional and constitutional arrangements left behind by the colonial powers were in most cases houses of cards easily blown down, most often by military juntas, less frequently (but more importantly) by popular revolutionary movements. Textbooks made attempts to describe the formal titles, offices, and organizational anatomy of some (noncommunist) Third World government, although by the time of publication that entire system might have been either completely overthrown and scrapped or drastically revamped. Moreover, even if the formal constitutional structures still remained standing, they usually were much further from the political reality than those that the Western powers had originally developed and attempted to transplant.

Another problem in treating the new African, Asian, and not-so-new Latin American governments in a traditional manner was that most of these systems were outright dictatorships, either military or military-backed. Back in the Cold War days, it was of course expected that a comparative text would describe the "totalitarian" and "dictatorial" nature of the USSR and other communist systems; these were the adversaries of Western democracy and could be described in very unflattering terms. On the other hand, many Third World dictatorships of the most dastardly variety (the Park regime in South Korea, the Suharto regime in Indonesia, the Pakistani military junta in the late 1960s, many South American dictatorships) have been the allies of the West in general and of the United States in particular in its struggle to contain communism. Most have received and continue to receive military and economic aid from the United States. To focus too directly on the obvious dictatorial nature of these systems would be both an insult to American allies and an embarrassment to American foreign policy. Was there not a more neutral, toned-down vocabulary that could be developed, one which would at once overcome the inadequacies of the constitutional/ institutional approach and avoid too-harsh judgments about these Third World systems?

SYSTEMS ANALYSIS AND FUNCTIONALISM

During the 1960s systems analysis and functional approaches began to overtake in academic popularity the traditional method of comparing political systems. The systems method views a political system as a sort of intermediate "black box" between political inputs, both supports and demands, and political outputs, policies, and programs. The system is recursive, which means that there is a continuous feedback loop from the effects of policy outputs in the political environment back to the set of supports for and demands on the system. The functionalist approach attempts to define a series of roles or functions that every political system must fulfill in order to maintain and perpetuate itself. Functions such as political socialization, recruitment, communication, rule making, rule enforcement, rule adjudication, interest aggregation, and interest articulation are presented in general terms, not tied to specific organizational or constitutional arrangements. Interest aggregation, for example, refers to the process of combining individual and small group interests into larger and larger coalitions of modified and wider interests. Interest aggregation could be performed by a government body, a parliament, a semipublic body, a political party, a private voluntary organization, a union, or a civic association. In nondemocratic systems interest aggregation could be perceived as being performed by a powerful dictator, the single legal party, or the military for the whole society.

The use of systems analysis or functionalism for comparative politics texts has several advantages. Both methods allow the observer of politics to focus on whatever groups or organizations seem to be *relevant* in fulfilling any given role or function. Activities of whatever type or source that strengthen the system's performance of interest aggregation are considered *eufunctional*. Those behaviors that weaken this vital role are seen as system *dysfunctional*. Thus, in comparing, for example, political rule-making roles in different nations, the researcher may be comparing an effective parliament in a Western liberal democracy, a party central committee in a communist system, and perhaps a military council in a Third World dictatorship.

Once the confines of the constitutional/institutional approach had been transcended, the observer of politics was somewhat freer to compare similar roles performed by very dissimilar groups. And the language of systems analysis and functionalism skirts some touchy problems of name calling in dealing with dictatorial regimes. As peaceful coexistence, later called detente, between the West and the Soviet Union developed in the 1960s and 1970s, this jargon was also extended to descriptions of communist systems, reflecting a change from the practices of Cold War scholarship. Systems analysis and especially functionalism can aid in the study of particular parts or subsystems of a polity, without the necessity of going into a description and analysis of the whole system.

Of course, after a while, criticism of these new approaches began to appear. While there were no institutional/constitutional confines to the study of political behavior, there were no clear guides, except the wisdom of the scholar, as to whether a group chosen for study was actually performing an imputed function adequately, insufficiently, or at all. How well is the American party system performing the function of interest articulation? What standards can be applied? Even if a given system collapses tomorrow, it is conceivable that some vital political functions were carried out admirably. Answers to these questions still remain either vague or trivial, partly because the main advantage of systems/functional analysis, its greater generality, allowing for broader applicability in the post-colonial world, has also been its greatest failing, namely, lack of specificity and standards. The very ease of forming functional comparisons across different systems without applying value-laden labels has led many to suspect that these new methods are incapable of getting down to the nitty-gritty of politics. The key questions, Who's in charge here? and What's the fuss all about? may be as distant from the clinical jargon of systems/functional approaches as they were from the constitutional/institutional tradition of comparative studies. Some critics have also claimed that both systems analysis and functionalism tend to stress roles that maintain the status quo while neglecting roles and behaviors pressing for radical or revolutionary change. While there is really little in the actual language or precepts of these approaches that would necessarily create a conservative bias, in actual practice this does seem to be the case, a situation that probably results from a biased selection of only certain potential uses from these approaches.

A second line of criticism has been directed against the dissection of political systems into partial roles/functions without evaluation of whole political systems. This criticism is certainly directed more against functionalism than against systems analysis, but since functionalism has probably been by far the more influential of the two, it is an important point to consider. What do we know of the real politics of any one country if we have read a study of its process of political socialization (perhaps compared with political socialization in one or more other countries)? Even if we have read articles on each political function deemed vital by functionalism, do we arrive at an integrated notion of the systems as an organic whole? Whereas traditional approaches often emphasized the "unique," sometimes "national" character of whole political systems (e.g., the deferential tolerance of British politics, the immobilism of French politics, the rugged individualism of American politics), systems/functional analysis has sometimes created an impression of interchangeable parts, resulting in what has amounted to a mechanical engineering guide to political systems. It is (probably) possible to mount a Honda engine in a Cadillac chassis fitted with a Dodge truck suspension and still get a motor vehicle (a motorized transport system) that runs. But is it possible to mount the British system of interest articulation and the Soviet system of political socialization into, say, the present Thai military dictatorship and still have any system at all? Clearly, some fewer combinations of subsystem types are compatible, while many many more would not even make good Edsels of the political realm. While some critics have called for a return to the traditional constitution/institutional methods, more have suggested that from among the many abstractly possible combinations of subsystems, comparativists develop integrated descriptions of those few patterns that empirically (actually) exist and are of substantive importance for understanding the workings of a number of national politics. These basic or *seminal* patterns could then be used to develop standards against which we could measure the performance of an individual country and still allow for some range of uniqueness with respect to particular segments or functions, which could be illustrated by individual countries within a given basic pattern.

WHOLE SYSTEM APPROACHES

Sweden, Britain, France, Japan, West Germany, and the United States would all be classified as liberal democracies having certain characteristics common to all systems of this basic pattern (see chapters 2-6), but with some very considerable differences in institutional structures, functional divisions of the political process, and policy inputs/outputs. In a limited biological analogy, liberal democracy might be seen as the general species, with the individual countries illustrating possible variants of subspecies still within the broader family. Attention is focused first on the development (evolution) of this general pattern of government. The description of various segments or aspects of national systems is thus placed under an individual integrated (umbrella) picture of the basic pattern as a whole.

The biological analogy is clearly limited, however, since in political life there does exist the possibility for basic change of patterns (through revolution or external conquest) as well as for continued within-pattern evolution.

One problem associated with this modified "whole system" or "seminal pattern" approach is the selection and definition of those few basic political system-types that we are able to recognize and that are important to an understanding of contemporary comparative politics. Feudal monarchy, for example, a quite distinctive and recognizable pattern predominant in Europe from the Middle Ages to the French Revolution, might not be considered important enough for inclusion (but cf. Gamer, 1976) since only a few nations (Saudi Arabia, Jordan, and perhaps Morocco) today fit this pattern, and in recent times monarchy (as in Iran and Ethiopia) often faces the choice of political "modernization" or revolutionary overthrow.

There is a consensus on liberal (or capitalist) democracy and communism as two seminal patterns of political development; these are systems-types whose basic features we can and will describe, that are quite distinctive, and that are fundamental to an understanding of modern comparative politics. Approximately twenty nation-states fall into each of these two basic patterns. Very commonly countries like France, Sweden, Britain, West Germany, the United States, and Japan are chosen to illustrate the variation within liberal democracy, while the Soviet Union, China, and Yugoslavia serve to highlight differences within modern communism. However, this recreates the problem of how to treat most of the Third World or developing nations. To be sure, some of the communist states like China, Vietnam, Cuba, and Angola are non-European and developing, nonindustrial societies, and yet their experience as communist systems is not illustrative of noncommunist Third World systems. A very few Third World countries (India, Venezuela) can be considered liberal democracies, though not as stable as their developed counterparts, but their experience as liberal democracies, while important in and of itself (especially in the case of India), is not representative of the great majority of Third World countries.

Some comparative texts using the whole system approach have simply decided to treat the liberal democratic and communist patterns, on the perhaps unwritten assumption that the Third World countries will over time settle into one or the other. It is clear that, despite detente and the Sino-Soviet split, there still exists a basic competition between liberal democracy and communism as model-types for other nations.

Other authors have included descriptions of a few selected Third World political systems, frequently Mexico, Nigeria, Tanzania, and India, either because these systems have been relatively stable for their region or because their population size seems to warrant their inclusion. Current academic etiquette probably dictates inclusion of some Third World systems as a necessary sign of respect, as a symbol of nonbias, and as an upgrading of the importance attached to the developing nations of Asia, Africa, and Latin America.

In this text, description of the political systems of the Third World is organized along the lines of the factors that appear to be dominant in Third World politics and basic to a realistic understanding of those politics: imperialism and dependency. This is hardly a novel approach for Marxists or radicals, but for some reason no one of this persuasion has yet seen his or her way clear to writing an introductory comparative politics text. Conversely, those of a conservative and liberal persuasion (and even some Marxists) have avoided this approach or have sidestepped the basic imperialist/dependency theme by treating it as stemming from pure propaganda, regrettable misunderstandings, or psychic frustration. Without going into detail here (see chapter 12), the persistence of imperialist/dependency relationships between the developed West (beyond the end of colonialism) and the nations of the Third World provides the common denominator among systems of the noncommunist developing world.

A description of imperialism and dependency supplies a general set of relationships, processes, and structures that helps to comprehend the political systems of the Third World. This general pattern is analogous to earlier descriptions of liberal democracy and communism as basic system-types. Within this general pattern examples can be drawn upon to illustrate the possible variations. Imperialism is the analytic link that allows for the comparison of regimes as organizationally/constitutionally different as the military junta in Thailand, the one-party KANU system in Kenya, the former dictatorship of Marcos in the Philippines, the multiparty democracy of Colombia, and the one-party dominant PRI system in Mexico. Dependency theory gives valuable insights into other features of many Third World governments: the inability of the government to promote the social welfare of the populace; the general instability of governmental structures, especially democratic structures; and the rise of revolutionary socialist movements as part of the anti-imperialist response. Additionally, information on the nature of both capitalist democracy and modern communism (especially in regard to foreign policy) is placed in a global perspective by the theory of imperialism applied to the Third World.

The choice of imperialism and dependency as a basis for discussing political development in the Third World departs from the conventional descriptions of political systems as internal mechanisms related only in terms of foreign policy toward other nations (except for extreme situations like invasion or annexation). Yet it is every day in every way more apparent that we live in an interdependent world. Although in theory every country is sovereign, and thus free to constitute its government and make policy as an internal matter, we know also that even the most powerful nations, the United States and the Soviet Union, are not free from external restraints, even beyond those that they exert on each other. We know, for example, the immediate impact on the industrial, wealthy nations caused by the OPEC oil boycott in 1973; we know the effect that worldwide publicity has on treatment of leading Soviet dissidents. No nation lives in a vacuum. Therefore it should not be surprising that extraterritorial forces exert a greater, even dominant, role in the political life of the Third World nations, which are economically, socially, and militarily more vulnerable than either the developed capitalist or communist states. The more debatable issue is whether this pattern of dominance/dependence characterizes generally and fundamentally the relations between the industrial West and the nonindustrial Third World. Not as debatable is the utility of the theory of imperialism in (1) bringing coherence and meaning to what are often pictured as random or chaotic political developments, (2) setting up standards for evaluation of political behavior, and (3) setting up broad predictions of future developments which the observer of politics can measure agains real world developments.

A Policy-Outputs Emphasis

The question remains as to just what substantive material should be presented for our three basic patterns of liberal democracy, communism, and imperialism/Third World. Since the early 1970s another trend in comparative studies has been the proliferation of comparative policy analyses or comparative politics with an emphasis on actual distribution of goods and services in different societies.

In the past these comparative policy studies were fueled by the thought that many of the advanced industrial nations, both communist and capitalist, faced relatively similar problems in ecology, energy, mass transit, and welfare, and that one might learn from cross-national studies of programs designed for meeting relatively similar goals. Some of these policy comparisons included only advanced capitalist democracies, but more recently comparisons drawing on data from communist states as well have been published. The bulk of these policy comparisons are limited to one policy area; for example, pollution, income distribution, or educational opportunity, although a few cover several areas and attempt to develop some generalizations about the policy-making process. Few include policy cases from the Third World, except occasionally with respect to income and land distribution policies.

The focus on political outputs, in the actual distribution of income, wealth, land, education, elite recruitment, health care, housing, and even criminal justice, a still young development in comparative politics, stems also from a feeling by some that neither formal institutions/constitutions nor political functions/roles were telling much about what politics meant in the daily life of the citizen.

Understanding the American federal Constitution and the functions of its three branches, the party system, and the free press, and so forth, still does not tell us that in fact before 1965 most Southern blacks were disfranchised by violence and terrorist threats, or that they could not sit at a Woolworth's lunch counter where whites were being served. But this factual knowledge is the bottom line of the political order, the set of political outcomes that affects the material and spiritual welfare of the citizen.

France and Sweden are liberal democracies, yet income distribution favors the wealthy far more in France. Both the Soviet Union and China are communist systems, yet only the Soviet Union has a serious social problem with alcoholism. Even within system-types these are important variations.

The presentation of each seminal pattern of political system dealt with in this text attempts to give as much attention as possible to the social reality of each system for the various groups or classes of citizens. Students of comparative politics usually come away from an introductory course with an abstract view of political systems divorced from the most basic outputs that they produce, maintain, and defend. To be sure, leadership struggles, who won and who lost and why, are often highlighted, and a few spectacular or crisis events are covered. But the victory of Kennedy in 1960, or Willy Brandt in 1969 in West Germany, or Leonid Brezhnev in 1964 in the Soviet Union, while important in terms of personal conflict at the top levels of the political elite, in themselves tell us little of the substance of American, West German, or Soviet politics. Likewise a great scandal like Watergate (or the German *Spiegel* affair, the Lockheed bribery scandal in Japan, the Solzhenitsyn deportation by the USSR), an attention-grabber because of the high human drama and symbolic morality issues involved, at most affect directly the careers of a hundred people, fewer than are tried for murder in any recent year in Detroit. The difference, of course, is that political history is routinely written about the events and crises of the famous and powerful, not about the rise and fall of the average citizen.

Given the above considerations and arguments, we have chosen to focus this text on the impact of the political system on the average citizen. This means that we will concentrate on items that affect the daily lives of the great majority of people, and not on the exciting scandals, political intrigues, campaigns for office, or heroes and villains of our time. For purposes of coherent organization, there are three main sections, dealing with the liberal democracies, the communist systems, and the Third World nations, in that order. Keep in mind the questions, "What difference does it make to live in a liberal democracy (communist system, Third World system)? What practical impact does the political system make on the life of the individual?"

Within each main section there are five chapters. The first chapter in each case gives a historical and theoretical overview of each system-type. This is a clear and necessary concession to the need for some background on the history, structures, institutions, and great events that have helped shape each system-type. The succeeding chapters of each main section then turn to a comparative presentation of system performance in four areas: (1) economic development; (2) social equality; (3) personal liberty; and (4) quality of life.

Economic development includes industrialization and urbanization, per capita gross domestic product levels, indices on standards of living, education, housing, health, and welfare programs. Although the necessity and even the desirability of continued high growth rates has been increasingly questioned in the West recently, economic development is certainly a key area of system performance, for without development, even the most free, unpolluted, and egalitarian society confines its people to a hard and immobile life. There is little questioning of the desirability of growth among the poor nations of the world.

Social equality concerns the distribution of income and wealth, social inequalities of class and minorities in education, elite recruitment, and justice. Special attention is given the sex inequalities and the record of each system-type in dealing with these inequalities. Equality in its many forms, equality of both opportunity and result, has become a political rallying point with particular strength in the postwar years, and it is now clear that social equity, as well as economic development, is a very important field of system performance. Even systems with good records of overall economic growth that fail to provide for social justice (not complete equality, but some public-ly acceptable level of inequality) may find themselves skating on thin ice.

Personal liberty is the third field of political system performance to be evaluated. Freedom of speech and freedom of the press, the right to vote in free and competitive elections, freedom of religion and freedom to travel, the right to organize into unions and other political groups, and the right to a fair trial are all included under this heading. Personal freedom, as has often been pointed out, does not feed or clothe a people, and it may not contribute to social equality either, but it is still a valued goal of millions in both the rich and poor nations of the world.

We have titled the fourth area of system performance the quality of life. Here we measure criminal behavior, problems of family breakup, drug addiction and alcoholism, environmental pollution, unemployment or job-lessness, and signs of social alienation. How free we are, and how free to enjoy material prosperity, can be severely limited by violent street crime and professional crime, air and water pollution, family problems, joblessness (even with generous unemployment compensation), loneliness, and social isolation. Ironically, quality of life items are usually measured negatively by the extent of social distress, rather than by any positive measures of personal security and safety, marital or familial bliss, environmental enjoyability, career satisfaction, or community spirit. Perhaps we take quality of life seriously as an area of system performance when crime, pollution, or alco-holism seem to threaten, often in ways not easily measured, the enjoyment of other values. Perhaps many quality-of-life items are taken for granted other-wise, so that we first notice their importance, their value to us, when we are deprived of them. In any case, we do not mean to suggest that quality of life should be measured by negative behavior indicators, just that most available statistics, especially for cross-national purposes, have focused on negative aspects in this field.

BASIC POINTS

As the following chapters present material on the performance of each political system-type in each area, keep in mind the following (arguable) propositions, which are the most important "lessons" of this text:

1. Each system-type has its own special pattern (syndrome) of perfor-mance in the economic growth, social equality, personal liberty, and quality of life areas. While there is considerable variation within each system-type (as will also be noted), the most basic differences in performance "mix" are those that exist between system-types.

2. No political system-type is able to maximize all performance areas at the same time. Each has its own special strengths and weaknesses that are inherent in the system-type. Performance failures in certain areas are not

regarded here as mistakes in policy or abuses by particular governmental leaders, but as part of an overall "package deal" of the entire system.

3. As a corollary to the above, contradictions exist within each system-type, which create basic performance successes and failings. Trade-offs among performance priorities must realistically be expected of any political system. The normal patterns of system trade-off or contradiction may be taken as a definition of the system itself. Development within a system-type will mean higher levels of performance in certain areas, but also will mean the heightening of contradictions seen in other areas.

4. Political system-types are not equal in overall balance of performance successes and deficiencies. It matters to people whether they live in a Western democracy, a communist system, or a Third World system. A (durable) change in the type of political system for a particular society is a momentous social decision, which will affect (both positively and negatively) the daily life and future hopes of its people.

The four performance areas discussed above cover a tremendous amount of ground, and a textbook can only introduce students to the basic features of system performance and basic comparisons. That is the main purpose of this text—to deal with basics of political system outputs as they affect average people. Tables of data can be both boring and impersonal if they stand alone. We can look at a chart that shows annual per capita income for India as $248 in 1983, and we know that this is low compared with that for the United States or the Soviet Union. But what does $248 per capita income really mean in real life? We hope the photographs that have been included will be worth many words (and many tables of data) in breathing some life into these numbers. Students should not pass over the photographs lightly, but should study them in some detail. These photos give some insight into the daily lives of people in different countries—their work, homes, family life, nutrition and health, schooling, and personal struggles for a better future. Of course, photographs, as well as statistics, can be deceptive and we have presented only a small selection of visual images. While the selection is too limited for any in-depth understanding of any nation, or system, or field of performance, what it can do is introduce American students to a daily life very different from anything they themselves have experienced or witnessed. This visual confrontation with a different reality can be a powerful and awakening experience, a motivating force for acquiring more information and deeper understanding. If this book achieves that much, it will be enough.

Chapter 2

Liberal Democracy—Theory and History

THIS CHAPTER OUTLINES THE TRANSITION FROM an agrarian feudalism to an industrializing capitalism in the societies of Western Europe and describes the relationship between economic and political elements of this transition.

DEMOCRATIC LIBERALISM AND CAPITALIST LIBERALISM

The emergence of liberal democracy as a new type of political system in Western Europe and North America (later in Japan) is inextricably bound up with the capitalist/industrial revolution and the passing of feudalism in those areas. It should not be surprising that theories of liberal democracy have borrowed heavily from the concepts of economic liberalism (classic capitalism).

The early theorists of liberal democracy (more likely to have been called republicanism) were proposing a radical, even revolutionary break with the political theory that described and supported the feudalist monarchies. Feudalism rested on rule by an aristocratic class (or estate) of titled landowners (barons, dukes, earls, counts, and such) capped by a royal family that provided the monarch (king or queen). The monarch was typically though not always assumed to rule by "divine right." In other words, God (always either Catholic or Protestant) had chosen this royal family and its heirs to rule over the nation, and the work of the monarchy was also the will of God. The royal family in turn supported (established) a state religion that was to be regarded as the only true religion of the land. Before the Reformation in the sixteenth century, this religion was Roman Catholicism throughout Western Europe. After the Reformation it became Anglicanism in England and Lutheranism in Prussia and Scandinavia. The state church, for its part, was almost without exception a staunch support for the monarchy, preaching obedience not only to the monarch but also to his or her helpers, the local lords of the manor. In feudal society each person was born into a station in life, a social caste (an estate), and there was little one could do to change that status. People were socialized from birth into accepting as divine fate their station in life. One could be a very good peasant, but to hope to be advanced

13

into the aristocracy or allowed to marry an aristocrat was insanity. On the other hand, even the most miserable lord would not be demoted to commoner or peasant.

The feudal system began to be challenged with the rise of a new class, which was an extension of the town burgher estate in the middle ages. This new class was the modern business or entrepreneurial middle class, which represented a new form of production, the factory system, and a new form of distribution, the free market system. As the economic power of this new bourgeoisie grew, new theories of government that reflected the changing social order also surfaced. One of the forerunners of these theories is the *Leviathon* by Thomas Hobbes. Hobbes wrote in the England of the seventeenth century, actually somewhat in advance of industrial capitalism, but in the midst of the challenge to the English monarchy posed by Oliver Cromwell and his New Model Army. Hobbes, perceiving that "divine right" doctrines were coming unstuck, attempted to justify the monarchy (and the absolute authority of the state) on other grounds, namely egoistic self-interest. Assuming that mankind is by nature egoistic but rational, Hobbes argued that people come together to found a civil society based not on the word of God but on a social contract that reflects their individual self-interest. To achieve their selfish ends, people agree (covenant) to give up certain natural rights (and retain others) in return for the state's (monarch's in Hobbes's day) assurance that all citizens will do the same, or be punished if they do not. The innovations in Hobbesian theory lie in the notions that: (1) the social order is a human, not a divine, construct; (2) that the egoistic self-interest of each adds up to the best social result; and (3) that one of the chief roles of the state is to guarantee the enforcement of contracts (covenants). Although Hobbes intended his *Leviathon* as a new rationale to support absolutist monarchy, his line of reasoning foreshadowed many features of later theorists of representative government. John Locke, for example, bases his call for republican government on the rational self-interest of the citizen; Locke's theory of the social contract is also a secular, or nonreligious, image, implying a separation of church and state and tolerance for religious pluralism. The secularization of politics, i.e., the removal of a state-supported religion, is one of the radical departures of liberal democratic thought from the feudal system.

Other early theorists of liberal democracy stressed in different ways the notion of competing interests as the foundation of political life and of a desirable social order. Montesquieu emphasized, for example, the separation of governmental powers into executive, legislative, and judicial branches. This checking and balancing of various branches of government has found much more favor in the American experience than in the European, but is not without its influence on continental parliamentary systems as well, particularly in the notion of an independent judiciary and nonpartisan civil service. Madison, in the *Federalist Papers,* asserts the need for a balanced contention of factions within society to avoid tyranny, one of the chief worries of the American founding fathers. No one faction of citizens should be permitted to gain a position from which it could subdue and suppress other factions. Competition of factional (special) interests in the political arena will balance out to the best result for the society as a whole. Let us note here that when Hobbes, Locke, Montesquieu, and Madison defend the social contract of the citizenry or the rights of the citizen to elect representatives to government, they took for granted that this citizenry would include only male property owners of some substance. *No one* among these early theorists of liberal democracy advocated or envisaged voting rights (the franchise) for the nonpropertied, for factory and farm workers, for women, and certainly not for slaves. The term "bourgeois democracy" describes rather precisely and objectively the limited extent of political participation intended by these proponents of early capitalist democracy; the bourgeoisie and its ideologists were fighting not for universal suffrage but for its own class rights. Only Jean Jacques Rousseau, among these early democratic theorists, stressed social equality as a presumption of the new proposed democratic system.

These early theories, then, with the exception of that of Rousseau, are in broad agreement with the economic theories of early capitalism, especially the Manchester School liberalism of writers like Adam Smith. Smith, in his classic *Wealth of Nations,* describes capitalist society as a competition of each against all, with egoistic self-interest the motivation for behavior. Through an "invisible hand" of the marketplace, however, the aggregation of individual self-interests ends up to be the optimal social outcome as well, Smith postulates. The laws of supply and (effective money) demand would assure production of those goods and services needed by the population, and competition among entrepreneurs would serve both to keep profit levels in bounds and to encourage new and more efficient production methods. In the governmental realm, Smith's main point was to call for limited government, one that could guarantee the sanctity of contracts and maintain law and order and a stable currency, but little else. As with Locke, Madison, and Montesquieu, one of the main goals of government as Smith saw it was the negative one of avoiding tyranny, especially the return to the absolute monarchy of feudalism. Certainly Smith did not want government messing around with the "invisible hand" of the marketplace. The affairs of the economy were best left to the judgment of entrepreneurs and consumers; two of the characteristics of liberal democracy in capitalist economies have historically been the basic separation of political rights and property rights, and the reluctance of government to infringe on the rights of property.

Once again, let us for the record make clear that while Adam Smith and others of his persuasion thought of capitalism as a progressive advance over feudalist production, the fruits of this progress were not destined for the working class. In fact, with the introduction of the factory assembly line under capitalism, Smith has the following rather pessimistic prediction for the modern industrial worker:

> THE understandings of the greater part of men are necessarily formed by their ordinary employments. The man whose whole life is spent in performing a few simple operations . . . has no occasion to exert his understanding. . . . He general-ly becomes as stupid and ignorant as it is possible for a human to become. . . . His dexterity at his own particular trade seems in this manner to be acquired at the expense of his intellectual, social and martial virtues. But in every improved and civilised society, this is the state into which the labouring poor, that is, the great body of the people, must necessarily fall. (Quoted in Tucker, 1972:287)

Of course, these are only some of the main points stressed by early democratic theorists. Over the course of the nineteenth and twentieth cen-turies, theories of liberal democracy have on the whole become remarkably more progressive, with more emphasis on equal opportunity for all citizens (in theory, at least) and social justice as well (Jeremy Bentham's "the greatest good for the greatest number" is a case in point). Only a few theorists, such as Friedrich von Hayek and Milton Friedman, still cling to the earlier, specifically capitalist goals of liberal democracy, and even then not *in toto*. Without tracing this development in any detail, let us turn now to the major events that have marked the historical emergence of liberal democratic po-litical systems.

THE ADVENT OF LIBERAL DEMOCRACY

It is difficult to pinpoint the first beginnings of liberal democracy. Some of the Italian and Greek city-states, and especially the merchant capitalist cen-ter of Venice, possessed many of the institutions and procedures that we associate with liberal democracy today. Iceland is considered by many ex-perts to have had the first and longest lived effective parliament. But the transformation of the British monarchy into a parliamentary democracy is surely one of the first and steadiest examples of the birth of liberal democra-cy. Britain was also the first nation to begin the industrialization process, and in Britain industrialization was more gradual and drawn out than in later industrializing countries. Most observers have related Britain's slow pace of capitalist development to its evolutionary political transformation. Characteristic of the British experience was the partial, step-by-step ad-vancement of the powers and rights of Parliament against the Crown. As early as 1265 the so-called Simons Parliament had assembled in revolt against King Henry III. In a series of confrontations, reforms, and sometimes rebellions (the Glorious Revolution of 1688), Parliament established its right to assemble on a regular basis and to control the administration of the king's government. Gradually Parliament and later the House of Commons (the lower chamber) within Parliament, supplanted the monarchy entirely as the basis for establishing a government. As the scope of powers of the House of Commons increased, so also did the electoral base from which it was elected and to whom the Members of Parliament (MPs) were responsible. The fact that this movement was gradual did not mean that it was always peaceful or that the privileged aristocracy or royal family gave way with grace and of their own volition.

The great Reform Act of 1832, which eliminated the practice of "rotten boroughs" (districts where seats in Parliament could literally be bought and sold) and established an expanded electorate of property owners who paid a certain uniform minimum level of property taxes, was passed by the Commons but was twice rejected by the House of Lords, until riots in the streets convinced the Lords to pass the bill on a third go-round. With the process of expanding suffrage to new social strata (the working class and finally women) came legal recognition of trade unions, the right to strike, and explicit protection of freedoms of speech, press, and assembly. Workers' political parties, despite some rough going initially, pushed their way into the party system.

We may forget that in the liberal democracies even today the struggle for the effective right to vote is not ancient history but either recent history or current politics. Women's suffrage in the United States, Germany, Sweden, and a number of other nations dates back only to the end of World War I. In Switzerland, one of the most stable and the most prosperous liberal democracy, women still cannot vote in certain cantons (states), although they can vote in national elections. In the United States, the de facto right to vote for southern black citizens began only with enforcements of the 1965 Voting Rights Act, which began to counter the violence and chicanery used to disfranchise black citizens in the South. Even now, residence and prior registration regulations in the United States serve to effectively *disenfranchise* millions of American citizens, and voter turnout in the United States compares poorly with levels of voting participation in most other Western democracies.

In other areas as well, there remains some unfinished business with regard to many of the liberties associated with liberal democratic theory. In West Germany, there is still religious instruction in the public schools, and parents in most areas must send their children to either the local Catholic or Protestant school; unless a citizen formally renounces his or her religion, a 10 percent tax surcharge is levied on his or her income tax by the government and given over to the church. Secularization of the political system, in other words, has not yet been completed in educational and tax affairs.

In France the government-owned television networks are notoriously progovernment in their news coverage, and though this lessened somewhat under former president Valery Giscard d'Estaing it was still far from the position of TV news coverage in most other liberal democracies. In West Germany, since an antiradical law (*Radikalenerlass*) took effect in 1972, there have been political firings or nonhirings of suspected or admitted radicals in the civil service, which includes all teachers and railway, postal, public transit, and public communications employees, as well as employees in all national, state, and local government offices. This virtual ban on practicing one's vocation (*Berufsverbot*) without having committed any crime whatsoever would be labelled a political purge if it took place in a communist country. The condition of liberal democracy still has room for improvement, even by its own standards.

STABLE DEVELOPMENT OF LIBERAL DEMOCRACY: SWEDEN

In some countries, this developmental process was relatively steady, and while not necessarily peaceful, was not reversed in any major aspect for any significant period of time. There were, in other words, no major retrogressions. Once unions were legally recognized, their legal status was not revoked. Once enfranchised, workers or women were not later denied the right to vote. Press freedoms, subject to serious infringement in both England and the United States at the start of the nineteenth century, were constantly broadened, and while there were some relapses (mostly in wartime), never was there any serious or successful attempt to establish a controlled press. In this group of nations, which includes Great Britain, the United States, Canada, Australia, New Zealand, the Netherlands, Belgium, Norway, Denmark, Switzerland, Iceland, and Ireland (since its independence in1922), stability of the democratic system has been highest. Even during periods of acute crisis (war, depression, acute political strife), the system has remained essentially intact. Belgium, the Netherlands, Norway, and Denmark did, of course, have fascist occupation regimes forced upon them after being conquered by Hitler's *Wehrmacht* in World War II. To be sure, during both world wars liberal democracies did impose more narrow limits on certain liberties, and some opponents of the war (Socialist leader Eugene V. Debs, for example) and some ethnic groups (e.g., the Japanese-Americans in World War II) were ill-treated and denied basic rights. And yet even these serious infringements, regrettable and probably unjustified and unnecessary even under duress of war, did not, in this group of democratic nations, threaten the basic evolution of the system.

One example of democratic development worth discussing at length is the Swedish system. In its broad outlines, the Swedish pattern of democratic development is certainly more typical of a successful system-transformation than that of the United States. Indeed, as will become clearer in the next chapters, the United States is an atypical case of political development, one that in many respects is unlikely and unsuited to serve as a model for emulation or export. In particular, the United States lacked the struggle of democratic forces with a feudal aristocracy, which was present in nearly all other cases of smooth (or nonsmooth) evolution of a modern democracy, and for which Sweden is a good illustration (see Giddens, 1973). While there are many similarities between the British and Swedish patterns, the Swedish example is presented for two reasons: first, its unfamiliarity to American students; and second, its multiparty system, which is a good point of comparison with the Anglo-American two-party systems, both because it is a stable multiparty system and because it has an array of parties that is typical of European democratic systems generally.

Like the British Parliament, the Swedish *Riksdag* has its roots in the early history of the Swedish monarchy. As Adams (1970) has noted, the kings of medieval Sweden were elected by a body called the *Riksmöte*, probably the first instance of national popular participation in an election. Acquisition of the throne by election instead of birthright clearly hindered the development of an absolutist monarchy. After 1371, the monarch was further limited by his oath of office and by a detailed feudal version of a policy platform (*Handfästing*), which the nobility exacted from the new king. Over the next two centuries, many kings were removed from office on grounds of breach of oath. The first *Riksdag* was convened in 1435, following a peasant uprising against the Danish monarchy, which then dominated Sweden as well as Norway and Finland (then the eastern province of Sweden). As Adams convincingly argues, the *Riksdag*, initially an emergency assembly convened by the Swedish Crown to deal with a particular crisis but kept in existence because of a plentiful supply of crises in the latter part of the sixteenth century, gradually became a regular fixture of the legal-political system, holding sessions every three years as required by a 1660 law. Four estates—the nobility, clergy, burghers, and peasantry—were represented in the *Riksdag*.

This should not give an impression of an inevitable or uncontested rise of the Swedish Parliament to dominance. Even in the most gradual and eventually most successful cases of parliament building, there were defeats and temporary setbacks. Nils Herlitz (1939) has outlined the major constitutional struggles between *Riksdag* and Crown since the assertion of an independent and unified Swedish nation-state under Gustav Vasa, elected King Gustav I by the *Riksdag* in 1523. At least twice the monarchy was able through various devices to reverse the progress toward a parliamentary system. In 1682 King Karl XI succeeded in uniting the clergy, burgher, and peasant estates behind him to impose an absolutist monarchy over the nobility. This was again overturned in 1719 after the death of Karl XII, when the *Riksdag* proclaimed an "Era of Liberty" and adopted a constitution limiting monarchial powers. As both Adams (1970) and Hancock (1972) agree, the initial experience with parliamentary ascendancy was not especially impressive. Two parliamentary groupings, the aristocratic and militarist Hats, said to have been in the pay of Louis XV of France, and the commoner-based and fiscally conservative Caps, said to have been bribed by the Russian tsar, were not really organized political parties but preparty foreign-policy factions, whose control of the *Riksdag* paved the way for the bloodless antiparliamentary coup (1772) by King Gustav III, which restored again the king's absolute right to veto legislation. Following the annexation of Finland by the Russian empire in 1808-1809, a formal constitution was adopted, confirming the division of the *Riksdag* into four estates. It was not until the 1860s that the *Riksdag* was restructured as a bicameral legislature (more in line with other European parliaments), with an upper house indirectly elected but with a limited franchise based on property qualifications. At this point (see Verney, 1957; Rustow, 1955) the overwhelming majority of the population (about 80 percent) were still not permitted to vote, and the system was still dominated by the king and land-owning nobility.

It took still another fifty years of keen struggle before the expansion of the franchise covered all adult males (1907-1909) and finally females as well (1919-1921). But by the early 1920s, the principles of parliamentary responsibility and parliamentary government had made their final breakthrough. Now the monarch was no longer the chief executive, but was forced to nominate as prime minister the leader of the majority (whether single-party or coalition) in the *Riksdag*. The cabinet under the prime minister now assumed in practice the daily control over the administration of government.

Hancock (1972:20-32) describes this period from 1870 to 1920 as one of fundamental economic, social, and party system development, which accompanied the ascendancy of liberal democracy. During this period the industrialization of the Swedish economy transformed the workforce from overwhelmingly agrarian to increasingly urban industrial. Those employed in agriculture declined from 72 percent of the economically acti population to 44 percent, while those engaged in industry and commerce rose from 20 to 50 percent. The system of isolated villages and farms producing food and handicrafts for immediate family consumption and local trade was giving way to commercial agriculture, factory production, and a money exchange economy. Modern rail transport and communications were especially important to Sweden in overcoming the isolating effects of terrain and climate to facilitate the growth of national export markets, although it also led to the appearance of cyclical economic crises associated with capitalist development. This in turn led to growing worker-owner conflict and to emigration, mainly to North America, for over a million Swedes during the nineteenth century. This period produced advances in a national education system and the spread of literacy skills to all classes; the growth of trade unionism (the feudal guild system had been abolished in 1842) as the mainstay of the new Socialist movement, the partial emancipation of women in the areas of education and of property holding and divorce rights; and the proliferation of new religious, temperance, student, and consumer cooperative groups associated with the new social order. As the old economic and social order declined, new political parties representing the working and business classes began to challenge the political order, which was still dominated by the aristocracy and challenged until then only by farmer interest groups. Brogan and Verney (1968: 50) describe the Swedish party system that developed in this period as quite appropriate to its traditions:

> BROADLY speaking, the four main social groups in Sweden—wage earners, salaried employees, farmers, and businessmen—are represented in the legislature by the four main parties—the Social Democrats, Liberals, Center (formerly the Agrarians), and Conservatives. . . . It is doubtless no accident that a people accustomed for centuries to being divided into four estates of the realm should after a generation or two of social and political transition (1865-1905) find a need for four political parties, each tending to depend on the support of one of the main social groups into which twentieth-century Sweden is divided. The age of individualism and of liberalism was short-lived. Sweden passed very quickly from a condition of semifeudalism to one of semisocialism.

The Swedish system of proportional representation, whereby a party's number of seats in the *Riksdag* (since 1971 a unicameral parliament) is determined by its percentage of the popular vote, has probably contributed to the maintenance, if not to the original appearance, of the multiparty system.

Only the party of the industrial working class, the Social Democrats, represented a clearly novel addition to the traditional estate system. The Communist party broke away from the Social Democrats in 1917, the year of the Bolshevik revolution, to form a second workers' party, but has remained a minor fixture of the party system (though of occasional importance both as support and competition on the left for the Social Democrats). The Social Democrats, on the other hand, have remained the largest single party since 1914, and governed, either alone or in coalition with another party, from 1933 until 1976, with only one short break of three months in 1936. Just when it seemed to some observers that Sweden, alone among the liberal democracies, was developing into "something of a one-party system on a national scale" (Adams, 1970:157) after forty-three years of social Democratic-led government, the three-party coalition of Liberals, Conservatives, and Agrarians finally succeeded in getting together (there are real differences of both interests and philosophy among them) and securing a narrow majority in the 1976 *Riksdag* elections. The Swedish case is sure evidence that neither a multiparty system nor proportional representation by themselves lead to political instability, any more than two-party systems or majority district electoral mechanisms produce political stability.

It should be emphasized that despite the existence since the 1920s of five parties, the popular conception of the Swedish party system has developed over the years into one of loose bipolarity, with the three bourgeois parties (Conservative, Liberal, and Agrarians) pitted against the workers' parties. "Bourgeois bloc" and "workers' bloc" characterize other multiparty systems in a useful manner as well and undercut some of the seeming differences between two-party and multiparty conceptual models. In fact, given the continued existence in Parliament of the British Liberals (getting 10 to 15 percent of the vote but only a handful of seats) and the German FDP (Liberals) in the *Bundestag* (5 to 10 percent of the vote and seats), only the United States among the liberal democracies has evolved a strict two-party system. In this sense the United States' experience is atypical within the general pattern.

A key element in the successful evolution and stability of the Swedish liberal democracy was the behavior of major parties and social classes at vital junctures of the political transformation in the late feudal or postfeudal period (see Giddens, 1973). On the one hand was the willingness of conservative elements of the old aristocracy and later of the industrialist class to give way and even to lend support and legitimation to basic sociopolitical reforms and not to resort to violence or abandon the parliament as the locus of struggle. Thus the Conservative party, unlike its namesake in Germany, supported the extension of the franchise in 1907-1909 and the establishment of parliamentary government in 1919-1921. Conservatives have learned to live with the extensive welfare state programs introduced over the years by Social Democratic governments and now would claim only to desire to administer such programs less bureaucratically, more efficiently, and perhaps with lower costs. At the same time, this tolerance on the right was in part facilitated by the reformist rather than revolutionary/radical approach of the working class unions and party organizations. From the early leadership of Branding through Hansson and Erlander to Palme, the Social Democratic leadership has committed itself to gradual change through strictly parliamentary means, concentrating on partial reforms within the capitalist economy rather than the radical transformation to a planned socialist economy. One exception to this general rule occurred in the Socialist pressure for change throughout Europe at the end of World War II. The Swedish Social Democrats put forward a twenty-seven-point program critical of capitalism and aiming at transformation of at least certain aspects of it but without denying basic rights of private ownership. Even this more radical proposal was dropped in 1948 after a heated campaign against it by the three bourgeois parties.

The break with Marxist theory occurred even earlier in Sweden than in socialist movements in France, Germany, or Italy and enabled the party to both expand its electoral appeal to members of the white-collar middle class and to form coalitions at times with the Liberal and Agrarian parties.

INTERRUPTED DEMOCRATIC DEVELOPMENT: GERMANY

Another group of contemporary liberal democracies has experienced a far more checkered pattern of development, marked by major upheavals and reversals. In France, Germany, Italy, and Japan (as well as in Greece, Spain, Portugal, and Finland), the movement toward democracy or the democratic system itself has been overwhelmed by the forces of reaction, and for a time democracy has been replaced by dictatorship, generally fascist in nature.

To better appreciate some of the factors related to a pattern of interrupted democratic development, we may take the example of Germany. To be sure, Germany is not necessarily typical in its pattern of interrupted or unstable democratization, and its experienced setbacks cannot necessarily serve as an explanation for French, Japanese, and Italian reversals of liberal democracy in their histories. Although there are similarities, it is perhaps understandable that the cases of deviation from the pattern of steady democratic growth form an even less homogeneous group experience than the original pattern itself.

One problem affecting German political development (the German problem) was that of establishing the modern German nation-state. The Germanic clan or tribal culture appears in recorded history before the birth of Christ in the struggle with the Roman Empire. The warrior tribes were the main bulwark against the Romans; the decline of Rome was associated with the migration of these Teutonic tribes throughout Europe (and even into North Africa). Toward the end of the fifth century the Frankish tribes under Clovis conquered Roman Gaul and united the territories of much of present-day France and West Germany. By the year 800, the German-Frankish chieftain Charlemagne (or Karl der Grosse) controlled an empire including France, Germany, Austria, Spain, and Italy and was crowned Emperor of the Holy Roman Empire of the Germanic nation by the pope. Soon after Charlemagne's death, however, his empire was split among his grandsons; the Holy Roman Empire included most of Germany, Austria, the Netherlands, Belgium, and Switzerland. Although geographically impressive, the empire was a loosely organized and shifting set of kingdoms, principalities, and city-states, dominated for most of its history by the Austrian house of Hapsburg (1273-1806), which provided the emperor. As such, effective government for most Germanic peoples was the *Landsherr* (or local monarch) and its feudal diet *(Landstand)*. Only in the free cities of the Hanseatic League did the rise of the burgher class of merchant capitalism produce for a time a trend toward political liberalism, with personal liberty and civil rights for all citizens. But these Hansa cities were cut off from influencing the states of the empire as a whole by their autonomy. In the fifteenth century they were for the most part attacked and incorporated into the monarchial territories. The French historian Vermeil (1969:56) suggests that "this enforced intergrada-tion in the territorial order cost the German people its political education. Little by little the proud and independent burghers were humbled. Had circumstances permitted, they might have made of Germany a great modern democracy."

The Reformation, while uniting Germans in some ways, served to divide them in other ways, almost always to the detriment of the peasants and townspeople and to the benefit of the provincial aristocracy. Martin Luther, who gave Germany a uniform written language, left behind a conglomera-tion of states with new religious cleavages between Protestants and Catho-lics. Lutheranism, potentially populist and democratic in tone, became a tool of the nobility and the aristocratic authorities (*Obrigkeiten*). As rebellious peasants challenged not only the Catholic church but the aristocracy itself, demanding abolition of serfdom, lower taxes, and elected parsons, Martin Luther turned against the masses, preaching hellfire and damnation for these "murderers and robbers who must be stabbed, smashed or strangled, and should be killed as mad dogs" (quoted in Heidenheimer, 1971:6). In the end, Lutheranism became institutionalized as an aid to monarchy, a rigid dogma supporting the established feudal order and forsaking the plight of the lower estates (classes). By the end of the Thirty Years War (1618-1648), the states of Germany were still divided, still dominated by the Austrian emperor, materially exhausted and falling behind economic developments in France, England, and the Netherlands.

In the eighteenth century, however, a German state of the northeast, Prussia, under the reign of Frederick the Great, built a well-drilled army and an efficient centralized bureaucracy, both staffed by sons of the landowning aristocracy (*Junkers*). It expanded its territory to the east, mostly at the expense of the Poles and Lithuanians, and in the nineteenth century was preparing to challenge both France and Austria for the role of unifier of a modern German nation-state.

The old Holy Roman Empire (the first German Reich), often cited by historians as neither holy, nor Roman, nor much of an empire, was finally to fall victim to the Napoleonic Wars of 1790-1815. During the period 1805-1815. Napoleon had forced the establishment of a Confederation of the Rhine, giving some major liberal reform impetus to the states of southwest Germany in particular. When the French revolutionary armies were defeat-ed in 1814-1815, with Prussia as one of the victorious coalition partners against Napoleon, the Holy Roman Empire was not resurrected. Instead, a

Germanic confederation of some thirty-eight states, both large (Hessia, Bavaria, Saxony) and small (Saxe-Coburg-Gotha, Lauenburg) was established, with no effective national political system yet in sight. The Austrian emperor assumed nominal executive control, but the Diet of the confederation required a unanimous vote before any decision could be taken. This doctrine of absolute state's rights made the confederation a rigid monument to the privilege of the local nobility, which is of course what it was meant to be as part of the post-Napoleonic restoration of the feudal order. In Baden, Bavaria, Wurttemberg, and Hesse-Darmstadt, however, the local monarchs had granted constitutions providing for essential civil liberties, Christian equality, and equality before the law for all citizens. Bicameral legislatures *(Landtag)* with an upper house reserved for the nobility and a lower house for the burgher class exercised some power of the purse, but without achieving any dramatic breakthrough to effective parliamentary democracy, even at the state level.

A customs-union *(Zollverein)* did facilitate freer trade within the confederation, and there was some modernization of agriculture and in the 1840s the introduction on a significant scale of machine production and the building of a national road network and postal service. Still, Germany lagged far behind France and England in industrial development at midcentury.

A first attempt at unification came with the revolution of 1848. In the wake of popular uprisings in Paris, Berlin, and Vienna that for a time had the ruling Prussian and Austrian aristocracies off balance and unable to do much about the course of events, a parliament was convened in the commercial city of Frankfurt/Main to draw up a national constitution. Composed mainly of educated and professional men, the Frankfurt Assembly produced a constitutional charter, after much haggling and many diversions, calling for a constitutionally bound monarchy, a bicameral parliament, one chamber representing the states and the other the national electorate able to challenge the executive's administration of government. The charter called further for separation of church from state and education, free enterprise, and individual liberties.

But the Frankfurt Assembly lacked an armed force to back its liberal ideals, and it never had the solid popular support of the citizenry. By the time it got around to offering the crown of a united but liberal republican Germany to the king of Prussia, the reactionary nobility had recovered their confidence, and the Assembly was dispersed by Austrian and Prussian troops. The liberal bourgeois revolution had failed to unite Germany; even in its failure at Frankfurt, as Krieger (1972) has rightly noted, the German idea of liberty was a compromise between monarchy and republican principles. It was not conceivable that Germany could be unified and attain at least quasi-parliamentary government except by playing off the crown against the local aristocracy. The people, it would seem, were not deemed capable of supporting the burden of sovereignty, even at the height of German liberalism.

The defeat of 1848 had a long-lasting effect on the politics of the German bourgeoisie. Observers from a variety of perspectives have remarked on the particular corporate authoritarianism of the German industrialist class, its acceptance of economic liberalism, of free enterprise and the most rational profit-seeking, without any commitment to political liberalism (liberal democracy) as was the case in England, Sweden, the Netherlands, and the United States. By the time of the unification of the nation under Bismarck's leadership in 1871, the older generation of intellectual liberal leaders had given way to a new generation of industrial capitalists concerned, if at all with politics, then with unity, order and stability. Already by the 1860s, "the middle classes still maintained connections with the older liberal ideals, but the pursuit of economic interests was already strong enough to shift the primary focus of political concern from liberal parliamentarianism to liberal nationalism" (Krieger, 1972:405). The German bourgeoisie, having failed to unite the country under the banner of liberal democracy, now turned in a different direction. They were ready to accept national unity under conservative aristocratic domination if it meant economic growth, strong state protection from the workers' movement, and, increasingly, protection against an effective popular democracy. Vermeil writes that the German capitalist class now "saw in the (Kaiser's) Reich ruled under Prussian hegemony nothing but a guarantee of economic progress, and in national unity nothing but the essential condition for certain bureaucratic and military achievements" (1969:199). This pattern of support for the political system on purely materialistic grounds meant that in times of economic crisis, loyalty to the system would be extremely problematic. While this was not responsible for the downfall of the Kaiser's empire, it was later to play a key role in the undoing of the Weimar democracy.

The modern German state is in large measure the result of Bismarck's political genius. In a series of confrontations with Austria (1866) and France (1870-1871) engineered by Bismarck, Prussia's armies defeated its major rivals for domination in Germany. In 1871 King Wilhelm accepted the imperial crown of the new German empire, but Bismarck, his chief minister, was wise enough to endow the new system with at least the trappings of a constitutional and preparliamentary system; real power rested with the crown, the military, and the bureaucracy, all staffed by the landed nobility. The constitution set up a national parliament, with a lower house (*Reichstag*) elected on the basis of universal male suffrage, progressive for its time. A multiparty system quickly emerged, and considerable press freedom was permitted. This popularly elected *Reichstag* was kept from effective power, however, by the sole jurisdiction of the emperor over foreign and military affairs and by the Kaiser's power to appoint the chancellor, who was head of governmental administration.

There was also a second chamber, the *Bundesrat,* with delegates representing the states of the empire and dominated by Prussia, which alone held seventeen of the fifty-eight votes. This more compliant upper house with considerable responsibility for both legislation and administration further weakened the position of the *Reichstag.* Finally, much domestic legislation and administration of matters most directly affecting the average citizen was left to the individual states. In the state of Prussia, for example, the state legislature was still elected according to feudal estate, with the nobility, a tiny minority of the population, electing one-third of the delegates, the burghers one-third, and the great majority of workers and peasants also one-third.

For the next twenty years, Bismarck, the so-called Iron Chancellor, was quite successful at keeping the *Reichstag* factions at bay through a never-ending series of shifting coalitions, confrontations and concessions (somewhat simplistically, a strategy of divide and rule). For example, in his battle with the rising working-class Social Democratic party (SPD), Bismarck first attempted outright suppression under the anti-Socialist law (1881-1890). During this period, the party was banned, union organization was severely constrained, and party and union militants were arrested or exiled. When Bismarck realized after a decade of police suppression that the workers' movement would not fade away under pressure but was in fact growing stronger, he reversed gears, dropped the police suppression, and initiated a series of far-reaching social insurance programs, the first of their kind in the West, to take the wind out of the SPD's sails and to cement the loyalty of the working class to the state.

As a point of contrast with the Swedish and American experiences, both national unification and the early foundations of a welfare program were associated in Germany with the authoritarian government of the Kaiser, not with achievements of liberal democracy or its parliamentary machinery.

The party system of the *Reichstag* reflected the class and religious cleavages of the society. The Conservatives (and smaller Reich party) represented the landed aristocracy; the National Liberals, the nationalist and increasingly conservative industrialists; the Catholic Center party, the religious Catholic minority; the Progressives, the still liberally oriented elements of the intelligentsia and bourgeoisie; and the Social Democrats, the urban working class. Recruitment of party leaders mirrored these divisions in class and religion, with little integration of interests across class lines. Still, this multiclass-based party system was also present in Sweden, without the same negative effects on liberal democracy. Factors other than multipartism were more important in the failures of democratization in Germany, especially the orientation of the modern business class, one of the growing social influences in the era of industrial expansion, toward liberal democracy and its realization.

As the Social Democrats grew stronger and the economic position of the aristocratic Junkers declined, the nationalistic industrialist class gradually threw in its lot with the old order to stave off the advent of both democracy and socialism, which were increasingly equated with each other. It may be said that the German bourgeoisie, having failed to achieve a liberal parliamentary system in 1848 before the rise of the organized labor movement in the last quarter of the century, came to actively oppose liberal democracy, which it now associated not with the rise of capitalism but with the rise of socialism.

In the United States, of course, the birth of liberal democracy preceded both industrialization and the union movement. In Sweden it would appear that it was the relative moderation of the aristocracy that made the difference. While we can point to certain factors, such as Sweden's earlier achievement of national unity, its religious homogeneity, and in particular its only marginal involvement in the power struggles of central Europe in the nineteenth century, that aided Sweden's democratic transformation, it must also be recognized that for Sweden, as for Germany, industrialization came at the same time as the crucial push for democratization, with the same possibility of opposition to democracy by the business class. Here we must, with Vermeil (1969), recognize some essential differences among capitalist classes across national borders between generations, differences that make the relationship between the development of capitalism and business class support for liberal democracy a contingent one rather than an automatic one. We shall return to this crucial point later, when we consider the prospects for liberal democracy in those nations yet to achieve an industrial revolution.

By the outbreak of World War I, the *Reichstag* still remained a deeply divided preparliament, unable to effectively check or balance the Kaiser and his ministers, though none of the chancellors after the forced resignation of the Bismarck in 1890 possessed his political talents.

The *Reichstag* still had not established itself as the basis for forming a government or for passing final judgment on policy and legislative matters. This breakthrough was only to come with the defeat of the Kaiser's armies in the course of war; in November of 1918, with the war lost and the populace "bled white," unrest began to spread throughout the land. The German High Seas Fleet mutinied, and workers began to occupy some major factories. The Kaiser abdicated and fled the country, leaving the prodemocratic forces to sign the humiliating Versailles Treaty and to try to pull the shattered country together. Although the young Weimar democracy survived early attempts at both socialist revolution and reactionary coups d'etat, it was clearly a system born under less than auspicious circumstances. Nevertheless, the Weimar Republic was the first full-blown system of liberal democracy to be established in Germany, with a universal adult franchise, abolition of many privileges of the aristocracy in the state governments, and with a majority in the *Reichstag* clearly the basis for forming a government and enacting legislation. As the German political historian Karl-Dietrich Bracher (1970) has pointed out, it was by no means the case that Weimar democracy was doomed from the start. Even with the disadvantages of an army general staff clearly disloyal to the republic and a bureaucracy and judiciary packed with reactionary and aristocratic elements also of dubious loyalty, it took the wrenching experience of the Great Depression to propel the Nazi party (National Socialist German Workers party) under Hitler from less than 3 percent of the vote in 1928 to 37 percent by 1932, and then a coalition of the Nazis with the party of wealthy landowners and big business, Hugenberg's National Conservatives and the Catholic anti-democratic schemer von Papen, to finally overwhelm the young democracy.

It was the Protestant middle and upper class that in troubled times, ever fearful of socialist revolution, had turned toward order and stability, this time in the form of fascist dictatorship. Lipset (1963) has documented the flight of middle-class voters from the liberal German Democratic party, the German Moderates, and the German Middle-Class party to the Nazis and to a lesser extent to the Nationalist Conservatives. More recent evidence from Hamilton (1983) has shown, however, that Nazi support was highest in the most wealthy Protestant upper-class districts. Already in 1931 a formal alliance of Nazis and Nationalist Conservatives illustrated which groups would eventually overthrow the Republic. Even the relatively conservative historian Golo Mann (1968:400-401) could not deny the collaboration of the capitalist class in the building of fascism:

> THE majority (of conservatives), under the party leader Hugenberg, entered into an alliance with the National Socialists whom they copied though showing a little more restraint; they talked of the "November criminals", of the "outrage of Versailles", of the treachery and inefficiency of democracy and the rest. Hugenberg was a rich man, the owner of an enormous publishing and newspaper business. . . . The concentration of all enemies of the Republic on the right was called the Harzburg Front after the spa where the whole gang, industrialists, generals, bankers, and party leaders met in 1931. What they had in common was hostility to the Republic.

With the naming of Hitler as chancellor, the disintegration of democratic institutions began, and at a pace and with a ferocity unequalled by the fascist regimes in Italy, France, and Japan. Within a matter of months, opposition parties were banned, starting with the Communists (KPD); opposition newspapers were shut down and nonoppositional media subjected to increasing censorship; civil rights of political, ethnic, and religious minority groups were first abused and then totally suppressed, leading ultimately to the establishment of concentration camps for the extermination of Communists, Jews, and Gypsies; labor unions were abolished and replaced with a bogus labor front (DAF) that openly favored business over workers' interests; the economy, which remained in private hands, was reoriented toward military production; in foreign affairs, an aggressive nationalism and lust for conquest characterized the new regime (see Bracher, 1970; Neumann, 1942). Schweitzer (1964) sees the Nazi regime, at least prior to the wartime mobilization, as a sort of four-way coalition incuding the Nazi party, the secret police, the generals, and big business, who agreed on the goals of "military and economic rearmament, the suppression of trade unions, and the invigoration of capitalist institutions" (504). The coalition consensus on higher profit for big business resulted in a sharp decline of wages and salaries as a percentage of national income, whereas income from property, entrepreneurial activity, and corporate profits rose from 30.4 to 39.2 percent between 1932 and 1939 (Knauerhase, 1972:129).

Only total defeat in World War II brought the system down. It is only since 1949 that a liberal democracy, reimplanted by the Western occupation forces in the Federal Republic, has grown and prospered and has over time come to be identified with political and economic success. Since 1949 the *Bundestag*, the lower house, has been an effective parliament, the party system gradually transformed itself into a two-and-a-half party system (Social Democrats, Christian Democrats, and the smaller Free Democrats) through a stepwise decline to insignificance of the radical left (Communists) and radical right (neo-Nazis). A temporary re-emergence of the radical right, the NPD, to between 5 and 10 percent of the vote during the recession of 1965-1966 was associated with the same lingering dynamic of economic crisis and authoritarian attitudes (Nagle, 1970) that posed a fatal threat to Weimar. But in the 1974-1975 recession, much worse and longer than the one a decade earlier, no such right radical (or left radical) movement emerged, and it may be that a new generation of Germans of all social classes have now positively identified themselves with liberal democracy for better or for worse, in good times and not-so-good times. In the 1980s, the rise of the environmentalist Greens as a new party in the *Bundestag* has affirmed the opportunity for the "new social movements" to enter the political arena, as well as the commitment of the Greens to compete within the parliamentary system.

Interrupted Democratic Development: Fascism

If we compare the duration of fascism in Germany with that in other major political systems whose process of democratic development has been interrupted by fascist or fascist-like takeovers in the last century, a rather consistent pattern appears. Since the founding of a unified Germany under Bismarck's leadership in 1871, German democratic development has been reversed for about thirteen years, under the Third Reich (1933-1945). Italy, which similarly became a unified modern nation-state under constitutional monarchy only after Garibaldi's successful military campaigns in 1860, suffered relapses under the fascist dictatorship from 1922, the date of Mussolini's seizure of power in his "March on Rome," to 1943, with the surrender of Italy to the Allies in World War II. Japan began its constitutional history only in 1890 with the first elections to a national parliament, and while there was never a formal fascist government established during the 1930s and 1940s, the ultranationalist military command virtually took over state power in the period 1930-1932 through a series of assassinations of leading political figures and the army's independent decision to invade Manchuria and transform it into a puppet state of the empire. This Tojo militarism was broken only with the unconditional surrender of Japan in 1945. France has, of course, suffered several setbacks in its democratic evolution, beginning with the degeneration of the Revolution of 1789 into the Directorate and then into the Napoleonic empire. The Bourbon monarchy was restored with the defeat of Napoleon by the combination of other European powers, and it was not until the revolution of 1848 that parliamentary government was once again attempted under the short-lived Second Republic. This republic was again overthrown by Louis Napoleon in his tragicomic coup of 1851 (cf. Marx, "The Eighteenth Brumaire of Louis Napoleon"), and a proto-fascist Second Empire established. The Second Empire, despite its infamous corruption and political folly, was not overthrown from within, but succumbed only after disastrous military defeat by the Prussian armies in the war of 1870-1871. The Third Republic (1871-1940) survived the first world war, but not the second, and it must be remembered that the Vichy regime of Petain and Laval represented a fascist regime (1940-1944) that governed effectively in its own right, making it unnecessary for the Nazis to occupy France (except for a few strategic points) until the advent of the British-American invasion late in the war. The Fourth Republic (1945-1956) was toppled by a military coup over the issue of Algerian independence and supplanted by the Fifth Republic, which survives today. We might agree then with Paul Sweezy (1942) that the normal form of government for these advanced capitalist systems is liberal democracy, with fascism representing a contingent system alternative for modern capitalism, especially in response to crisis situations.

Fascism has been interpreted in many ways. Some have seen it as a revolt against modernity, against both finance capitalism and socialism, and against big corporations and big labor unions. Marxists have often described fascism as the last resort of the bourgeoisie for staving off the advent of socialism. Along psychological lines, fascism has appeared as an "escape from freedom" (Fromm, 1940) and as a racist supernationalism.

There are, however, some general features of fascism not in dispute. Fascism destroys freedom of the press, party organization (except for the ruling party), speech, and free assembly. It undermines the independence of the courts and utilizes police and paramilitary street gangs (black shirts, SA-brown shirts, Action Française, death squads) to suppress dissent and terrorize potential opponents, using a quite visible degree of actual violence. Authentic labor unions are outlawed and replaced, if at all, by a regime-controlled labor front. Labor leaders and leaders of leftist parties are hunted down and imprisoned, executed, or forced into exile. On the other hand, the capitalist class is generally in a favored position under fascism and has historically collaborated with these regimes. Fascism does not challenge the private ownership of industry or commerce, although it may seize the holdings of dissident or ethnic minority businessmen. The economy under fascism remains a capitalist economy, with the full force of organized coercion on the side of the employer. Industrialists, bankers, and in some countries large landowners, are able to utilize the repressive capabilities of fascism for their economic interests, and while it is unfair to say that capitalists invariably turn to fascism in times of deep crisis, it is true that big business does not oppose fascism in power, nor does it hesitate to profit from the system.

Besides the support of the business class, fascism has historically had either active or passive support, and never active resistance, from the Catholic church and the professional military. In General Franco's fascist uprising against the Spanish Republic in 1936, Franco's three pillars of support were the military, the bourgeoisie, and the church. In Germany and Italy, the military looked on from the sidelines as Hitler and Mussolini took and abused political power; indeed in both cases the fascists could not have succeeded without the disloyalty of the professional military to the constitutional republic. In Japan, the military was the vanguard of the fascist regime. The church, which in Italy had made it a sin to vote in a free election, signed a concordat first with Mussolini and later with Hitler. As long as the church organization was left intact by the fascists, they preached submission to the regime. This does not exhaust the list of supporters of fascist parties and regimes; many ordinary workers and peasants also voted for the Nazis, the Fascists, the Falange. But the great majority of the working class continued to vote for Socialist or Communist parties until free elections were suppressed.

It should be emphasized that all of the major fascist systems in Germany, France, Italy, and Japan came to their demise through military defeat, not through internal rebellion. This is not to say that internal rebellion or revolution against fascism is impossible, only that fascism in its major appearances met its demise through its aggressive militarism and not through longer-term internal transformations. The collaboration of the capitalist class with the fascist regime has presented a problem for business at the demise of fascism and the re-establishment of democracy. Capitalism in Germany, Italy, and France especially was heavily discredited at the end of

World War II, and several of the most prominent collaborators (Renault in France, Krupp in Germany) had their economic empires broken up or nationalized. The Socialists and Communists, who in all cases had formed the main internal resistance groups both before and during the war, emerged to participate in coalition governments; much social legislation was enacted to redress the abuses that the working class had suffered under fascism. Still, the Western Allies resisted the call for wide-ranging nationalizations of industry that would have meant an end to capitalism, and the United States Marshall Plan was predicated on economic recovery for capitalism in Europe.

PARLIAMENT—CENTERPIECE OF LIBERAL DEMOCRACY

Certain institutions may characterize a political system-type. Liberal democracy has long been identified with the development of a national parliament or legislature that is the focal point of political debate and broad policy making. As the centerpiece of liberal democracy, the parliament serves as a forum for contending interests, factions, or parties. It is the assemblage of openly elected representatives of the citizenry. Early struggles of bourgeois democracy, as cited previously, were histories of the emergence of a politically effective and competitively elected parliament (in England the House of Commons, in Germany the Reichstag, in Sweden the Riksdag, and in the United States the Congress).

In the twentieth century, many other political institutions have developed within the industrial democracies of the West to challenge or transcend the important roles of the parliament. A consolidated two-party or multiparty system has at times seemed to signal a decline of parliament in favor of effective policy making within the party organizations, especially during periods of one-party dominance, as in the forty-year period of government by the Social Democrats in Sweden, or the long period of Republican dominance in the United States after the Civil War, or during the Adenauer era of the 1950s and early 1960s in West Germany. In these periods, the party organization seemed to dominate the parliament as the focal point for political decision making.

The executive branch of government has also challenged the central role of parliament, especially in crisis or wartime situations and under inspired or forceful leadership. President Roosevelt during the Great Depression and World War II, Winston Churchill as the British wartime prime minister, President de Gaulle in the first decade of the Fifth French Republic, and Chancellor Adenauer in West Germany overshadowed both their own parties and the parliament, certainly in popular attention and political initiative. In the latter 1960s, under both President Johnson and President Nixon, it was feared that an "imperial presidency" was developing in the United States, able to conduct government affairs in virtual disregard for Congress and through a creeping takeover of Congress's legislative functions.

Finally, the growth of government bureaucracy, necessary for administration of the vast array of welfare and regulatory programs and for expanded peacetime military establishments and state-run industries, has appeared to place much political decision making beyond the reach of any elected government body. In some systems, notably the French Fourth Republic (1945-1958) and the postwar Italian democracy, both noted for frequent turnover in coalition governments, the higher civil service was viewed as a source of political continuity. In Britain also, the top echelons of the civil service provided a continuing expertise and administrative experience for state-run industries that outlasted any particular Labor or Conservative government and that was of growing importance as a center of decision making.

All of these perceptions have some validity, and they describe some of the basic additions to parliamentary democracy over the past century and a half. Yet the Congress, the *Bundestag,* the House of Commons, and the *Riksdag* have always rebounded from periods of weakness and responded to challenges from particular parties, prime ministers, and presidents, and even from bureaucracy. Other political systems, both communist and Third World, may have an effective party organization, or a strong executive, or a stabilizing civil service. But it is the historic birth of an elected parliament and its continued vitality that mark liberal democracy as a political system-type. Conversely, the demise of liberal democracy, as in Germany in the 1930s, Italy in the 1920s, or the Second Czechoslovakian Republic in 1949, has been marked by the demise of an effective parliament.

The democratic parliament tends to be an institution of moderation and partial reforms generally incapable of leading any radical social change, whether revolutionary or counterrevolutionary. In this sense, also, parliament has been the instrument of "moderate" parties from the conservative right to the social democratic left, those parties whose goals could be achieved by incremental reforms within the existing capitalist system. The parliament of liberal democracy is in many ways the ideal institution for avoiding basic social change. Its openness assures that competing social interests will try to counteract any policy movement that might adversely affect their own interests. Moreover, those interests that benefit most from the status quo are generally the best positioned to press their case and are free to use their considerable financial resources to influence both legislators and voters. The necessity for periodic re-election of representatives biases parliament against programs calling for short-term (or long-term) sacrifice in order to achieve longer-term goals. Even a reform-minded party with a parliamentary majority must try to avoid drastic shifts in policy that would, in the short run, lead to economic disruption and social disorder, which would lead either to some loss of electoral support or to a military coup. The politics of broad consensus building are preferred to the politics of class polarization. Successful parties and leaders in parliamentary systems are typically, though not always, those who occupy the middle ground, not those who advocate controversial programs. Politics tends to chase after short-run public favor, at the expense of either constant programmatic action or political education. Social and economic planning is hindered by parliamentary democracy, though not entirely ruled out. This is, we would posit, one of the functions of the institution: to discourage notions of social and economic planning, which might develop the capability for a transition to socialism.

Governing parties cannot risk carrying out radical social policies if they wish to remain in office and maintain the liberal democratic system. Parliamentary democracy limits its scope of "normal" policy choices to those that do not question the existing social order, but that try to amend it through partial measures. Parliament is not an institution designed for political mobilization of have-not groups in the society; rather it is best suited to diminish, but not eliminate, the impact of lower-class demands and to increase the likelihood of stalemate or watering-down of radical proposals. Parliaments as institutions have not always survived periods of severe economic and social crisis; there are limits to the containment of both lower-class demands for basic change and bourgeois support for fascist suppression of militant worker organizations. By the same logic of moderation, parliament has limited impact in shaping its own political environment. Almost by definition, it cannot take decisive action to resolve impending class violence, revolutionary upsurge, civil war, or fascist coup. But within the postwar period of growth and increasing prosperity in the developed capitalist nations, parliament plays a central moderating and consensus-building role in the liberal democracies.

THE GEOGRAPHY OF LIBERAL DEMOCRACY

Liberal democracy, although expressed in terms that could be applicable to any society and any culture, has largely been limited to Japan and the advanced capitalist nations of the North Atlantic. Beyond this community of prosperous industrialized states, the record of democracy is limited. In just the last thirty years, most of the nations of the developing Third World that had either attained liberal democracy or were struggling to establish such a system have succumbed to right-wing dictatorship, usually backed by the military. In the Latin America of the 1950s, for example, Chile, Argentina, Uruguay, and Brazil were still governed by elected civilian officeholders. There was multiparty competition in elections, a relatively free press, and independent trade unionism. Chile was, of these systems, perhaps the most stable and most similar to the European democratic pattern. In 1970 the Marxist candidate of the Popular Unity coalition of Socialist, Communist, and Radical parties, Salvador Allende, won a three-way race for the presidency, the first Marxist government to come to office through strictly electoral means. After three years of political and class polarization, the Chilean military, with considerable help from its American sponsors, overthrew the Popular Unity government and murdered President Allende. Support for the coup came from the Chilean bourgeoisie and the Catholic church. Since 1973 Chile's military junta under General Augusto Pinochet has done everything expected of a fascist regime. It has killed and tortured leftist political opponents and abolished political parties, free trade unions, and freedom of the press. Its policies have been extremely hard on the working class while benefiting both wealthy Chileans and foreign investors in Chile. The Chilean case is important in that liberal democracy had seemed to have taken root there more firmly than in most Latin American nations, let alone the only recently independent states of Africa and Asia.

In Chile respect for civilian government by the military was a fairly well-established tradition. If that tradition collapsed under the strains of class polarization amidst social reform, can liberal democracy be expected to survive or develop elsewhere in the Third World? Naturally, there are particular aspects of the Chilean experience that are not found in other Third World systems, and no one would claim that Chile represents the last word on the possibilities for democratic survival with social reform in the developing nations. Some would say that since social reform under Allende aroused class polarization and therefore the coup, democracy must not attempt social reform if it wants to survive. This notion of democracy, which prizes stability above all and neglects the popular demand for social justice, is a mechanistic vision of democratic freedoms, one rejected by this author. If democracy by definition cannot be used by the lower strata as a means to express and press their demands and needs, it will calcify and ultimately fail as a democracy.

In South Korea, Thailand, Indonesia, Ghana, Nigeria, Pakistan, Peru, Argentina, Uruguay, and Brazil, all with at least some experience in democratic institutions during the post-World War II years, military dictatorships have interrupted the process of democratization for extended periods. Only a few countries (Colombia, Venezuela) have convincingly re-established liberal democratic processes after a period of military rule. For most of the Third World, the entire postwar era has been one of either colonial domination or, upon the attainment of independence, one-party rule or military dictatorship.

Liberal democracy will reappear in some of these countries. The fact that it has been overthrown for the present does not imply that there is no future whatsoever for liberal democracy or parliamentary government in the Third

World. Military juntas and personalist dictatorships make enough mistakes and enough enemies to be ousted with some regularity. In some instances states introduce or reintroduce democratic government, as in Thailand in 1973, Pakistan in 1971 and Argentina in 1983. It should be noted that the military regained power in Thailand in 1976 and in Pakistan in 1977. Yet it is doubtful that we can even speak of a highly interrupted pattern of democratization in these countries, since, with few exceptions, democracy had been the anomaly, dictatorship the rule. We shall in fact argue, in chapters 12 and 16, that there is little reason to hope for popularly responsive, let alone liberal democratic, government in these nations so long as they remain so dependent on the developed nations of the North Atlantic region. For now, it is enough to establish the historical boundaries up to the present of the pattern of political development called liberal democracy.

Chapter 3

Economic Development—
Affluent Consumerism

THE ECONOMIES OF WESTERN DEMOCRACIES have undergone significant transformation since the early industrialization of the nineteenth century, which has pushed them ever further from the idealized laissez-faire model of Adam Smith. These economies must still be described as capitalist, since they are characterized by private profit and private ownership of the means of production as the main organizational principle for determining investment, employment, prices, and wages.

One trend in the development of capitalism has been the growing complexity of corporations and the accompanying concentration of economic power among the largest enterprises. The business enterprise has now progressed through several stages in the past century, including (1) growth of professional management, (2) growth of more impersonal stock ownership, (3) widening of a firm's market, both nationally and internationally, and (4) widening of product array, both through internal diversification and corporate merger.

In industry and in agriculture, small and middle-sized family_owned and family-operated businesses have lost out to a much smaller number of large and more complex corporations. The local family firm has been superseded by the nationally based corporation, which in turn has been progressively integrated into the multinational conglomerate, largely self-financing and with increasing operations abroad for resources, manufacturing, and marketing. Large multinationals such as Exxon, General Motors, Thyssen, Unilever, and Nippon Steel have annual sales that exceed the total annual production (GNP) of most nations. From one sector of the economy to another, sales and profits have been concentrated in the hands of perhaps three or four giants. Rather than a multitude of small enterprises fiercely competing to survive under the "invisible hand" of the market, a monopoly capitalism tends toward collusion and price setting as the rational way for the largest corporations to maximize and stabilize profits and sales. Smaller firms are still subject to a market they cannot control, however, and their profit margins are correspondingly the lowest. (In the United States profits have been negative for the smallest businesses since the end of World War II).

A second trend has been the growth of government and its role in maintaining economic prosperity. The Great Depression of the 1930s ended the orthodoxy of an unregulated market capitalism. Through a combination of new economic theory, trial and error, and wartime government intervention in the economy, the liberal democracies have assumed a new and growing responsibility, widely recognized as legitimate, for limited intervention in the marketplace. The whole point of Keynesian economics, developed in the Depression era, was to moderate the excesses of capitalist development, especially to avoid another Great Depression. Since the free market clearly could not guarantee this, Western governments undertook means to regulate the economy, to ensure that economic slowdowns, a normal part of the business cycle, did not spiral into catastrophe, or that economic booms did not overheat and then suddenly burst. Four main aspects of governmental activity can be identified with the new "Keynesian" orthodoxy: (1) regulation of economic activity, (2) welfare spending, (3) military spending, and (4) government employment.

Regulatory activity of banking and finance operations, stock exchanges, labor-management relations, and general marketing practices were designed to prevent the recurrence of unsound stock speculation and banking practices and class violence that marked Western capitalism prior to 1929. Monitoring the economy closely, government now attempts to provide a climate of both investor and consumer confidence for stable but moderate growth.

Welfare spending, apart from its humanitarian goals, serves as a major support for consumer spending among the elderly, the jobless, the sick and disabled, and the retired and thus provides support for business activity. During the Depression, consumer spending dried up as joblessness increased, adding to the downturn in production and employment. Welfare spending is one major avenue for maintaining consumer demand even in, or especially in, the event of recession.

Large-scale military spending is an additional means of governmental support for business activity. Military contracts provide a considerable source of sales and profits for many of the largest corporations, especially in the United States (President Eisenhower warned, in 1960, of a growing "military-industrial complex"). Government military spending in the liberal democracies did not return to prewar peacetime levels and serves now as an element in an overall "Keynesian" strategy.

In the liberal democracies, government has also become a sort of "employer of last resort" in two ways. Government (nonmilitary) bureaucracy has increased markedly with the growth in welfare programs and regulatory bodies, producing a large increase in civil service employment. In Britain and Italy especially, many bankrupt or unprofitable businesses in automaking, steel, and shipbuilding have been "saved" through nationalization, primarily to maintain employment levels. In the United States, where nationalization is ideologically unacceptable, the federal government has nevertheless provided billions to the railroads, to Lockheed International, and to the Chrysler Corporation, and for essentially the same reasons.

These trends, taken together, have produced a monopoly capitalism in a welfare state: Liberal democratic governments have assumed the role of stabilizing the economy at high levels of employment and business activity, while not actually planning the economy as a whole. In the 1970s, to be sure, there was considerable criticism of the growing power of the large corporations from consumer organizations (Naderism in the United States), of energy companies from environmentalist movements, and from antiwar or antimilitary spending groups. In the 1980s, on the other hand, we are witnessing growing criticism of government regulations and welfare spending (not military spending) from conservative and neoconservative (i.e., once liberal) groups in many Western democracies. In Great Britain this movement has produced a Conservative government under Prime Minister Margaret Thatcher that, unlike earlier Conservative governments, has begun in all seriousness to reverse many of the trends in government policy that have characterized the postwar period throughout the West. In the United States, the administration of Ronald Reagan has produced a similar attempt.

Nevertheless, even if public criticism and public antagonism against the large oil companies, the utilities, and other corporate giants has grown, the trends toward greater corporate complexity, greater international involvement, and greater concentration of economic power have not been reversed. And, even if one takes the rhetoric of both Prime Minister Thatcher and President Reagan to be actual policy goals, the Conservatives of the 1980s are not (yet) suggesting an abandonment of the most basic welfare programs of the postwar era, nor are they suggesting that the government is not responsible for trying to maintain or improve economic performance levels.

AFFLUENCE IN THE LIBERAL DEMOCRACIES

Probably the most basic and most outstanding feature of the advanced liberal democracies is economic wealth. A quantitative comparison between the liberal democracies and the developing world is astounding and even shocking to those who have not seen it before. In the 1970s, the per capita GNP (Gross National Product) of Sweden was twenty times that of the Philippines, eleven times that of Colombia, nineteen times that of Egypt, fifty times that of Burma, thirty-four times that of Pakistan, twenty-six times that of Kenya, fifteen times that of Ghana. The general ratio in per capita income between the rich, developed nations and the poor, developing nations is roughly 20 to 1 presently, according to economist Rosenstein-Rodan (1972). This does not take into account that there are middle-class people in the rich nations living well above their countries' averages and that the poorest strata in the poor nations live below their national averages, so that between a middle-class Swede and a Philippine peasant, the income gap is actually on the order of 100:1.

As startling as the huge gap in income is the fact that it is a relatively recent historical phenomenon. Rosenstein-Rodan estimates that in the early nineteenth century, the nations of Western Europe and North America, already the wealthier nations, had per capita income levels only twice those of the poorer nations. In the last 150 years, the rich lands/poor lands gap has grown tenfold, from 2 to 1 to 20 to 1. Western democracies, by the 1970s, had all reached the level of mass consumer societies. With some relative differences, of course, within this community of nations, family ownership of large consumer durables such as an automobile, television, radio, refrigerator, and a mixed variety of other appliances has been realized for a substantial proportion, and sometimes overwhelming majorities, of the population. These material outputs of advanced capitalism are generally accessible to average members of the blue-collar working class and white-collar employee class as well as to higher social strata of professionals and business owners, and in quantity/proliferation unheard of in the most prosperous periods of the pre-Great Depression years.

Within the community of the affluent nations are some basic features worth special note. One is that the American standard of living, measured in gross national product (GNP) per capita, was surpassed by the 1970s in both Sweden and Switzerland (see table 3.1). The differences between American GNP/capita and GNP/capita in West Germany, Holland, Denmark, and Norway were also minor by the mid-1970s and fluctuated with changes in the exchange rate of the dollar against the various European currencies. The most rapid growth of GNP/capita has been achieved, however, by the Japanese, who by 1987 had even surpassed the United States in GNP/capita ranking. (We should note here that GNP/capita figures do not tell all. If one takes into account the varying prices of consumer goods from country to country, the United States consumer may still be considered most favored in purchasing power for a given "market basket" of goods.) The position of the United States at the end of the Second World War was something of an anomaly, arising from the widespread losses of personnel, production facilities, and markets among the European nations (and Japan), including neutrals like Sweden and Switzerland. This anomalous position has now been normalized.

In many ways, as we stressed in the previous chapter, the American experience has been unique, unlikely to be duplicated as an entire pattern or model, but this does not mean that the United States, even in aggregate terms, should be assumed to be the leader in productivity (per capita) or that the United States leads in fields such as health care, welfare, education, or housing. In many fields the United States does lead, and here the other liberal democracies may be (and already have been) able to profit from American experience. In other fields the United States has been the laggard and could well consider how other systems have managed to do better. This statement should not rekindle the notion of "interchangeable parts" in what are, after all, highly complex social and political systems or of the "social engineering" approach criticized earlier. Yet nations with similar levels of development and overall patterns of governments should be able to learn from each other.

Table 3.1 Selected Indicators of Affluence

	Switzerland	West Germany	United States	Britain	Sweden	France	Japan
GNP/CAP[a] (1975)	14,281	9,093	12,027	7,771	11,334	8,543	6,904
GNP/CAP[a] (1983)	15,552	10,903	13,492	8,693	11,850	9,896	9,149
TVs/1,000 (1982)	370	354	646	457	387	369	560
Radios/1,000 (1982)	370	392	2,133	986	853	854	696
Autos/1,000 (1983/84)	398	412	535	282	371	352	226

a. In 1982 dollars.

SOURCES: UN *Statistical Yearbook*, 1983/84; *Statistical Abstract of the United States*, 1986.

The growth of the rich/poor gap between the world's nations is one of the most basic changes of the last century and a half and is related to two straightforward factors. First, the nations of Western Europe and North America (plus Japan) were the first to experience industrialization under capitalism, and the productivity increases of an industrial economy have increased the differentials between rich and poor nations. Second, the political-economic-military imperialism practiced by the industrial economies in the underdeveloped Third World has widened differentials between rich and poor nations.

Analysis of the second factor will have to wait until our discussion of political systems in the Third World. For now it is enough to establish correlates of industrial growth in the leading capitalist nations in the historically quite modest time span of one hundred fifty years. Table 3.2 presents a variety of aggregate data that describe some broad demographic features of the liberal democracies. The liberal democracies were the first to successfully industrialize their economies, the way in which things are produced. In all the liberal democracies, 30 to 40 percent of the male workforce is employed in the manufacturing/mining sectors of the economy. As industrialization has advanced since the turn of the century, this percentage has stabilized and in some countries, particularly the United States, has even declined somewhat. Since the early 1900s, the sector of the workforce with the most rapid growth has been the nonmanual or white-collar employee sector, which includes office personnel, most government workers, sales and distribution personnel, managerial/supervisory, and professional/technical employees. With the decline of older industrial areas and the displacement of new industrial investment overseas, the workforce of the liberal democracies has more and more been concentrated in the broad "services" sector. Since the Second World War, the category of professional/technical employee has grown most noticeably within the nonmanual occupations, reflecting the increasing importance of specialized training and technical expertise in the functioning of government, corporate, and educational complexes.

Between 10 and 25 percent of the employed male workforce now hold positions characterized chiefly by a higher education. The growth of the white-collar and technical intelligentsia has meant a continuing decline in the percentage of those employed in agriculture, at the same time that mechanization and agricultural technology has raised agricultural productivity to support an increasing urban and suburban population. Whereas 75 to 85 percent of the population were engaged in agriculture in these nations in the early 1800s, now less than an eighth are still active in farming. In the most highly industrialized nations (Britain, West Germany, the United States) the figure is less than 6 percent. While there are still sizeable agricultural populations in Japan, Italy, and France, with holdovers from the peasantry of feudalism and the small farmer (smallholder) of early capitalism, agriculture has on the whole been modernized along commercial-industrial lines, most conspicuously in the United States, where the Jeffersonian ideal of the independent yeoman tiller of the soil has become an endangered species, and farming is dominated by huge agro-corporations. It is not only in the urban economy but also and perhaps as vitally in agricultural production that the economies of the liberal democracies have been transformed over the last century and a half.

Table 3.2 Occupational Structure and Residence (1984)

	Switzerland	West Germany	United States	Britain	Sweden	France	Japan
Population (millions)	6.4	61.2	237.0	56.4	8.3	54.9	120.0
Percentage of workforce in:							
Industry	39	44	31	38	33	35	34
Agriculture	6	6	4	3	6	9	11
Services	55	50	66	59	62	56	55
Urban population (percent)	60	86	74	92	86	81	55

SOURCE: Adapted from World Bank, *World Development Report,* 1986.

Industrial society is, or has been so far, an urban society, and the liberal democracies are overwhelmingly urban cultures. This is important, because in Western civilization (and most others as well) it has been the cities and towns that have contained the concentrated educational, cultural, and material wealth of the society and have been the center of political power as well. While this might seem rather exaggerated in an era (in the United States) of urban decay and broadcast technology, the process of urbanization in the West brought larger and larger numbers of people into contact with new possibilities, new desires and needs, and new skills than did (or could) the village or farm. The bright lights of the city have become the goal of millions of ex-villagers in modern history, and this is not in any way limited to Western capitalist society. From the Soviet Union to Brazil and from Nigeria to Indonesia, cities are growing by leaps and bounds.

One difference, and an extremely vital one in this "age of the city," is that in the West, as urban areas expanded, so did productive industrial and commercial activity, generating millions of new jobs for the millions of new city-dwellers. Even counting the severe depressions of the 1890s and the 1930s, and the many lesser recessions caused by the cyclical development of capitalism, it is still clear that creation of urban employment kept rough pace with urban population growth. While this is also true for the communist systems, it is definitely not true for most Third World nations. Urban growth is not necessarily a sign of economic progress in those nations.

From Elite to Mass Education

All of the items that will be discussed below are interrelated (autocorrelated) with the contemporary achievement of an advanced capitalist economy with a liberal democratic system. There is no intent to imply any one-way causality from economic growth to educational, health, housing, or welfare fields. Such descriptions oversimplify a complex pattern of mutual reinforcement and organic interdependence. The particular historic development of the industrial democracies exhibit a pattern of interrelationship among these elements, however, that is not being duplicated in today's developing nations and that has been significantly altered in the communist or state socialist systems.

In the West, literacy was already fairly widespread at the point of industrial takeoff. Gutenberg's invention of movable type for printing in the fifteenth century represented a technological revolution for literacy skills far in advance of industrial capitalism. But as Western societies urbanized, more and more members of the middle and lower classes were drawn into an expanded, national educational system. In the city, in the factory, and in the store the modern worker or employee had to be able to read, write, and reckon. Replacement of the local subsistence or village barter economy with the mass-market, currency-based exchange system required attainment of new skills on a mass scale, at least for males. Literacy in Britain in the early

1800s may have been around 30 percent; by 1841-1845 literacy reached nearly 70 percent among adult males and among females about 50 percent; by 1920 literacy rates were over 90 percent for all the Western industrial powers except Italy. Near-universal literacy was reached before World War II.

In the last three decades, the expansion of the educational system and of educational opportunities has occurred at the secondary (high school, gymnasium, lycee, grammar school) level and in higher education (college, university, higher technical institute). In the European school systems of the early 1950s, pupils were generally channeled at an early age (ten to eleven) into either college preparatory secondary schools or general education and technical vocational schools. Overwhelmingly, the children of upper-middle-class, well-educated parents filled the prestigious college prep schools, while the sons and daughters of farmers, workers, and white-collar employees ended up in the secondary schools that led only to vocational or technical skill schools at best. This process is known as "class channeling" and tends, of course, to make upward mobility much more difficult for children of lower social origins. Perhaps only 2 to 5 percent of college-age young people actually attended a college or university in the early 1950s, and they were overwhelmingly from higher social backgrounds. Class channeling makes clear at a very tender age who are the winners, the upwardly mobile, and who are the losers, the underclass of the society. In West Germany, the student cultures of the *Hauptschule* (general education), *Realschule* (technical/vocational), and *Gymnasium* (college-track) are social worlds apart. In the first there is a sense of harsh but realistic adjustment to a lesser future (or tough talk and rebelliousness); in the last there are pride, self-esteem, and wide horizons, coupled with better manners and respectful treatment from teachers. British sociologist Frank Parkin (1971:64) gives a good summary of the impact of class channeling on ambitions among English schoolchildren:

THE evidence suggests that from a fairly early age low status members are *taught* to narrow their social horizons. The selection of "appropriate" reference groups is

Table 3.3 Education Spending and Literacy Levels

	Switzerland	West Germany	United States	Britain	Sweden	France	Japan
Percentage GNP spent on public education:							
1965	3.6	3.4	5.3	5.1	6.4	3.7	4.9
1983	5.1	4.5	6.7[a]	5.3	8.4	5.8[b]	5.7[b]
Literacy (percent)	100	99	99	99	100	99	98
a. 1981							
b. 1982							

Sources: UNESCO *Statistical Yearbook*, 1986; *World Handbook of Political and Social Indicators*, 1972.

then likely to follow as the children become adult. By this time they will have received reasonable training in the art of not "seeing" the privileged for purposes of comparison.

In the United States, on the other hand, with the exception of a relatively small number of elite prep schools such as Exeter, Groton, and Choate for the offspring of the rich, there has historically been little class channeling within secondary schools (this statement will be amended somewhat in the following chapter). Secondary education in the United States has been comprehensive, meaning that generally all who attend the public schools go through the same institutions. Here again, the lack of a feudal past has made the American experience unique and, in this case, progressive. Heidenheimer, Heclo, and Adams (1975) have outlined the political struggles in Britain, West Germany, and Sweden in changing over from a class channeling to a comprehensive secondary school system in recent decades.

In Sweden (and Norway) Social Democratic governments in power for decades were able to complete the transformation and thus to raise opportunities of higher education for working-class children as well as to expand them markedly for middle-class children. In Sweden, the proportion of university students of working-class origins rose from 8 percent in 1947 to 16 percent by 1963, with the upward trend expected to continue (Parkin, 1971:111). In Britain, after some modest beginnings in the 1950s, the Labour government of Harold Wilson was able, in the 1964-1970 period, to put into motion a stronger trend toward "comprehensivization" in the secondary schools. Despite some rearguard delaying actions by the succeeding Conservative government (with Margaret Thatcher as minister of education), the number of comprehensive high schools rose steadily from 262 in 1965 to 1,835 by 1973, enrolling nearly half of all secondary school students (as opposed to less than 10 percent in 1965). The long-run effects of British education reform at the secondary school level on working-class representation in the universities remain to be seen, since the transformation at the secondary level is far from complete.

In West Germany, attempts to create comprehensive schools under the SPD-FDP social-liberal government of Willy Brandt (1969-1974) failed rather miserably, even in their final, extremely watered-down format. Rigid opposition from the Christian Democrats, secondary school teachers, and middle-class parents, coupled with the SPD's recent and still-tenuous leadership in national government, led in 1974 to the tacit admission by Brandt's successor, Helmut Schmidt, that plans for educational reform of the secondary school system were being abandoned. The brief momentum of the late 1960s had not achieved a breakthrough.

Of all the Western European schooling systems, as both Parkin (1971) and Tomasson (1965) assert, only Sweden and Norway have fundamentally transformed the class-channeling system, although it may be that the British comprehensive system will in the not-too-distant future achieve some moderate gains for working-class children. The schooling systems with the least class channeling, then, would seem to be those of the United States, where the political system had no feudal past to contend with, and those of Norway and Sweden, where the strength and durability of ideologically committed social democratic movements, in power for decades without interruption, were able to achieve basic reforms.

Table 3.4 Enrollments in Higher Education 1955-1984

	West Germany	United States	Britain	Sweden	France	Japan
	Percentage of Age Group in Higher Education					
1955	3	18	4	5	4	—
1965	9	40	12	13	18	13
1983	30	56	20	39	28	30
	Students per Million Population					
1965	6,320	28,400	4,847	9,230	10,420	11,100
1984	24,650	52,810	16,000	26,510	21,140	20,060

SOURCES: UNESCO Statistical Yearbook, 1986; World Bank, World Development Report, 1981, 1986.

Apart from the postwar issue of comprehensive versus class channeling in the secondary schools, the total number of places in higher education has expanded markedly in nearly all the liberal democracies. As table 3.4 indicates, between the mid-1960s and the mid-1980s the percentage of the college-age population enrolled at the university level doubled, tripled, and even quadrupled. In the United States and Sweden, the two leaders in higher education, roughly 40 to 60 percent of young men and women of college age were in fact attending some institution of higher education. Higher education in the United States and Sweden had been transformed from an elite institution to a mass institution. In some individual states, for example, California, where 80 percent of high school graduates went on to a college of some sort, higher education had become a nearly universal phenomenon.

MORE CORRELATES: HEALTH AND HEALTH CARE

One of the most significant changes in the course of the industrial development in the West since the early 1800s has been the increase in life expectancy. In late feudal Europe, average life expectancy was generally between thirty and thirty-five years for males and thirty-five to forty years for females. Infant mortality rates were extremely high, so that even with high birthrates, population growth was minimal. Even then, life expectancy was somewhat higher in Europe than in Mexico, India, and China. As table 3.5 clearly shows, in the cases of England and Sweden the advent of industrialism has been associated with a dramatic doubling of life expectancy.

Part of this revolution in longevity can be attributed to increases in economic resources available through the preindustrial merchant capitalist or early factory system economy, which improved basic nutrition, clothing, and shelter for the general population. Economic historian T. S. Ashton (1948:4-5, 64) attributes the decline in death rates in England, and especially infant death rates, to the introduction of cheap cotton underwear and lye soap. These increased personal hygiene possibilities for great numbers of people, reducing the risk of infection, a common cause of early death. Ashton notes also the improvement in nutrition through the introduction of the potato from the New World and through the availability of wheat instead of inferior grains such as rye and barley for daily consumption. Use of brick walls and slate roofs instead of timber and thatch also reduced the incidence of disease-carrying pests in the home, which had been another source of mortal danger to infants in feudal agrarian society. Although by all accounts working-class housing in the early urban manufacturing centers left much to be desired, Ashton argues that "larger towns were paved, drained, and supplied with running water; . . . and more attention was paid to such things as the disposal of refuse and the proper burial of the dead" (1948:5). All of these factors, hardly associated yet with advanced technology or even industrialism per se, had reduced the death rate by nearly half between 1740 and 1820 in Britain, creating a growing population with far more children surviving infancy.

Table 3.5 Average Life Expectancy

	SWEDEN			ENGLAND AND WALES	
Year	*Male*	*Female*	*Year*	*Male*	*Female*
1755-76	⁓33.2	35.7			
1816-40	39.5	43.6	1841	40.2	42.2
1901-10	54.6	57.0	1901-10	48.5	52.4
1936-40	64.3	66.9	1937	60.2	64.4
1983	73.6	79.6	1981-83	71.3	77.3

SOURCES: *Encyclopaedia Britannica*, 1953 ed., vol. 7, p. 114; *UN Statistical Yearbook*, 1983/84.

It is important to note that quite in advance of "modern medicine" and miracle drugs produced by advanced technology, these relatively simple and straightforward additions to nutrition, clothing, hygiene, and housing possibilities had already done much to improve life expectancy. Health care includes not only what a professional health service system can deliver, but also (perhaps even more fundamentally) basic necessities that are available to the populace, from the highest to the lowest social strata. In the West, the provision of these basics preceded the development of national medical systems, either private or socialized, able to provide modern medical technology for health care. This is doubly important, for in the Third World the process has been at least partially reversed. Medical technology is relatively easy to export, and the training of a corps of competent doctors and paramedical personnel is within the reach of even the poor nations. What is lacking, and perhaps even declining, in the Third World is access by the poorest classes to adequate amounts of the basics of nutrition, housing, clothing, and sanitation. Until these are available, the power of medical technology is limited and may in some instances only complicate the problem of development (see chapter 13).

The progress and breakthroughs of modern science included the field of medicine. As society became more urban, more interdependent, less locally self-sufficient, the role of national medical organizations and public health authorities expanded. The variety of approaches to providing access to professional medical care has been considerable, although all the Western industrial nations have participated in the trend toward some form of comprehensive health system that could loosely be called socialized medicine. Heidenheimer et al. (1975:9) have provided a useful sketch of Western European experience in establishing public health services:

1. Conservative monarchs introduce a national hospital plan to maintain the health of soldiers and ex-soldiers and then extend the services to the general population (Sweden, eighteenth and nineteenth centuries).
2. Conservative politicians introduce public health insurance programs in an attempt to deprive rising socialist parties of an appealing issue (Germany, 1883).
3. Liberal parties introduce health insurance partly in an attempt to keep organized skilled workers from defecting to either conservative or labor parties (Britain, 1911).
4. Social democratic governments take the lead in transforming health systems partially financed through public sources into comprehensive, integrated public systems that supply almost all the health care in the country (Britain, 1948; Sweden, 1970s).

The United States has been the notable laggard in this field. Extreme opposition from the powerful American Medical Association (AMA) and private insurance companies has prevented the establishment of any comprehensive national health insurance program. Public health expenditures, which stood at 0.4 percent of U.S. GNP in 1913, stood at 0.7 percent in 1932 and were still less than 1 percent by 1964 (Heidenheimer et al., 1975:18). For veterans, a special case, socialized medicine has been a reality for some time in the

United States. More recently, the aged under Medicare and the poor under Medicaid have received at least basic coverage. The majority of Americans purchase some medical insurance coverage from private insurance carriers, and a significant percentage (20 to 25 percent in recent estimates) are uninsured and depend on personal finances for purchases of medical care.

Table 3.6 Health Care Indicators

	Switzerland	West Germany	United States	Britain	Sweden	France	Japan
Life expectancy 1981-83							
Males	72.7	69.5	71.0	71.3	73.6	70.2	74.2
Females	79.6	75.4	78.3	77.3	79.6	78.5	79.8
Population per physician	390	420	500	680	410	460	740
Infant mortality/ 1,000 live births	8	10	11	10	7	9	6

Sources: UN *Statistical Yearbook*, 1983/84; World Bank, *World Development Report*, 1986.

Some relatively significant differences exist in the medical emphases of the various systems in the liberal democracies. The British National Health Service (NHS), as Odin Anderson (1972) has shown, has emphasized the role of the general practitioner (GP) physician. The United States has the highest proportions of surgeons (and specialists generally), and Sweden has poured prodigious resources into its hospital centers. It should be added that, in the 1970s, each of these three health systems showed some ability to adapt and re-evaluate its priorities. Under the Labour government of Harold Wilson in the 1970s, the Health Ministry has built up the number and role of local health centers. Hospital-centered care, the most expensive format of health care services, has now been somewhat de-emphasized by the Swedish government in favor of more decentralized health centers. And in the United States, repeated criticisms of large-scale unnecessary surgery performed by a surplus of surgeons has led medical schools once again to emphasize training of doctors in primary medical care fields (internal medicine and pediatrics). The democracies have now committed themselves to providing decent (not necessarily equal or best-quality) medical care to all their citizens, regardless of individual ability to pay.

In reviewing some basic statistics of health care in the liberal democracies, it should be clear that there are only minor differences in longevity, population/physician ratios (except in the case of Japan), and infant mortality rates. Again, the significant differences on a worldwide scale are between the developed nations, both capitalist and communist, and the nations of the

Third World. The lack of major differences in the statistics of the liberal democracies would indicate that, contrary to the propaganda of the AMA, the socialized medicine of our European neighbors has not produced a decline in health standards. To the contrary, as Heidenheimer and others have noted, the United States now trails many, if not most, of the liberal democracies in areas such as infant mortality rates. This is, in turn, attributed not to the aggregate amounts of spending on health care or to the numbers of trained doctors in practice, but rather to the less equitable geographic and social distribution of accessible physician care in the United States as compared with Sweden and Britain.

MORE CORRELATES: HOUSING

Decent housing and a healthy home environment is an important element in the daily welfare of every person. Any discussion of housing conditions in the contemporary liberal democracies should be set in the perspective of how dramatically current circumstances diverge from those of early capitalism or late feudalism. Most observers agree that the housing conditions of the early working class were terrible. T. S. Ashton, a scholarly celebrant of capitalism, nevertheless admits the decline in urban housing standards in England of the early 1800s:

> AFTER 1793 the import of timber from the Baltic was restricted and the price of labour of bricklayers and carpenters went up. . . . This meant that if dwellings were to be let at rents which the workers could afford to pay they had to be smaller and less durable than those of the eighties (1780s: J.N.). The rows of ill-built, back-to-back houses, into which the rapidly growing population of the towns was pressed, were largely the product of wartime conditions [i.e., the Napoleonic wars]. (1948:160)

In some early manufacturing towns such as Manchester and Liverpool, which had large numbers of poor working-class Irish, 10 to 15 percent of the population were living in cellars. Cellars of those times were dark, dank, filthy places, the poorest of housing.

The young Friedrich Engels gave this stirring eyewitness account of the working-class district of Manchester in the year 1842:

> EVERYWHERE half or wholly ruined buildings, some of them actually uninhabited, which means a great deal here; rarely a wooden or stone floor to be seen in the houses, almost uniformly broken, ill-fitting windows and doors, and a state of filth! Everywhere heaps of debris, refuse, and offal, standing pools for gutters, and a stench which would alone make it impossible for a human being in any degree civilised to live in such a district. . . . Passing along a rough bank, among stakes and washing lines, one penetrates into this chaos of small, one-storied, one-

roomed huts, in most of which there is no artificial floor; kitchen, living and sleeping-room all in one. In one such a hole, scarcely five feet long by six broad, I found two beds—and such bedsteads and beds!—which, with a staircase and chimney-place, exactly filled the room. In several others I found absolutely nothing, while the door stood open, and the inhabitants leaned against it. Everywhere before the doors refuse and offal; that any sort of pavement lay underneath could not be seen but only felt, here and there, with the feet. This whole collection of cattle-sheds for human beings was surrounded on two sides by houses and a factory, and on the third by the river, and besides the narrow stair up the bank, a narrow doorway led out into another almost equally ill-built, ill-kept labyrinth of dwellings.

Enough! The whole side of the Irk is built in this way, a planless, knotted chaos of houses, more or less on the verge of uninhabitableness, whose unclean interiors fully correspond with their filthy external surroundings. And how could the people be clean with no proper opportunity for satisfying the most natural and ordinary wants? Privies are so rare here that they are either filled up every day, or are too remote for most of the inhabitants to use. How can people wash when they have only the dirty Irk water at hand, while pumps and water pipes can be found in decent parts of the city alone? . . .

Such is the Old Town of Manchester, and on re-reading my description, I am forced to admit that instead of being exaggerated, it is far from black enough to convey a true impression of the filth, ruin, and uninhabitableness, the defiance of all considerations of cleanliness, ventilation, and health which characterise the construction of this single district, containing at least twenty to thirty thousand inhabitants. And such a district exists in the heart of the second city of England, the first manufacturing city of the world. (Reprinted in Tucker, 1972: 432-34)

This description by Engels, we should note, attests to poor housing conditions well after the end of the Napoleonic Wars, which Ashton cited as the cause of bad housing conditions for workers earlier in the century. Certainly over the next century housing conditions gradually improved for the population, including the working class.

In both Europe and Japan, but not in the United States, tremendous losses in urban housing during World War II created drastic shortages in the early postwar years, which had to be made up before advances beyond the prewar level could be achieved. In most major German and Japanese cities, over 80 percent of prewar housing had been either destroyed or heavily damaged. In France, Britain, and Italy, war damage was less extensive, but shortages resulting from low levels of construction during the Great Depression and near zero levels during the war still called for major housing programs. In the United States as well, inexpensive Veteran's Administration and Federal Housing Authority loans fueled an unprecedented housing boom. However, the balance of public-to-private housing construction has varied considerably in each country. In Europe, the prewar political reluctance to get government involved in housing construction to any significant degree gave way first to the necessity for making up for wartime losses, then to the increased demands for housing created by a growing percentage of elderly citizens (no longer living with their children) and by the postwar baby boom (Heidenheimer, 1975). In Britain, Sweden, France, West Germany, and the Netherlands, among others, public and quasi-public (largely nonprofit, government regulated) housing-starts in the early 1970s still constituted between one-third (West Germany) to two-thirds (Sweden, France) of all new housing.

Again, the experience of the United States is the anomaly, where opposition to major government efforts has kept public housing to less than 1 percent of total housing. This is, of course, partly explained by the lesser need for an immediate massive postwar program of housing construction in the United States, untouched by war damage. It is also partly explained by the ideological reluctance of both major American political parties to oppose private construction firms, real estate interests, apartment owners, and private banks in financing and building public housing on more than a minimal scale. In Europe, Labour, Socialist, and Communist parties have from both ideological heritage and the lessons of practical politics backed low-cost public housing, or public housing in general, against the interests of the capitalist housing marketplace. Parties of the working class have backed the notion of decent housing as a basic right of the individual that should be protected through government. Even Conservative, Gaullist, and Christian Democratic governments find it easier to keep public housing programs going than to face stiff opposition by curtailing them drastically. Finally, it must be recognized that in the United States public housing (as with many aspects of welfare) continues to be identified with a black racial minority long the object of discrimination and hostility. In American society, as in no other Western democracy, this association has stigmatized the very concept of "welfare" and confounded efforts to create public housing programs that would benefit not only blacks but other lower income groups as well.

The final message of this section, however, must again be directed to the relative abundance of decent housing for citizens of the liberal democracies in comparison with that for the other peoples of the world, especially the Third World. With French and Italian achievements somewhat lower and United States, Swedish, and West German conditions somewhat higher, the supply of basic modern housing in the democracies stands apart from that of the rest of the world. It is understandably difficult for most Americans to appreciate the housing revolution that has accompanied urbanization and industrialization over the past one hundred fifty years. In the United States, most average housing over a century old has been torn down and replaced with newer constructions. But in Europe, despite the destruction of both world wars, there are still examples of housing that date back to feudal times. In small towns in West Germany, for example, such as Linz or Detmold, there are neighborhoods with houses of eighteenth-century vintage intact and inhabited. These are not only the townhouses of the rich, but more modest houses of the lower classes. Here one has the opportunity to examine feudal-period dwellings, with small central rooms, small windows and doors, and sleeping lofts. These cramped lodgings once housed large families with many children and sometimes an aged grandparent or two. Originally they had no indoor plumbing, running water, or electricity. Most are now modernized. In some historical museums, one can see replicas of the rural huts of peasant families or the covered carts in which shepherds slept, which were their only housing.

CORRELATES: THE WELFARE STATE

In addition to education, health care, and housing, we can identify other government programs that can be subsumed under the general heading of welfare. A 1964 study by the U.S. Department of Health, Education, and Welfare (HEW) lists five categories of welfare benefits: (1) old age, invalidism, death; (2) health care; (3) work disability compensation; (4) unemployment compensation; and (5) family allowances. The HEW study omits housing as an area of welfare concern, perhaps because system commitment to public housing in the United States has been so weak. By the 1960s, all of the Western democracies had developed some programs or coverage in all of the five areas, with the exception of the United States, which had no programs in the category of family allowances (Groth, 1971: 162-63). In the late 1960s, the Nixon Administration proposed a Family Assistance Plan (FAP), which would have provided uniform assistance to needy families with children. Heidenheimer et al. (1975:204-5, 218-19) describe the defeat of the FAP proposal by an alliance of liberals, who complained that too little was being offered, and conservatives, who wanted to kill the proposal outright. Support from the White House also faded in the course of the struggle over welfare reform, and the proposal was lost. However, a Supplementary Security Income program to be administered by the existing Social Security Administration was passed, though it was limited to the categories of the elderly, blind, and disabled poor. The food stamp program was greatly expanded, with provisions for a uniform minimum income level for family participation. Heidenheimer et al. (1975:219) report that by 1975 "the food stamp program covered more persons (including working family heads) than the original highly controversial FAP proposal, cost as much, and offered benefits at least as large."

The welfare state in the advanced capitalist nations has been in the process of development for nearly a century. Its first major or large-scale origins can be found in Bismarck's social insurance programs for health, the aged, and disabled of the 1880s. The purpose of these programs, as mentioned earlier, was to blunt the appeal of the rising socialist movement in the Kaiser's Germany. Most observers (see Groth, 1971:158; Heidenheimer et al., 1975: 194-95) ascribe the first passage of an unemployment insurance program under the British Liberal government in 1911 to an attempt to win over the workers from the growing Labour party. Once again, the basic motivations were not altruism or humanitarianism (although these were of course widely advertised), but a political response to the perceived threat of socialism and a recognition of the determination of a growing and militant industrial working class. Even so, the breadth of the coverage and the benefit levels of social programs before the Great Depression were quite modest. This was a pre-Keynesian era of economic thinking in the West, and government welfare outlays were not generally viewed as an integral part of government action that would maintain (or even raise) consumer spending, vital to a healthy economy. Thus these early welfare programs did little to avert or alleviate the downward spiral of unemployment and suffering of the Depression era. Even the reforms of the 1930s by the New Deal and other Depression-era governments in the West were insufficient to spark an economic recovery. Most observers agree that only the massive defense spending for the military of World War II provided the impetus for a return to prosperity.

It is only in the post-World War II period that the commitment of the liberal democracies to significant welfare spending levels on a variety of programs has gained a political consensus and become a fiscal reality. Quantitative comparisons of government outputs in the welfare field are likely to be complex and often controversial, depending on definitions of what gets included or excluded as welfare spending. Questions of whether welfare programs produce any greater income equality are even touchier. Fortunately, there are some figures available that give rough impressions of the extent of welfare spending within nations over time and of the variation among nations by political system-type. Table 3.7 documents the upward trend of social spending as a percentage of gross domestic product (GDP) since World War II. In all cases there has been a significant rise, but with some equally important differences in levels and rates of growth. Some leaders in welfare spending in the early 1950s, West Germany and France, have remained relative leaders. Some nations, the United States, Japan, and Switzerland, have remained pinch-penny laggards, despite rises in spending levels as a percentage of GDP. Sweden, now popularized as the prototype of the welfare state, occupied only a middling position twenty-five years ago and became only gradually a welfare leader. The Dutch, relative laggards in 1950, experienced in the 1960s an explosion of welfare reform, which by 1970 placed them among the big spenders of the liberal democratic community.

Occasionally the "creeping socialism" or welfarism feared by conservatives not only creeps but also gallops. It is not necessarily the case that certain nations, by virtue of some unchangeable "individualist" or "collectivist" political culture, are destined to remain at the low or high end of the spectrum of welfare spending among the liberal democracies. In fact, comparative studies of levels of welfare spending have found relatively few correlates of welfare spending that would explain the differences within the liberal democracies (see Wilensky, 1975; Heidenheimer et al., 1975; Pryor, 1968; Groth, 1971; Jackman, 1975).

Table 3.7 Social Security Expenditures as Percent of GDP, 1960-1980

	1960	1970	1980
Switzerland	7.5	10.1	13.8
West Germany	15.4	17.0	23.8
United States	6.8	9.6	12.7
Britain	10.8	13.8	17.7
Sweden	10.9	18.8	32.0
France	13.2	15.3	26.8
Japan	4.9	5.4	10.9
Netherlands	11.1	20.0	28.6

SOURCE: ILO, *Cost of Social Security, 1978-80*, 1985.

More important than the still-considerable differences that currently exist among the rich democracies of the West is the cleavage globally between the rich and poor nations. In a survey of sixty-four nations for the year 1966, Wilensky (1975:19) finds that the top quartile of nations in terms of per capita GNP spent an average of 13.8 percent of that GNP on social security programs, whereas the two bottom quartiles spent only 4.0 percent and 2.5 percent respectively. All nations in the top quartile were liberal democracies, including the United States, Sweden, Switzerland, West Germany, France, Britain, and the Netherlands. In the second richest quartile of nations, the level of welfare spending averaged 10.1 percent of GNP for all sixteen nations, but this aggregate of semirich countries was a mixed bag of communist, liberal democratic, and developing nations. For the five developed liberal democracies in this quartile (Japan, Italy, Austria, Ireland, Israel), average welfare spending was 12.8 percent of GNP; for the seven richest and most industrialized communist nations (USSR, Czechoslovakia, East Germany, Hungary, Poland, Bulgaria, Rumania) the average was 11.5 percent of GNP; but for the four developing nations (Venezuela, Spain, Greece, Trinidad-Tobago), the average fell to 5.9 percent, much closer to the general averages for the poorer nations of the bottom thirty-two nations in the study. In other words, on a global scale, there are two categories of nations that qualitatively lead in levels of welfare spending: the developed liberal democracies and the developed communist nations (for further discussion of welfare spending in the communist countries, see chapter 8).

Without going into the effects of welfare or the manner of its application and distribution among the various programs, all of which are more debatable points, it can be stated that there is general agreement that welfare spending reaches the highest levels on a global scale among the developed nations, both democratic and communist. While it is problematic to speculate on what levels of welfare spending would be found in a contemporary industrial fascist system, Groth (1971:171-74) notes that the fascist regime in Italy and the Nazi regime in Germany "spent less [on welfare] in proportion to national income than their predecessors" (173). This was, in part, consistent with the fascist tendency to extoll "survival of the fittest" notions, which relegate the weak and poor to continued oppression or extinction by the strong. But Groth also remarks: "The relative niggardliness of fascism and nazism was rooted not only in the social philosophy of its leaders but in the social and economic conservatism of many of their backers, allies and supporters" (174).

If we concentrate only on differences in levels of spending for welfare within the community of liberal democracies, there are two explanations that scholars in this area have uncovered. The first is that the earlier welfare programs were instituted (Heidenheimer et al., 1975:189), the higher the current levels of spending for those programs. The basic reasoning is that once initiated and established, administrative "incrementalism" tends to widen the base of coverage and raise the levels of support over time (i.e. "creeping socialism" or the "foot in the door" notion). Typically, coverage is initially extended to limited and less well-off portions of the population (the poor, aged, blind, disabled) and broadened stepwise into comprehensive plans for most or all citizens. Because of the prosperity of the postwar era, and especially in the inflation-prone years of the latter 1960s and 1970s, there has been a tendency to link benefits to current living standards and living costs. This has been done by raising benefit levels to a more contemporary living standard and by linking benefits to rates of inflation, assuring increased spending in proportion to inflation rates. This has also acted as a considerable drain on the funding for social security systems. In the United States and West Germany, two of the most powerful capitalist economies, the financing of social security had become an acute problem by the mid-seventies, with major new taxation required to refinance the system.

A second factor has been related in some studies (Pryor, 1968) to levels of welfare spending is the proportion of aged people in the society. The proportion of the population over the age of sixty-five has grown considerably because of increased life expectancy and declining birthrates since the inception of social security programs in all the liberal democracies. Pryor's data (1968:466) indicate that in the late 1950s, over 60 percent of welfare expenditures went to the aged in one form or another in the United States, West Germany, and Austria. Thus a rise in the proportion of the elderly has a major impact on levels of welfare spending.

Beyond this, there is little that can be definitively said about the reasons for the relative positions of the liberal democracies in welfare spending. The work of scholars such as Jackman, Wilensky, Heidenheimer, and Pryor has refuted many myths about the supposed effects on welfare spending of "individualist" versus "collectivist" ethics, military spending versus welfare spending, or centralized versus decentralized political systems. Wilensky (1975:113-19) is particularly effective in knocking down fallacious arguments about the harmful effects of welfare spending on democracy itself, while not ignoring the real possibilities of middle-class taxpayer revolts against welfare.

We cannot begin to untangle many of the most interesting but complex issues of welfare spending here. It is enough to close out this chapter with the overriding conclusion that the liberal democracies are among the leaders in aggregate levels of welfare spending, one more correlate in the configuration of the political system.

Chapter 4

Social Equality—Opportunity
versus Results

CHAPTER 3 DEALT WITH THE ACHIEVEMENTS of liberal democracies in advanced capitalist societies in the general area of economic development; even
areas of public health and welfare spending were seen to be correlates of
economic development. Nothing in this chapter negates or "cancels out"
these achievements. But, as we shall show, entrepreneurial liberty for the
individual and its defense in a profit-oriented capitalist economy has effects
on social inequality. Higher levels of average per-capita income do not imply
that everyone is sharing general economic growth equally, equitably, or at
all. The poor, the unemployed, racial/ethnic or regional minorities, and
women may not be gaining or may be losing ground even if the economy
overall is "booming." This depends on the extent of social inequality in the
system and on the ability and commitment of the system to reduce social
inequities.

In this chapter the distribution of wealth and income, justice, health/
education/welfare, political elite recruitment, and the situation of minorities
and women in the liberal democracies are discussed under the heading of
inequality. Under the general umbrella of quality of life (see chapter 6), such
problems as crime, drugs/alcoholism, pornography, divorce rates, social
isolation, unemployment, and pollution are discussed. In part, this is clearly
an artificial division, since the ill effects of crime, drugs, alcoholism, pollution, joblessness, and even the loss of family values fall more heavily on the
poor, the urban working class, and the minorities than on the wealthy,
suburban, dominant strata. To be sure, drug addiction and alcoholism are
also problems of the well-to-do and especially of their offspring, but the
upper-middle-class youth addict in all probability avoids the criminal justice
system and gets first-rate treatment and understanding for his or her addiction along with repeated chances to pursue a promising career pattern.
Pollution and crime can threaten virtually any neighborhood or community,
but the more affluent residents have the resources to run away to newer,
safer, cleaner areas, taking their resources with them and even further hindering the ability of their ex-neighborhood to meet the threat of crime or
pollution. Still, there are at least some limits to the ability of those in higher
social strata to escape the problems that typify modern capitalism and

quality-of-life issues. The division is probably valid as a relative distinction, certainly not as an absolute one.

Inequality: How Much and Is It Changing?

The liberal notion of equality that developed in the writings of Locke, Montesquieu, Madison, and Jefferson was specifically limited to the legal-administrative sphere of society. Its radical, even revolutionary, character lay in its opposition to the legally sanctioned privileges of the aristocracy and the church, which were privileges of birth and state-sponsored religious dogma rather than of achievement or free choice. As one author put it recently:

> The classic liberal concept of equality implies equality before the law, where there are no legally designated differences in status, reward, or privilege without regard to performance. Specifically, it originated as a middle-class concept that entailed opposition to aristocratic privilege, promotion of individual liberties against perceived governmental oppression, and promotion of the rules that the same legal standards are applicable to all males. In its more advanced manifestations, liberal equality entailed such political goals as extension of the suffrage. Equality in this sense is not concerned with differences in opportunity that are the result of differences in the distribution of social and economic resources. (Mayer, 1977:136)

Even this statement probably gives too much credit to classic liberalism, since, as described in chapter 2, liberalism was quite content to limit the suffrage to male property holders. It was primarily the not-always-peaceful agitation of the labor movement and later the women's suffrage movement that forced the gradual step-by-step expansion of voting rights. Still, it is clear that classic liberalism raises no objections against gross inequalities of wealth, income, education, housing, and health care as long as these disparities are not fixed by law. In fact, classic liberalism has been most consistent in its objections to any political efforts to ameliorate social inequality. Economist Gaston Rimlinger (1971:305–31) shows that at best, classic liberalism is compatible with some forms of social security financed by wage-earners themselves, as long as they *do not decrease levels of income* or wealth inequality, but attempt only to better manage the scarce market resources of individual citizens.

The feudal order, which liberalism opposed, contained some rather elaborate tradition-based reciprocal obligations between lord and peasant, which included not only a paternalistic *noblesse oblige* on the part of the aristocracy, but in many cases detailed arrangements for the provision of protection and welfare of the masses in cases of armed attack, drought, plague, and other calamities. In its period of ascendency, therefore, liberalism sought to break down notions of class (social) obligations, paternalistic or otherwise. Classic liberal theory, supported by the doctrines of Parson Malthus and of Social Darwinism, in fact opposed even those elements of social welfare that were patently nonredistributive:

> THE liberal capitalist civilization that emerged in the late eighteenth century rejected the traditional protectionism of the old social order. It denied the poor man's claim to a right to protection by society; it discarded the concept of paternal responsibility of the rich for the poor. In the liberal industry state, every man was to be free to pursue his fortune and was to be responsible for his success or failure. (Rimlinger, 1971:35)

Liberal theory, a forerunner of liberal democracy in the West, fought against claims of social obligation and social justice. It is in the area of social inequalities that liberal democracies have been most reluctant to act and in which liberal democracies are most likely to be half-hearted in actions to mitigate inequalities.

THE WEALTH-AND-INCOME GAP

We can start most reasonably with a discussion of disparities in income and wealth that characterize the Western democracies. Economist Martin Schnitzer expresses the importance of wealth distribution as a key to understanding disparities in other areas quite nicely, as well as the problem that wealth inequality raises for the meritocratic claim of democracy:

> ALTHOUGH wealth in itself is not a bad thing, there is certainly a conflict between the way in which it is concentrated in the hands of a few and the American belief in equality of opportunity. With wealth goes economic power and prestige. The wealthy can afford to send their children to the best schools and provide them with the right contacts in employment. Inheritances also compound inequality through generations. Those who are wealthy can finance their own or others' campaigns for political office and thus successfully obtain political power. In no country is this more pronounced than the United States. The wealthy can hire expensive and successful lawyers to widen the scope of legitimate tax avoidance for themselves and also to resolve in their favor any legal conflicts with the less wealthy. (1974:43)

Although Schnitzer's evaluations are limited here to the United States, we shall show that his remarks are applicable with some modifications to the liberal democracies in general. The effects of wealth disparity go beyond the ability to "buy" various benefits; rather they constitute together the basis for the continuation (although at a high level of overall development and economic well-being) of a class-divided society.

First of all, however, we should establish some definitions of wealth and income and then try to measure the actual extent of inequality that exists currently in a number of liberal democracies. By wealth we mean the sum total of all assets owned by individuals (or families). This includes land, buildings, factories, stocks and bonds, homes, jewels, every imaginable kind of commodity, as well as cash on hand. By income we mean reported individual (or family) earnings in a single year. These include income from work such as wages and salaries, and income from wealth, such as interest, capital gains, dividends, and rents. Despite some rather complex issues of reporting accuracy, valuation, and cross-national units of measurement for income and wealth in various societies (see Schnitzer, 1974; Cromwell; 1977, for some cogent explanations), we can make some reasonably accurate calculations and comparisons among the liberal democracies in this area.

Two tools frequently used by economists to summarize the degree of inequality in the wealth or income (or any other commodity) distribution are the Lorenz curve and the Gini ratio. In figure 4.1, a solid line represents the Lorenz curve for an entirely equalized distribution of income (which exists in no country and serves only as a polar extreme). This straight line indicates that any given percentage of the population receives the same percentage of the national income. The "lowest" 20 percent gets 20 percent, the "top" 20 percent gets 20 percent, the bottom 60 percent gets 60 percent, and so on.

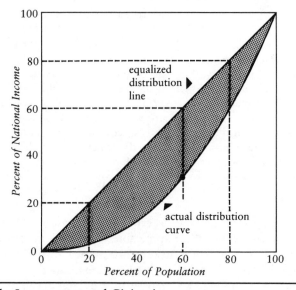

Figure 4.1 The Lorenz curve and Gini ratio.

The dotted line indicates an hypothesized Lorenz curve for an income distribution in which the bottom 20 percent on the income ladder receives only 5
percent of national income, the top 20 percent receives 40 percent, and the
bottom 60 percent gets 30 percent of national income. In this hypothesized
example, the shaded area between the actual Lorenz curve and the completely equalized Lorenz curve (actually a forty-five degree angle straight line)
represents the amount of inequality in the system. This area of inequality can
be expressed as a ratio to the maximum theoretically possible amount of
inequality and is called the Gini ratio. The greater the Gini ratio, which runs
from a minimum of zero to a maximum of unity, the greater the inequality of
income distribution.

Figure 4.2 gives the Lorenz curves for the distribution of income in the
United States for 1971 and the distribution of wealth in the United States for
1962. The Gini ratio for income in 1971 was .34, while for wealth in 1962 it
was .75, or more than twice the level for income. The lesson here is that
wealth, which is a more basic indicator of the distribution of total resources
capable of being applied to a variety of goals, is far more unequally distributed than annual income.

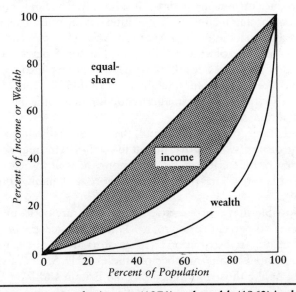

Figure 4.2 Lorenz curves for income (1971) and wealth (1962) in the United States

Some figures for other liberal democracies would indicate that generally
wealth is far more concentrated in the hands of a tiny minority than is
income. In Britain, for example, the Gini ratio for pretax income in 1967
was .33, while the Gini ratio for wealth distribution was 0.85, again more
than double the income index. Table 4.1 gives some Gini ratios for a number

of Western democracies in a variety of estimates. Clearly, the share of total income going to the richest 10 percent of the population is greater than the share going to the poorest 40 percent; France and Australia seem to have the greatest disparities and West Germany and Japan the smallest among those listed.

Finally, there are some estimates of income distribution after the tax systems in each country have worked their will. There is only a fairly narrow range of Gini ratios for family income in most of the liberal democracies. France is the exceptional case, having a far greater degree of inequality of income than any of the other advanced democracies. France is far from the *égalité* notion expressed by the French Revolution of 1789, the farthest of any liberal democracy. The Gini ratios for pretax reported income indicate that much of the inequality in income is relatable to income from property, which is in many cases nonreported and untaxable income. These ratios also serve as a benchmark against which to measure the effects of government taxation on income distribution.

In the case of Sweden, the tax system, including national and local income taxes and contributions to the national old-age pension program, are structured so as to reduce income inequality considerably. The Gini ratio in 1970 drops from .36 on pretax income to .26 on after-tax income. The bottom 40 percent of Swedish income earners received only 15.3 percent of pretax income, but 20.4 percent of after-tax income. The top 5 percent of income earners in Sweden accounted for 17.1 percent of pretax income, but only 10.8 percent of after-tax income (Schnitzer, 1974:85–86). In Britain and West Germany also there is some smaller reduction in income inequality as a result of national tax structures.

In the United States, on the other hand, there is virtually no reduction of levels of income disparity from government tax policy. This may seem rather surprising in view of loud cries of anguish among the well-to-do of confiscatory or punitive tax rates. Such protests come more reasonably from middle-income families.

How is it possible that a progressive income tax rate of 14 percent to a maximum rate of 70 percent (prior to 1981) failed to achieve *any* measurable degree of income redistribution? The reasons are both clear and have been well documented in any number of studies of U. S. tax laws. United States tax laws, unlike those in Sweden or even Britain and West Germany, have massive tax loopholes that lower considerably the tax rates actually paid by the wealthy. In particular, capital gains (on sale of assets held six months or more) are taxed at only half the rate applied to wages and salaries; also, interest on state and local bonds is entirely tax-free. In both areas, the average citizen does not have sufficient capital to benefit from these tax loopholes. Only those who already hold wealth can and do benefit from these tax provisions that permit income from wealth to be taxed not at all or less than income from work. Philip Stern (1973:94) has noted that for those fortunate citizens with annual incomes of over $1 million, all tax loopholes added together provide an average *savings* in taxes (tax avoidance) of $720,490 yearly and reduce the effective rate of taxation to about half the official rate. Estimates of losses in tax revenue range from a low of $36 billion to a high of $97 billion for the year 1971. As both Stern and Schnitzer have noted, the effect is that the progressivity of the income tax is reduced, and at the very top of the income scale some $2 billion of tax welfare is doled out to the three thousand richest American families. This is, for comparison, equal to the total amount spent by the federal government in 1971 to provide food stamps for the needy (Schnitzer, 1974:47). If welfare for the rich balances welfare for the poor, it should not be surprising if the degree of income inequality remains unchanged. Those in the middle tend to be the greatest tax losers.

Table 4.1 Gini Index for Income Distribution in the Liberal Democracies

		Pretax Reported	*Percent of Income Going To*	
			Top 10 Percent	Bottom 40 Percent
United States	(1971)	.34	23.3	17.2 (1980)
Sweden	(1970)	.36	28.1	20.5 (1981)
Britain	(1967)	.33	23.4	18.5 (1979)
West Germany	(1968)	.39	24.0	22.4 (1978)
France	(1962)	.50	30.5	16.4 (1975)
Japan	(1962)	.39	22.4	21.9 (1979)
Australia	(1966–67)	.30	30.5	15.4 (1976)

SOURCES: Schnitzer, 1974; Howe, 1975:215; World Bank, *World Development Report*, 1986.

The existence of tax loopholes for the rich is not, of course, an exclusively American phenomenon. Undertaxation of capital gains in particular constitutes in all liberal democracies, with the exception of Sweden, "the most important area of inequality in the treatment of various income sources" (Musgrove, 1969:197). In Britain and West Germany there are similar opportunities for the wealthy to avoid any heavy taxation of capital gains income, and again it is only the wealthy who can profit from such loopholes.

Among the most regressive tax systems in the liberal democracies is the French, which only compounds the greater inequality of pretax income in that country. Richard Musgrove, in a study of fiscal systems in Britain, Sweden, West Germany, France, and the United States (for 1961), found that real rates of taxation were most regressive in France. In terms of the difference in effective rates of taxation for those earning $100,000 as opposed to those earning $3,000, the French difference was only 29 percent versus 38 percent for the United States, 41 percent for West Germany, 48 percent for Sweden, and 57 percent for Britain. The French government, in an OECD study for the years 1965–1971, relied least on income taxes for its revenues, and the income tax, even with all its failings, is still the most progressive form of taxation. In 1971, only 10.8 percent of French tax revenues were from personal income taxes, versus 25.6 percent in West Germany, 32.1 percent in Britain, 35.1 percent in the United States, and at the top of the list 45.8 percent in social democratic Sweden (cited in Heidenheimer, et al., 1975:232). France is also one of the few liberal democracies that has still not instituted an income tax withholding system, with the result that French tax authorities are basically unable to check on reported income of taxpayers. In France, tax-reported income makes up only 23.8 percent of total personal income, compared with 75.1 percent in Britain, 79.3 percent in the United States, and 92.3 percent in West Germany (Tanzi, 1969:78–80). In France, as in Italy, there is massive tax evasion through nonreporting of income, especially by the wealthy, although also by lower-income marginal workers. As Heidenheimer et al. suggest, this is a reflection of the ability of the well-to-do to flout tax laws with impunity: "The French system of tax collection . . . assumes from the start that several of the most important non-salaried groups subject to income tax—the well-to-do, small businessmen, and professionals—will not declare anything like their real incomes no matter what the law says" (1975:237).

Despite the introduction since the turn of the century of nominally (officially) quite progressive income tax laws in all of the liberal democracies and the expansion in the post-World War II era of total levels of taxation (of all kinds), there are some notable differences in the effects, if any, of taxation on the levels of income inequality. In Sweden, in fact, a progressive and strictly enforced tax system does produce significant equalization in the distribution of income. In France (and Italy) massive tax fraud by the rich is tolerated by the government, which thereby increases the burden of taxation on the average income earner. In the United States, and to some degree in Britain and West Germany, tax loopholes offer what amounts to tax welfare for the rich, which again shifts the burden of taxation to middle-income groups.

Even as the costs of government have risen as a percentage of GNP from the 1950s to the 1980s, the propertied interests (except in Sweden) have been able to shift tax burdens from their shoulders enough to avoid any significant reduction in income inequality. Propertied interests have had the power, in one way or another, to offset the potentially progressive effects of higher income taxation with increased tax welfare for themselves.

The current situation is clear enough. Despite all the rhetoric about equality in the modern welfare state, there exists a considerable degree of income inequality in all the liberal democracies, with Sweden having the most equal income distribution (after taxes) and France the most unequal.

With respect to wealth, by almost any standard there is a tremendous degree of concentration of assets in the hands of a tiny minority, and tax policy has had precious little effect on this inequality of wealth. It has already been pointed out that in all the liberal democracies (and in all nonsocialist economies in general) wealth distribution is far more concentrated than income distribution. How extreme this concentration is can be illustrated by data from the United States, Britain, and West Germany (see table 4.2). In each case, the bottom half of the population owns only 5 to 10 percent of the nation's wealth. In the United States, the bottom 25.4 percent of the population owns zero assets, having debts that offset their ownership of homes, cars, and other personal possessions; the bottom 8 percent of the population actually have negative net wealth, owing more than they are "worth." At the other end of the spectrum, the top 1 or 2 percent of the population hold title to between 30 and 40 percent of all the national wealth, and the top 20 percent own in the neighborhood of 80 percent of their nation's assets. This very high polarization of wealth adds significantly to income inequality, since income from property is even more concentrated than property itself. Most assets of average families are in the form of homes, cars, and life insurance policy equity, none of which earns income.

Table 4.2 Distribution of Wealth in the United States, Britain, and West Germany

UNITED STATES (1962)[a]		BRITAIN (1970)		WEST GERMANY (1968)[a]	
Population	Wealth Held	Population	Wealth Held	Population	Wealth Held
Top 0.5%	25.8%	Top 1%	20.7%	Top 0.4%	23.8%
Top 1.4%	38.7%	Top 2%	28.0%	Top 1.1%	33.7%
Top 7.5%	59.1%	Top 5%	40.9%	Top 3.6%	49.8%
Top 18.7%	76.2%	Top 10%	51.9%	Top 20.5%	79.1%
Top 43.1%	93.2%	Top 50%	90.2%	Top 55.7%	95.0%

a. Percentages calculated from absolute figures cited.

SOURCE: Schnitzer, 1974:44, 129, 195.

Income from property overwhelmingly goes to the rich, increasing their wealth further. Corporate stock, state and local bonds, rentable properties, land, in short almost all forms of wealth that are income-producing are concentrated in the hands of a very small minority. Even in the United States, where stockholding has the widest base, it is the rich who receive the lion's share of stock dividends. Socialist critic Michael Harrington describes the situation thus: "The top 1 percent of the wealth holders own 62 percent of all publicly held corporate stock; the top 5 percent have 86 percent, the top 20 percent have 97 percent. So much for our stockholder democracy" (1976:277). One study calculated that in Britain in 1959 fully 60 percent of all income from property went to the top 1 percent of income earners, and 99 percent of all income from wealth went to the top 10 percent on the income scale (Meade, 1964:table 1; cited in Schnitzer, 1974:197).

Granted that there still exists an enormous concentration of wealth in the liberal democracies, and lesser but quite formidable concentrations of income as well, isn't there a trend toward greater equality? Some have argued that as the modern welfare state has emerged in the Western democracies, distribution of income and wealth has become gradually more egalitarian, although few, given the data above, would argue that we have reached any sort of egalitarian state of affairs as yet. Economist Simon Kuznets (1950) theorized several decades ago that as traditional agrarian societies begin to industrialize, the degree of income inequality rises initially (in the era of robber baron capitalism) and then tends to decline as the industrial society matures. Daniel Bell has boldly claimed that "a sticky fact of Western society over the past 200 years has been the steady decrease in income disparity among persons" (cited by Harrington, 1976:276).

However, it is clear from careful work on income distribution in the United States by Williamson and Lindert (1976) that it is nonsense to speak of any steady decline in income disparity over the past two centuries. As recently as the 1920s there was a marked trend in the opposite direction, and there have been substantial periods since the late eighteenth century (e.g., 1820–1860) of sharply increasing inequality. There are, however, some data that support a much more modest thesis of decreasing income and wealth inequality since World War I. In Britain, a 1975 royal commission report shows a decline in the before-tax income of the richest 1 percent from 17.1 percent of national income in 1938–1939 to 10.6 percent by 1949–1950 and to 6 percent by 1972–1973. After-tax shares of income for the top 1 percent were 11.7, 5.8, and 4 percent respectively (Harrington, 1975:270). This is attributed to the egalitarianism of the British Labour party acting through governmental policy. In the area of wealth ownership, the holdings of the top 1 percent declined from 69 percent of total wealth in 1911–1913 to 42 percent in 1960. Wealth still remained heavily concentrated among the richest 10 percent. In 1911–1913 the top decile in wealth held 92 percent of all assets, and in 1960 they still held fully 82 percent. Another study by Robert Lampman (1960) indicates that in the United States in 1922, the top 1 percent owned 31.6 percent of all wealth versus 26.0 percent by 1956. Bell (1974:451) has argued that the decrease in disparities among persons has come "not by distinct policies and judgments about fairness, but by technology, which has changed the cost of products and made more things available to more people"; others (discussed by Parkin, 1971:114–28) have cited industrialism in general and in some instances (Sweden, Norway, Britain) the effects of a strong socialist/labor party ideology of egalitarianism.

But the facts that seem to indicate a long-run trend toward greater equality in income and wealth are partial and are contradicted by other studies. Gabriel Kolko insists that there was "no significant trend towards income equality in the United States between 1910 and 1959" (1962:13). Parkin (1971:120), citing evidence from Britain and Norway, concludes that while there may have been some movement toward greater equality in the immediate post-World War II years, this trend was not strong and was reversed in the late 1950s. Peter Henle (1972) of the Library of Congress, in a comprehensive study of income distribution in the United States from 1958 to 1970, found that the Gini ratio for wages and salaries for all male workers increased from .328 to .356 and that the Gini ratio for total earnings for males increased from .399 to .428 over this period. Schnitzer's (1974:112) data for West Germany indicate that the distribution of after-tax family incomes had a Gini ratio of .396 in 1950, .384 in 1955, .380 in 1960, .387 in 1968, and .392 in 1970. In a major study of wealth concentration in the United States, sponsored by the Joint Economic Committee of the U.S. Congress, the degree of wealth inequality was found to have increased between 1963 and 1983. In 1963, the richest .5 percent of the population controlled 25.4 percent of the nation's wealth, and this increased to 35.1 percent by 1983. The richest 10 percent owned 65.1 percent of the wealth in 1963, and this rose to 71.7 percent by 1983 (Kloby, 1987:7). If the value of private homes is excluded, to give a picture of the distribution of potential income-producing wealth, the inequality is much greater still. In 1983, the top .5 percent of the population owned fully 45.1 percent of all private assets (excluding family homes), and the top 10 percent owned 83.2 percent.This partial information indicates that the *current trend* in income and wealth distribution in West Germany and the United States, and perhaps generally in the liberal democracies, is in fact *towards greater inequality*.

It may well be that because of the Great Depression, which ruined many of the rich, and World War II, which quickly produced full employment and higher wartime wages in a scarce labor market, there was a shift toward greater income equality in several of the liberal democracies between 1929 and 1945 (see Harrington, 1976:277; Schnitzer, 1974:57; Williamson and Lindert, 1976:73–77). It would appear that by the late 1950s and early 1960s, despite the growth of welfare programs and increased levels of taxation, the trend toward greater equality had been halted and then reversed in countries such as the United States and West Germany. Despite the significant rise of the standard of living for the population as a whole, there would seem to be no general movement toward income or wealth equality in the post-World War II period. Capitalism, even in the modern welfare-state democracy, seems to have (or better, seems to have retained) a strong tendency toward greater inequality, which requires strong and committed government policy backed by a well-organized and determined working class (as in Sweden) to counterbalance.

Most pieces of information that show reductions in income-wealth inequality come from the Depression-World War II years, and it is doubtful whether economic disaster and world war can be considered as rational tools of the political system in promoting greater equality.

Government policy in the liberal democracies thus has to run very hard just to keep income/wealth inequality at its present concentrated levels and to counterbalance strong free market tendencies toward even greater concentrations. The fears of some (Bell, Glazer) and the hopes of others (Wilensky) that the liberal democracies are sliding into radical or even noticeable egalitarian redistribution of income-wealth are probably unfounded and good only as political mythology of the welfare state. Parkin has summarized it quite well:

> THUS, if the first post-war decade was a period characterized by a certain degree of income equalization, the second decade was one in which the trend went into reverse. This appears to have been a general West European pattern, and one which has not been noticeably checked by Social Democratic administrations. Speculation concerning the drive towards income equalization seems to have been greatly influenced by the conditions of the early post-war period. But the recent concern with the extent of poverty in affluent societies marks a distinct change in mood and underlines the point that the drive towards inequality, inherent in a market system, is not easily held in check. (1971:120–21).

EDUCATIONAL INEQUALITY: MONEY VERSUS MERIT

We began this discussion of inequality in the liberal democracies with a quote from Martin Schnitzer on the ways in which money can be transformed into occupational, educational, and political privilege. In this section we will detail some of the disparities in life opportunities due to inequalities of wealth. It must be emphasized at the start, however, that for the overwhelming majority of the well-to-do, young and old alike, wealth is inherited, not self-made. The rags-to-riches dream of America especially and to some extent of all capitalist societies has indeed been fulfilled for a few in each generation, yet all the data we have on the wealthy in *every* liberal democracy indicates that the wealthy were born into wealth. The advantages that money confers are thus unearned by these individuals, which contradicts both the norm of equality of opportunity and the standard of merit achievement.

One area of conferred privilege is education. We have already recounted the "class channeling" system of many European school systems (chapter 3). Parkin's study shows that only small minorities of university students in Britain (25 percent), Norway (25 percent), Sweden (16 percent), Denmark (10 percent), France (8 percent), Austria (8 percent), the Netherlands (5 percent), and West Germany (5 percent) were of working-class backgrounds at the beginning of the 1960s. In Britain, with a larger-than-average proportion of working-class university students, only 2 percent of all working-class children got as far as the university versus 20 percent of all middle-class children (Heidenheimer et al., 1975:131). Even these figures underestimate the disparity of educational opportunities, since the definition of middle-class is a relatively broad one and includes some fairly modest positions. A definition of the really well-to-do upper middle and upper class would show much more than a ten-to-one advantage.

The expansion of the higher education system in the 1960s and 1970s in many if not all of the liberal democracies undoubtedly gave many individuals greater opportunities both in education and in career choices, yet recent studies have concluded that the expansion of college-level education has not and cannot by itself produce greater equality. The reasons are many. In the first place, those best able to take advantage of the increases in college and university enrollment were the sons and daughters of the middle class, regardless of merit or innate ability. A study by David Cohen (1972, cited by Harrington, 1976: 273) shows that of U.S. high school seniors in the bottom 20 percent according to IQ scores and whose families were in the bottom 20 percent on the income scale, only 10 percent went to some sort of college. Of those seniors in the bottom 20 percent in IQ scores but whose parents were in the wealthiest 20 percent, 40 percent went on to college. In the European school systems there exist elite private secondary schools that provide quality university-track preparation for the offspring of the affluent.

Even in the United States, where most middle-class children are likely to go to public schools, the wealth related property-tax system of public school financing provides similar disparities in quality of education between middle-class and working-class districts. James Coons, in a study of public schools in Ohio, which does more state funding of its schools than most states, concludes: "In Ohio a child's public education is dependent for its quality upon the private wealth of its district. It is as simple as that" (1970:80; cited in Heidenheimer et al., 1975:132). This is compounded in the United States by the racial factor, so that poorer schools, especially in the inner cities, also tend to have overwhelmingly black enrollments. Table 4.3 illustrates the double correlation of family income and racial composition with percentages of students in college prep/honors tracks. The percentage of students aiming for college education is close to the percentage of non-black students in each case, but it also climbs steadily by neighborhood income bracket.

Table 4.3 Family Income, Race, and High School Education *(Washington, D.C., 1964)*

High School	Median Neighborhood Income	Percentage of Black Students	Percentage of Students in College/Preparatory Honors Tracks
Dunbar	$3,900	99.8	15.6
Anacostia	$6,000	61.0	39.0
Western	$8,600	42.7	58.9
Wilson	$10,400	2.3	92.2

SOURCE: Adapted from Heidenheimer, Heclo, and Adams, 1975:134.

As the number of colleges and universities has increased, moreover, the quality of the college or university has become increasingly more important than the fact of college attendance. Studies by Coleman et al. (1966), Little and Westergaard (1964), and Jencks (1972) have indicated the strong influence of social class background in affecting the quality of education received. Wilensky expresses surprise that any sociologist should by now have failed to perceive the inability of even universal college education "to effect by itself a major redistribution of income or a revolution in equality" (1975:4). Wilensky notes that in California, community colleges turn out graduates for such occupations as bank clerks, chefs, technicians, and lower-level white collar positions; the state colleges and universities provide the economy with middle-level personnel in teaching, commerce, industry, and government. Graduates of the elite campuses (Berkeley, Stanford) are overwhelmingly programmed for higher professional and executive posts. For a career at the top or elite levels of the occupational ladder, the quality education required is still very much class related; that is, recruitment to top jobs through the higher educational system, even in its much-expanded form, is largely a self-recruitment process from within the top strata. British sociologist Anthony Giddens, in a comparative study of several Western democracies, summarizes the situation.

IN the capitalist societies, the educational qualifications associated with recruitment to elite groupings will tend to be very much those associated with a background of material privilege. What influences elite recruitment is not that the aspirant recruit possesses a degree in physics or engineering, but that the degree is conferred at Oxford or Harvard; and, whatever the variability which may exist in degree of "closure" of elite recruitment between different societies, it is everywhere true that ownership of wealth and property continues to play a fundamental part in facilitating access to the sort of educational process which influences entry to elite positions. (1973:263–64)

FITNESS TO RULE: INEQUALITY IN ELITE RECRUITMENT

Elite recruitments include top jobs in industry, commerce, the high-paid, high-status professions, the military, judiciary/civil service, and elective government. Comparative studies on the background of elites in the liberal democracies agree on the tremendous overrepresentation of the upper and upper-middle class in all of these different elite groupings.

A variety of analyses has shown the extent of overrepresentation of higher occupations, higher social origins, and higher educational attainment among members of both elective and nonelective elites in the liberal democracies. In one of the best recent syntheses of research findings, Robert Putnam (1976:ch. 3) states that in the United States, Britain, Italy, and West Germany, only 1 to 3 percent of national legislators had had manual occupations, while 60 to 65 percent of the working population were in the manual job category. This might be expected, since it could well be that the skills necessary for legislation are not those necessary for manual occupations. Yet if one looks at the social origins of legislators (see table 4.4), Putnam finds, as have other researchers, that there is no equality of opportunity for those of lower-class origins to rise to political elite status.

Table 4.4 Social Origins of National Legislators *(Percentage figures)*

	United States	Canada	United Kingdom	France	Italy	West Germany
Higher managerial/ Professional	73[a] (44)[b]	81	46 (58)	56	48 (28)	42 (35)
Manual working class/Farmer	11 (18)	12	15 (22)	9	11 (36)	17 (30)

a. estimates from Blondel.
b. estimates from Putnam.

SOURCE: Adapted from Blondel, 1973:160–62, and Putnam, 1976:23.

As has been pointed out in cross-national elite comparisons by Nagle (1977), Miliband (1969), and Bottomore (1966), the United States political elite is considerably more closed to the working class than is the case in nations like Britain or Italy, where strong socialist, labor, or communist parties have afforded citizens from humbler backgrounds at least some opportunities for advancement through politics. The United States never developed a working-class party. Thus, despite a much-advertised "log cabin" myth of American political leadership, there has never been at any time during the history of the Republic any significant recruitment from the lower social strata. The American Congress, the cabinet, and governorships have been dominated, with little alteration from industrialization, immigration, boom, or depression, by businessmen and professionals, overwhelmingly lawyers (Nagle, 1977; Matthews, 1954).

In Germany, on the other hand, the Social Democratic party (SPD) and, during the Weimar period from 1919 to 1933, the Communist party (KPD) sent considerable numbers of deputies to the *Reichstag* who were not only from humble origins but from working-class occupations. As the SPD grew in strength from 1871 to 1912 in the Kaiser's Germany, the share of deputies from blue- and white-color occupations increased considerably (table 4.5). The direct representation of industrialists and nontitled landowners peaked at the height of industrialization about the turn of the century and the share of seats held by the aristocracy declined gradually. The German "Revolution of 1918" dramatically increased the direct presence of worker/employee types in the *Reichstag*, and the KPD deputy faction, especially after the proletarianization of the party in the 1920s, was made up almost entirely of young radicalized workers. As prosperity returned to postwar West Germany in the 1950s, however, recruitment of workers, blue collar and white collar, became less and less common, and by the 1960s recruitment came overwhelmingly from higher occupational strata.

Table 4.5 Occupations of Reichstag/Bundestag Deputies, 1871–1983

	1871	1893	1912	1919	1932	1949	1961	1972	1983
Worker/Employee	0	6	15	30	37	49	13	15	19
Landowner/Business Owner	15	31	19	14	17	14	19	8	13
Manager/ Professional	37	30	46	49	41	32	63	72	65
Aristocracy	42	25	14	(a)	—	—	—	—	—
Other	6	8	6	7	5	5	5	5	3

a. After the fall of the Kaiser in 1918, the small percentages of deputies with titles were included under their nontitled occupations.

SOURCE: John D. Nagle, *System and Succession: The Social Bases of Political Elite Recruitment* (Austin: University of Texas Press, 1977), pp. 128–29. Reprinted by permission of the publisher.

Despite the political turmoil that has marked much of German history in the last century, other nations of the West have shown a roughly similar pattern. With the impact of industrialization the political role of the aristocracy has been weakened, though with some considerable variation in time lag from country to country. Nontitled representatives from the new business class and even more from the upper echelons of management, civil service, and the professions have become attractive candidates from conservative, Christian Democrat, and liberal parties. Most of the early working-class parties, including the German SPD, the British Labour party, the French Socialists, and the Swedish Social Democrats, which once sent mostly workers to parliament at the beginning of the century, have, ever since achieving some national power, and especially in the period of post-World War II prosperity, nominated more and more of their candidates from higher occupational strata. Through this process of *embourgeoisement,* British Labourite MPs, for example, who were 80 to 100 percent workers between 1900 and 1920, were only 30 to 40 percent workers between 1955 and 1975. It would appear that the phenomenon of Eurocommunism, by which the Italian, French, and Spanish (in post-Franco Spain) communist parties are attempting to make themselves acceptable governing parties in the Western democracies, also brings with it a decline in the recruitment of worker deputies from these parties (Putnam, 1976:179). The transformation is most notable in the Italian Communist party, which has had both the will and the opportunity to practice the strategy of Eurocommunism in a liberal democratic setting. As a result of both the *embourgeoisement* of the major parties of the left in their leadership recruitment and the decline of the aristocracy in the leadership pool of conservative parties, the trend has been toward consensus recruitment of political elites in the West from those of higher (but nonaristocratic) social origin and higher managerial/professional occupations. In the United States, this position was arrived at "prematurely" under special circumstances, namely, the absence of a feudal nobility for the new bourgeoisie to displace, and later the absence of a working class party that might have served, at least in the early period of industrialization, to elevate members of the working class to national office.

Administrative, nonelective elites tend to be at least as unrepresentative as elected political elites, and in some cases significantly more so (table 4.6). In Britain, West Germany, and France, where the senior civil service enjoys great prestige and power, recruitment is quite class-selective, and the social composition of this elite is more biased in favor of the upper classes than is the elective political elite. Evidence from Guy Peters (1978:92–93) on the social origins of senior civil servants in several other democracies, while not strictly comparable because of shifting definitions and different years of sampling, confirms the general picture. Percentages of administrative elites from working-class origins are relatively scarce in Switzerland (15 percent in 1969), France (17 percent from 1953–1968), the Netherlands (15 percent in 1973), Canada (13.2 percent in 1957), and, surprisingly, very scarce in early postwar Denmark (4.3 percent in 1945) and Sweden (3.0 percent in 1949). Peters attributes much of the upper strata over-representation to the inequalities in higher education, which "despite attempts to make post-secondary education more available . . . still remains a sanctuary of the upper and middle classes" (94). In those countries like the United States and more recently Sweden, that have comprehensive secondary school education and much-expanded higher educational opportunities, a somewhat higher proportion of the administrative elite might be expected to come from working-class origins, but even here, no great qualitative shifts can be anticipated, for there are noneducationally based social biases at work in the elite levels of the bureaucracy:

> LIKE all organizations, they tend to replicate themselves, and there is a strong tendency to recruit people who are like those already in the positions. This type of organizational bias is perhaps especially strong during the personal interviews generally required for appointments to upper-echelon positions. (Peters, 1978:94–95)

There is sufficient evidence to state that it is not only the university degree but also the degree at the right (most prestigious) university that affords entrance into the top administrative elite. Miliband (1969), Bottomore (1966), and Peters (1978) have demonstrated the preponderance of Oxford and Cambridge (the Oxbridge connection) graduates who constitute two-thirds of all top British administrators, and the dominance of Paris university graduates, who make up three-fourths of entrants to the elite Ecole Nationale d'Administration. In Japan nearly 80 percent of the senior civil service graduated from Tokyo Imperial University (Kubota, 1969). In the United States the senior civil service as a whole does not have the same prestige, and there is no elite university connection comparable to that in France or Britain; only in the high-status U.S. Foreign Service do Ivy League school graduates tend to dominate.

By all accounts, this class bias in nonelective elites holds for judicial and military elites as well, with some minor differences (see Miliband, 1969:61–62, and Bottomore, 1966). For example, recruitment to the American military leadership has been from "the upper-middle rather than truly higher or definitely lower classes. Only a very small percentage of these are of working-class origins" (Mills, 1956:192). This compares with a somewhat more exclusive and still aristocratically-tinged basis of advancement into the British, West German, and French top officer corps.

Table 4.6 Social Origins of Administrative Elites *(Percentage Figures)*

	United States	Canada	Britain	France	Italy	W. Germany
Bourgeois	63[a] (47)[b]	87	77 (35)	80	83 (42)	81 (42)
Working class	21 (18)	13	19 (18)	17	5 (9)	0 (8)

a. estimates from Peters.
b. estimates from Putnam.

SOURCES: Putnam, 1976:25, and Peters, 1978:92–93.

In the area of economic elites, which includes business owners, corporate executives, and leading professionals, the picture of class dominance is even stronger. Westergaard (1965:89), Giddens (1973:170–71, 181–82), and Parkin (1971) have emphasized that studies of social mobility in the liberal democracies have found that "virtually all movement, whether upward or downward, inter- or intragenerational, across the nonmanual/manual division, is 'short-range'" (Giddens, 1973:181). Miller (1960) reports that generally less than 5 percent of sons of manual workers make "the big leap," a long-range upward move, to higher business circles and top professions. A high figure of 8 percent was reported for the United States, giving credence to the notion of greater fluidity of class lines in American society, although Giddens (1973:170) reports that long-range mobility from working class to elite positions seems to be generally higher in Japan as well as the United States compared with most European societies. Studies in West Germany, Japan, Britain, Canada, and the United States show that generally three-quarters of current business and professional elites come from upper- and upper-middle-class backgrounds, while less than 10 percent are from working-class homes. One can always find success stories of self-made men and women, but these are statistically quite infrequent. Among the more specialized subelites of contemporary Western societies, only the union leadership comes from distinctly more working-class origins.

While all elites, with the minor exception of union leaders, in contemporary capitalist society are quite unrepresentative of the general population along class lines, a general rule of thumb suggested by Putnam (1976:24–25) is that elected political elites are somewhat less unrepresentative than administrative elites and that economic elites are least representative of all. It would appear further that with respect to political elites, the trend since World War II has been toward greater inequality in the social basis of recruitment in several democracies, including West Germany and Britain. Indeed, in West Germany, the return to economic prosperity and the institutionalization of the Bonn democracy was matched step for step by the progressive closing out of the working class from political elite recruitment, by Social Democrats as well as by Christian Democrats.

THE HIGH COST OF JUSTICE: INEQUALITY BEFORE THE LAW

One area of equality is supported with some enthusiasm by liberal theory and widely held to be not only compatible with both capitalism and democracy but a basic foundation of liberalism. This is equality of the individual before the law, the notion that due process of law, the administration of justice, and the enforcement of criminal statutes and government regulations should be impartial, blind to the social origins and circumstances of the individual. Yet even here it is all too evident that wealth is able to transform itself into influence in the legal system, to provide a class-biased administration of the law in favor of the rich to the detriment of the lower classes.

In all the liberal democracies, the overwhelming proportion of those persons actually arrested for crimes, those convicted of criminal behavior, and those serving time in prison are of lower social origins, poorly educated and from largely unskilled and semiskilled occupations. There is, in fact, relatively little official recording of crime by the well-to-do. Is it simply that criminal behavior is relatively infrequent among the upper classes? American criminologist Edwin Sutherland (1974) answers that the bias of the criminal justice system assures that most police effort goes toward fighting, however efficiently or inefficiently, crimes committed by lower-class individuals, that criminal prosecutions are more likely against blue-collar transgressions of law, and that jail sentences are much more likely and longer for the lower-class convicted. Sutherland coined the phrase "white-collar crime" to cover the range of illegal activities engaged in by people of high social status, whether prosecuted by the criminal justice system or not. He estimated from his case-by-case survey of white-collar criminality in the United States that such crimes as falsified company balance sheets, security fraud, real estate fraud, fraudulent bank security transfers, insurance fraud, tax fraud, and price-fixing cost the citizenry much more than even the most spectacular bank robberies, burglaries, or hijackings, yet they seldom, *even when discovered,* lead to penalties as severe as those for these crimes, if they lead to penalties of the criminal justice system at all. Sutherland's landmark study of seventy large corporations and their unlawful practices involving over one thousand legal or administrative decisions against them led him to the following conclusions:

> THE upper class has greater influence in moulding the criminal law and its administration than does the lower class. The privileged position of white-collar criminals before the law results to a slight extent from bribery and political pressures, principally from the respect in which they are held and without special effort on their part. The most powerful group in medieval society secured relative immunity by "benefit of clergy," and now our most powerful groups secure relative immunity by "benefit of business or profession." (1974:43)

Donald Cressey, a research colleague of Sutherland who helped to advance the study of white-collar crime and develop a sociological theory of criminal justice, gives this summation:

> WHITE-COLLAR crimes—crimes committed by persons of respectability and high social status in the course of their occupations—also are extremely widespread, but an index of their frequency is not found in police reports. Prosecution for this kind of crime frequently is avoided because of the political or financial importance of the parties concerned . . . or because of the difficulty in securing evidence

sufficient for prosecution, particularly in the areas of crimes by corporations. (1974:40)

This inequality before the law for corporate criminals is all the more glaring since opinion polls show that the public regards white-collar and executive crime as serious offences, more serious even than many "blue-collar" crimes such as burglary and robbery (Clinard and Yeager, 1980: 5–9). Most estimates of the costs to the public of corporate crime show that it is far greater than that of street crime; for example, one case of illegal corporate price-fixing among plumbing fixture manufacturing businesses cost consumers over $100 million, whereas the largest sum netted from a robbery was only $4 million, involving a Lufthansa warehouse in New York City in 1978. Yet, Clinard and Yeager, at the end of their recent study of corporate crime, conclude:

> THE corporate executive runs little risk of a criminal conviction or prison sentence for his illegal actions on behalf of the corporation. Complex legal and social features, as well as bias within the system, operate in such a manner that corporate officers are largely insulated from the consequences of their socially harmful actions. . . . (1980: 297)

The authors add that corporate criminals, even when caught and convicted, are often welcomed back into top positions in the business community and do not lose their social standing, nor do they consider their actions "criminal," but rather just part of the corporate necessities of doing business.

According to Cressey (1974) and Gurr et al. (1975) business fraud is on the increase in Western Europe and the United States in the postwar era, but is not accurately reflected in official statistics, which indicate only the tip of the iceberg. There are differing opinions as to the cause of criminality generally (see Gordon, 1977: ch. 6; Quinney, 1970) as well as of criminality among the upper classes, who do not suffer from economic deprivation, social discrimination, or any apparent mental pathology. But among the specialists who have studied white-collar criminality, there seems to be a broad consensus that the application of criminal statutes, prosecution of offenders, and punishment of the guilty is markedly biased in favor of those from the top levels of society. Gilbert Geis's (1967) close analysis of the 1961 antitrust case against General Electric and Westinghouse and Bacon and Mays's (1970) and Schafer's (1976) analyses of differential treatment by social class of criminality agree on the class bias of the criminal justice system.

There is rather firm evidence from studies in Sweden, Norway, Finland, the United States, and England that with respect to juvenile delinquency as well social class is a deciding factor as to whether delinquent behavior is subject to criminal prosecution or is treated as a private (noncriminal) matter: "The kinds of offenses that middle-class youngsters commit may be similar to those lower-class children commit, i.e., damage to property, petty theft, etc., but they tend, in the main, to be dealt with not as crimes, but as childish indiscipline" (Bacon and Mays, 1970:133).

In recent years it has come to public attention that those in high public office, even when caught with hand deep in the public till, are seldom criminally prosecuted and even less often jailed if prosecuted. Spiro Agnew, former vice-president of the United States under Nixon, is free today without having been required to serve any jail sentence for his crimes of bribery and extortion. Former Prime Minister Tanaka of Japan, who has been tried and convicted in the multi-million-dollar Lockheed bribery scandal from the 1970s, has not served any prison sentence and until a recent heart attack continued to be a top political leader in the governing LDP, because his wealth and political clout permit the endless delay of "justice." The same is true of the Italian defense ministry officials, including two ministers of defense bribed by Lockheed who have not been charged to date with anything. While there are of course some spectacular cases of court convictions of the rich and powerful (Governor Mandel of Maryland, Billy Sol Estes of a former era), these are rare exceptions. They are the occasional showpieces that are supposed to symbolize an equality before the law that does not, and never did, exist.

NONEMANCIPATION OF WOMEN AND MINORITIES: SOME SPECIAL INEQUALITIES

Inequality of opportunity in the liberal democracies extends, of course, to groups other than social classes, most notably to women and to certain ethnic, racial, religious, and regional groups. The case of American blacks is both a clear and, despite the indisputable gains of the civil rights movement, continuing example of severe racial inequality. Inequality based on religious background can be demonstrated for Catholics in Northern Ireland and has been noted for non-European Jews (Sephardim) who fare poorly in Israel (see Putnam, 1976). But for purposes of cross-national comparisons on the widest basis, we will concentrate here on the patterns of inequality for women in the liberal democracies, since women constitute approximately half the population in each country and since many, though by no means all, of the factors limiting the emancipation of women in the West are similar in nature if not strength.

The field of politics has always been dominated by men in the liberal democracies. Women were among the last groups of adults to gain the right to vote (about 1920). Generally speaking, the percentage of women in cabinet positions and national legislatures has remained at token levels (less than 5 percent), and in some Western democracies, notably West Germany, has even declined in the post-World War II period. Only in progressive Scandinavia has the percentage of women in both cabinet and parliament climbed to levels above marginality. In Sweden, for example, women held 21 percent of the seats in the *Riksdag*, the high-water mark for the liberal democracies in the 1970s (Means, 1976:382). In the 1980s, the Norwegian parliament had 35 percent women deputies, and eight of eighteen cabinet members, including Prime Minister Gro Harlem Brundtland, were women. This proves that liberal democracies are capable of better results than those generally obtained, but it also shows that only in the most progressive democracies has even this much progress occurred.

Data on occupational roles filled by women are not much more encouraging. In the professions and higher management, women are still a small minority. Time-series data presented by Bernard (1971) and Iglitzin and Ross (1976) indicate that in several of the liberal democracies, notably the United States and West Germany, there was even some worsening of the economic position of women between 1950 and 1970. In the United States, for example, 11.4 percent of natural scientists in 1950 were women, but by 1967 only 8 percent were women. This decline accompanied a rapid growth in the 1960s of the demand for and pay scale of scientists. Likewise, in 1950 more than half of elementary school principals were women, but this figure declined dramatically by 1970 to less than one in five (Mandel, 1975:125-26). This decline occurred in a period of improving status and pay scale for public school administrators and teachers. An insultingly low 1.4 percent of U.S. high school principals in 1970 were women. Bernard, among others, has hypothesized that when occupational roles gain in status and salary, women will be squeezed out by men, whereas women will be permitted to fill jobs of primarily low or declining position on the job hierarchy.

The figures on employment for selected high-status occupations in several liberal democracies show some relative differences, however (table 4.7). It must first be noted that each category is relatively crude and conceals the fact that women tend to be clustered at the lower end of the considerable range of income and responsibility that exists within the categories of doctor, lawyer, manager, and judge. It would appear that the United States and Japan are relative laggards in equal occupational opportunity for women, while again Scandinavian nations, such as Sweden and Finland, are leaders.

The women's movement in the 1970s has made some headway in employment opportunities in some of the liberal democracies, and there are generally greater proportions of women in higher education now than in previous decades. Women constitute a growing percentage of the total workforce, reaching nonwartime peaks in many countries. But much of this increase has been in low-paid and part-time employment, and it remains to be seen whether the women's movement will develop enough strength to make lasting qualitative improvements in professional, managerial, and political opportunities for women.

Table 4.7 Representation of Women in High-Status Occupations *(Women as percentage of all persons in occupation)*

Occupation[a]	1	2	3	4	5	6	7	8	9
Country									
United States	2	‹2	0[b]	5	3	7	15	22	17
West Germany	6	-	-	-	5	20	-	6	-
France	2	‹2	0[b]	-	18	20	-	20	-
Japan	3	‹1	-	-	3	10	1	18	5
Finland	22	3	0[b]	4	-	9	-	14	5
Sweden	14	3	-	-	7	12	-	-	10

a. *Occupational code:*

    1. elected office—national parliament
    2. high civil service
    3. corporate management—officers and board members
    4. labor union leaders—officers and board members
    5. lawyers and judges
    6. doctors
    7. primary and secondary school principals
    8. college faculty
    9. managerial level positions

b. less than 0.5 percent

SOURCE: Adapted from OECD. *The Role of Women in the Economy*, 1975.

Table 4.8 Earnings of Full-Time Female Employees as Percentage of Male Employee Earnings by Economic Sector

Country	Year	Sector					
		1	2	3	4	5	6
France	1978	62	70	68	75	66	84
West Germany	1981	66	68	65	77	77	-
Sweden	1981	72	72	92	93	86	88
Switzerland	1980	66	75	63	78	73	79
Britain	1980	53	54	56	50	61	-
United States	1980	61	56	60	46	65	-

Sectors:

1. Manufacturing
2. Wholesale trade
3. Retail trade
4. Banking
5. Insurance
6. Government service

SOURCE: Adapted from OECD, *The Integration of Women into the Economy*, 1985: 84.

In terms of income inequality between full-time employed women and men, there is still much room for improvement in the liberal democracies. Among the most progressive is Sweden, with ratios ranging from 72 to 93 percent by economic sector of employment. Among the most backward are the United States and Great Britain, with ratios ranging from 46 to 65 percent. Especially disappointing in these two nations is the recognition that in banking and insurance, two modern service sectors where job growth has been high, the female/male earnings ratios have not been generally higher than other, declining sectors. This is not an encouraging sign for the future. In terms of longer-term trends, in the United States, the overall ratio of women's incomes has fluctuated in a narrow range of 59 to 65 percent over the period from the mid-1950s to the mid-1980s. The most recent gains have only brought the gap back to what it was thirty years ago.

Table 4.9 Median Total Money Income of Males and Females[a] (full-time workers) United States, 1956–1985

Year	Male	Female	Female/Male Ratio
1956	$4,462	$2,828	.63
1960	5,435	3,296	.60
1965	6,479	3,883	.60
1970	9,184	5,440	.59
1975	12,934	7,719	.60
1980	19,172	11,590	.60
1985	24,999	16,252	.65

a. Income in current prices

SOURCES: U.S. Bureau of the Census, *Current Population Reports,* Series P-60, annual issues (U.S. Government Printing Office).

No assessment of women's emancipation in the liberal democracies would be complete without noting the emerging poverty among women and children in single-parent female-headed households. A recent study by Sylvia Ann Hewlett (1986) indicates that particularly in the United States, the rise of divorce rates and the move into the job market by large numbers of women with small children has led to the growth of poverty for children and for mothers with small children. Hewlett points out that after divorce, the material standard of living of ex-husbands rises by an average of 42 percent, but declines for the ex-wives and children by 73 percent. Further, two-thirds of custodial mothers receive no child support from the father, and legal authorities are notoriously ineffective in enforcing court-ordered child support. Maternity leave and day-care facilities in the United States are less available and less generously supported than in the European democracies, and in the 1980s, the Reagan Administration cut back federal support for day-care and nutrition programs. Public support for day care actually fell by some 25 percent from 1980-1986. The result is that 77 percent of those below the poverty line in the United States are women and children. While similar tendencies are also visible in the European democracies (and in the Soviet Union, cf. chapter 9), they are less pronounced, and government efforts to aid needy mothers and children have generally been stronger.

Chapter 5

Liberty—High-Water Mark of Individualism

LIBERTY IS TAKEN HERE IN THE CLASSIC SENSE of freedom from arbitrary coercion for the individual. Although individual liberty has never been realized in the absolute, certainly there is a tremendous range of system tolerance for individual behaviors across the span of history and nations. Democratic liberty is fairly easy to define in its essence: the right to dissent against authority and the right to be different—to choose among real choices. There's nothing very tricky about liberty as a concept; it's the practice of liberty that is so difficult. Whenever one dissents from authority, it's likely to cost something.

By living in society, we agree not to do certain things, such as commit murder, loot, or attack our fellow citizens. These are deprivations of liberty that savages and wild animals possess. But we are better off, we think, living in society under these limitations (Hobbes). If we kill, pillage, or commit arson, the authorities (i.e., the state) are empowered to (try to) catch and punish us. There are many laws and regulations that we are supposed to follow, and if we do not, we may be penalized. Our liberty is always circumscribed by law. Every individual's liberty is limited by the rights, and mere existence, of others in society. However, the ability of the liberal democracies to tolerate dissent within quite broad limits, and in many cases to make public facilities and monies available for expressions of opposition groups, is certainly a quality that is admired by citizens of nations where such individual freedom does not exist.

On the other hand, lest we forget the real world of liberal democracy, two things should be noted. One is that the resources for exercising liberty are not equally distributed (see chapter 4). Mr. H. L. Hunt, a now-deceased billionaire could (and did) buy up a string of newspapers (over one hundred) to bring his views to society. Only the rights of purchasing power in a market economy gave him the possibility of converting wealth into political influence.

While it is true that a person is free to use his or her personal (even if limited) resources to be heard, to try to organize with others of similar opinion for the purpose of convincing opponents and more likely the great apathetic majority to support some position, it is not true that dissent does

87

not cost something beyond the few dollars put into it. A person's opinions, if they are known to and unpopular with an employer, could cost that person a job, or a promotion, or maybe just a raise. Indeed, while most people in the liberal democracies (or perhaps in most nonrevolutionary societies) are not dissidents and most are not union, feminist, or gay rights activists, most studies of public opinion in the liberal democracies (Stouffer, 1954; Nagle, 1970) show that strong pluralities or majorities would in fact deny rights of free speech and assembly to many unpopular minority groups. This makes the record of the liberal democracies all the more impressive, since in many areas suppression of civil liberties for certain minority groups has been politically popular. Here the independent judiciary, a check on the executive and legislative functions of government, has been particularly important, especially in the United States, in protecting and expanding the rights of blacks, women, workers, atheists, radicals, and homosexuals, to name a few, to a level more comparable with those of nondissident or nonminority groups.

It is not an easy thing to defend the liberty of someone or some group that you disagree with, perhaps very strongly, especially when you have majority sentiment on your side. Yet, as Rosa Luxemburg pointed out long ago, democracy is the practical right to be in the minority and not be suppressed. Dr. Martin Niemoller, the German Protestant theologian, after the experience of the Nazi Third Reich, made an astute observation on the costs of the failure to defend the liberty of the other person. When the Nazis first suppressed the Communists, Niemoller hesitated to voice opposition, because he was not a Communist and opposed the Communists. When they began rounding up Socialists, he hesitated again, because he was not a Socialist and opposed Socialism. When they persecuted the Jews, he hesitated again. But when the Nazis came after him, the pattern of social and political suppression of dissent had already been established, in part through his earlier silence.

A GLOBAL SURVEY OF PERSONAL LIBERTY

The development of individual liberty, even if limited both in extent and by social class initially, has been closely associated with the evolution of liberal democracy as a political system. Liberal democracy in turn has been generally more loosely associated with the development of capitalism in the West, in Europe, in North America, and in European-offspring nations such as Australia and New Zealand. In the pre-1945 period, however, advanced capitalism was also associated with fascism and authoritarianism in countries like Germany, Italy, France, and Japan; in these countries liberal democratic systems were restored only by external force after their complete defeat in the last world conflict.

Since 1945, as in no previous era, we can associate the achievement of wide personal liberties with all the advanced capitalist systems, which serve at the same time as the boundary of the stable liberal democracies. Western capitalism (plus Japan), even with the remaining issues of voting rights for women in Switzerland and the purges of dissidents from public service jobs in West Germany, has become virtually coterminous with guaranteed protection of a wide variety of political and civil liberties.

Freedom House, a conservative American think-tank, issues periodic reports on the status of both political and civil liberties in every nation. Each country is subjectively ranked on a scale of 1 (greatest protection of liberty) to 7 (greatest restriction on liberty), so that different degrees of effective personal liberty are recognized. The School of Journalism at the University of Missouri has developed a separate Press Freedom Index that attempts to measure the independence of each nation's press, radio, and television and in particular their ability to dissent from government policy. For each nation, a judging panel of newsmen ranks the media by means of criteria (extent of government ownership, types of censorship, licensing) from a high of $+4$ (most free) to a low of -4 (least free). The judges' scores are then averaged for each country to arrive at a final Press Freedom Index.

While these judgments are of course debatable for individual nations, and are admittedly measured by *current Western standards,* they nevertheless can be useful for illustrating our point about the global extent of liberty and its post-World War II association with Western advanced capitalism. This connection is a result of two polarizing trends: (1) the strengthening and expansion of personal liberty in the western democracies, and (2) the decline of personal liberty in several other regions where either communist, military, or other one-party regimes have come to power.

Table 5.1 shows the Freedom House ranking of selected nations on political and civil rights for 1975 and the Press Freedom Index for 1966. The major point to note is that almost all of those ranked highest (1 or 2) on both civil and political liberties are the advanced capitalist systems, and no advanced capitalist system scores less than a 2 on either scale. Rankings for press freedom are more varied among system-types, but again the advanced capitalist democracies always rank high and never fall into the negative (unfree) side of the scale. On the other hand, only one communist nation (Yugoslavia) makes it onto the positive side, and all other communist nations are ranked negatively on the scale. Press freedom in the Third World is evidently much more varied, with both positive and negative ratings.

The World War II defeat of European and Japanese fascism has solidified the advanced capitalist nations into a more homogeneous grouping of political systems. The postwar decolonization in the Third World has meant formal independence for nearly a hundred "new" nations. But Western hopes for the adoption of Western-type political systems, with the same

Table 5.1 Indicators of Liberty in Selected Nations

	Political Rights (1973-79)	Civil Rights (1973-79)	Press Freedom Index (1966)
United States	1.0	1.0	+2.72
Britain	1.0	1.0	+2.37
West Germany	1.0	1.1	+2.43
France	1.0	1.7	+1.92
Italy	1.4	1.7	+1.98
Japan	2.0	1.0	+2.44
Sweden	1.1	1.0	+2.83
U.S.S.R.	6.6	6.0	−3.08
Czechoslovakia	7.0	6.4	−2.51
East Germany	7.0	6.9	−3.20
Poland	6.0	5.7	−2.54
Cuba	6.9	6.6	−3.02
Yugoslavia	6.0	5.7	+0.08
India	2.1	3.3	+0.98
Indonesia	5.0	5.0	−0.40
Brazil	4.3	4.7	+1.25
Mexico	4.1	3.4	+1.46
Egypt	5.6	4.7	−2.32
Algeria	6.1	6.0	−3.26
Tanzania	6.0	6.0	+0.87
Kenya	5.0	4.6	+1.20
Iran	5.6	5.7	+1.03

SOURCES: Gastil, 1976:15; *World Handbook of Social and Political Indicators*, 1983.

priority attached to personal liberty, have not been realized. Communist revolutions in Eastern Europe, Asia, Africa, and Cuba have produced systems with sharply divergent views of personal liberty (as well as other matters). Personal liberty, as defined and practiced in the wealthy capitalist world, has simply not been as attractive or as practical as might have been expected. Freedom House spokesman Raymond Gastil, in a rather discouraging world survey of personal liberty, comments that "in ranking countries in terms of civil and political rights we do not mean to imply that these rights exhaust the definition of a good or desirable political system. Some free states may be less desirable to live in than some unfree states, especially where the unfree state provides a more adequate standard of living or a more challenging future" (1976:12).

Personal liberty, as a goal, is in competition not only with economic development but also with the goals of social equality and quality of life. People may favor greater social equality at the expense of lesser personal liberty; they may favor a greater effort in fighting crime (a quality of life item) at the expense of personal liberty. The choice comprises a complex, many faceted array of values. And it is not always the case that the sacrifice of one goal necessarily improves progress toward another goal. Some losses of liberty, especially in the Third World nations, would seem to have been pure losses. Certainly the records of the communist systems and Third World dictatorships are very different in this respect.

DEVELOPMENTS IN LIBERTY SINCE 1945: THE UNITED STATES

The early 1950s in the United States were the heyday of McCarthyism and red-hunting. Members of the Communist party were arrested and sent to jail under the Smith Act for allegedly plotting to overthrow the government. Radicals, Socialists, and even progressive liberals were purged from the AFL and CIO union leaderships, from the civil service, from colleges and public schools, from the entertainment world, and from television, radio, and press establishments. Not only did these people (including people like Pete Seeger, Zero Mostel, and Will Greer), convicted of no crime whatsoever, lose their jobs, but they were also blacklisted so could not find new ones. The era of the fifties, of the "silent generation," was one of heavy-handed treatment of dissidents to the left of anticommunist liberalism.

Those purged and blacklisted served, of course, as a warning to others who might be tempted to express similar opinions. In legal parlance this is called a "chilling effect" on free speech, but this phrase does not adequately express the human suffering and injustices of the "red scare" purges of the period, which went far beyond the tragicomic anticommunist crusade of Senator Joe McCarthy (see Wolfe, 1973). Today, in the Soviet Union, when a Soviet Jew applies for an emigration visa, he or she loses his or her job immediately as a punishment and as a warning to others. In the 1950s, when a singer in the United States expressed opinions or sang songs deemed radical or socialist, he or she was blacklisted in the industry. Of course, the Soviet Union is still a one-party dictatorship despite destalinization, and the United States in the 1950s was certainly a liberal democracy, yet both dissidents lost their jobs and for not so dissimilar acts.

In the 1950s, throughout the South and much of the rest of the United States, blacks were denied basic rights through racial exclusion enforced either by legal statute or by Ku Klux Klan terror. Blacks were denied access to housing in certain neighborhoods; and public services, including schools, garbage collection, street maintenance, and police protection, were basically neglected in black ghettoes by an all-white government. The black American was definitely discriminated against in his or her own country with the open support of federal, state, and local governments. If you were born before 1965, you were alive when a black citizen might be murdered for attempting to register to vote in Mississippi; when a black was not allowed to take an empty seat in the front of a public bus in Montgomery because that seat was reserved for whites only; when a black person could not get counter service at a southern Woolworth's, where only whites were served. The degradation of the black American was a systematic part of American life, as American as apple pie. It was not occasional, or accidental, or a "misunderstanding."

Through the 1950s and 1960s, however, pressure for change built up. The civil rights movement, through the NAACP (National Association for the Advancement of Colored People), made some progress in the courts against school desegregation. Yet, despite the 1954 Supreme Court ruling that all segregated school systems must integrate "with all deliberate speed," a decade later little actual compliance with the law had taken place. Both in the South and elsewhere white school and local authorities had defied the law with impunity. By the early 1960s, more militant civil rights groups such as CORE (Congress of Racial Equality), SNCC (Student Nonviolent Coordinating Committee), and Martin Luther King, Jr.'s SCLC (Southern Christian Leadership Conference) had begun to push the civil rights cause through the tactics of economic boycott, sit-ins, mass marches, and demonstrations. A strategy including large-scale but nonviolent civil disobedience was introduced to attempt to force federal government attention to the issues of equal rights for black citizens. By the mid-1960s, however, black anger began to erupt into urban rioting, looting, and burning.

One could reasonably mark the point at which white government authorities began to respond positively to civil rights with the Watts riot of 1965. By 1968, urban black rioting was becoming unprofitable for at least some segments of the white business class, and it was at this point that real if partial advances in civil rights came to *de facto* realization. One corporate executive summed up the rationale for action on civil rights:

> SINCE the Detroit and Newark riots in 1967, a closer identity has sprung up between the needs of the ghetto economy and the needs of the normal economy. The riots now reach beyond the black or "grey" areas of the cities and threaten the entire American economy. Curfews and enforced closings of businesses undermine downtown real estate values. Riots now mean massive losses of profits, millions of forfeited wages, and cancelled conventions for entire cities. (Quoted in Wolfe, 1973:46)

The real enforcement of and compliance with the 1964 Civil Rights Act and the 1965 Voting Rights Act marked the beginning of the end of officially sanctioned racial discrimination, although it is clear that even today some discrimination in schooling, housing access, and especially jobs still exists through entrenched resistance from local school boards, real estate agencies, unions, and businesses. Yet the fact remains that on a variety of fronts, progress has been made. Herbert Gans (1973:136–37) argues that the ghetto rebellions were responsible for the temporary upsurge in government and business programs to alleviate the effects of racism. This is also part of the American (and European) heritage of liberal democracy, going back to the bitter and violent union struggles of the period from the mid-nineteenth century through the Great Depression years. The gains in civil liberties have been won in hard struggle against those who dominate in the economy and in government. They are the result of contradictions in the society that boil up at certain points and must be addressed and resolved, at least partially or for the short run.

In the late sixties, the escalation of American intervention in Vietnam and the corresponding growth of the antiwar movement at home brought with it a widening of civil rights in other respects. In the earliest antiwar protests, marchers in demonstrations were often attacked by supporters of government war policy while police stood by and watched, often later arresting only the antiwar demonstrators (see Parenti, 1974, ch. 8). Sometimes police would themselves "rough up" protesters. Public officials who freely granted march or parade permits to prowar groups such as the Veterans of Foreign Wars or the American Legion refused the same to antiwar groups. All manner of chicanery was employed to keep antiwar candidates or antiwar propositions off the ballot in local, state, and federal elections; petition signatures would mysteriously "disappear" after being handed in to election officials, or some "irregularity" would be manufactured to invalidate the petitions. Eventually, however, the antiwar movement became too strong, too widespread, and too militant to be stopped, short of the murderous type of force that was only briefly and tragically applied at Kent State and Jackson State.

But there was another reason for the acceptance of civil protest as a legitimate form of dissent against the war policy, and that was the split within the established political leadership itself. United States intervention in Vietnam was a bloody and costly disaster from start to finish; it was wrong from a multitude of perspectives. Gradually, established public officials already holding high office and long a part of the national political scene, figures like Eugene McCarthy, George McGovern, Robert Kennedy, and Ted Kennedy gave their support to the movement, making it more difficult to discount or denounce it as extremist or communist-inspired or treasonous. Civil rights leaders such as Martin Luther King, Jr., Coretta King, Stokely Carmichael, and Dick Gregory added their voices and joined at least partially the civil rights and antiwar efforts. Some relatively progressive unionists like Leonard Woodcock of the UAW, the independent electrical workers (UE), and some AFL-CIO chiefs who defied George Meany's hawkish stand on the war lent working-class support. The system grudgingly conceded greater opportunities for voicing opposition—marching, petitioning, running candidates, and speaking on radio and television. By the early

1970s, the right to publicly voice dissent was being practiced by millions with far less fear or probability of reprisal, but again it was a gain made through struggle.

The machinery of liberal democracy was not the unbiased, neutral, "conversion process" pictured in theory; it never was and never will be, so long as it is run by people who themselves have a strong interest in the outcomes produced by democracy. The increases in individual liberty have usually, though not always, been accompanied by bitter confrontations, often including individually targeted violence, rioting, and even rebellion. From the revelations of Watergate and the post-mortem dissection of the Vietnam issue, we now know that the United States government, through the CIA, FBI, IRS, and a host of state and local agencies, engaged in a wide variety of illegal and unconstitutional acts directed against civil rights, antiwar, and leftist organizations. Not only President Nixon engaged in and encouraged such practices as telephone taps, FBI and CIA burglaries, and IRS tax intimidation. The FBI had a long-standing program of counterintelligence (COIN-TELPRO) and disruption, threats, and break-ins directed against groups such as the Socialist Workers party that FBI Director Hoover considered "subversive." Hoover also considered Martin Luther King, Jr. subversive and had anonymous threatening letters sent to King suggesting suicide as the only way out. Violent repression of the Black Panther party is a matter of record (Wolfe, 1973). The murder of Black Panther leaders Mark Clark and Fred Hampton in their beds by Chicago police in December of 1969, officially an "accident" for which no one has been convicted, must be seen as part of the known and now exposed overall program of repression against the Black Panthers.

The results of pressure for greater personal liberty have not been reversed, even in the conservative political era of the 1980s. Younger conservative leaders do not advocate a return to racial segregation or the suppression of blacks' voting rights. The greater personal liberty afforded to gays and women, while opposed by many conservative and ultra-conservative political and religious fundamentalist organizations, have not been directly attacked by the conservative Reagan administration. Even the older generation of conservative political leaders like Ronald Reagan and Barry Goldwater, who opposed federal desegregation measures and civil rights legislation, do not now call for a reversal of these historic measures.

This is not meant to imply that the struggle for the maintenance of personal liberty is over or that there will be no threats to personal liberties in the United States in the future. Indeed, the AIDS epidemic has in recent years raised the possibility of a political backlash against the gay community. It may be tempting for some political leaders to use public fears of the disease to mobilize public support for suppression of civil rights for homosexuals. Still, in the latter 1980s, public health officials have in general resisted this trend, and have insisted on treating AIDS as a public health problem and not as a weapon against gays. This is a remarkable change in the public health field from just a generation ago, when homosexuality was treated as a disease.

Alan Wolfe has done an excellent job of describing the types and extents of repression in liberal democracy and of relating this repression to the interests of the economic and political system:

> THE history of liberalism has been a struggle between those who controlled the society and found the tenets of a limited liberal state perfectly to their liking and those who wished to share in the blessings of liberal society but were not allowed to do so (or were permitted to do so only after a struggle) because they had no base of private property from which to act. For this reason, many of the victories of liberal society were won through the martyrdom of groups that were not liberal. The IWW, for example, a syndicalist and socialist organization, did more to establish the right to speak freely on a street corner than any other group in American history. . . . When people choose to remain powerless, they refuse to claim the benefits of liberal society for themselves. But what happens when oppression is no longer accepted, when the demands are made? Then the fundamental contradiction of liberal society asserts itself. Liberalism can work only by being restrictive, particularly to those in power. Each attempt to extend the principles of liberalism to a powerless group has been convulsive. (1973:229)

Wolfe rightly notes that gains made through struggle are important gains, though they did not change the fundamental nature of the social order. Herbert Gans (1973:136–37) fears the backlash effects of attempts to achieve progress in civil rights or social welfare through disruptive activities, while admitting the short-term victories connected with convulsive confrontation. The record shows, however, that violence, intimidation, and disruption are practiced by the authorities in liberal democracy against dissident groups who try to participate in the political system in order to both improve their economic situation and challenge existing policies.

It is comforting to think that progress toward greater individual liberty could be made through entirely peaceful means; that would eliminate the unpleasantness and personal risk to which those in the forefront of unionist, civil rights, and antiwar movements have historically been exposed. Many early union leaders, socialists, and black activists were shot or lynched; they never lived to enjoy the rights for which they fought. Many personal accounts of early struggles for workers' rights attest to the reluctance of most to get involved for fear of reprisal. *The Autobiography of Mother Jones* (1925), the story of an early union organizer, recounts the repeated attempts to travel the road of entirely peaceful organization, electoral participation, and court cases to get the system to work by its professed ideals. Yet, in the face of violence, terror, and official bias against them, workers were faced with the tough choice between submitting or responding in kind to government and company violence.

West Germany: Liberty in a Reconstructed Democracy

The greatest postwar gains in personal liberty in the industrialized capitalist nations have been made in West Germany, Italy, Japan, and France, where the defeated fascist regimes were replaced by reconstructed parliamentary systems. In 1949, after four years of government by the Allied occupation authorities, the Federal Republic of Germany *(Bundesrepublik)* held its first elections for a new parliament *(Bundestag)*. Many parties ranging from the far right to the Communist party of Germany on the left were permitted to compete in the elections, and only the Nazi party was outlawed from reorganizing. Under the new federal government, freedoms of press, assembly, speech, party competition, union organization, fair trial, religious practice, and emigration, all suppressed between 1933 and 1945 by the Nazi regime, were restored and supported by the internal political system (as opposed to the Allied occupation command). Despite some restrictions and retrogressions to be discussed below, the West German democracy has since 1949 provided the same general level of protection of personal liberty that characterizes the more stable liberal democracies, such as Britain and the United States. Germany's expansion of personal liberty continues to dwarf all other trends and (together with that of Japan, Italy, and France) represents the most significant development in personal liberty in the industrial world, and perhaps in the entire world, since World War II.

The first years of the *Bundesrepublik* coincided with the heightened East-West tensions of the Cold War. West Germany was integrated into the anticommunist alliance forged by the United States. While McCarthyism was rampant in the United States, in West Germany, too, communists, leftists, and left liberals were purged from positions of leadership in the unions, the schools, and the media. The Communist party of Germany was outlawed in 1956, and many of its leaders were persecuted for presumed disloyalty to the constitution (Basic Law). The era of Chancellor Adenauer's leadership in the 1950s and early 1960s was one in which dissent and nonconformity, in life-styles as well as politics, were discouraged, sometimes through the power of government. A turning point in this trend toward authoritarian conformity came in 1962, when Adenauer's defense minister, Franz Josef Strauss, seized the offices of *Der Spiegel,* a left-liberal news magazine, after the publication of a story on secret West German/Spanish military arrangements. Had Strauss's actions been allowed to stand, freedom of the press would have been dealt a major blow. But, amidst national and international protest, Strauss was forced to back down and to resign from the cabinet, although he remained head of the powerful Bavarian

Christian Social Union (CSU). The Spiegel Affair, rather than resulting in a defeat for press freedom, served to encourage investigative reporting and lively criticism of government policies.

Through the 1960s, the exercise of personal and political liberty increasingly and openly challenged not only the CDU-dominated governments of chancellors Adenauer and Erhard, but also the perceived lack of effective choice among the three parties (Christian Democrats, Free Democrats, and Social Democrats) represented in the *Bundestag*. From the radical right, the National Democratic party (NPD) denounced the institutions of liberal democracy as responsible for the "moral decline" of German society and advocated a nationalist and reunited Germany similar to the Germany of 1939. Founded in 1964, a tiny remnant of earlier right-wing groups, the NPD suddenly won 7 to 10 percent of the vote in several state-level elections in 1966–1968. This was a period of mild recession and the so-called grand coalition government of the two largest parties, the Christian Democrats and Social Democrats (see Nagle, 1970). Many feared that the NPD, like the Nazi party of the Weimar Republic, would build voter support on popular fears and prejudices (against foreign workers and foreign influences and against communists, Jews, and homosexuals) and on an appeal to nationalist and militarist sentiment. Some advocated a legal ban on the NPD to forestall this possibility, citing the experience of Weimar. However, the NPD strongly professed its loyalty to the Basic Law and had committed few overt acts of violence. Indeed, in the 1969 election campaign, NPD speakers often had to be protected against anti-NPD demonstrators. In many localities, pressure from major parties, unions, and businesses was used to deny access to meeting halls for NPD gatherings, and NPD election posters were torn down and destroyed much more frequently than those of the major parties. The governing CDU-SPD coalition ultimately resisted the temptation to outlaw the NPD, and the right-radicals received only 4.3 percent of the national election vote, failing to get any seats in the *Bundestag*. By the 1970s the National Democratic party had shrivelled to insignificance.

The New Left, often termed the Extra-Parliamentary Opposition (APO), also challenged the social and foreign policies of the CDU-SPD grand coalition. Inspired in part by philosopher Herbert Marcuse, and led in part by Rudi Dutschke, a student of Marcuse, the APO attacked the government's support for United States intervention in Vietnam and the close relationship with the Shah of Iran. They called for democratization of economic life, for student participation in university government, and for sexual emancipation from middle-class conventions. One demonstration protesting an official visit to Germany by the Shah in 1967 resulted in the shooting of one student by police. In some respects, the demonstrations by the APO in the latter 1960s, like the Spiegel Affair of the early 1960s, served to widen the scope of practical personal liberty in that after some initial violent confrontations, police and local government officials gradually accepted street demonstrations as a normal part of democratic political life, and police reactions became more restrained. The New Left, which was quite hopeful that far-reaching change might be possible in the 1960s, was largely disillusioned by the inability of SPD Chancellor Willy Brandt (1969–1974) to carry out even a modest educational restructuring and industrial reform *(Mitbestimmung)*. Promises and plans for student participation in university governance were largely abandoned in the more conservative atmosphere of the latter 1970s.

West German politics in the 1970s was one of mixed gains and setbacks for personal liberty. On the one hand the government has become obsessed with maintaining security for public officials in the era of Baader-Meinhof kidnappings and murders of political leaders, judges, and businessmen. Barbed wire around government ministries, armored car patrols, and machine-gun sentries have produced a palpable feeling of uneasiness, particularly in the capital city of Bonn. The Baader-Meinhof terrorism may have partially succeeded in one of its goals, namely that of goading the government into treating all citizens as potential security risks.

As has been stated elsewhere, this attitude is reflected in the administration of a 1972 decree prohibiting "radicals" from public employment at any level. Since school teachers, university professors, railroad engineers, bus drivers, telephone and telegraph personnel, employees at the several state-owned iron and coal facilities, plus all members of the federal, state, and local civil service are part of governmental employment, "radicals" can be barred from a good number of jobs, which essentially bars them from practicing their professions *(Berufsverbot)*. In applying for public employment, an applicant must pass a loyalty test. Standards change from state to state, and from year to year, depending on the political climate. Teachers in particular have been denied jobs for simply belonging to leftist organizations or for legally demonstrating against the Vietnam War. The loyalty hearing may bring forth stories from professional "informants" or personal enemies, and they certainly have a chilling effect on critical social analysis in the schools.

On the positive side, new citizen coalitions *(Bürgerinitiativen)* have emerged that promote a wide series of issues on which the main parties did not offer much choice. Environmentalist and antinuclear groups (led by the BBU, the Federal League of Environmental Citizen Initiatives) have forced questions of nuclear reactor safety, reactor siting, energy planning, and especially nuclear waste disposal onto the political agenda through actions ranging from court suits and public hearings to mass demonstrations and civil disobedience. In the 1980s, the new Green party has begun to contest elections directly, with modest success. The Greens held about 8 percent of Bundestag seats after the 1987 national elections and represent a variety of "new social movements," including peace activists, environmentalists, and feminists, at both the federal level and in most states (Länder). Although split into several factions, the Greens are evidence of a "new politics" which favors more direct and active citizen participation in governing. After initial attempts to vilify the Greens as either communist or know-nothing, the main parties, especially the SPD, have started to rethink their positions and have called for more public dialogue on nuclear power. These are signs that increasing numbers of West Germans perceive liberty as going beyond voting once in four years and are willing to participate in politics beyond the organization of the major parties. Now nearly forty years old, West German democracy has avoided several temptations to stifle the expression of liberty in the name of security or order, but the continuing ban on "radicals" in public employment remains an inconsistency in that record.

The stretching of liberty to its current bounds in liberal democracy has been a turbulent process. And this is the second lesson that needs to be stressed. In the postwar era, the practice of dissent has been broadened in all the Western democracies; those in positions of power have made concessions rather than continue or escalate a repressive strategy. This was by no means the only possibility and is in fact a relatively rare turn of events in the last century in world political developments.

Even in the advanced industrial nations, there is the alternative of fascism compatible with capitalist economics and at times suitable to the business class. If those who dominate the present order are not willing to make concessions as a necessary price for maintaining the essentials of the economic and social hierarchy intact, they may well opt for a more aggressively repressive system. One might argue that this is what whites (the propertied class) in Rhodesia (Zimbabwe) and South Africa chose to do. And it is instructive to note that these white settler groups are the offspring of British and Dutch political cultures, which in Europe have relatively unblemished records of steady democratic development.

In general, in the aftermath of World War II, the fascist alternative has been in disrepute in the industrial West, and despite some occasional stirrings on the neofascist right (the NPD in West Germany, the National Front in Britain, the MSI in Italy, the Poujadists in France, and perhaps elements of the Wallaceite AIP in the United States), it is still correct to say that the broad postwar consensus against fascism remains intact. The military defeat of the fascist alternative in Germany, Japan, Italy, and France has, at least for the prolonged period of economic growth after the war, decreased the ability of the "haves" to overtly coerce or threaten the "have nots" or to silence dissent. And in limiting the options of repression, compromise and concession become more likely. At the present time, individual liberty is at a highwater mark in the community of Western democracies. Never before has it been so true that individual liberty is a correlate of liberal democracy in advanced capitalism.

Chapter 6

Quality of Life—The Dark Side of Modernism

EVEN IN A RELATIVELY PROSPEROUS AND FREE society, problems of crime, drug addiction, alcoholism, family disintegration, alienation, unemployment, and pollution may severely hamper or even negate the enjoyment of both formal liberty and material affluence. Some of the keenest observers of Western societies, such as Erich Fromm (1955), David Reisman et al. (1950), Herbert Marcuse (1967), and Daniel Bell (1974, 1976) have argued from a variety of political perspectives and psychological, economic, and cultural approaches that the worship or fetishism of material goods is itself at the root of a "cultural crisis of modern liberal capitalism." The theme of "having more, but enjoying it less" has been voiced often, usually in loose terms, so that it is somewhat difficult to know just what should be examined under the heading "quality of life." There is disagreement as well on the causes and cures (if any) for the various problems most often subsumed under this heading.

Some have argued that most, if not all, of these ills are the result of a competitive, hedonistic, and class-divided capitalism and that a humanitarian socialist society (probably quite different from any socialist society now existing) would reduce those problems to manageable proportions. Others contend that capitalist industrial society is to blame and that a return to nature and the countryside, either to small farm or communal life, is the answer. The communes founded in the 1960s and early 1970s by young Americans were symptomatic of these attitudes. Despite the demise of most such experiments after a few years, the longing for a simpler, less competitive, less bureaucratic life, is still evident not only in the United States but in West Germany, Sweden, and Britain as well.

Others argue that these problems are inherent in modern, urban, mobile societies in general, whether capitalist or socialist, and that we must simply learn to live with and perhaps adjust to them if we want to continue to enjoy the material benefits of our complex and highly productive economy. This advice may sound either hard-hearted or tough-minded, depending on personal preference, but it does often provide an antidote to the scaremongering prevalent in many discussions of the problems of modern industria. Some would question whether frequent divorce is a social ill at all and would argue that drug experimentation is a mind-expanding and creative new freedom, indeed a question of personal freedom (for a good discussion, see Bakalar and Grinspoon, 1984), that pollution is much exaggerated and not a serious danger, and that unemployment no longer means severe material deprivation. Hardly anyone contends that violent crime is good for us, but some (Bell, 1953) have seen nonviolent and "victimless" crimes (such as gambling, prostitution, and graft) as quite functional or even necessary and discount apparent recent crime waves as statistical illusions. In this section we will contend with these divergent viewpoints as we present data on crime, family breakdown, unemployment, pollution, and alienation and loss of community in the midst of material wealth. We can scarcely hope to come to any fine judgments as to the sources of all these phenomena of modern liberal democratic societies. Our main purpose is to gain a better idea of the magnitude and trends in each of these areas.

CRIME AND NONREHABILITATION: THE DARK AT THE END OF THE TUNNEL

Any cross-national comparison of crime in contemporary societies runs into problems of definitions and statistics. Crimes may be differently defined and laws differently enforced in various nations, especially in decentralized legal systems like that of the United States or West Germany. Laws change over time, and the enforcement of laws also changes. We know that crime statistics, that is, crimes reported to the authorities, are only a fraction of total crimes actually committed. Homicides in the developed West are well reported, but many burglaries and thefts, and perhaps most corporate crimes, go undetected or unreported. The underreporting of rape is attributable to social pressures on the victim and the perception that involvement with the authorities will bring further agony and little chance of justice. Many thefts, burglaries, and assaults never come before the criminal justice system for a variety of reasons, but primarily because of a belief that the police will not catch the thief or assailant and that if they do, the courts will not punish (or rehabilitate) the offender or protect the victim from further harm. Gurr (1977:16–17) estimates that official crime statistics in Britain and the United States underestimate the total volume of criminal behavior by ratios from 2:1 to 10:1. Surveys of crime victimization for the general population reveal these discrepancies between official and actual criminality. Gurr argues, however, that reported crime statistics do correspond to relative frequency of criminal behavior and that they can thus be used, with caution, to tell us about trends in the incidence of crime.

In a most careful long-term analysis of crime in the cities of London, Stockholm, Sydney (Australia) and Calcutta from the early 1800s to the present, Gurr, Grabosky, and Hula (1977) note a common pattern for the more developed Western societies, a pattern from which Calcutta deviates sharply. They find that there has been a dramatic rise in criminality, both violent and nonviolent, in the West since the Great Depression, with the greatest increases occurring in the latter 1960s and early 1970s. The upward trend for white-collar crime began during the Depression itself and continued to accelerate through the post-World War II era. The rate for known white-collar crimes increased in London by 700 percent between 1945 and 1970 and in Stockholm also by 700 percent between the late 1920s and the early 1970s (1977:635–36).

In the field of violent crime, London experienced a tripling of the murder rate between 1950 and 1970 and Stockholm had a 500 percent increase in assaults from the 1940s to the 1970s. In Sydney, the rise in violent crime was somewhat more delayed, but in the 1960s there was a 40 percent jump in homicides and serious assault and a staggering 800 percent leap in armed robbery. Robbery, that most common of crimes, was up by 3,000 percent in London between the 1930s and the early 1970s and by 600 percent in Stockholm over the same general period. Sydney again experienced a somewhat delayed rise in "common crime," with a doubling of larceny and a tripling of burglary from just 1960 to 1970. Gurr and his associates find these data generally in line with trends in reported crime from France, England, and Wales generally, the United States as a whole, and with specific studies for a number of cities such as Boston and Chicago (646–47).

More startling than the massively documented and publicly perceived growth of criminality of all types in the post-Depression West is the reversal this represents vis-à-vis the declining crime rate for Western societies overall from the early 1800s to the 1920s. According to Gurr, the low point of criminality in Western societies was probably reached in the 1920s, ending a century of sometimes erratic but nevertheless considerable declines in reported criminal behavior in London, Stockholm, Sydney, Boston, Chicago, and Buffalo. It would appear that after bottoming out in the immediate pre-Depression years, the rate of criminal behavior began to climb again in the developed West, slowly at first, but with a sharp acceleration in the 1960s during a period of unprecedented affluence (figure 6.1).

This increase in crime and criminal violence now in some areas effectively limits the freedom of many, especially women and the elderly, who fear to go outside their homes after dark or even during daytime. Vandalism of both private and public property, seemingly senseless brutality in the neighborhood and increasingly in the schools, massive shoplifting, and repeated armed robbery against local merchants have created a climate of fear and despair, a tangible if not easily quantifiable loss of community morale. In the 1980s, in the United States, there has been a leveling off or slight decline in crime rates, which is generally attributed to a leveling off or decline in the proportion of young adult males in the population. In West Germany, on the other hand, Interior Minister Friedrich Zimmerman reported (*The week in Germany*, Feb. 24, 1988) a strong rise in criminality from 1.9 million cases in 1966 to 4.4 million in 1986 and saw no end to this current trend.

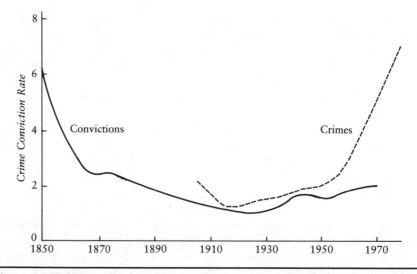

Figure 6.1 Common trend in crimes and convictions for theft and violence in the West, 1850–1970, based on studies for London, Stockholm, and Sydney, Australia.

SOURCE: Adapted from T. Gurr, P. Grabosky, and R. Hula, *The Politics of Crime and Conflict* (Beverly Hills, Calif.: Sage, 1977), pp. 60–61.

Nevertheless, crime rates remain at a new and higher plateau in most of the liberal democracies at a time not of economic depression or collapse but during the period of greatest economic affluence in their histories.

An additional negative feature of the new criminality is the recognition, now widespread, that the criminal justice system does little to actually rehabilitate, or reform those criminals who are apprehended. Rather, prisons often harden criminal behavior patterns, and when prisoners are released at the end of their sentences, they are quite likely to commit further crimes. This pattern of repeat criminality, called "recidivism," means that in the United States, about 70 percent of convicted criminals will commit more crimes (and be caught). One general factor which seems to decrease criminal behavior on the part of released convicts is the aging process. With increasing age, especially for males, the likelihood of further crime declines, but this is hardly a success for the prison system, which in 1986 incarcerated 547,000 people in the United States, as compared to 133,000 in 1945 and 210,000 in 1965. This includes federal and state prisons only, but not city and county jails, which in 1986 held an additional 273,000 inmates as compared to 86,000 in 1950. The United States is somewhat unusual among the liberal democracies in terms of the prisoner population per capita. While the number of prisoners has grown in other liberal democracies in the postwar period as well, the growth in numbers, both in absolute figures and per capita, has been much more modest. In England and Wales, for example, the inmate population numbered 21,000 in 1951 and grew to 43,000 by 1981; in West Germany, the inmate population hovered around 48,000 in the 1960s. These are significantly lower levels per capita than in the United States.

Explanations for the post-Depression rise in crime are varied, but not too varied to be summarized briefly. Radical criminologist Richard Quinney (1969, 1970, 1977) and economist David Gordon (1977) have argued that crime is endemic to a class-divided capitalist order, that criminality is partly functional to the system at levels of corporate price fixing, political bribery and corruption, even tax evasion and is partially a sign of class conflict at levels of common street crime, especially in poor working-class districts. Gurr (1977) argues from the viewpoint of a political scientist that the goals and interests of political elites are also important factors in determining how public order will be maintained. In the face of rising crime rates and public responsiveness to "law and order" slogans throughout the West,

> THE elite and governmental response has been relatively tolerant. At least two plausible explanations come to mind. One is paralyzing lack of agreement among interested parties about the most effective policies to follow. Second, elites and officials are in fact relatively little concerned about these kinds of crime because their costs—unlike the cost of civil strife—are sustained mainly by the ordinary citizens, who are most likely to be assaulted and who bear, directly and indirectly, most of the costs of personal and commercial theft. (683–84)

Sociologist Daniel Bell (1974, 1976), psychologist Erich Fromm (1955), and political analyst Richard Goodwin (1974), among a host of others, have criticized the hedonist individualism and fetishism of commodities and things (cars, clothes, houses, swimming pools, country clubs—Veblen's conspicuous consumption) that increasingly characterize the social spirit of Western capitalism. The breakdown of the Protestant (and Jewish) ethic of work and frugality, and of the Catholic ethic of social obligation and family values generally, has given way to the ascendancy of possessive individualism as the modern capitalist expression of freedom. For the well-to-do corporate executive and the poor urban working-class youth alike, the objects of success are material possession (and their flaunting), and the means employed to get them are secondary and purely utilitarian considerations. Since law enforcement is lax or nonexistent against corporate crime and ineffectual against common crime, illegal means are, from an economic viewpoint, increasingly popular.

Still another view emphasizes elements of the urban environment in encouraging deviant or antisocial behavior, of which crime is one subset. Gurr (1977) and Nettler (1974) point to cultural heterogeneity, overcrowding, anonymity, and intergroup friction as factors of Western urban civilization that might explain increases in crime and strife. Cultural heterogeneity and the mobility/anonymity of urban society promote the decay of normative standards and greater possibilities of deviant behavior, while urban population densities and close group contact provide fuel for aggressive behavior. Gurr (1977) argues that social scale and cultural heterogeneity, taken together with the economic imperatives of system and the goals and interests of political elites, provide the important elements that condition the extent and treatment of public and social disorder.

Observers like Gurr, Bell, Fromm, and Goodwin are not optimistic about the future of Western democracy in fighting criminality. Bell sees this as a cultural crisis of capitalism, a historic disjunction between the still-successful world of productive capacity and the new hedonism of consumption. The liberal dream of rehabilitation of criminals seems now a utopian failure, and there is little hope that prisons in any Western society do or ever can reassimilate inmates into productive life. On the other hand, a return to the brutalizing punishment of criminals common two centuries ago is politically unrealistic and would probably escalate criminal disorder into civil rebellion in several countries, as Gurr suggests (1977:767). Here there is consensus among observers of Western society. High and perhaps climbing crime rates are further correlates of affluent capitalism in the liberal democracies.

THE FAMILY AS AN ENDANGERED SPECIES

The family is the basic building block of most civilizations. People the world over, at very different levels of economic development and facing a variety of problems and possibilities, when asked what they aspire to in life, include a happy and healthy family life. Pollster Hadley Cantril (1965) in his twelve-nation cross-national comparison of the patterns of human concerns, concludes that "in nearly all the countries studied, the major hopes and aspirations are those involved in maintaining and improving a decent, healthy family life" (35). Yet modern Western society in many ways disrupts or erodes traditional family structures and roles, without replacing them with some functional alternatives. The extended family, with several generations living under the same roof, has given way to the nuclear family, encompassing only the parents and their minor children. The elderly grandparents and widowed aunts and uncles live apart and increasingly in communities (or ghettoes) of the aged. More women have gone out to seek employment in recent years in most liberal democracies, methods of birth control and abortion have become widely available, and birth rates have fallen steadily, in many countries to below zero population growth (ZPG) levels. Economic rationality, maximizing of personal income, pursuing a satisfying and lucrative career, and freedom to "do your own thing" or "be your own person" militate against having and even more against personally raising children.

The result is that, given competent birth control techniques, the average family size is getting smaller and smaller.

These trends are more advanced in the United States, Sweden, and West Germany, less so in Japan, where the traditional family order and modern industrialism seem to coexist. Of course, what is economically most rational for each individual, namely, abstaining from child rearing entirely, is ultimately suicidal for the society at large. The possibility that the population of West Germany might shrink from 65 million to 22 million by the year 2070 (*The Times,* London, April 27, 1979, p. 7), with an increasing percentage of aged and an increasing burden on a dwindling younger generation, reveals one of the many contradictions of modern industria. The rise of the self-interested individual means also the decline of the collective (or social) sense of belonging and obligation necessary to keep societies, communities, and ultimately families together.

It is apparent that today there is simply not the same effort made to save troubled marriages as there was a generation ago, nor does the presence of small children in the family delay or prevent a family breakdown. A generation ago it was common, especially among middle-class families in the United States, West Germany, and Britain, to keep a marriage together "for the sake of the children," or simply to avoid the greater social ostracism that divorce brought. The children of such troubled marriages did not always benefit from socially imposed pressures against divorce, but there should be no pretense that children of divorced parents are today beneficiaries of better home care and greater parental guidance and affection. There is no need to exaggerate the extent to which the traditional bonds of marriage and family life have declined in the West, and there is no good reason to idealize a golden past of family life, either (see Sussman, 1972, for typical argumentation that divorce is a healthy sign of personal problem solving and searching for a newer life-style). Divorce rates throughout the liberal democracies are on the rise and have been since the late 1950s (table 6.1).

Table 6.1 Divorce Rates per 1000 Population, 1946-1984

	1946-48 peak	1955	1965	1975	1984
United States	4.35	2.30	2.40	4.75	4.96[a]
Sweden	1.04	1.21	1.24	3.14	2.44
West Germany	1.88	.92	.93	1.73	2.14
France	1.41	.67	.71	1.16	1.89
Britain	1.36	.59	.73	2.43	2.89
Japan	1.02	-	.79	1.07	1.49
Switzerland	1.04	.89	.83	1.39	1.79[b]

a. 1985
b. 1982

Source: *UN Demographic Yearbook,* 1954, 1975, 1985.

In a comprehensive study of divorce and the law in several societies over long periods of time, Max Rheinstein (1972) points out that while formal divorce rates were low throughout the West in the nineteenth century, informal divorce through abandonment or migration was common among the lower classes. We cannot be sure that family breakup is at an historic peak for Western civilization. We can be sure that there has been a significant increase in marriage breakups since the 1950s throughout the Western democracies generally.

After a flurry of broken war-time marriages in 1946–1947 in the United States, Britain, Germany, and France, divorce rates fell off dramatically and remained low through the fifties. This began to change in the late fifties and early sixties. Divorce rates have been on the rise ever since, with some clear differences in magnitude among the liberal democracies. Catholic societies such as France, Italy, Switzerland, and West Germany, which is half Catholic, and traditionalist Japan, are still well below the divorce levels presently experienced in the United States, Sweden (and Scandinavia generally), and Britain. It must be noted, however, that in Catholic societies, the official divorce statistics underestimate the rate of actual family breakup very considerably. In Italy the number of "unofficial" divorces made liberalization of the divorce laws a national issue in the 1970s. By the mid-seventies, divorce rates in the United States, Sweden, and Britain had reached all-time highs, surpassing even the immediate post-World War II divorce splurge.

In Scandinavia and the United States, between one-third and one-half of all marriages will end in divorce. Rheinstein (1972:307–13) and Sussman (1972) attribute the increase in divorce in the West to the breakthrough in the 1960s of the ethic of "individualist liberalism." Rheinstein concludes that changes in the legal statutes on divorce are not causes but symptoms of this new ethic, which is related in turn to: (1) changes brought about by the industrialization of the economy; (2) the new economic position of women; (3) the declining relevance of religion; and (4) greater individual geographic mobility. Since these factors are more prevalent in some cases in the more industrial communist societies of Eastern Europe, we should expect to find (and do find) that rising divorce rates are not peculiar to the capitalist West. This would also imply, as Marcuse argues in his *One Dimensional Man* (1967), that individualist materialism is common to both modern capitalist and communist societies (see chapter 11).

Unemployment: Return of a "Solved" Problem

Even as per capita GNP continues to rise to unprecedented levels in the liberal democracies, there exist at the bottom of the socioeconomic ladder a considerable and, in the 1970s and early 1980s, a growing mass of chronically unemployed and underemployed workers. Mass unemployment, one of the classic symptoms of a boom/bust capitalism from its inception through the Great Depression, had seemed on the way to a satisfactory, though not complete, resolution through the postwar triumph of Keynesian economics and active government intervention in the marketplace economy. Through a series of fiscal and monetary policies designed to spur capital investment, promote job creation by private industry, government welfare, other spending to keep consumer demand high, direct job creation by the government as employer of last resort, and government nationalization and subsidization of bankrupt industries, a "mixed" capitalist system would be able to keep unemployment levels down. Additionally, much-expanded un-employment and welfare benefits would change unemployment from a per-sonal and family catastrophe to an unpleasant but much more manageable situation for those few who still faced joblessness.

For over a quarter of a century, this optimism seemed to be justified. With the partial exception of the United States, where unemployment remained qualitatively higher, the Western democracies, after the reconstruction of the war-shattered economies of Germany, France, Italy, and Japan, all enjoyed high growth rates and low, even miniscule, unemployment levels by the 1960s. In West Germany, the *Wirtschaftswunder* brought domestic unem-ployment to less than 1 percent and attracted over 4 million foreign workers *(Gastarbeiter)* from Spain, Italy, Greece, Turkey, and Yugoslavia to Ger-many, mostly for menial or factory work that Germans were no longer willing to perform. The European Common Market countries together at-tracted over 8 million foreign workers. In Japan, the larger companies have in the postwar prosperity virtually guaranteed life-time employment (tenure) to their workers after an initial trial period, so that even in less favorable times a firm would not lay off workers to cut costs. In progressive Sweden (see Schnitzer, 1970) government reserve investment funds and extensive and effective job retraining and job placement at government expense added to the array of tools available in the liberal democracies, and also succeeded in reducing unemployment to nearly 1 percent by the 1960s. In Italy and Britain, governments followed a policy of extensive nationalization of finan-cially troubled industries and government subsidy to preserve jobs. In Italy also the Christian Democrats made government an employer of last resort for millions through its patronage system. Even in the United States, with chronic high unemployment especially among blacks and with greater ideo-logical blinders against national planning for full employment (nationaliza-tion, or direct job creation by government), unemployment was forced down below the 4 percent mark between 1966 and 1969. This was, of course, related to massive military spending on the Vietnam War and the drafting of hundreds of thousands of young men into the armed forces and thus represented no real solution to unemployment.

The price for keeping unemployment low in the post-World War II liberal democracies was a modest inflationary trend. The Keynesian approach to steering or guiding the economy called basically for a reversal of the disastrous balanced budget policies followed by both conservative (Herbert Hoover in the United States) and social democratic (Hermann Müller in Weimar Germany) governments during the Great Depression era. But frequent pump-priming through deliberate deficit spending would very likely also create a general upward drift of prices and a climate of inflation as the norm. While this bothered Conservative and Christian Democratic parties somewhat, by the 1960s even Republicans in the United States (although not the Goldwater wing), Conservatives in England, Christian Democrats in West Germany, and Gaullists in France had grudgingly accepted the basic notions of Keynesianism as the new orthodoxy. In the perceived political choice between modest inflation and the danger of severe recession or even depression, parties from moderate Conservative to Social Democratic seemed to share a consensus in favor of keeping unemployment down. While the business cycle had not been eliminated, there was confidence that it could be "damped down" or kept within acceptable bounds.

Then came the OPEC oil embargo of 1973, the quadrupling of oil prices, and the recession of 1974–1975 throughout the noncommunist world. This was the most serious recession since the Great Depression and was different from previous recessions in several aspects. First, the recession hit virtually all of the liberal democracies simultaneously (with the partial exception of Sweden). Previously, recessions in the developed West, as in the United States in 1957–1958 and West Germany in 1966–1967, had been more isolated occurrences; still-healthy economies could help bring the afflicted (most frequently Britain and Italy) out of their most difficult times through loans, imports, and investments. Now the economies of the industrial West were, more or less, in lock step, and there was much wrangling and paralyzing disagreement over who should or could afford to help whom out of the recession. After nearly three decades of growth and freer trade among the nations of the West, there is now a serious danger of protectionist trade conflict, a breakdown on international currency exchange policies, and a loss of undisputed American leadership in Western affairs generally.

Second, unemployment rose to postwar highs in the 1974–1975 recession, not only in the United States, but also in West Germany, France, Britain, and the Netherlands, where in the 1960s joblessness had been at very low levels. Figures from Sweden indicate that a determined and progressive social democracy was able to avoid the general trend of unemployment (though at the cost of severe inflation), while the figures for Japan illustrate the effectiveness of conservative but benevolent paternalism of large Japanese corporations in minimizing official joblessness.

Third, the 1974–1975 recession introduced a new phenomenon into the lexicon of Western economists—"stagflation." Generally speaking, mainstream economists had seen inflation and unemployment as trade-offs, so that recessionary high unemployment should have damped down inflationary pressures in both wage and price areas. The mid-1970s recession, however, combined both high unemployment and high (not modest) inflation rates. Inflation for the years 1974 through 1977 averaged 18.8 percent in Italy, 17.6 percent in Britain, 12.3 percent in Japan, 10.9 percent in France, 8.8 percent in Canada, 7.6 percent in the United States, and a comparatively mild 4.9 percent in West Germany. And while inflation remained high, the "recovery" years 1976 and 1977 did not reduce unemployment to prerecession levels throughout the liberal democracies generally. In 1976 in fact, unemployment increased in Canada (to 7.1 percent). France (up to 5.0 percent), Italy (up to an official 3.7 percent), and Britain (to 5.5 percent), while remaining at high postwar levels in the United States (7.7 percent) and West Germany (4.6 percent). The worldwide recession of 1981–1982 pushed unemployment figures to even higher levels than those experienced in the mid-1970s recession. In many of the liberal democracies, the jobless rate passed 10 percent, and in Great Britain, Ireland, and Belgium, it reached closer to 15 percent by late 1982. These are levels comparable to the first (but not worst) years of the Great Depression, and even in the economic recovery of the mid-1980s unemployment rates have not declined to levels of the pre-1973 period. Each new business upturn since the mid-1970s seems to have had less strength, and each downturn has thrown larger numbers of people out of work. The optimism of two decades, of *Wirtschaftswunder,* the Great Society, and *Il boom,* of confident Keynesianism, has been shattered. Paul Lewis (1978:35), reviewing the forecasts of the Organization for Economic Cooperation and Development (OECD), concluded: "At best, the new forecasts show the industrial countries making disappointingly slow and uneven progress in escaping the high unemployment and inflation that have trapped them for the past few years. At worst, the numbers could mean they are at the brink of another recession, without even the consolation of low inflation to show for it."

Table 6.2 Official Unemployment Rates, 1965-1985

	1965	1970	1975	1980	1985
United States	4.5	4.9	8.5	7.2	7.2
Sweden	1.1	1.4	1.4	--	2.8
West Germany	0.6	0.7	4.7	3.4	7.4
Britain	1.6	2.7	4.5	7.0	13.2
Japan	0.8	1.2	1.9	2.0	2.6
France	1.4	1.7	2.4	6.3	10.3
Canada	3.9	5.9	6.9	7.5	10.5

SOURCES: UN Statistical Yearbook, 1983/84; *Statistical Abstract of the United States,* 1987.

Some comments on the official jobless statistics are necessary to interpret the real extent of the human problem of being unemployed or underemployed. In Italy, official joblessness is only the tip of the iceberg, due to the creation of literally millions of do-nothing slots in an already-bloated government civil service and in the nationalized industries. These positions are unproductive (parasitic) from any economic point of view, and their wages and salaries are really surrogates for unemployment or welfare payments. In West Germany, in addition to the million-and-a-half unemployed workers, there are also many more workers on short-time, that is, workers who had full-time jobs but are now forced to work only part-time. In the United States, the official unemployment rate does not count workers who are too discouraged about job prospects to be actively looking for work, workers who are involuntarily working part-time, and the working poor, those who are working full-time but are earning incomes below the poverty level. David Gordon (1977:70–75) estimates that even the lowest, most conservative estimates of total underemployment in the United States in 1975 would come to 17 percent, or double the official jobless rate. Moreover, unemployment in the liberal democracies is not evenly spread among all social groups, but is much higher among young workers, women, and some ethnic/racial minorities. Official black unemployment in the United States is double white unemployment.

As for the human meaning of unemployment or underemployment, any number of studies show the high correlation between joblessness or marginal employment and almost every other social ill, from poverty to trouble with the law to drug abuse and alcoholism to family disintegration and mental disease. And while no one can seriously relate unemployment in the liberal democracies to the threat of starvation anymore, it is by no means clear that the subjective loss of self-worth and alienation is any less damaging. As many theorists of relative deprivation have pointed out, the welfare poor and unemployed "on the dole," whether in the black ghettoes of Watts, Hough, and Harlem, in the poor Irish and working-class districts of Liverpool, Manchester, and London, or the shantytowns around Rome and Naples, do not compare themselves to the sidewalk-dwellers of Calcutta or Frantz Fanon's "wretched of the earth" in the Third World. They do not necessarily feel fortunate by comparison with the lowest of the low, especially when they live in close proximity to the luxury townhouses and apartments, shops, entertainment spots, and restaurants of the rich. In a constantly changing society, the definition of what is minimally acceptable for a human being or a family also shifts, not only for the upper and middle classes, but for all social strata generally. In the West, the middle class of the 1930s or 1950s measured its success, its modicum of well-being, in terms of housing and appliances, cars and vacations, leisure and travel, at levels that would be considered hardship by many of today's middle classes. Although there are certainly areas in the liberal democracies where poverty is accepted with a traditional fatalism, it must be assumed that expectations of the working class as a whole have risen substantially above Depression era levels.

POLLUTION: THE SOLVABLE PROBLEM

For the purposes of this book, pollution has been included in the catalog of quality-of-life issues because of the attention it has drawn over the last decade and because of the wide array of literature that almost monotonously tells us of some new poison or pollutant that may threaten our well-being. While air, water, nuclear waste, and even noise pollution are indeed social problems and political issues worth discussing, the message of this subsection is, in brief, that pollution is one of the more manageable ills of industrial society. In the field of pollution politics, as British social analyst Barbara Ward puts it:

> THERE is an optimistic school for which its opponents coined the phrase "techno-fixers"; there is a pessimistic school whom the techno-fixers tend to dismiss as "doom-sayers." In between lie as many nuances, differences of emphasis, and varying priorities as can be observed in the battle of ideologies. But the broad distinction between hope and despair sets the direction of the debate. (1976:69)

While optimism is called for as far as the developed nations are concerned, pessimism may be more appropriate for the Third World. In fact, pollution may be an issue in the affluent West in some measure because we have already attained material abundance and can afford to spend more energy, time, money, and skills on environmental quality.

First of all, pollution is hardly a new phenomenon or limited to the most industrialized nations. Air pollution in Mexico City, on a good day, runs ten times the permissible health limit established for cities of the United States. Cynthia Enloe (1975:ch. 4) has emphasized the notion that caring about the environment is for most of the world's nations a luxury issue. Both air and water pollution in Calcutta, São Paulo, and Lagos are at harmful levels daily, without becoming a political issue. When we talk of polluted air and water, stench, and deafening noise, we should be aware that these are found in their worst form in the cities and slum-cities of the Third World (see Ward, 1976: part 4, and ch. 16).

It is probable that the worst cases of local pollution in the Western nations are already in the past. Engels's description, cited earlier, of working-class Manchester in the mid-nineteenth century left little doubt of the intolerable degree of filth, stench, fouled water and air, and unabated factory noise that characterized daily life in working-class districts. John A. Loraine (1972), in his thoughtful balance sheet of pollution of different varieties, points out that London and Nottingham suffered from air pollution as early as the thirteenth century due to the burning of soft coal (with high sulphur content) for domestic heating. (Calcutta develops a similar but much intensified pollution from the burning of animal dung for domestic heating.) London's air pollution problems were increased tremendously during the industrial revolution. The first recorded killer smog occurred in London in 1873, when a dense, immobile mass of polluted air hanging over the city killed approximately one thousand people. Other bad bouts of air pollution were recorded in London in 1880, 1882, 1891, and 1892 and in Glasgow in 1909, where Dr. Harold Antoine De Voeux first coined the term "smog" (smoke and fog). Photochemical smog began to appear over Los Angeles in the 1940s. Occurrences of heavy air pollution combined with a thermal inversion (where a layer of cold air sits on a layer of warmer air, trapping air pollutants) killed sixty people on the River Meuse in Belgium in 1931 and killed twenty people and hospitalized hundreds more in the small industrial town of Donora, Pennsylvania, in October of 1948. The worst case on record, however, occurred in London in December of 1952, when a thermal inversion plus a week-long smog killed approximately four thousand people.

Pollution disasters continue, of course. In Japan in the early 1970s, four separate court cases brought to public attention and politicized the disastrous effects of industrial pollution, which resulted in over one hundred deaths and nearly two thousand injuries from mercury poisoning ("Minimata disease"), cadmium poisoning, and petrochemical air pollution (Enloe, 1975:321–32). In 1976 in Seveso, Italy, an entire village was evacuated after an explosion in a chemical plant, which poisoned the air, ground, and water for miles around. The wreck of the supertanker *Torrey Canyon* in 1967 in the English Channel fouled fishing grounds and beaches with over 30,000 tons of crude oil. Eleven years later the breakup of another supertanker, the *Amoco Cadiz,* carrying 220,000 tons of crude oil, destroyed many miles of French coast for fishing and resort industries. And even though it is probably true that urban air pollution levels are lower now than at the peak of the industrialization drive in the late 1800s or even the first half of the twentieth century, the fact that more people now live in urban areas combined with the fact that an increasing percentage of the population is over sixty-five (and more susceptible to respiratory ailments) could mean that more people are harmed by these lower pollution levels. In any case, reductions in current air pollution could produce a meaningful improvement in well-being.

Yet there is good evidence that since the belated and in most cases forced recognition of the pollution problem by governments in the United States, Japan, Sweden, and to some lesser extent Britain, effective steps have been taken in several areas that have already had some significant (i.e., measurable) effects in reducing pollution and guarding against pollution. In *Death of Tomorrow* (1972), John Loraine singles out the three main sources of air pollution as industry, motor cars, and domestic fuel consumption. The mix of villains differs by country and by locality in each country. In the United States, the decline in the use of coal for both home heating and industry has meant that automobile use has risen in importance as a source of air pollution. Government-mandated controls on the amount of lead permissible in gasoline in the United States and other Western nations, as well as requirements for emission controls on new cars, have been making a dent in measured levels of air pollution in such cities as New York and Los Angeles.

Barry Commoner (1987), in a summary of the progress made in environmental pollution control in the most recent period, cites several hopeful signs. For example, from 1975 to 1985 in the United States, lead emissions dropped by 86 percent, sulfur dioxide emissions by 19 percent, and carbon monoxide emissions by 14 percent. In the area of air pollution, therefore, Commoner argues that recent history teaches us that progress is possible given governmental, technical, and social effort. On the other hand, in the area of water pollution, only one-fifth of some four hundred river testing locations showed improvement in water quality between 1974 and 1981. In the area of toxic chemical pollution, the banning of the agricultural pesticide DDT reduced the levels of DDT in human body fat by 79 percent between 1970 and 1983. In other words, increased awareness of environmental issues and hazards in selected areas has produced, in a fairly short time span, notable changes. In other areas, such as toxic chemical production, waste disposal, and radiation exposure, little overall progress, and some regression, has taken place. Commoner sees a long struggle ahead, but takes some satisfaction in the growth of political movements such as the Greens, who now hold seats in parliaments and/or regional and local governments in West Germany, Switzerland, and Italy, and which are linking environmental decisions to basic questions of the economics of production technology. While Commoner emphasizes the tremendous changes that must occur to safeguard the environment for human society, this is one area where the liberal democracies, because of their tremendous social wealth and their high level of opportunity for political dissent, may be better able to cope than in most other quality-of-life issues.

Signs of Alienation and Loss of Community Morale

Other aspects of liberal democratic society are just as much signs of decay and sickness as crime, divorce, and unemployment. In the post-World War II period, drug addiction has grown to qualitatively new levels throughout the west. While drug addiction is most severe in the United States (with Sweden apparently a close second) with an estimated 150,000 to 600,000 heroin addicts alone, there are large and relatively open addict communities in

Stockholm, Berlin, and Amsterdam as well as in New York, Washington, and San Francisco. In the years from 1960 to 1980, drug usage took a "great leap forward" in the West. Drug arrests in the United States, despite some trend toward decriminalization and police nonenforcement in some localities, increased from 31,000 in 1960 to 230,000 by 1969. Drug arrests of persons under eighteen climbed from less than 2,000 to nearly 60,000 in the same period (Wald and Nutt, 1972:27). In some black ghettoes hard-drug addiction is a mass phenomenon. Holahan (1972:288) estimates that between 8 and 12 percent of all black males aged fifteen to thirty-four in Washington, D.C., are drug addicts. In Britain, where drug addiction has never reached anything like American or Swedish proportions, the number of officially registered heroin addicts climbed from a mere 62 in 1958 to 2,240 by 1968, and cocaine addicts from 25 to 564 (May, 1972:349). Stockholm has an addict population of some 10,000, which means that even if there were no addicts in Sweden outside of Stockholm, Sweden would have almost as many addicts per capita as the United States. The highest addict death rate from overdose, however, is found in West Germany and especially in West Berlin.

The German Addiction Center in Hamburg reported in 1981 that there were an estimated 300,000 to 600,000 addicts to some drug, of which 50,000 to 70,000 were heroin addicts. Some trends in addiction included drug (and alcohol) use at earlier ages, more women involved in illegal drug use, and greater usage of two or more drugs at the same time. Forty percent of addicts in West Germany were under twenty-one years of age (*The Week in Germany,* March 20, 1981).

Alcohol abuse remains the most common form of dependency and the most dangerous in terms of deaths caused. It is estimated that there are about 11 million alcohol-dependent people in the United States, while in West Germany the estimate is 1.2 to 2.8 million. Alcohol abuse in West Germany is responsible for sixteen times more fatalities than drug abuse, and approximately 90,000 people become alcoholics each year.

Modern chemistry has created some new hallucinogenic drugs in the postwar era, such as LSD and more recently PCP, that can be manufactured with relative ease in small garage or home workshop laboratories. These new drugs have added a new dimension of faddishness to the recent rise in addiction. More important, however, is the change in the composite picture of the addict in the affluent liberal democracies. Nils Bejerot, in his wide-ranging study of drug addiction in different countries, summarizes the situation about 1950 as follows:

UNTIL about twenty years ago dependence on sedative and stimulant drugs was a phenomenon largely confined in economically advanced countries to two relatively well-defined groups. In most countries there was a group of addicts drawn from the upper and professional classes, including a substantial group from medical or allied occupations, who had ready access to narcotics and stimulant drugs prone to cause dependence. In some countries, and the U.S.A. in particular, there was a much larger addiction problem closely associated with poverty and underprivilege. (1970:v)

Given this profile in the early postwar years, one might have expected for drug addiction "a decline in parallel with the eradication of poverty and disease and the improvement of living conditions," suggests Bejerot. What has emerged in the 1960s and 1970s, however, Bejerot finds, is a new population of drug users from fifteen to twenty-five years old and from all social classes—the well-to-do, the middle class, and the working class, as well as the poorest in society. Drug addiction and drug usage have grown to be symptomatic characteristics of the sickness of society in general, not just the deviant behavior of the ghetto poor or upper-class medical practitioners. Drug addiction today in the West reflects not despair of bitter poverty but a wide-ranging sense of alienation of the middle-class user from society. Illegal drug trafficking has in the 1980s become a giant economic network. In the United States, its sales volume has been estimated at $100 billion to $150 billion, which makes it larger than the automobile industry in economic power and which enables it to influence various elements of law enforcement, courts, and banking to suit its needs.

Drug usage is of course not confined to heroin, cocaine, LSD, PCP, etc. Millions of men and women seek to forget their anxieties, relax their tensions, produce pleasant sensations, or simply get through the day by the use and abuse of legally obtainable uppers and downers, stimulants and tranquilizers, and of course alcohol.

To many if not most observers of the liberal democratic societies, the average citizen is fast losing his or her sense of social or community belonging and feels incapable of personally getting involved to solve problems of crime, drugs, delinquency, pornography, and loneliness. The world was shocked in 1964 when in New York City Kitty Genovese was stabbed to death by a street assailant while some twenty-nine people witnessed the slaying in progress and did nothing to help the victim. No one came running, no one shouted out a window for help, no one called the police. No one wanted to get involved, each hoped only to escape harm or inconvenience by remaining isolated from the immediate tragedy. Escapism, whether by the abandonment of the cities or troubled neighborhoods by the well-to-do or the middle class, or through drugs, alcoholism (and divorce?), through noninvolvement behind bolted doors, or through extreme subordination of self to any number of cults is a sign of the times, an abandonment of community effort or at times a grotesque attempt to find a collective existence. It is a recognition, explicit and implicit, of the decline of local control over events that affect the quality of life in the immediate environment.

Roland Warren (1972:9–10), in a many-faceted study of the changes in community in America (with general lessons for the developed nations), lists five major functions that are relevant to a locality: production-distribution, socialization, social control, social participation, and mutual support. Warren details in his work how communities have lost their autonomy to larger, vertically structured state and national organizations, both private and public. A series of transformations, including increased division of labor, increasing systemic relationships of locality to the larger society, bureaucratization/impersonalization, transfer of functions, urbanization and suburbanization, and changing values, which Warren collectively labels the "great change," have contributed to the decline of the community model. More important, despite the renewed interest in community development and community control in the 1960s in the United States and elsewhere in the West, which signalled a conscious recognition of this loss of community, Warren is not optimistic that the problems that afflict community morale and lower the quality of life can be brought under control by purposive (planned) action. First and most basic, these problems are not just local but state and national problems, and there is no sign that they are manageable at any level under existing circumstances. Second, the reform attempts of the 1960s were of an adaptive type, which "at best alleviate the side effects of the more basic change" (363). Finally, Warren comes to the conclusion that those who seek to alleviate community problems through local citizen participation and effort often run up against powerful vested interests that have a great stake in keeping things as they are:

1. Collaborative strategies will result only in programs and policies which the existing power configuration finds acceptable.
2. Power will not voluntarily be given up by elites.
3. Attempts by the poor, agency clientele, youth, etc., to participate in community decision-making often will not be resisted so long as they do not pose threats to the well-being of those in power, or threaten to change the power configuration.
4. Where such threats are posed through broader participation such broad participation will be co-opted, controlled, or fiercely attacked by those in power. (388)

Conclusions

This chapter has presented several areas of citizens concern in the affluent liberal democracies. Of the issues of criminality, family breakup, pollution, unemployment, and personal alienation, there are signs of improvement only in the area of pollution (mainly of air and water). This is because pollution is at least in part manageable as a technical problem and does not directly involve social, class, or interpersonal relations. Liberal democracies are much more able to deal with technical and aggregate economic issues than with questions of either social equality or social morale. This must be seen as a price paid for the encouragement and protection of individualist materialism and personal liberty. Since these are core values of the liberal democracies, we must doubt whether, in the absence of some basic shifts in values, the serious problems presented here can be solved. Further, any significant shift in core values that would challenge rights of property ownership and personal freedom in favor of equality and community will run up against, as Warren points out, determined resistance from very powerful and established interests.

Chapter 7

Communism—Theory and Origins

MODERN THEORIES OF SOCIALISM AND communism were developed chiefly in the nineteenth century after the ultimate failure of the French Revolution and the final defeat of the Napoleonic armies in 1814–1815. This period, from 1815 to 1914, was one of relative peace and industrialization in Europe. Economic developments such as the expansion of the free market system, first in England and France, later in Germany and northern Italy, were changing the social and political anatomy of Western Europe as well as of the United States and Japan. But the benefit brought by increased production, new inventions, and greater personal liberty had to be balanced against the costs of miserable living and working conditions for the new urban working class and against the constant specter of unemployment. The rise of industrial capitalism, celebrated by liberal economic and political thought, looked very different from the perspective of working-class Manchester.

The suffering of the working class in nineteenth-century capitalism stood in sharp contrast to the opulent wealth of a handful of plutocrats (the captains of industry) such as Thyssen and Krupp, Morgan and Vanderbilt. Those who criticized the suffering and inequities associated with capitalism were not always socialists. Some were aristocrats hoping for a return to (or the salvation of) agrarian feudalism and monarchy. Others, following Adam Smith, regarded the misfortunes of the working class as a necessary price of progress. The socialists constituted a group of critics who wanted to build a more just society fundamentally different from capitalism, without returning to feudal monarchy. Among those socialist (or communist—the terms were at that time interchangeable) theorists there was considerable disagreement over the strategy for bringing about the transition from capitalism to socialism. Marx emphasized, though granting some possible exceptions, the revolutionary overthrow of capitalism and the bourgeois state by a mass uprising of the urban working class, the proletariat. English industrialist Robert Owen and his followers, on the other hand, set up socialist communities (New Lenark, New Harmony) in England and the United States to act as models for the rest of society. The Frenchman Pierre Proudhon emphasized a decentralized syndicalist system based on a workers' takeover of the factories. The Russian nobleman Mikhail Bakunin sought to bring an end to capitalism through terrorism and assassination of high government officials. His new socialist society was cast in an anarchist image, that is, having no formal government, but rather direct self-government by the people.

Socialist thinkers disagreed also in their basic attitudes about technology and urban industrialism. Marx believed that the new technology of capitalism was a revolutionary breakthrough for mankind and that it offered the possibility for eliminating poverty, disease, and ignorance throughout the world if only it could be applied justly and rationally through socialism. Agrarian socialists (often called populists) believed that the new industrial technology and the crime-ridden, crowded, dirty cities being spawned by it were the root of the evils of capitalism. They hoped to reverse urbanization and industrialization, to revive the communal (that is, socialist) spirit of the villages and small towns. The Owenites favored using industrial innovations, but on a more decentralized small-town or small-city basis, to avoid pollution and overcrowding.

There is scarcely room here to describe the many different and interesting plans for building a new society to replace capitalism; there was consensus perhaps only on the idea that this society would be more just, and therefore more egalitarian, than capitalism. This may sound like very little to agree on, yet the immorality and unfairness of capitalism appeared so great that this made (and is still making) the concept of socialism a powerful and motivating force for a more just society. It is today quite likely that those pressing for greater social equality will call themselves socialists. Even those who mainly want to legitimate their claim to support greater social equality will appropriate the socialist label. And on the other side of the fence, the wealthy and privileged in most societies are also the most dependably and violently antisocialist, the most opposed to any form or element of socialism. Only in a few countries, most notably the United States, do leading proponents of greater social justice still disclaim all forms of socialism and consider themselves liberals.

MARXIST SOCIALISM

Of all the theories of socialism that arose in the last century, certainly those of Karl Marx have had the greatest impact to date in the real world. In fact, one of the basic developments in political theory over the past century has been the rise of Marxism as the leading theory of socialism. In Marx's own time, there was no one predominant theory of socialism; Proudhon, Owen, and Bakunin probably had greater followings than did Marx in the mid-nineteenth century. Even today there are several non-Marxist socialist movements and political parties, including the Fabian socialists in England, the Spanish anarcho-syndicalists, and the Zapatistas in Mexico. Many of the governing social democratic parties of Western Europe (and elsewhere) have anti-Marxist, non-Marxist, and Marxist factions in varying mixtures; indeed in all cases the Marxist wing is not the dominant group. Yet the popular identification of socialism with Marxism is a historic development that has for some time overshadowed the socialist thought of Marx's competitors.

Marx (1818–1883) never lived to see socialism, of any type, in operation in any country. Most of his writings dealt with the workings of capitalism and the reasons for the predicted overthrow of capitalism. They do not give a detailed blueprint for the operation of a socialist society. Marx said that the proletariat itself would have to work out the details through actual practice. In the *Communist Manifesto,* Marx and Engels did outline some general policies that would start society down the road to socialism once the bourgeoisie had been overthrown:

1. Abolition of property in land and application of all rents of lands to public purposes.
2. A heavy progressive or graduated income tax.
3. Abolition of all right of inheritance.
4. Confiscation of the property of all emigrants and rebels.
5. Centralization of credit in the hands of the State, by means of a national bank with State capital and an exclusive monopoly.
6. Centralization of the means of communication and transport in the hands of the State.
7. Extension of factories and instruments of production owned by the State; the bringing into cultivation of waste-lands, and the improvement of the soil generally in accordance with a common plan.
8. Equal liability of all to labour. Establishment of industrial armies, especially for agriculture.
9. Combination of agriculture with manufacturing industries; gradual abolition of the distinction between town and country, by a more equable distribution of the population over the country.
10. Free education for all children in public schools. Abolition of children's factory labour in its present form. Combination of education with industrial production, &c., &c. (Tucker, 1972:352)

Radical as these proposals were for their time, Marx related them to the transitional phase of the "dictatorship of the proletariat," before full communism is achieved. Only in the era of full communism would humanity apply the general ethic of "from each according to his abilities, to each according to his needs." Eventually humankind would reach a fully classless society, with no one born into great wealth or stultifying poverty, a society that would have overcome exploitation of workers, racial or ethnic groups, and women. Production would be socially planned; the means of production (factories, farms, offices) would be collectively owned rather than in private hands. Marx believed that under full communism, government bureaucracy, including police and military, would "wither away" as volunteer citizen groups took over the tasks of social administration. In such a society all would participate in governing, not just a few "professionals." In short, there would be no full-time politicians, bureaucrats, or generals; all these roles would be performed by ordinary citizens on a short-term or rotating basis.

Even with the most modern technology and automation of much back-breaking work, there would still be some tedious and unenjoyable work, but no one would consistently get stuck with these chores. In a rather idyllic passage from one of his earliest works, Marx contrasts the place of occupation in capitalist and communist societies:

> HE is [*in capitalism*] a hunter, a fisherman, a shepherd, or a critical critic, and must remain so if he does not want to lose his means of livelihood; while in communist society, where nobody has one exclusive sphere of activity but each can become accomplished in any branch he wishes, society regulates the general production and thus makes it possible for me to do one thing today and another tomorrow, to hunt in the morning, fish in the afternoon, rear cattle in the evening, criticize after dinner, just as I have a mind, without ever becoming hunter, fisherman, shepherd, or critic. (Tucker, 1972:124)

In such a society people would be able to develop many talents, using both manual and mental labor, hand work and brain work.

Evolutionary Socialism

Marx was disappointed in his hopes for socialist revolution in Europe. He had never considered the possibility of a socialist revolution succeeding in one country, but had hoped that a socialist revolution, following the pattern of the French Revolution of 1789, would sweep across national boundaries, becoming an international workers' uprising. Underestimating the forces of nationalism, he had helped to found the Workingman's International to promote socialism throughout Europe and to build international working-class solidarity. By 1895, when Engels died, it was becoming clear that many of the predictions for revolution would not be fulfilled, at least for a while. To be sure, workers were rebelling against poor wages and working conditions by building union organizations against formidable odds. But the union movement and the socialist and labor parties that it supported in various countries were for the most part not revolutionary. Gradually, though not without a good deal of violence, unions and working-class parties received recognition and were able to push through partial reforms on child and female labor, voting rights for working men, factory safety, hours and wages, and union bargaining rights. Daily life for the urban worker and his or her family at the turn of the century was still no bed of roses, but it did seem as though the working class could begin to share the benefits of industrialization by working and struggling within the capitalist system. From this perspective, one branch of socialist thought, now generally called social democracy, extensively revised Marx's ideas and eventually abandoned Marxism.

Eduard Bernstein, a close friend of Engels and a prominent publicist for the German Social Democratic party (SPD) until the 1930s, advanced a major critique of Marx, which arrived at the conclusions that: (1) capitalism was not about to explode from its own internal contradictions; (2) a workers' revolution had become very difficult, if not impossible, because of advances in military technology (especially the machine gun and breech-loaded cannon); and (3) a gradual democratization of the political and economic system could create a more just society (socialism) without revolution. The key to this "evolutionary socialism" was education of workers, promotion of the union movement, and support for workers' parties. Socialism would come through ballots rather than bullets. Social democrats and laborites would be the loyal opposition, which would someday become the governing party, playing by the rules of the system itself. Of course, this meant giving up notions of international working class solidarity when it clashed with the "national interest" or with the spirit of nationalism in electoral politics. It meant, for example, that Social Democrats in Germany supported the conquest of new colonies in Africa and Asia by the kaiser as a proper part of Germany's new great-power status. Subjugation and exploitation of Third World peoples was not something that Social Democrats really approved of in principle (how could they?), but as long as the British, French, Americans, Dutch, and Japanese were cutting up the Third World into colonies and "spheres of influence," Germany should not be disadvantaged. After all, every great power needed its "place in the sun."

The great test of the social democratic movement (organized as the Second International) came in 1914 at the outbreak of World War I. It was clear that the war would be a disaster for the working class. They would be the ones to die by the thousands (eventually by the millions) in the front lines, while industrialists and aristocrats amassed war profits and directed the battlefield slaughter from safe vantage points. The question for the socialist and labor movements in Germany, Britain, France, Russia, Italy, Austria, and later the United States was whether to unite (via the Second International) to oppose the war in the name of the international working class or to individually support the national war policies of their own nations in order to prove their nationalist loyalty. In nearly every case, the revisionist social democrats voted with liberals and conservatives to support the war. One of the few exceptions was the American Socialist party, which refused in 1917 to abandon its opposition to American participation in the war, an action for which socialist leader Eugene V. Debs was jailed. Lenin's Bolsheviks in Russia also opposed the war and were subsequently denounced as traitors and as German agents. A minority of socialists who opposed or came to oppose the war formed the beginnings of the communist parties of Western Europe. Rosa Luxemburg and Karl Liebknecht, for example, split off from the Majority Social Democrats in Germany to form the Spartacus League, which in 1919 became the German Communist party. Indeed, World War I marks the historic split in the international socialist movement into revisionist social democrats and revolutionary communists. This split has continued, with moderate Social Democrats like Willy Brandt, François Mitterrand, Golda Meir, and Olof Palme as recent representatives of the Second International and the heritage of evolutionary socialism. The communist parties, on the other hand, joined together in the Third International under the tutelage of the Bolsheviks and have been associated ever since with the theories of Lenin as well as Marx (hence the title Marxist-Leninist).

LENINISM

Just as Bernstein had found it necessary to revise Marxism and develop a different strategy for social democrats in the industrial West, so Lenin adapted Marx to the changed conditions of capitalism in the late nineteenth century. Lenin also noted the diminished revolutionary possibilities in the more developed West and even remarked on the growing prospects of a "labor aristocracy," a relatively well-to-do segment of workers, in these nations. But Lenin explained this as a result of imperialism, whereby the developed West between 1875 and 1914 had divided up the Third World into colonial empires and spheres of influence.

During this period the British Empire, largest by far, stretched from the Cape of Good Hope in South Africa to Cairo, from India, Pakistan, and Burma in South Asia to the subcontinent of Australia, Malaya, Hong Kong, and Singapore in East Asia, and finally to Jamaica, the Bahamas, British Honduras, and British Guyana in the Caribbean area. The French conquered much of Saharan and sub-Saharan West Africa, as well as Indochina. Latecomers like Germany claimed some territories in Africa (Tanzania, Namibia, Cameroun, Togo) as well as some Pacific islands and "spheres of influence" for economic exploitation in Turkey and China. The United States, already having attained its Manifest Destiny of stretching from coast to coast at the expense of native American Indians and Mexico, reached out to establish its hold over Hawaii and the Panama Canal Zone and to Cuba, Puerto Rico, and the Philippines. The United States gradually became the economic and political force in Latin America generally, with the power to intervene in the affairs of various nations (Mexico, Nicaragua, Panama, the Dominican Republic). Even Belgium claimed for its monarch the huge and mineral-rich Congo in central Africa. The great ancient empires of the Ottomans in the Middle East, India, Persia, and China were either totally swallowed up, or dismembered, or subordinated to the industrialized West (plus Japan). In Africa, only tiny and resource-poor Liberia escaped being gobbled up. Tsarist Russia, while itself an imperialist power in China and the Balkans during this period, became increasingly open to economic exploitation by French, German, and British finance capital. Lenin and other revolutionaries as well considered Russia an economic sphere of influence of the advanced Western powers.

Through the exploitation of cheap native labor and resources, Western capital was able to find new sources of profit, allowing it to make concessions to the working class in the developed metropolises of Europe and North America. This decreased the revolutionary tendencies in these most advanced nations, so that, contrary to Marx's expectations, the proletariat was becoming less radicalized. Lenin argued that the locus of revolution had been displaced from the developed West to the less-developed nations now dominated by Western imperialism and its corporate multinationals. As the Third World peoples were forcibly integrated into the world capitalist system and subjected to patterns of development dictated by the Western multinationals, they would organize to defend themselves and liberate their countries from imperialism, both political and economic. Lenin predicted that wars of national liberation would erupt to deprive Western capitalism of its sources of profits, and that these revolutions in the underdeveloped world would then lead to the re-emergence of the class struggle and working-class revolution in the West. Lenin, of course, was working and planning for a revolution in Russia (the weak link in the chain of international finance capitalism), but always with the hope that this would be the spark to ignite a revolution in Europe (especially Germany). A socialist Europe could then aid, on equitable terms, in the industrial development of Russia. Like Marx, Lenin did not envisage building socialism in Russia, but considered international-scale revolution a necessity.

The opportunity for wars of national liberation to succeed would be enhanced by conflicts among the imperialist powers, conflicts that according to Lenin would lead to wars among the imperialists over the division of spoils in the Third World. Already, at the turn of the century, hostile clashes in Africa (for example, the Fashoda incident) between British and French, the rising challenge of Germany to British naval power, and the rivalry of Russia and Japan to dominate Korea and Manchuria gave evidence of the potential for a major war. Secret treaties detailed how one coalition of powers intended to take over the colonies of another power. These intraimperialist struggles between Germany and England, France and Germany, Italy and Austria, Japan and Russia, and so on, would give the liberation movements improved opportunities for success.

Preparing for revolution in tsarist Russia, or in the underdeveloped nations generally, would require a different type of organization from that of

Western social democratic parties. In tsarist Russia there existed no freedom of speech, no free elections, no rights of union organization; instead there were extensive secret police spying and torture and violent suppression of dissent, a qualitatively different political atmosphere compared with the kaiser's Germany. There was little room for an open, public, democratic socialist movement to operate. The conditions to which Bernstein was responding in Western Europe (even in authoritarian Germany) simply did not exist in most of the underdeveloped world. Lenin saw the need for a vanguard party of a new type, a tightly organized, disciplined cadre of professional revolutionaries, dedicated to the revolution above all. The Leninist party member would be willing to suffer deprivation, jail, and worse over long periods when revolution seemed hopeless, so that when the conditions for revolt appeared, the chance would not be missed. The rebellious workers (and perhaps even peasants) would have a coherent, even paramilitary, leadership, able to topple the old order. Even the most corrupt and hated regime, Lenin argued, does not simply abandon power and disappear. A final shove must be given, an armed shove that would be able to overcome the well-armed military and police resistance. Without a vanguard party, the revolutionary upsurge may be delayed or diverted, giving the old order time to regroup or (as frequently happened and still happens) call for outside help.

Marx had not fully appreciated (as Engels, Bernstein, and Lenin later did) the extent to which modern technology, applied to weaponry, had changed the balance of power between a poorly armed proletariat rising in spontaneous rebellion and a professional military. Lenin's vanguard party would have to be as professional and as capable in the use of force as its opposition if the revolution were to succeed. The Leninist party would be governed according to a set of rules called democratic centralism, which provided for: (1) election of party leaders by the membership, (2) regular reports by leaders to members, (3) open debate of issues before deciding on a policy line, and (4) strict obedience to leadership and policy decisions.

This "party of a new type" and its democratic centralism ran into heavy criticism within the European socialist movement. The objections to Lenin's theory of the vanguard party were twofold. First, social democrats like Julius Martov and Eduard Bernstein argued that a socialist revolution in still-underdeveloped nations like Russia in the early 1900s was wildly premature. These countries first had to go through the capitalist stage, which was still in its infancy. Each stage of development as outlined by Marx is necessary and cannot be skipped. Lenin was accused of being a modern Jacobin, trying to push for revolution where the social conditions were not yet ripe. In such a case, as with the Jacobins of the French Revolution, the revolution would have to resort to terror to maintain power, and even then it would fail, as had Robespierre's regime. This could lead to a degeneration of the revolution into a military dictatorship (Napoleon) or it could end with the restoration of the *ancien regime* (as in France in 1815), all at tremendous cost in human suffering and discredit to the original ideals of the revolution.

A second objection was raised by Rosa Luxemburg and those more sympathetic to revolutionary socialism. Luxemburg was concerned that Lenin's vanguard party would continue in power as a new ruling class after the old order had been overthrown. Marx had originally foreseen a spontaneous workers' revolution that would be quickly victorious and would produce not a new governing elite, but rather a governing majority, the proletariat. Luxemburg feared that Lenin's professional cadre of revolution-makers would not disband after leading the revolution, but would provide a new undemocratic and dangerous obstacle to building socialism. Needless to say, these objections continue to provide much controversy among socialists and to be relevant to questions of revolution and the building of socialism.

THE RUSSIAN REVOLUTION—FIRST AND ALONE

The first political system to call itself socialist was established by the 1917 October Revolution in Russia. The autocratic tsarist system had been challenged by revolutionary upheavals before World War I, in 1905–1906, but had managed with the help of the army to survive for another decade. At the beginning of World War I, in fact, it seemed that an upsurge in nationalistic patriotism would restore some measure of popular support for Tsar Nicholas II. However, the fortunes of war quickly eroded this early optimism when Russian losses at the front mounted to disastrous proportions. Meanwhile, the tsar's corrupt and inept government lost whatever public confidence it had held, and the economy became both overloaded by the war effort and shattered by the loss of industrial facilities to the advancing German armies. In February of 1917, popular unrest in the capital city of Petrograd came to the boiling point. One day, an international women's day march, a demonstration of steel workers from the huge Putilov works, and food riots combined to overwhelm the local tsarist authority. Rather than firing on the masses, most soldiers joined the demonstrators, and in a few days the tsar had lost control of the effective use of coercion. But as Nicholas II abdicated, national political power was split. The Provisional Government composed of conservatives, liberals, and some agrarian reformers took control of the civil bureaucracy and national ministries. Local revolutionary councils (soviets) of workers, peasants, and soldiers sprang up, as in 1905, to challenge the legitimacy of the Provisional Government. In the following months, a power struggle developed between the more moderate Provisional Government and the revolutionary soviets. Lenin's Bolsheviks and other revolutionary groups were constantly increasing their influence. The Provisional Government made several mistakes during this period that showed it was out of touch with mass sentiment. In particular, it kept Russia in the war, refusing to sign a separate peace with Germany, although it was clear that it could not stop the German advance. It refused also to expropriate and redistribute the vast landholdings of the nobility and the Russian Orthodox church, although it was clear that peasants were already taking matters into their own hands, whether the government approved or not. By late fall, Lenin and Trotsky had finalized plans for an armed uprising to topple the Provisional Government. On October 25, 1917, armed units of Red Guards took over the major banks, telegraph offices, rail stations, and ministries and stormed the Winter Palace in Petrograd. A coalition Bolshevik-Left Socialist Revolutionary government was proclaimed, and when the Russian troops at the front signalled their support, the second revolution of 1917 was complete.

Up to this point, there had been surprisingly little bloodshed from either the February or October revolutions (apart from continuing war losses at the hands of the Germans). But this did not last. The Bolsheviks had promised "Bread, Land, and Peace." In their first months in office, they expropriated the holdings of the church, the nobility, and big industrialists without compensation and legalized the redistribution of land to the peasantry. After several months of debating the war and peace issue, Lenin's government signed a peace treaty with Germany at Brest-Litovsk. Under the terms of the treaty, Russia surrendered huge chunks of former Russian territory to the Germans. Lenin regarded this treaty as a necessary device to give the revolution some breathing room. He intended that after a short while it would become a meaningless scrap of paper. But in the meanwhile it also caused a rupture in the Bolshevik-Left Socialist Revolutionary coalition and the beginning of the civil war. The Left Socialist Revolutionaries, who favored continuing the war against Germany, unleashed a wave of terror against supporters of the treaty, assassinating several top Bolsheviks and the German ambassador and shooting Lenin in the head. The Western allies of wartime Russia used the separate peace as an excuse to invade Soviet Russia with expeditionary armies and to finance an attempt at a comeback by the reactionary tsarist elements (the White armies). American forces occupied Murmansk in the North, British troops took control of the Baku oil fields, and Japanese armies marched into Siberia. Germany still controlled much of European Russia. At its low point in 1918, the Bolshevik government controlled only about one-seventh of the territory of the old Russian Empire.

Lenin had hoped that revolution in Russia would ignite revolution in Europe (especially Germany), and there were indeed uprisings in Germany and Hungary in 1918–1919 in the aftermath of the defeat of the Central Powers in World War I. Revolutionary councils were set up in Berlin and Munich, many of the large factories in the Ruhr were taken over by workers, and a Soviet Republic was established for several months in Hungary. Ironically, however, but in keeping with revisionist thinking, the majority Social

Democrats in Germany used the reactionary military command of the kaiser (who had fled the country) to suppress the socialist revolution, and revolutionary leaders like Rosa Luxemburg and Karl Liebknecht were assassinated by right-wing paramilitary death squads.

This policy sealed the fate of the 1918 socialist uprising in Germany, as well as crippling the new Weimar democracy, and left Soviet Russia alone and encircled by hostile capitalist powers. Against these apparently long odds, the Bolsheviks won the civil war of 1918–1921. Trotsky became a self-taught military genius, built the Red Army to a strength of 5 million men, and along with other Bolsheviks defeated the White armies and forced the British, Americans, and Japanese to withdraw. The White terror was more than answered by the Red terror of the Cheka (forerunner of the People's Commisariat for Internal Affairs, the NKVD). And the Bolsheviks had considerable popular support, primarily from the small but concentrated industrial working class but also from the poor peasantry. Western support of the most reactionary and anti-Semitic opponents of the Bolsheviks only increased tacit or active support for Lenin's government among Russian Jews, for example, as the lesser evil.

By early 1921, the Bolsheviks faced a situation unanticipated by Marx, Lenin, or Bernstein. A socialist revolution had succeeded in a backward underdeveloped country, a huge multiethnic collection of peoples. But the revolution had failed in Europe. Soviet Russia was alone and isolated, the target of total economic blockade by the West. On the other hand, although the Bolsheviks had indeed been forced to use terror to maintain themselves in power, the revolution had not lost its base of popular support, nor had it degenerated into military dictatorship. The Leninist vanguard party had shown extraordinary ability to make and then defend the revolution, even without aid from socialist revolution in Europe.

What would be the future course of a socialist revolution in this predominantly peasant society? Through most of the 1920s the Bolshevik party debated this issue. The New Economic Policy (NEP) adopted in 1921 made major concessions to the more entrepreneurial peasantry (the kulaks) and to businessmen in retail trade. This was initially a program of reconstruction designed to bring the war-ruined economy back to its prewar levels of output, which it did by 1926–1927. But it was becoming apparent that the NEP could be continued only by further concessions to the kulaks and that industrialization would be slowed considerably if this course were taken. Still, there was a significant faction of the party that favored doing just this in order to maintain the good will of the peasantry (including the kulaks). Another faction proposed rapid industrialization and collectivization of agriculture, with both agriculture and industry centrally managed through five-year plans. This would mean austere consumer levels for many years and forcible expropriation of kulak lands, but it was seen as a necessary economic prerequisite to building Russian socialism and defending it against a hostile foreign environment.

This industrialization debate was intensified and complicated by the death of Lenin after a series of paralyzing strokes in January of 1924. The major factions and leaders, notably Trotsky, Stalin, Zinoviev, and Kamenev, fought not only over policy alternatives but also over leadership succession. Originally Stalin had favored a continued NEP, which he labelled "Socialism in One Country." Trotsky had favored the "New Course" program of rapid industrialization. In an economic crisis that arose in 1927–1928 after Stalin's faction had defeated Trotsky politically, Stalin reversed himself and adopted many of the "New Course" ideas, but in extreme form. He then put into effect, in 1928, the first Five-Year Plan for industrialization, collectivization, and urbanization at levels far more ambitious than had originally been proposed. This evoked massive resistance from the kulaks in the countryside and their bloody suppression and liquidation by the Red Army.

The rupture of the worker-peasant alliance was followed in the 1930s by Stalin's purges of other (real and imagined) opponents in the party, government, and military, and even of the secret police (NKVD) itself. Massive labor camps were set up to accommodate millions of Stalin's victims, who labored in the mines, lumber camps, and construction projects run by the NKVD camp administration (GULAG). Alexander Solzhenitsyn has eloquently described the horrors of the Stalinist forced labor system.

Yet, with all of its terrors and paranoia, Stalin's regime pushed Russia's economic development ahead at an impressive, even unprecedented, rate. The combination of "terror and progress" (Moore, 1966) did produce a decisive break with the agrarian peasant society in which the 1917 revolution had been formed, and the Soviet Union was irreversibly on its way to becoming a modern industrial giant. Despite the purges, despite the economic deprivation in consumer goods and the forced savings for industrial investment, and despite the even greater human sacrifices and economic losses during World War II inflicted by Hitler's Wehrmacht, the USSR by the early 1950s had emerged as an industrialized economic and military power. Western analysts often discount or overlook the popular support that the Soviet system retained and mobilized for the industrialization and war efforts. But it is clear that the Communist party (Bolsheviks), even as it purged millions and demanded sacrifice and hard work from nearly everyone, also had strong support among the urban working class and the poorer peasantry, which made the first five-year plans possible.

For over a quarter century until the end of World War II, the USSR remained (with the minor exception of Mongolia) by default *the* model of socialism, and yet the Soviet experience was in most respects very different from what theory had predicted. Under extremely trying circumstances, the Bolsheviks had succeeded in defeating a variety of internal and external enemies during 1917–1921. After close to a decade of debate, it had embarked upon a program of industrialization, an economic revolution, which Marx had seen as the historic task of capitalism, not socialism. Stalin had directed this industrial revolution with a dictatorial will and a pliant party apparatus in which open intraparty factionalism and even individual dissent were forbidden. Marx had foreseen a socialism (even if called the dictatorship of the proletariat) more democratic than the bourgeois democracy it superseded. Russia had no tradition of bourgeois democracy to follow, but rather a long heritage of autocratic tsarist rule.

It should not be surprising that the socialism of the Soviet Union under Stalin was so far from the theories of Marx. But if Stalinism did not provide a model of Marxist socialism, it showed that a centrally planned industrial revolution in a backward nation was possible without a bourgeois class of industrialists, business owners, and landowners. It is this alternative for economic modernization that made the Soviet Union a competitive model for the less-developed nations. The Soviet economic breakthrough of the first two Five-Year Plans (1928–1938) was all the more impressive when compared with the Great Depression that the Western capitalist societies were suffering at that time.

EXPANSION AND POLYCENTRISM

Following the defeat of fascism in World War II at the hands of the war-time alliance between the Soviet Union and the Western democracies there emerged several new communist systems. Between 1945 and 1950 communist parties professing Marxist-Leninist principles came to power in Poland, Rumania, Bulgaria, Hungary, Yugoslavia, Albania, Czechoslovakia, East Germany, North Korea, China, and North Vietnam (though not recognized until the final defeat of the French in 1954). For a short time communist parties in France, Italy, and other Western democracies served in postwar coalition governments, and even after being ousted with the onset of the "Cold War" in 1947 they remained strong opposition parties, popular among workers and respected for their resistance to fascism.

In Eastern Europe (and North Korea), the Soviet Army of occupation in several cases imposed a communist regime as the postwar political system. Although there is disagreement as to the exact internal strength of local communist movements, it is generally agreed (by noncommunist observers) that in Poland, Rumania, East Germany, and North Korea, the local communist parties came to power largely through the aid of an occupation force, the Red Army. In several places, however, local communist parties developed mass popular followings of their own and were able, after the end of World War II, either to directly assume control of the government (as in Yugoslavia and Albania) or to defeat their opponents in a more protracted revolutionary war (as in Vietnam and China). In China, Mao's People's Liberation Army defeated Chiang Kai-shek's American-supported Nationalist armies, and in North Vietnam, Ho Chi Minh's Viet Minh were able to overcome French attempts to recolonize Indochina.

A third pattern includes Czechoslovakia, Hungary, and Bulgaria. In these countries, local communist parties had widespread popular support and built impressive records of resistance to both reactionary aristocracies and fascism. Yet the presence or near-presence of the Soviet Red Army clearly assisted these parties in defeating and eliminating the local opposition to the establishment of a communist system.

Since 1960, several communist systems have emerged in Latin America, Asia, and Africa, making the geographical scope of communism worldwide. In the 1960s, Cuba, under the leadership of Fidel Castro, turned to the Soviet Union initially for military aid against American intervention (the CIA-sponsored Bay of Pigs invasion), then for economic aid to counteract the United States-organized economic blockade. These factors gradually transformed the radical revolution that overthrew Batista into a communist system. Cuba is one example of the self-fulfilling prophecy involving an American counterrevolutionary foreign policy, whereby American hostility to a serious reform-minded regime pushed it into the communist camp and made it into the communist system that the United States feared in the first place.

In the 1970s, in the aftermath of the failure of American intervention in Vietnam, Cambodia, and Laos, the puppet governments of those countries were overthrown by indigenous communist movements, resulting in a reunited Vietnam and Khmer Rouge and Pathet Lao governments. In Africa, more than a decade of guerrilla warfare led to the overthrow of the Salazar-Caetano dictatorship in Portugal and to the withdrawal of Portuguese colonial forces in 1974, leaving the Front for the Liberation of Mozambique (FRELIMO) virtually uncontested to form the first independence government in Mozambique. In the wake of the Portuguese's departure from Angola, divisions among three major contenders for power led to a brief civil war with considerable outside intervention by the United States, Zaire, South Africa, the Soviet Union, and Cuba. With Soviet-Cuban aid, the Marxist Popular Movement for the Liberation of Angola (MPLA) of Augostinho Neto won out over the CIA and Zaire-backed National Front for the Liberation of Angola (FNLA) and South African-backed National Union for the Total Independence of Angola (UNITA).

There are currently several other states in which parties, movements, or military regimes espousing Marxism, Marxism-Leninism, or revolutionary socialism have attained control of government. These include Mengistu's Marxist military regime in Ethiopia, the Sandinista regime in Nicaragua, and Marxist-Leninist South Yemen. In these cases, however, the ideological orientation is either still in doubt or there is reason to question the durability of the present political system.

The post-World War II expansion of communist systems to all continents has meant several things. First and foremost, it has led to the phenomenon of "polycentrism," or multiple independent centers of communist politics and "models" of communism (see Bertsch and Ganschow, 1976).

First to challenge Soviet claims to sole leadership of the communist movement was Tito's Yugoslav League of Communists. In 1948 Tito's regime refused to integrate Yugoslavia into the military and economic bloc being promoted by Stalin. Although originally fashioned along Soviet lines, Yugoslav communism over the years has developed its own quite distinctive program, which includes a private noncollective agriculture, decentralized management of industry through factory-elected worker councils, liberalized travel and trade policies, and nonalignment in foreign policy.

Next to challenge Soviet authority within the communist world were the Maoists (joined, until recently, with the Albanians). The Sino-Soviet split developed gradually during the 1950s, in large part out of Chinese disapproval of destalinization in the USSR, launched in 1956 by Nikita Khrushchev. To Mao this meant betrayal of world revolution (through detente with the West) and the restoration of capitalism in the Soviet Union. Mao no longer considered the USSR to be a communist system, but rather a restored capitalist system with aggressive designs for world domination that made it even more dangerous than the United States. China's split with the USSR has now grown to such proportions that, at least in terms of foreign policy, Peking now seeks alliances with other governments, parties, and movements primarily on the basis of anti-Soviet orientations. Only in the past few years has the Chinese leadership moderated its criticism of Moscow somewhat and shown some interest in dispute resolution.

Within this Sino-Soviet split, several ruling communist parties have shown their independence by remaining neutral. Cuba, Rumania, North Korea, and North Vietnam for a long time refused to take sides in the debate and tried to cultivate friendly relations with both sides. In recent years, Cuban collaboration with the Soviets to aid the MPLA in Angola and the Mengistu regime in Ethiopia has led to Chinese denunciation of Castro and Cuban communism. China also chose to side with the Khmer Rouge in their border conflict with Vietnam, thus pushing Vietnam into clearer alliance with the USSR. And Albania, Peking's long-time ideological ally, has now split with China and is steering its own independent course.

Finally, from Western Europe's major communist parties has come the challenge of Eurocommunism (an explicit break from Moscow's policy line), continued and extensive criticism of the Soviet system, and firm commitments to parliamentary democracy as the only path to socialism in countries like Italy, France, and Spain. The postwar years have witnessed a decline in the USSR's influence in the Italian Communist party, which now gets up to one-third of the national vote and governs in several regions and most major cities. Most recently USSR influence has eroded in the French Communist party, which gets 10 percent of the French vote, governs in several cities, and in uneasy alliance with the French Socialists became a minor partner for three years in the Mitterrand government after the victory of the left in the 1981 elections.

On the other hand, the Soviet Union has protected its dominance on several occasions by intervening directly with military forces (Berlin, 1953; Hungary, 1956; Czechoslovakia, 1968) in Eastern Europe. Even in this region, however, the Soviet Union has had to accept Rumania's independent course as well as the maverick Yugoslav system. And it is clear from the "Prague Spring" in Czechoslovakia, introduced and led by the Czech Communist party, the Soviet Union is not simply or consistently able to manipulate these parties. The birth of the independent trade union Solidarity in Poland in 1980 is an expression of both rejection by Poland of the Soviet model and support for a "Polish model," a decentralized, democratic, and self-managing economic and political system. The emergence of Solidarity, although clearly related to the special circumstances of Polish history and society, lends further evidence to the potential for political conflict within communist systems, and especially those in Eastern Europe that were imposed from outside by the Soviet Union.

In recent years polycentrism has meant not only criticism of the Soviet system from within the communist world and open debate over the correct model for building socialism among both ruling and nonruling communist parties, but also, as demonstrated in the border clashes between Vietnam and Cambodia, China and the Soviet Union, and China and Vietnam, armed confrontation between communist states. It would appear that the divisions within the communist world have grown with the expansion of communism to the point of a possibility of war between communist nations.

THE VANGUARD PARTY—CENTERPIECE OF COMMUNIST SYSTEMS

The characteristic institution of communist systems is the Leninist vanguard party. The roles of the Leninist party in communist political systems include: (1) making the revolution, (2) suppressing political opposition, and (3) modernizing economic and social structures. As predicted in Lenin's theories, the vanguard party has been capable of leading a socialist revolution to victory in armed conflict. Even against strong coalitions of internal and external enemies, Leninist vanguard parties in Russia, China, Yugoslavia, and Vietnam have achieved effective control of government (state power).

Once in power, the vanguard party has not disbanded, relinquished state power, or allowed political competition from defeated or newly emergent parties or groupings, but has consolidated and become the only organized political force in the society. As Lenin's critics had said, the vanguard party has opted for suppression of political dissent in the name of defending the revolution.

In most communist systems (with the partial exception of Yugoslavia's market socialism), the vanguard party in power has served as the key for mobilizing and organizing the society for industrialization. With major productive facilities in the hands of the state, the party has directed the planning of the economy, sometimes with greater centralization, sometimes with less, but with a thoroughness and directedness that sets communist industrialization apart from that of other developing nations.

Not all Leninist parties have played all three major roles, nor have they played them in the same fashion. In Cuba, still something of an anomaly, revolution was made without a communist party in the lead, and the Cuban Communist party that was built only several years later is still somewhat of an unknown in the Cuban system. In Yugoslavia, the party largely abdicated its central planning of the economy in the 1950s while still suppressing dissent, though with relative mildness. In China, the approach to economic development has varied considerably, depending on whether Maoist or anti-Maoist factions in the party were in charge. And in Czechoslovakia, in 1968, the Czech Communist party abandoned press censorship and suppression of dissent before a Soviet-led invasion overthrew and dismantled the Prague Spring.

It is possible, therefore, for Leninist parties to deviate from the fulfillment of certain typical roles. Reform and restructuring programs in the People's Republic of China under the post-Mao Deng leadership and more recently in the Soviet Union under the Gorbachev leadership indicate that the ruling Leninist parties are capable of significant changes, including reductions, in the economic and political roles of the party, as the result of lessons learned from past experience and experimentation both at home and in other Communist systems. Questions are now even being raised as to what are the essential elements of socialism that cannot be abandoned by the ruling party. And yet, the vanguard party continues to be the most identifiable feature of communist systems as diverse as those of the USSR, China, and Yugoslavia. It remains the center of political decisionmaking and the arbiter of future development, even in those cases where it has chosen to abdicate certain roles.

Politics of communist systems are centered, therefore, not in the formal offices of government, such as the prime minister and his cabinet, nor in the parliament, for these offices are subordinate to decisions made within the party. Individuals who hold important government positions are not unimportant, however, for usually they are also important leaders in the party. But some of the most important political leaders, such as Leonid Brezhnev or

Mao Zedong, held no government position for many years, but were responsible for top-level party organizations. Authoritative policy decisions and considerations of alternatives take place within the Politburo of the party and are sometimes referred also to the next-lower level of the Central Committee. The Secretariat, which is responsible for staffing party organizations with full-time party workers (cadre), is a particularly important focal point of political power, since power over personnel appointments implies considerable ability to manipulate or at least bias policy decisions. National party congresses, which in Lenin's day were also the forum for lively debate and candidating, now serve to announce the party leadership's program for the next several years, often for a new Five-Year Plan.

Politics in the Leninist vanguard party are typically closed to individuals and groups outside the party. This holds for all three major functions outlined above. The logic of closed decision making, of general impenetrability, seems difficult to break. For purposes of leading armed revolution in backward and undemocratic systems, a closed and even clandestine political style may be a crucial advantage. For purposes of suppressing dissent and maintaining a monopoly over political debate, the party presents a publicly maintained unity and refuses candid discussion about internal party debates. Antithetic to parliamentary democracy, which invites dissent (and political immobility) through openness, the vanguard party discourages dissent through opaqueness of the system. And in the party's role as organizer and mobilizer for development, especially in the earliest phases of industrialization, the closed nature of decision making facilitates long-range planning requiring consumer austerity and hard work. If these choices were publicly debated, if they were more able to be influenced by public opinion, they would be more difficult to make.

Once the industrialization of the economy has been largely completed and the direct threat of counterrevolution has diminished, a closed and monopolized decision making process within the Leninist party may become a hindrance to further development. This was recognized by the Czech Communist party in 1968. Since 1985, Soviet General Secretary Gorbachev has also initiated a campaign for "openness" *(glasnost)*, which may lead to a new stage of evolution for the Soviet party. The Leninist party, as described here, will evolve in response to a changed environment, both domestic and international. But for a noncapitalist strategy of industrialization and social mobilization, the vanguard party is as central to communist systems as parliament is to the liberal democracies.

Some Conclusions

We can now draw some general conclusions from the historic growth of communism as a political system-type. This system-type is not nearly so uniform or monolithic as it is often assumed to be. Practically from the first appearance of other communist systems besides the Soviet Union, new and conflicting approaches to building socialism have appeared. Even in the Soviet Union, since destalinization there has been some evolution away from the Stalinist model and toward a more moderate political and economic system. It would appear that, except for the nationalization of the large factories and large landholdings of the church, aristocracy, and bourgeoisie, and the dominance (with some variations) of a Leninist vanguard party over the political system, there is little consensus on the path to socialism. This second factor could well change if a Eurocommunist-oriented government were elected in Italy or France. Certainly the Soviet model has had little success in maintaining its predominance in the expanding communist community of nations. Rather, the post-World War II period has brought about the realization of numerous paths to socialism, adapted to the circumstances of each communist nation. Nations that became communist through the efforts of local parties or revolutionary movements have not copied either the Stalinist or post-Stalinist Soviet system. Some regimes (Rumania, North Korea) put in power initially by the Soviet Red Army have later developed independent policies. If this historic record is any guide, we can predict that new communist regimes will continue to innovate, that communism is still evolving as a political system, and that it is less and less limited to the Soviet experience.

Communist political systems now encompass a quite diverse set of nations, economically, culturally, and historically. Some, such as East Germany and Czechoslovakia, are highly industrialized and fairly wealthy societies. Others, including Cuba, Yugoslavia, and North Korea, have semi-industrialized economies with middle-level standards of living on a world scale. Still others, such as China, Vietnam, and Mozambique, are still among the poorest and least developed nations. The geographic scope of communism has changed dramatically since World War II. Revolutions that have led to the establishment of communist systems are no longer limited to large societies like the USSR and China or to smaller nations on their peripheries. Small noncontiguous nations like Cuba, Angola, or Mozambique can, with aid from established communist regimes, make and defend socialist revolutions (though certainly at considerable cost and not without setbacks). Before the emergence of the Soviet Union as a world superpower, a revolution in a country like Cuba would have had no place to turn for help against invasion and economic blockade by the major capitalist nations. The liberation struggle in Vietnam, despite the tremendous determination and organization of the Vietnamese communists, could scarcely have been successful against massive American intervention without large-scale Soviet and Chinese aid (even though this aid amounted to only one-tenth the resources that the United States poured into that conflict).

So far, communist systems have emerged almost exclusively in the less developed nations on the periphery of the world capitalist economy. In Czechoslovakia and East Germany, it is questionable what sort of system would have emerged after World War II without the Soviet presence. In Western Europe it still remains to be seen what will come of Eurocommunism. New communist nations may be limited for some time to the Third World. This is, of course, both the fear of United States foreign policy and the hope of Soviet foreign policy.

We may now categorize the types of events that are associated with the emergence of communist systems. Here it is vital to note that we have still not witnessed a proletarian revolution in an advanced capitalist nation as a result of the internal breakdown or collapse of the capitalist economy (as, for example, during the Great Depression). Moreover, where liberal democracy has been firmly established, a communist revolution has not yet been able to seriously threaten let alone overthrow it. Clearly Marx's conditions for the coming of proletarian revolution have still not materialized. On the other hand, Lenin's theories of the vanguard party and of imperialism have made a major impact on political developments in this century. Wars of national liberation against fascist regimes, against autocratic despotism, and against colonial domination have characterized the successful communist revolutions. In Eastern Europe, it was the war against the Nazi occupation of Poland, Czechoslovakia, Yugoslavia, and Albania (and the local collaborators with the Nazis) and against the fascist allies of Nazism in Hungary, Rumania, and Bulgaria that opened the way for communist revolution after the military defeat of Hitler's armies. In China and Vietnam, it was again the armed struggle against the Japanese invaders that gave both Mao and Ho Chi Minh their greatest opportunities for developing a liberated zone under communist control and eventually for defeating both internal and external opponents in long civil wars after the defeat of Japan.

In more recent years communist systems have appeared in response to external military intervention by the West or to attempted suppression of anticolonial independence movements. The victory of the Khmer Rouge in Cambodia was almost certainly produced by the American invasion in 1970 and the United States-supported replacement of Prince Sihanouk by General Lon Nol. Up to that time the Khmer Rouge had been a minor factor in Cambodian politics, with no prospect for making a successful revolution. In Cuba, American attempts to assassinate and overthrow Castro transformed that revolution into a communist system. Cuba is the only example so far of a communist system being established without being led by a Leninist vanguard party, although it may be that this pattern could occur elsewhere (e.g., in Ethiopia). In Africa, where relatively peaceful decolonization (with the exception of Algeria) in no case produced a communist postindependence government, the refusal of Portugal (backed by secret CIA aid) to relinquish her colonies led to armed revolt in Angola, Mozambique, and Guinea-Bissau. In all these cases, the liberation movements were much more radical, and in Angola and Mozambique communist systems have emerged. When popular liberation movements that attempt to overthrow either feudal aristocracies, colonial white racist regimes, corrupt dictators, or foreign occupation are opposed by the Western democracies, they will very likely become radicalized, may seek military and political aid from communist nations, and may end up establishing new communist systems. This applies, currently, to all of Southern Africa (i.e., Zimbabwe, Namibia, and South Africa), to Ethiopia, to Nicaragua, to Chile, to the western Sahara, and perhaps to the Philippines as well.

Armed force or coercion against either communist or progressive movements has been, since World War II, less and less effective in preventing communism and may sometimes even have enhanced the prospects of a local communist party for making a revolution. The great successes of counterrevolution—of overthrow or defeat of popular, radical, or progressive nationalist governments in the Third World through external intervention (Guatemala in 1954, Iran in 1952–1953, the Dominican Republic in 1965)—are becoming more difficult to repeat as the worldwide balance of military power moves toward superpower parity and as the ability to aid liberation movements by the expanded community of communist nations has increased.

Chapter 8

Economic Development—
Non-Capitalist Roads to Modernization

FOR PURPOSES OF SIMPLIFICATION, WE CAN concentrate on three variants of communist economic systems: the Soviet, the Yugoslav, and the Chinese. It is still too early to judge whether the more recent communist systems, such as Vietnam or even Cuba, will produce their own distinctive variants.

The original model of a centrally planned economy, from which lessons of both success and failure have been derived, remains the Soviet. In most of Eastern Europe, as well as North Korea and Albania, the Soviet model has been applied. (Poland's private agricultural sector remains an anomaly.) Economic development in these nations is steered by a central planning agency (GOSPLAN is the name of the Soviet central planning body), which sets output quotas for factories, state and collective farms, and other state-owned facilities. There are still, in most Soviet-type economies, some small areas of private business, such as small private plots in agriculture, and some very small businesses, which are outside the command structure of Five Year Plans and which are, as in Soviet agriculture, still of considerable importance. But for most sectors of the economy, a GOSPLAN-type agency sets prices and wages, allocates basic investment, supplies, and personnel, and determines the rules for meeting production quotas.

The first great task of the Soviet central planning system was to mobilize both human and natural resources for rapid industrialization of the economy. In this process, maximum investment was channeled into heavy industry (steel, iron, coal, electric power, machine-building, and defense industries) while investment in agriculture, consumer goods production (light industry), and housing construction were deliberately held down. Generally, a collectivized agriculture has been used as a control mechanism to ensure sufficient foodstuffs at low state-set prices for the growing urban industrial workforce.

Until the death of Stalin in 1953, the Soviet and other East European economies were heavily committed to this extensive development phase of growth through mobilization of previously unemployed and underemployed resources. Canadian economist Alan Abouchar (1979) points out that one major achievement of the Soviet economic system has been greater control of economic fluctuations that afflict more affluent capitalist economies.

Abouchar (1979:40–42) calculates that Soviet long-term growth rates (increase of gross national product per capita per year) averaged 4.7 percent over the period 1928–1975, even including the tremendous destruction of World War II. This growth record surpasses the long-term growth rate of all the major capitalist economies, including the United States (1.6 percent 1839 to 1962), Germany (1.7 percent 1871 to 1962), and Japan (2.2 percent 1879 to 1962). Even over the shorter term period from 1950 to 1962 when Western capitalist economies were enjoying a postwar recovery from the Great Depression, Soviet per capita growth rates averaged 5.3 percent per year, compared with 3.3 percent for the United States, 2.3 percent for Great Britain, 4.9 percent for France, and 7.3 percent for West Germany, among the major Western systems.

In Poland, Hungary, Bulgaria, and Rumania, which were largely agrarian peasant societies before World War II, the Soviet model has achieved a decisive industrial breakthrough. East Germany and Czechoslovakia were in the main already industrialized before the war, and the Soviet model has brought some additional industrialization, perhaps even overindustrialization. In Asia, North Korea appears still to be engaged in this first phase of Soviet-type development, as is tiny Albania, one of the most orthodox Stalinist economic systems despite its independence from Moscow.

In East Germany, Czechoslovakia, Poland, and Hungary, as well as the Soviet Union, the drive for extensive industrialization has been completed. Since Stalin's death communist leaders have paid increasing attention to expanded consumer production, welfare spending, improved housing, and more plentiful foodstuffs (especially meat). Khrushchev's economic program, dubbed "goulash communism," was an early but limited move in this direction in the 1950s and early 1960s. A set of reforms, most often associated with Soviet economist E. G. Liberman, were proposed to partially decentralize economic planning and to introduce some elements of marketing discipline and profit mechanisms at the enterprise level. These modest reforms were opposed, however, by party and state "conservatives" on grounds of both ideological and institutional self-interest and were introduced only in a diluted form, mainly in the textile sector. Premier Alexei Kosygin, in the latter 1960s and 1970s tried to push similar reforms, but again without much success. The transition from a set of institutions and mechanisms aimed at *extensive* industrial growth to a system aimed at *intensive* consumer-oriented growth has been difficult for the Soviet system and for the East European nations that are still tied to current Soviet practices.

Attempts by East European systems to advance too far beyond the current Soviet model, as was the case in Czechoslovakia in 1968, and perhaps again now in Poland in the 1980s, have been vigorously opposed by Moscow conservatives, and the Czech liberal reforms were canceled after the Soviet-led invasion. In Hungary, however, where a New Economic Mechanism (NEM) has been gradually and cautiously introduced over a long period under the steady leadership of Janos Kadar, market- and consumer-oriented reforms have moved partially beyond the Soviet model, but with strict limitations for experimentation. It would appear that until the Soviet system implements a significant economic reform package, which has now been generally available and under discussion for a quarter century, it will pay a considerable and perhaps growing price in both agricultural output and consumer goods manufacturing. The slowdown in Soviet growth rates in the 1970s and 1980s is one reflection of the impasse of Soviet economic performance. Under the Gorbachev leadership in the 1980s, a new economic restructuring effort *(perestroika)* has been launched to introduce greater incentives for "intensification" of production methods and greater reliance on market-type mechanisms. In 1987, small private businesses were permitted to organize, mainly in the service sector. An individual contracting system with collective farmers, begun several years earlier, has been expanded. And a new law covering about 60 percent of all enterprises and giving more autonomy and responsibility for self-financing went into effect in January of 1988. However, there is still bureaucratic resistance to this new wave of economic reform, and it remains to be seen how far the new reforms can go in the restructuring of the Soviet economy. According to Soviet social scientists, there is also mixed popular support at best for these reforms, which in the short run will produce layoffs and price hikes on heavily subsidized consumer items before they begin to show tangible benefits. Certainly, any major reform of the huge Soviet economy will take considerable time to reach fruition and will run into numerous difficulties and setbacks, as Gorbachev and his economic advisors have admitted. Still, it is clear that after the generational shift from the older Brezhnev coalition to the younger leadership cohort around Gorbachev, the Soviet regime is seriously attempting to promote economic innovation. The relative success or failure of *perestroika* will be an historic indicator of the ability of the party to act as a leading political organization for the Soviet Union in the postindustrialization era.

Experimentation with different variants of a socialist economy has come from those communist systems which arose from independently made revolutions, namely Yugoslavia and China. Initially, however, both of these nations were committed to the Soviet economic model, and in the first years after their revolutions, both Yugoslavia and China began relatively orthodox Soviet-style industrialization programs.

Tito's break with Stalin in 1948 did not immediately signal the emergence of the new Yugoslav model of "market socialism." But, beginning in the early 1950s, the Yugoslav League of Communists moved to implement, with some setbacks along the way, many of the market and profit-oriented reforms that have been blocked for so long in the Soviet Union. Yugoslav central planning was greatly weakened, agriculture remained in private hands, though redistributed from prewar ownership, and the prices of most goods and services were freed from both control and subsidy. The Yugoslav model developed its own unique emphasis on the role of workers' councils, which were directly elected at all larger enterprises and which were given increasing responsibility for overseeing the operations of individual factories with workers sharing in the enterprise's profits or losses. This process of developing a self-managing society has also been extended to elected community social councils.

The Yugoslav leadership opened the economy to extensive trade with the West, permitted free emigration for its citizens, and allowed a good deal of small-scale free enterprise, particularly in tourist and service sectors. In larger self-managed factories, profit-making rather than quota-meeting governs the success or failure of the enterprise.

The Yugoslav economy, since the inception of "market socialism," has been notable for its development of Western-style consumerism, especially among the more prosperous social groups and the more economically advanced regions (republics that are the component parts of a federal system and that are also ethnic divisions). Yugoslav manufacturers are also more competitive with Western quality standards, as they must be to provide exports to the West, which enable Yugoslavia to import Western consumer goods, pay for Western technology, and attract Western investment. A basic feature of the Yugoslav economic model is its integration into the international capitalist market, as opposed to the much greater "delinking" from the West experienced by the Soviet economy and other East European economies during the postwar period.

Yugoslav "market socialism" has provided for: (1) greater worker participation in a decentralized economy; (2) greater availability of Western-style consumer goods; (3) greater room for private initiative and small business and agriculture; and (4) more flexible market-oriented price and wage systems. The costs of these reforms are also fairly clear and are seen by most observers as inherent features of the Yugoslav experiment: (1) the return of mass unemployment, 10 to 15 percent for the past decade; (2) chronic inflation tied to the inflationary environment of western economies; and (3) a growing foreign debt burden related to the need for importing Western goods and technologies. (Poland experienced some of these same costs in the 1970s under the Western-financed industrial program of Edward Gierek, but without the benefit of internal Polish reforms that would have at least constituted a coherent system.)

It is important to note that the Yugoslav leadership adopted an economic program in basic respects similar to reforms unsuccessfully advocated in the USSR and Eastern Europe for many years, but at a much lower level of industrialization and extensive growth than that achieved in other nations.

While the Yugoslav experiment may hold many lessons for other nations, we should remember that "market socialism" was introduced without first going through the phase of centrally planned industrialization.

Chinese communist development also began with an imitation of the Soviet model. Only in 1957, after Mao Zedong's split with the Khrushchev regime, did the Maoist faction of the Chinese leadership launch its Great Leap forward, which marked several significant economic departures from Soviet practice. Mao, however, was opposed in his radical economic experiments by a strong "bureaucratic-technocratic" faction of the party, and Chinese economic development has experienced several shifts in direction, depending on which faction in the "two-line struggle" was dominant at the time. From 1949 to 1957, Chinese development followed a relatively orthodox Soviet model, with significant contributions of Soviet aid. This phase was followed by the radical Maoist development of huge peasant communes as the focal point for a rural-based strategy of both self-sufficiency and intermediate technology-industry. In contrast to the centralized, urban-based, heavy industry orientation of Soviet plans, Mao's model was decentralized to the peasant communes of about 20,000 people. These communes were elevated to an active, leading position in the Chinese economic plan of development, whereas the Soviet Union's collective and state farms had been passive, subdued elements in the Soviet industrialization drive.

After three years ("three lost years," according to Mao's opponents), the failure of several aspects of the Great Leap Program, the "bureaucratic-technocratic" faction associated with Liu Shaoqi and Deng Xiaoping regained control and reduced considerably the scope of the Maoist experiments. For the next several years, expertise, growth rates, and managerial efficiency was raised in priority. On the other hand, however, the Soviet economy, which had been denounced by Mao as having reverted to capitalism, was no longer seen as an appropriate model to emulate. During this period, it appeared that Mao was gradually being eased into political retirement.

Then, in 1966, Mao began a political comeback with the aid of a mass campaign led by self-organized Red Guards and directed against bureaucratic and technocratic elites in government, economic management, universities, and even the party itself. At the cost of considerable economic and educational disruption, the Great Proletarian Cultural Revolution forced the leaders of the anti-Maoist faction from office and placed priority on correct "politics" (equality, anti-elitism, shaping a new culture) over practical economics (high growth rates, production efficiency, deference to expertise). The mass campaign of the Red Guards lasted for nearly three years, but the dominance of the radical party faction continued until Mao's death in 1976. (Zhou Enlai's position in all of these shifts is somewhat open to interpretation, although he probably played an important role as conciliator, preventing blood purges of the Stalinist variety from erupting. Zhou died of cancer in 1976.)

Immediately after Mao's death, a power struggle ensued, in which the so-called Gang of Four, including Mao's widow Jiang Qing, were defeated by a resurgent Deng Xiaoping and his associates. Since 1976, this "moderate" faction has reversed, bit by bit, the policies of the Cultural Revolution and put forward a program of "four modernizations" (in agriculture, industry, national defense, and science and technology), which ambitiously aim at making China a modern industrial power by the year 2000. Respect for higher education and formal training, hierarchy in management, priority to growth rates, and individual incentives, in short "economics in command," have been elevated to top importance, and Mao's economic ideas have been publicly criticized.

The Chinese economy, which from 1966 to 1976 had been virtually cut off from the outside world, has been increasingly opened to Western trade and tourism, investment, and technology. Tens of thousands of Chinese students are being sent abroad to gain Western educations. Some elements of the Yugoslav model, stressing decentralization (though not workers' councils), profit motivation for enterprises, greater wage differentials, a consumer goods orientation, and even some small-scale private enterprise and private agriculture have been introduced experimentally in some provinces and in some industries. The Chinese leadership again considers the Soviet economy to be "socialist," which is to say worthy of consideration as a model, even though Chinese foreign policy remains vigorously anti-Soviet.

The post-Mao leadership, since the introduction of the new "responsibility system" in December of 1978, has reported strong gains in both industrial and agricultural production. Western observers (see Hinton, 1983; Schell, 1984) have noted the rapid growth of small private businesses (restaurants, small hotels, services, transport) in the cities and the dismantling of commune agriculture in favor of family-centered, privatized, and mostly small-scale farming in the countryside. There is agreement that under the new responsibility system, enterprising individuals and families are able to earn considerable incomes unthinkable during Mao's time and can purchase a wider array of consumer goods, which are also much more in evidence as a part of Chinese society. For those families with higher incomes, an affluent and even stylish standard of living now has become a possibility. Chinese cities and villages now bustle with small- and middle-sized individual and family businesses, markets are better stocked with food, clothing, and consumer goods for sale at market prices, and China's enterprises, both state and private, have become much more tied into the world trading system. China, in relative terms, is going through a mass consumer binge that is unprecedented and that contrasts sharply with the austerity, collectively organized production, and controlled equality of the Maoist period.

After several years of the "four modernizations" program, some difficulties have begun to emerge. The gains in production and the decentralization of economic decision-making have not produced enough jobs for China's growing population, and chronic unemployment has re-emerged as a social ill, especially among urban youth. Further, as Hinton (1983) emphasizes, the new pattern of small family farming has begun to show the classic side effects of overcultivation of small plots and overgrazing of pasture land. Pressure for short-term productivity on the land has neglected maintenance and improvement of agricultural infrastructure (dams, roads, irrigation systems, conservation programs). Despite some "readjustments" in the early 1980s, including cutbacks on purchases of Western technology projects, the party leadership remains committed to the basic outlines of the "four modernizations" programs.

DIVERSITY IN STANDARDS OF LIVING

The liberal democracies, as pointed out earlier, are the wealthiest of the world's nations, taken as a group. Among the communist nations there is tremendous diversity in levels of development and in the accompanying standards of living for the average citizen. Czechoslovakia and East Germany are by most standards also among the "rich" nations of the world, with the USSR and Hungary not far behind (see table 8.1). In terms of net national product per capita, which measures the annual value of goods produced and is translated roughly into a dollar per capita figure, these nations are already among the well-to-do nations of the world, though considerably below the wealthiest of the liberal democracies (Sweden, Switzerland, or the United States). (There are some difficult problems in trying to

Table 8.1 Communism: Indicators of Economic Growth

	USSR	East Germany	Hungary	Czechoslovakia	Yugoslavia	China	Cuba
GNP/capita[a]:							
1975	$5,799	7,262	5,909	6,910	2,113	314	--
1983	6,490	8,800	6,570	7,511	2,594	376	1,864[b]
TV sets/1,000	307	344	262	280	210	6	164
Radios/1,000	504	385	352	308	219	64	317
Autos/1,000	35	189	126	170	125	c	21

a. These dollar GNP estimates, despite their seeming accuracy, should be treated as rough approximations. Both ideological and practical problems produce a wide range of such estimates.
b. 1980
c. Less than 0.5

SOURCES: *Statistical Abstract of the United States*, 1986; Sivard, *World Military and Social Expenditures*, 1983; *UN Statistical Yearbook*, 1983/84.

get an exact dollar comparison between outputs of capitalist market economies and centrally planned economies, but the figures in table 8.1 are probably accurate enough for most comparative purposes.)

Radio and television ownership is widespread and at levels comparable
with most of the European liberal democracies. On the other hand, the most
apparent difference in consumption rests with private automobile ownership levels, which are still modest in these nations. Soviet output has only
recently passed the mark of one million passenger cars produced per year,
and this represents a distinct shift away from Khrushchev's earlier emphasis
on free mass transportation and rental-car systems as the desired forms of
personal transportation. Khrushchev wanted to avoid the automobile-cen-
tered consumer culture of the West, but it appears to the dismay of some
communist theorists (Robert Haveman in East Germany, for example) that
communism in Eastern Europe is also bending to consumer desires for
privately owned cars. This is perhaps one more example of the strength of
consumer desires even in the supposedly "command" economies. At present,
however, this transition is still in an early stage.

Noticeably lower on the scale of affluence is the Yugoslav economy,
which is at a semi-industrialized or intermediate level. At the same time it is
well above the levels (per capita) of affluence reached by the Chinese system.
Despite the undoubted growth in production in China over the past three
decades, the Chinese economy is still concerned with producing the basic
necessities for decent health, clothing, nutrition, and housing and can afford
little in the way of luxury items, such as televisions, radios, or private
automobiles. This is not itself a criticism of the Chinese system, for the
equitable provision of essentials to a population of one billion, starting from
the conditions inherited by the regime in 1949, is a remarkable achievement.
Any diversion of human or material-technical resources to luxury goods
production was firmly resisted by Mao, and much Chinese criticism of the
East European and Soviet economies was aimed at their emulation of Western-style consumerism. Under the post-Mao leadership of Deng, however,
consumerism has been encouraged, indicating a desire to move China's
economy beyond the level of subsistence production.

Basic indicators of industrialization and urbanization show that the more
wealthy communist countries are those that have succeeded in industrializing and now have the capacity to turn their modern economies toward
greater consumer output (table 8.2). In China, on the other hand, the majority of the population is still engaged in agriculture, and agriculture continues
to provide more than half the gross national product (net material product).

One interesting difference between the communist industrial nations and
the industrial liberal democracies lies in urbanization patterns. While the
Soviet Union, East Germany, Czechoslovakia, and Hungary are relatively

Table 8.2 Communism: Industrialization and Urbanization Levels

	USSR	East Germany	Hungary	Czecho-slovakia	Yugo-slavia	China	Cuba
Population in Millions:							
	275.0	16.7	10.7	15.5	23.0	1029.2	9.9
Percentage of workforce in:							
Agriculture							
1960	39	17	39	26	57	69[a]	33[b]
1980	20	11	18	13	32	69	24
Industry							
1980	39	50	44	49	33	19	29
Services							
1980	41	39	38	37	34	12	48
Percentage urban:							
	66	76	55	66	46	22	71

a. 1966
b. 1965

SOURCES: World Handbook, 1972; World Bank, World Development Report, 1986; ILO, Employment, Growth, and Basic Needs, 1976.

urbanized societies, there is greater emphasis on middle-sized towns and cities and less growth of larger (over 100,000) urban centers. Part of this may be related to the continued existence of a sizeable peasantry in the USSR and Hungary (about one-fourth of the population), yet the differences remain even for East Germany and Czechoslovakia when compared with West Germany. In this respect their urbanization pattern seems closer to that of Switzerland or Sweden than to the more highly concentrated urban societies of Britain, West Germany, the United States, or even Japan.

The communist economies are a very mixed group in terms of level of industrialization and economic affluence. At the top end are the industrial, urban societies of Eastern Europe, which have already achieved their industrial revolution and are now concerned with the transition to a more intensive, consumer-oriented pattern of economic development. At the bottom end are the war-torn economies of Vietnam, Laos, Cambodia, Angola, and Mozambique, desperately poor agrarian societies in which the primary task remains the dependable production of subsistence essentials. In between are China, Cuba, Yugoslavia, Rumania, and North Korea, which are at differing levels of industrialization and urbanization, but which are committed to completing the modernization process.

Heavy Investment in Education

One feature that unites all the communist systems (with the partial exception of China) is a heavy emphasis on education, both basic and advanced. On achieving power, communist parties launched large-scale programs for adult literacy, expanded elementary school enrollments with the goal of including all school-age children, and later moved to expand secondary and higher education as institutions of mass education. This emphasis on education as a basic investment for development and human emancipation from ignorance, consistent with Marx's original call for universal and free education, is demonstrated by high literacy rates achieved in Eastern Europe (less so in China, where the Chinese pictographic language is more difficult to master than western phonetic languages), high rates of school enrollment, and especially the high percentage of the gross national product spent on public education (see table 8.3). The Soviet Union, which spends 7 to 8 percent of its GNP on education, and Cuba, which has spent 6 to 9 percent, are among the most generous in their budgeting for education, while the Chinese are relative laggards among the communist nations.

Table 8.3 Communism: Educational Spending and Literacy

	USSR	East Germany	Hungary	Czecho-slovakia	Yugo-slavia	China	Cuba
Literacy percentage	100	99	99	99	90	66	95
Percent of GNP spent on education:							
1975	7.6	5.1	4.1	4.7	5.4	1.8	5.7
1983	6.6	4.5	5.4	5.1	3.9	2.8	5.9

Source: *UNESCO Statistical Yearbook*, 1986.

China's exception to this general pattern of heavy emphasis on education was especially pronounced during the period of the Cultural Revolution. The universities were almost closed down for several years and the Maoists were most suspicious, even hostile, toward higher education systems, perceiving them to be institutions for elitism. As in many other areas, Mao emphasized the priority of "politics" over "economics," which in education meant a stress on correct political thinking over technocratic expertise (i.e., the priority of being "red" over being "expert"). While fostering the expansion of primary education, the Maoist faction of the Chinese Communist party tried to integrate the school system into the lives of the peasants and workers. This meant that in the communes and factories, "barefoot teachers" or "worker teachers" ran the schools as part of their regular occupation, in many cases bypassing or uprooting more highly trained and technically competent teaching personnel. Chinese advances in nuclear technology and earth-orbiting satellites demonstrate that in certain top-priority cases, highly educated scientists and engineers were probably insulated from Mao's experiments in education. But on the whole the Chinese commitment to expanding higher education, at least until recently, has been qualitatively different from, and less than, that of other communist systems. This was consistent with the Maoists' de-emphasis on advanced technology and rapid expansion of urban heavy industry, which would have required and could have employed new legions of technically trained college graduates. Only in the post-Mao period has China under Deng's leadership established a higher priority for education, especially higher education.

The expansion of higher education in the communist systems has increased opportunities for working-class children. This means greater change in the social origins of students in higher education than has been produced in the liberal democracies by erosion of the "class channeling" system. In the Soviet Union, the polytechnical institutes founded in the 1920s and 1930s were filled by the sons and daughters of workers and peasants, while offspring of the out-of-favor bourgeoisie and nobility were denied college/university entrance. These restrictions were largely dropped in the 1930s, when entrance to higher education began to rest on merit examination scores (table 8.4). Some studies of student social origins in the USSR indicate that children from nonmanual backgrounds (that is, professional, white collar, and technical) are most over-represented in higher education, as in the liberal democracies. But children of manual (that is blue-collar) families are also overrepresented, whereas they are underrepresented in Western colleges and universities. Underrepresented in both communist and liberal democratic systems are the children of farmers/peasants (Feldmesser, 1957; Lane, 1971). Khrushchev, as part of his destalinization campaign, attempted to improve educational opportunities for the collective farm family, but his reforms ran into a good deal of resistance and were passed only in watered-down form.

Table 8.4 Communism: Enrollments in Higher Education

	USSR	East Germany	Hungary	Czechoslovakia	Yugoslavia	China	Cuba
	Percentage of Age Group in Higher Education						
1960	11	16	7	11	9	–	3
1983	21	30	15	16	20	1	20
	Students per Million Population						
1965	16,740	4,660	5,030	10,010	9,480	1,220	3,280
1984	19,180	25,820	9,360	11,290	16,500[a]	1,380	21,230

a. 1983

SOURCES: *World Handbook*, 1972; UNESCO *Statistical Yearbook*, 1986; World Bank, *World Development Report*, 1981, 1986.

A second feature of higher education in the communist nations has been the emphasis on technical education as opposed to education in liberal arts or business administration. In part this reflects the planned linkage of education with economic development and the key role of science and technology in the modernization process. The formal training of engineers, scientists, and technicians was not in response to an already-developed industrial system, but was begun at the outset of the modernization process and reached a level not attained by the liberal democracies until later years, and not even then in many areas.

Education under communism has become the path of upward mobility. In a system where no one can inherit and live off family wealth, educational attainment is all the more necessary for improving one's position. Lane (1971: 508–9) has summarized the main features of Soviet education, which can be applied generally to communist systems:

> EDUCATION has become universal, ensuring widespread literacy, and Soviet education has emphasized technological competence. In all societies, education is a major determinant of the individual's life chances. This is particularly so in the USSR where the family has no legal rights over property. While Soviet education has attempted to bring down the barriers which barred deprived social and national groups from higher education, the cultural forces generated by family and parental occupation have asserted themselves. As in western societies, though perhaps to a lesser extent, professional strata pass on the advantages of their own education to their children thereby making them more educable, more worthy of "merit." . . . The main characteristics of Soviet education are its manifest connexion with economic and political institutions, and its emphasis on technological training and political socialisation. It is meritocratic, and now largely determines the life chances of the Soviet citizen.

CORRELATES OF COMMUNISM: HEALTH CARE

Next to education, provision of health care through a comprehensive system of socialized medical services has been a high priority of all communist systems. The training of doctors and other medical personnel, the construction of hospitals and clinics, in short the entire public health system is financed and planned by the government. Medical education is free, as is education generally in the communist nations. Physician services and hospital and sanatoria stays are free to the citizen, although the patient may not have much choice of which physician will treat him or her. There are in some systems small charges for medicines. And in most systems, the patient may opt for private treatment by a physician of choice, but then must pay for physician fees out of his or her own pocket. Generally speaking, there are several differences between socialized medicine in the communist nations and Western health care or fee-for-service arrangements:

1. In the communist nations, socialized medicine has been introduced comprehensively and at an earlier stage of economic development than in the West, where, with the exception of Germany, it has been built up by piecemeal reforms.
2. Socialized medicine in communist systems tends to emphasize preventive medicine as opposed to curative medicine; that is, more effort is placed on preventing illness or health problems than on dealing with the sickness after it has appeared.
3. There seems to be somewhat greater emphasis on medical care for children and the working-age population than on health care for the elderly, which is somewhat more the emphasis in the West.

The commitment to adequate health services available to all has produced significant rises in life expectancy and declines in infant mortality (table 8.5). The Soviet example, with the longest experience, has been summarized by Lawrence Mayer (1977) in his comparative study of industrial societies:

THE system of medical care in the Soviet Union is formed around a network of polyclinics and is considered by many observers to be among the most effective in the world at giving basic medical services to the general population. Doctors, who are state employees, work together in these clinics to serve patients who are assigned to them with very little freedom of choice on either side. There are problems, such as the apparently shorter and less thorough training period and the fact that medications and facilities are not always the most modern ones. On the other hand, the Soviet Union is proud of the number of doctors (among the highest in the world in either absolute or relative terms) and of the fact that virtually everyone has access to a physician. Thus, while much of the freedom of choice is removed, the Soviet system seems to do well in its goal of providing basic medical services to virtually the entire population. (361)

Table 8.5 Communism: Health Care Indicators (1980-1985)

	USSR	East Germany	Hungary	Czechoslovakia	Yugoslavia	China	Cuba
Life expectancy:							
Males	64[a]	69.5	65.6	67.1	67.7	65.5	71.5[b]
	42(1926)		55(1941)			35(1930)	
Females	74	75.4	79.5	74.4	73.2	69.4	74.9
	47(1926)		58(1941)			35(1930)	
Population per doctor:	267	472	390	345	644	1,769	722
Infant mortality/ 1000 live births:	28[c]	10	14	12	29	33	15

a. 1972
b. 1978
c. 1974

SOURCES: *UN Statistical Yearbook*, 1983/84; Sewell, 1977.

Recently, there have been reports of an increase in infant mortality in the Soviet Union, and there is evidence that Soviet medical technology is below the level of that of the Western democracies. The Soviet Union stopped providing statistics on life expectancy since 1972, a clear sign that more recent figures are unfavorable. This may be related to the difficulties the Soviet economy is having in general with technological innovation, to the diversion of resources to military spending, and to the adverse health effects of widespread alcohol abuse (see chapter 11). This does not negate the advances made since 1917 in providing publicly funded health care to Soviet citizens, but does suggest that unless the Soviet system addresses these basic issues, health care will not make further headway and may suffer some reverses unusual for an industrial nation.

Once again the Chinese model provides the clear exception to the general pattern of communist health care systems. Maoism created for China a mixture of traditional medicine (including herbal medications and acupuncture) administered by thousands of "barefoot doctors" and "worker doctors" who were not full-time or professional physicians but talented peasants and workers with paramedical training. In three-month training sessions (usually two) these selected workers and peasants learned how to take care of most routine ailments in the communes and factories where they continued to work. Serious illness is referred to either the commune or the city hospital. Some foreign observers (Gaaster, 1972:137–38) have praised the competence of these barefoot doctors.

Another aspect of China's health system has been its use of mass campaigns in public hygiene, such as the "four-pest" campaign to kill flies, mosquitos, rats, and bedbugs (initially also sparrows). Visitors to the People's Republic have often remarked on the cleanliness that separates China, a still poor society, from other poor (and not so poor) nations, where uncollected garbage, polluted water, stench, and vermin are a part of daily life for the average citizen. There is evidence that, in recent years, the "barefoot doctor" system is being replaced, though rather unevenly, by a fee-for-service system between doctor and patient. What is not clear is whether social health care services are still available for those too poor to pay for individual physician care.

PROBLEMS AND ACHIEVEMENTS IN HOUSING

While the communist systems do well in comparison with the liberal democracies on educational and health programs, they compare less favorably on housing. Average housing accommodations even in the more well-to-do communist states of Eastern Europe are less spacious and have fewer amenities than in the liberal democracies of the West. Still, on a worldwide basis of comparison, the communist nations have done a good job in providing basic housing for their populations, and in countries like East Germany, Czechoslovakia, and even the USSR, housing standards are now reaching levels above the essential minimum.

Some of the problems and shortcomings in the housing field can be attributed to the tremendous destruction suffered in World War II in Eastern Europe generally, but there was also great war damage in parts of Western Europe (West Germany and Italy, less in France and Britain) and in Japan. Two other factors were more basic to the lag in housing construction and in the quality of housing in the communist nations. First, until Stalin's death in 1953, housing had a low priority in the centrally planned economies. With top priority given to heavy industry, investment in new housing was treated as a residual to be minimized, not maximized or expanded. The quality of both materials and trained personnel assigned to housing construction was also lower than in high-ranking industries. Thus, for a decade after the end of the war, these economies consciously let housing limp along as best it could, with all effort possible put into industrialization. A second factor was the large-scale urbanization that accompanied the industrialization drive and that would have required great urban housing efforts just to keep the standards from falling. In societies that are either already highly urbanized or are not urbanizing, the necessity for new housing arising from rural-urban migration will be modest. In the Soviet Union and Eastern Europe until the latter 1950s, however, the pace of urbanization related to the industrial revolution created a tremendous backlog of urban housing needs at the same time that investment in the housing sector was being deliberately held down. Groth (1971:108–9) points out that in a comparison of Poland and Portugal in 1969, Poland had poorer housing statistics (and fewer private cars) despite its much higher levels of industry, education, and health care.

One measure of housing conditions used widely in Europe is total living space per person. Living space is measured in square meters (1 square meter is about 10 square feet) of floor space in state-owned apartments, private homes, or cooperative apartments, but does not include space taken up by kitchens, bathrooms, toilets, and halls. In the Soviet Union, 9 square meters per capita was established in 1922 as the minimum desirable norm. As of 1950, actual average living space per person was only 4.7 square meters, or about half the desirable minimum, and below what it had been in 1922. Construction efforts begun after Stalin's death raised the average to 6.8 square meters in 1964 and to 8.2 square meters by 1975. But, as one critic has said, "Man cannot live on floor space alone" (Jacobs, 1975:74). And there is wide disparity in housing facilities between the more urban and industrial areas and the provincial villages and countryside. Thus, as of 1971, of all public housing in Moscow, 100 percent had electricity, 99 percent had central heating, 99 percent had sewers, 99 percent had gas, 84 percent had bathtubs, 63 percent had hot water. On the other side of the coin, in the predominantly rural Chuvash Autonomous Republic of the

USSR, only a small percentage of housing units had bathtubs or showers, running water, or central heating. In these rural areas, most people still live in one-story privately owned homes with few amenities, and even public housing standards in these regions are still quite low. And as a number of Soviet and Western observers have noted, the quality of housing construction, although certainly rising in the 1970s, still leaves much to be desired. Most complaints are related to frequent repairs needed, especially to roofs and to the overloading of hot water, gas, and sewer systems.

On the brighter side for Soviet citizens (and for citizens in other communist nations as well), the cost of housing is among the lowest in the world. Because public housing is heavily subsidized by the government, an average family spends only 4 to 5 percent of its income for an apartment. Thus, it takes a worker only 8 hours on the job to earn enough to pay the monthly rent in Moscow, as opposed to 55 hours for a worker in New York City, 53 hours in Munich, 62 hours in London, and 102 hours in Paris (Bush, 1975:56).

It is difficult to characterize the housing situation in China with any precision, since there are virtually no reliable statistics available. Two rather broad conclusions verifiable by visitors can be made, however. First and foremost, the Chinese communist system has produced a much more equitable distribution of housing than was true under the nationalist government that it replaced and has eliminated the phenomenon of "homeless" or "roofless" people and families so prevalent in poor societies like India in the Third World, of which China was a member as of 1949. By all accounts housing is clean and orderly, a major factor in China's public health program and again a feature that distinguishes China from most noncommunist Third World nations, even those with significantly higher levels of GNP per capita. Second, housing remains austere, lacking most of the amenities that are commonplace (and taken for granted) in the liberal democracies and in the more industrialized communist countries of Europe. Running water, indoor plumbing, even electrification are absent from the homes of the rural Chinese family, and this covers the great majority of the population. The Chinese system, in housing as in so many other respects, has shown both how much can be accomplished at low levels of economic development through political and social organization (social will-power) and what cannot be done without a major modernization of the way in which things are produced (industrialization).

COMMITMENT TO SOCIAL WELFARE

A final feature of communist political systems has been a high commitment to social welfare programs, which include: elderly and invalid care, medical care and maternity benefits, work injury compensation, and income supplements to families with small children. Except in Yugoslavia's "market socialism," where there is considerable unemployment, no programs exist for unemployment compensation, since central planning has eliminated the phenomenon of mass unemployment. As in the liberal democracies, levels of welfare spending rose during the 1950s and 1960s, both in absolute figures and as a percentage of annual gross domestic product. As in the liberal democracies, there are some leaders and some laggards in welfare spending among the communist systems. The most affluent industrial communist states, Czechoslovakia, Hungary and East Germany, are among the high spenders on social welfare, while the Soviet Union, at least by 1980, was a relative laggard. Poland, Bulgaria, and Yugoslavia occupy a middle ground. There is no available data for China. One might note that while there are no industrial communist states that rival Sweden or the Netherlands in percentage expenditure effort on social welfare, there are no welfare laggards to compare with Japan or the United States (compare tables 3.7 and 8.6).

Table 8.6 Communist Social Welfare Expenditures as Percentage of GDP, 1960-1980

	1960	1970	1980
Soviet Union	10.2	11.9	14.1
East Germany	12.8	13.1	17.0
Hungary	8.8	11.0	18.2
Czechoslovakia	15.4	18.0	18.9
Poland	8.9	10.7	15.7
Bulgaria	10.7	13.7	15.1

SOURCE: ILO, *Cost of Social Security, 1978–1980*, 1985.

American political scientist Alexander Groth has summarized social welfare in the communist political systems as follows:

> EVEN though each of these systems subsumes a wide variety of levels of economic development, as between East Germany and North Vietnam, for example, or between Albania and Czechoslovakia, they all exhibit high welfare commitments. With the exception of the category of unemployment insurance (allegedly unnecessary in their planned, full-employment economies), all these states, excepting Red China with no general family allowance program, provide coverage under each of the remaining four categories of social insurance. Moreover, they do so with a generosity that apparently exceeds the contributions of many noncommunist regimes, whose wealth in terms of per capita GNP is considerably superior to theirs. (1971:164)

Other aspects of welfare programs and welfare spending in the communist countries have been dealt with by scholars such as Pryor (1968) and Wilensky (1975), and by the International Labor Organization (ILO). We cannot deal further with these issues here. Rather we have attempted to present a pattern for the development of welfare programs that differs from the "incrementalist" road taken by most of the liberal democracies. In the communist systems, social welfare programs have been introduced more quickly and comprehensively than in the liberal democracies. They have been financed across a much wider range of development levels than was the case in the experience of the liberal democracies. It is now proven that even in poor and semi-developed nations, social welfare is possible for the average citizen if the political system makes a firm commitment and has the will to carry it through. The political system-type that has done this in practice is the communist system.

Chapter 9

Social Equality—
Achievements in Social Justice

ONE GOAL OF COMMUNISM IS THE BUILDING of a classless society where earlier divisions and systematic conflicts between opposing classes, between capitalists and workers, between ethnic and racial groups, and even between men and women have been transcended. No communist system has yet reached full communism or even makes such a claim. What these systems do claim is that they are overcoming class barriers and reducing the social inequalities that characterize the much more affluent liberal democracies. In this process of overcoming class barriers to individual achievement and individual life chances, they are creating a more egalitarian society.

Marx foresaw the ultimate goal of communism not as an enforced equality, but rather as a classless solidarity in which the free development of each person was essential to the free development of the society. Under full communism the rallying cry would become "From each according to his abilities, to each according to his needs." This does not assume that all people have exactly the same needs or that the distribution of goods should be exactly equal. It assumes that people's needs are independent of the "market value" of the work they perform. Thus a factory worker's needs may be no less than a scientist's, even though the scientist's skills may be more scarce. Even under full communism, *complete* material equality is neither the goal nor even considered to be desirable. But there would not be the great material inequalities of capitalist societies.

In the transition to communism, the "dictatorship of the proletariat" would have as its motto: "From each according to his abilities, to each according *to his work.*" This recognizes continuing material inequality based upon differences in the amount and quality of work contributed to society. Able-bodied persons with some exceptions (e.g., housewives) are expected to hold down jobs. The communist systems emphasize the value of work as the rationale for both personal and social progress.

INCOME AND WEALTH DISTRIBUTION

In terms of income distribution, the communist countries are the most egalitarian in the world. Yugoslavia's "market socialism" is less egalitarian

161

in this respect than centrally planned East Germany, Czechoslovakia, Poland, and Hungary, but still more egalitarian than its Western capitalist neighbors (table 9.1). For example, the Gini ratio for family income is .24 in East Germany and .42 in West Germany (Cromwell, 1977). Remember that a Gini ratio of 0.0 would mean complete equality; a ratio of 1.0 would mean the greatest possible inequality. Thus there is about 43 percent less inequality in income distribution in East Germany than in capitalist West Germany. In a comparison of six liberal democracies and five communist systems, E. S. Kirschen (1974:86) concludes that in wages and salaries (not counting income from property) there is 36 percent less inequality in the communist systems.

Table 9.1 Communism: Income Distribution

| | Gini Ratio | Percent of National Income Going to: | |
		Top 10 Percent	Bottom 40 Percent
Soviet Union	.24–.30 (1979)[a]	—	
East Germany	.24 (1964)	16.9	26.3 (1970)
Czechoslovakia	.25 (1964)	17.4	27.4 (1964)
Bulgaria	—	18.8	26.6 (1962)
Poland	.26 (1964)	21.2	23.4 (1964)
Hungary	.27 (1969)	20.5	20.5 (1982)
Yugoslavia	.32 (1968)	22.9	18.7 (1978)

a. The Soviet estimates by Vinocur and Ofer (1987) are derived from interviews with 2,793 Soviet emigrants.

SOURCES: Howe, *United States and World Development* (1975); World Bank, *World Development Report* (1986); Vinocur and Ofer (1987)

Available data indicate that communist systems result in a qualitative shift toward greater income equality. To be sure, considerable differences in income and standard of living are still found in all communist societies, but not the huge gaps that separate the wealthy business and professional classes from the poor worker or ghetto dweller groups in the advanced liberal democracies. Gerhard Lenski (1966:312-13) reports, for example, that in the Soviet Union the highest income for any individual may be as much as 100 times the average income. This is certainly a great range, yet nowhere near the United States figure, where maximum income is 7,000 times average income.

While there are several reasons why income is more evenly distributed under communism, one basic factor is the elimination of the private property wealth of the capitalist class. In the communist nations, income from property has been almost totally eliminated. There is no longer a tiny minority of the rich and superrich (the top 2 percent or so) that derives extremely high incomes not from work but from interest, dividends, rents, and capital gains. In communist nations, most income comes from work. There are some exceptions; banks do pay a small interest on personal savings, and in small businesses and farming, some income can be derived from private wealth.

Kirschen's evidence indicates that even discounting income from property, in the post-Stalin era, wages and salaries are more equally distributed in Eastern Europe than in Western Europe. This second basic feature of income distribution in communist systems has varied considerably over time. The debate over the appropriate level of wage and salary inequality has been a central issue of communist development. In many communist nations, the debate has passed through several stages and is far from being resolved (if that is even possible). In the earliest stages of the Russian Revolution (1918-1921), income differentials were dramatically cut, and in some areas or industries wages were completely equalized. With the rise of Stalin to power in the USSR and the drastic industrialization drive of the 1930s, however, this trend toward equalization was halted and then reversed. The Stalinist regime denounced "equality mongering" and introduced wage rates that provided strong material incentives for workers, managers, and engineers in top priority industries like steel, iron, and electricity, and great material disincentives for people working in consumer goods production and agriculture. Changes were made in inheritance and tax laws so that skilled workers and professionals could pass on their personal savings to their children. In the distribution of scarce goods like housing, appliances, and even food and drink, top managerial and administrative personnel were definitely favored, whereas previously they had been placed at the end of the waiting line (especially if they came from bourgeois social origins).

As a part of the destalinization campaign of the 1950s, this trend toward increasing wage inequality was again reversed. Through the post-Stalin period generally there has been a trend toward greater income equality, especially marked in the Soviet Union in comparison with the Stalinist period, less so in the other European communist states, where the shifts in income policy have been less pronounced (Parkin, 1971:144). This turn toward greater equality has been implemented primarily along two paths: first, the establishment and then the raising of minimum wages for the poorest sector of the population, the collective farmers (while holding top salaries constant); second, the lowering of wage differentials in specific industries, so that, for example, in the ferrous metal industry the ratio of highest-paid to lowest-paid worker has fallen from 3.6 to 1 to 2.6 to 1 since the 1950s (Lane, 1971a:398).

English economist Peter Wiles (1975:25) has estimated that the ratio of income between the top 10 percent (decile) of Soviet citizens and the bottom 10 percent grew from 3.82 in 1928 to 4.15 in 1934 at the end of the first Stalinist Five-Year Plan, to a peak of 7.24 in 1946, and then declined again to 4.4 in 1956 after Stalin's death, and to between 2.7 (1968) and 3.2 (1970) by the latter 1960s. More recent estimates by Chapman (1979) for the 1970s confirm this general range but indicate no further equalization. Some recent estimates of Soviet income inequality from interviews of 2,793 former Soviet citizens (Vinocur and Ofer, 1987) have concluded that income in the USSR is more equally distributed than in the Western democracies, with stronger positions for the bottom 10 percent and bottom 20 percent of households in terms of national income shares. They also find that there has been no further equalizing trend during the 1970s. Lack of publicly available Soviet data hinders more precise calculations. It would appear that under the most recent Gorbachev reform proposals, greater income inequality as an incentive to harder and more efficient work is likely, but this remains to be seen.

Using decile and semi-decile ratios, Wiles (1975) also indicates that among the East European systems, the USSR has a somewhat greater income inequality than is the case for Hungary, Czechoslovakia, or Bulgaria (see also Lyall, 1979).

The post-Stalin trend toward greater income equality has not been unopposed, however, and opposition has come not only from die-hard Stalinists but from "liberal" or "reform" communists as well. Thus, as Yugoslavia introduced a more liberal communism utilizing many market features, income differentials between highly qualified white-collar workers and unskilled blue-collar workers increased from 2.38 to 1 in 1954 to 3.33 to 1 by 1961 (Parkin, 1971:173). There is some evidence that the liberal communist Dubcek regime, which introduced the 1968 Prague Spring (socialism with a human face), also planned to shift the income structure in favor of professionals and managerial personnel. Finally, although we have relatively little hard information, Deng Xiaoping and his associates have discarded the radical egalitarianism of Maoism in favor of greater rewards for successful family farmers, small businessmen, and the highly educated in professional, government, and managerial positions. Thus, either a Stalinist-type emphasis on greater reward differentials deemed necessary to promote rapid expansion and modernization of industry or the introduction of extensive market-type mechanisms related to economic and perhaps political liberalization have over the history of the communist systems opposed the trend toward greater income equality introduced by a communist revolution. Given the fact that social inequality still exists in the communist nations, the main dispute, as Lane says, "has been over the ratio between the richest and poorest and in practice this ratio is now very much lower than in western societies" (1971a:417).

Much has been made in the West over the various advantages that party, state, and managerial elites enjoy in communist societies. And it is true that the "new class," as Milovan Djilas (1957) has termed it, benefits from privileged access to housing, tourist shops, and special hospitals and spas. They often have at their service a state-owned car, telephones, and expense-account travel and entertainment possibilities. Many receive an extra month's salary each year and superior pension benefits. Yet, if one adds up all these extras, the conclusion of one competent anticommunist observer is that "the Soviet elite, in 'capitalist' terms, if not in the context of Soviet society, is a poor elite. True, there are many ways of getting around the law and the possibilities of doing so appear to improve with social position. Some people do have two or more dwellings, a large boat, or an invaluable collection of eighteenth century porcelain. But spectacular American-style consumption and accumulation patterns are virtually unknown" (Matthews, 1975:133).

This is, for critics of communism, a difficult admission to make, for even very poor societies have supported a ruling minority who live in the finest opulence amidst poverty and even starvation. This was true in tsarist Russia, and it is true today in nations like India, Mexico, Egypt, and Kenya. If the ruling communist elites are so powerful, as they are in many ways, why have they not used (or been able to use) that power to gain a much more opulent life-style for themselves? There is not the slightest doubt that countries as developed as the European communist states could easily produce and sustain a wide array of luxury goods, grand estates, fine jewels, and elegant clothes for its top elites.

Dr. Mervyn Matthews attributes the relative poverty of the Soviet elite to three factors: (1) the normative power of Marxism or communism; (2) strict controls on individual earnings; and (3) controls on property, which make it unlikely that anyone could accumulate (much less openly enjoy) great wealth without attracting the attention of the authorities. But this clearly begs the question, since a really powerful elite would be able to either change the laws or the system to allow for greater self-enrichment or to flout the laws by massive corruption of the court, tax, and finance authorities, as has been done for many years in Mexico.

We must conclude that the communist systems, up to now, have maintained a strong internal logic, which has made it impossible for the ruling party-state elites to enrich themselves to anywhere near the same degree as capitalist or aristocratic elites have done. The only explanation is that the normative power of Marxism/Leninism with regard to social equality is either so great among the populace that communist elites dare not attempt capitalist-style self-enrichment or that the elites themselves share the norms of greater social equality and choose not to attempt Western-style elite luxury at the expense of the proletariat.

EDUCATIONAL EQUALITY

In a communist society, where wealth or a secure position in the family business cannot (with minor exceptions for owners of small farms and shops) be inherited, there is correspondingly more emphasis on personal achievement for success. In the East European and Soviet systems, but not in China under Mao, this has meant a strong role for education as a means of improving one's lot. In the early years of these communist systems, the educational system inherited from the old order was radically restructured. The old class channeling system, which had effectively deprived children of lower-class parents of chances for higher education, was abolished and replaced by a comprehensive school system, which was then expanded to include all school-age children. At first, admissions to higher education were deliberately tilted in favor of working-class and peasant children as a redress for past lack of opportunity and out of consideration for political loyalty. After the initial period of political consolidation, however, entrance to institutions of higher education rested on merit entrance exams without regard to class background. As this happened, the percentages of students from lower-class and especially peasant origins began to decline, so that now children of white-collar employees and professionals are overrepresented in institutions of higher learning. Table 9.2 illustrates, in the case of Poland, the dramatic rise in educational opportunities for working-class children between the Pilsudski dictatorship of the 1930s and the People's Republic of the early 1960s. As of the latter 1960s, Giddens (1973:236-37) reports that over half of all students in schools of higher education in Poland, Hungary, and Yugoslavia came from worker or peasant families. In the USSR about half of all students came from these backgrounds. This upward mobility represents a remarkable breakthrough for the lower classes and should be recognized as one of the bases of working-class support for these systems. Communism has given many citizens life chances that they would never have known under the old order. This counts as freedom in a system that in liberal democratic terms is oppressive and unfree.

Table 9.2 Social Origins of Polish Students *(Percentages)*

Family Origin	1935-36	1960-61	1976-77
Manual workers	9.5	29.2	30.5
Peasants	5.0	18.5	11.9
Petty proprietors, craftsmen	12.0	4.6	
White-collar workers	38.0	46.5	54.1 (intelligentsia)
Upper class	35.5	1.2	3.5 (other classes)

SOURCES: A. Sarapata, in Szczepanski, 1966:46; Szczepanski, 1978:15.

At the same time, most observers (Lane, 1976; Giddens, 1973; Parkin, 1971) note that even given the relative equality compared to Western Europe, children of white-collar (nonmanual) family backgrounds are more prevalent in the universities, where they study law, humanities, and the arts, while those from blue-collar families are more prevalent in the polytechnical, mining, railroad, and economics institutes. Thus it appears that blue-collar students more frequently go into applied fields in industry, whereas white-collar students tend toward the higher-status professions.

Another area of concern for educational equality is ethnic representation. We have seen how this issue remains a problem in the United States, and to lesser degrees in other liberal democracies. The Soviet Union is also a highly differentiated, multiracial and multiethnic society. Included in its 1970 census were some 129 million Russians, 41 million Ukrainians, 9 million Belorussians, 9 million Uzbeks, 6 million Tatars, 5 million Kazakhs, 4 million Azerbaidzhanies, 15 other nationalities with more than 1 million people each, and 103 smaller ethnic groups, each with under a quarter million members. In the late years of the tsarist regime, there was extreme inequality in education among the various nationalities, with almost universal illiteracy and no institutions of higher education among the Islamic peoples (Uzbek, Kazakh, Kirghiz, Tadzhik, Turkmen) of the Central Asian provinces. Public policy in the development of the USSR has aimed at bringing these groups into the mainstream of Soviet development in terms of both economic and educational equality. Aspaturian (1968) has calculated an index of representation for different ethnic groups among students in institutions of higher education for 1927, 1956, and 1965 (see table 9.3). An index greater than 1.0 indicates overrepresentation of an ethnic group, and an index less than 1.0 indicates underrepresentation.

Table 9.3 Ethnic Representation of Students in the USSR

Nationality	1927[a] Index	1959[b] Index	1965[c] Index	1959/65 Increase (thousands)	1959/65 Percent Increase
Russian	1.06	1.13	1.11	1,527	183
Ukrainian	.69	.75	.81	379	211
Uzbek	.11	.82	.83	65	213
Kazakh	.07	.94	1.06	48	218
Georgian	2.00	1.41	1.38	46	196
Kirgiz	.12	1.00	.80	10	149
Tadzhik	.08	.71	.57	11	157
Armenian	1.81	1.07	1.14	41	203
Turkmen	.21	.80	.80	10	174
Jewish	7.50	3.73	2.18	43	83
Tatar	.40	.75	.71	45	202

a. Total students = 168,000
b. Total students = 1,341,000
c. Total students = 3,866,000

SOURCE: Adapted from Aspaturian 1968:177.

Aspaturian's data show a trend toward ethnic parity in higher education, with the Central Asian nationalities making considerable gains, although Jews, Georgians, Armenians, and Russians are still somewhat overrepresented. Lane (1976:94) notes that even though Jewish overrepresentation in higher education has fallen, the number of Jewish students rose from 51,600 in 1956 to 94,600 in 1965 as a result of the considerable expansion generally of college-level enrollments.

We might summarize the pattern of educational opportunities in communist systems as being more open to working-class children than is the case in the liberal democracies and therefore more egalitarian, though there is still a tendency for the intelligentsia to pass on through the family environment a greater "educability" to their children. In the absence of a radical restructuring of the family, as was proposed by some early Bolshevik leaders like Alexandra Kollontai, it is likely that children of well-educated parents will continue to have better chances for a higher education.

EQUALITY IN ELITE RECRUITMENT

Aside from income distribution and educational opportunities, social inequality appears in all societies in the selection of some people to positions of authority, whether in government, party offices, economic management, military leadership, or educational and cultural institutions. Communist systems of all varieties recruit a much larger share of their elites from the lower classes (workers and peasants) than do the capitalist democracies. Even severe critics of these systems, such as Huntington and Brzezinski (1963) and Djilas (1957) recognize this basic fact. Djilas argues that even though the "new class" of party-state elites monopolizes political power and economic planning, it is not self-recruited from its own ranks:

> THE new class is actually being created from the lowest and broadest strata of the people, and is in constant motion. Although it is sociologically possible to prescribe who belongs to the new class, it is difficult to do so; for the new class melts into and spills over into the people, into the lower classes, and is constantly changing. (1957:61)

In other words, communist elite recruitment is far more open to the lower classes than elite recruitment in the capitalist democracies, which, as Giddens (1973:240-41) has pointed out, leads to a different (and less pronounced) class structure within the communist societies. This alone would make it different from Western elites, which are largely self-recruited from the upper strata of society.

Some of the most extensive information on the social background of various leadership groups in communist systems comes from a study of

Table 9.4 Social Origins of Yugoslav Elite (1968)

(Figures are indices of representation among elites relative to proportion of the general population.[a])

Social Origin	Legislators	Administrators	Party Leaders	Economic Leaders	Intellectuals
Nonmanual worker	1.38	2.12	1.39	1.19	3.10
Manual worker	1.11	1.04	1.28	1.39	.92
Peasant	.69	.50	.56	.55	.20

a. An index greater than one indicates overrepresentation; an index less than one indicates underrepresentation.

SOURCE: Based on Lane, 1971a:117.

Table 9.5 Social Origins of West-East German Military Elites, 1967

FATHER'S STATUS	WEST GERMANY (percentage)	EAST GERMANY (percentage)
Aristocracy	13.3	0
Professional, upper middle class	63.3	12.5
Lower middle class	16.7	6.3
Worker	0	62.5
Peasant	0	6.3
Not ascertained	6.7	12.5

SOURCE: Adapted from Hancock, 1973:13.

legislative, administrative, party, managerial, and intellectual elites in Yugoslavia in the late 1960s. These data indicate that party and economic leadership is, relatively speaking, the most proletarian, with the administrative and especially the intelligentsia elites more likely to be recruited from nonworking-class social backgrounds. Among all the elite groupings, the peasantry is still considerably underrepresented, despite its undoubted gains since the establishment of the Yugoslav communist system.

One grouping that is vitally important and that was not included in the Yugoslav study is the military leadership. The difference that a communist system can make in terms of elite recruitment is illustrated by Donald Hancock's (1973) comparison of the paths taken by capitalist West Germany and communist East Germany in the rebuilding of their armed forces after the dismantling of the Nazi *Wehrmacht*. In West Germany, recruitment to top military posts of the *Bundeswehr* came from the aristocracy and upper-middle classes, which also formed the social basis for the general staff of the Kaiser's *Reichswehr* and Hitler's *Wehrmacht*. All of the West German officers in Hancock's study had in fact served in the old *Reichswehr* or

Wehrmacht. Only a few had opposed Nazism at any time. In sharpest contrast, the great majority of the East German *Volksarmee* leadership comes from lower-class origins and had been active opponents of Hitler's Third Reich. It has been generally noted that the communist military command is almost as heavily proletarian in origin as the party leadership. Since in most of the precommunist systems the officer corps was dominated by the aristocracy and upper-middle classes (in varying mixtures), the communist system has brought a radical change in this special area.

One characteristic of communist political elites, with the exception of those in China under Mao, is that over time their educational levels have risen considerably. Among the original leaders of the Bolshevik party were people like Lenin, Zinoviev, and Trotsky, who had attended a university. But by the end of the civil war in 1921, the Bolshevik leadership had itself been proletarianized, and a majority of the Central Committee membership had only a primary- or secondary-school education. This situation remained until the launching of the great industrialization drive of the 1930s, when the politically loyal but poorly educated were replaced (many through the Great Purge) by younger cadres who were of proletarian origin and politically loyal to the system but also had the requisite technical expertise to oversee the new industrial economy (table 9.6).

Table 9.6 Educational Level of Soviet Central Committee Members, 1930, 1952, 1986

EDUCATION	1930 (percentage)	1952 (percentage)	1986 (percentage)
Primary/secondary	67	24	8
Technical institute	4	39	59
Military institute	—	5	11
Teacher/medical/law institutes	17	24	8
Party higher school	—	3	2
University	12	5	12

SOURCE: Adapted from Nagle, 1977:66, 90.

Since Stalin's death in 1953, this "expert trend" toward a political elite with higher education, predominantly in applied fields, has continued. This again is in contrast to Western elites, whose higher education is most often in the field of law, followed by other liberal professions and business administration. The Chinese experience during Mao's time stands in contrast to the Soviet and Yugoslav patterns and the pattern of Western elite recruitment. Mao distrusted the "expert trend" and viewed this as a return to the "capitalist road" of development in Eastern Europe. In China, Mao struggled against Liu Shaoqi and Deng Xiaoping as Chinese advocates of a technocratic elite.

It may be that in the post-Mao period China, too, will experience a Soviet-style transformation in the educational qualifications of its leading personnel in party and government.

Although the trend toward a technically trained political elite is most dramatic over the longer lifetime of the Soviet system, it characterizes the experience of the other European communist regimes as they have matured. This has led some observers, like John Kenneth Galbraith and Daniel Bell, to assert a certain "convergence" of capitalism and communism into "postindustrialism," insofar as real authority seems to rest with a new technocratic elite. While this is not the place to evaluate either the concept of "convergence" or of "postindustrialism," it is worth noting the qualitative differences that persist between the most advanced capitalist systems and the communist systems, despite the undoubted influence and importance of technically competent specialists to both paths of development. Whether these differences are great and fundamental or secondary and marginal compared with the similarities of all advanced economies remains a separate issue.

Women's Emancipation

The liberation of women has been one of the explicit goals of communism since the days of Marx and Engels. Indeed, Marx and Engels considered the domination of men over women as the first form of class oppression, and they saw the liberation of women as a "bench mark" for the development of a humane and classless society in general. Lenin had specifically called for the employment of women in all phases of the economy and the liberation of women from household chores as necessary steps toward sexual equality. Unlike the theorists of capitalism or liberal democracy, the earliest advocates of communism explicitly supported women's liberation as an integral part of building a new society.

How well communist systems measure up to the goal of sexual equality depends on what yardstick is used.

There are four basic ways to judge the progress that women have made under communism. First, there is the standard of absolute equality in all areas. This is used by ardent anticommunists (Jancar, Dallin) so that any deviation from absolute equality is counted as the failure of communism to live up to its promises. Then there is the standard of progress achieved since the revolution. This measures the achievements of women under communism against the position of women under the usually reactionary policies of the tsarist, Nazi, or Kuomintang regimes. This is probably the easiest standard for the communist regimes to score well on. A third index compares the status of women in communist societies with that of women in the liberal democracies, the chief ideological competition of communism. This can be instructive but may fail to capture the most current trends in either system-type. A fourth standard does examine the current trends in the situation of women as a sort of "what have you done for me lately" focus. None of these standards taken alone can reveal the complex and often contradictory changes in women's status since the introduction of communism.

In the first years of nearly all communist systems, most of the legal and semilegal (religious, traditional) barriers that oppressed women were officially removed. Marriage by consent, free divorce, abortion, equal rights of citizenship and personal property, equality before the law, equal pay for equal work were all passed into law or even guaranteed in the new constitutions. The crudest forms of commercial exploitation of women through concubinage, prostitution, and pornography were eliminated. Even today, mass sexually oriented advertising and inane beauty contests are in general not found in communist nations.

But legal equality does not automatically produce actual equality, so we must look for evidence of concrete gains for women. In the Soviet case, the evidence is overwhelming that women have moved into new fields in larger numbers and percentages than in any other society, communist or noncommunist. With the industrialization of the USSR came unparalleled occupational breakthroughs for women, which have continued beyond the Stalinist industrialization drive and the war-time emergency. The percentage of higher professional positions held by women in the USSR has risen from 28 percent in 1928 to 52 percent as of 1974. Over 4.6 million Soviet women are employed as engineers, doctors, lawyers, teachers, economists, agronomists, and other professionals (Dodge, 1977:206), and 63 percent of all semi-professional jobs (technicians, accounting, legal, medical personnel) are held by women (some 8 million). About 72 percent of all doctors, 69 percent of teachers, 64 percent of economists, 40 percent of agronomists, and 31 percent of engineers are women. By contrast, in tsarist Russia of 1913, only 10 percent of doctors were women. In the mid-1920s only 1 percent of engineers were women, although this had already risen to 13 percent by 1939 (Mandel, 1975:135). Soviet women have broken the sex barriers in blue-collar occupations as well; 29 percent of construction workers, nearly 38 percent of railroad workers, and 17.3 percent of machine construction workers are also women (Sacks, 1977:202). According to Mandel (1975:106) a third of all Soviet crane, derrick, and forklift operators are women, as are a majority of streetcar, bus, and subway train drivers. In 1926 less than one-eighth of typesetters were women; by 1959 nearly four out of five compositors were female.

The Soviet Union compares favorably not only with Western democracies in its occupational and educational opportunities for women, but also with other communist nations. In higher education, which is the key to entering professional occupations, women account for 49 percent of all students in the USSR, compared with 45.3 percent in Bulgaria, 44.5 percent in Hungary, 40 percent in Cuban colleges and 50 percent in Cuban universities, 42 percent in Poland, 40 percent in Yugoslavia, 38 percent in Czechoslovakia, 34 percent in East Germany, 32 percent in Mongolia, and 27 percent in one leading university in China. In those fields of engineering and technology that in the West are almost exclusive male preserves, women make up 38.3 percent of student majors in the Soviet Union versus 28.5 percent in Cuba, 20 percent in Poland and China, 17 percent in Czechoslovakia, and only 8.6 percent in East Germany. Remember that Sweden, with 6.4 percent women among its engineering and technology majors, is *tops* among the liberal democracies (Mandel, 1975:322).

Despite this undoubted advance toward emancipation of women in educational and occupational opportunities, especially in the USSR but to lesser degrees in all the communist nations, there are still many areas where sex inequality continues to burden women. First, and perhaps most apparent, is the relative absence of women among the political elite. In the USSR, women represent only about 27 percent of party membership and hold less than 3 percent of Central Committee seats and no Politburo positions. The picture in other communist nations is little different, except for an occasional, one might say token, female cabinet or Politburo member, usually in a not very important ministry or party function. Here the sexual pattern of political recruitment hardly differs from that in the liberal democracies, and politics remains a male domain. Second, even though women are better represented in the professions and in formerly "masculine" jobs generally, they are less in evidence as one goes higher in each occupational hierarchy. Thus, while Soviet women make up nearly all the nursing personnel and seven of ten doctors, they account for a lesser 57 percent of heads of hospitals and head physicians and only 25 percent of neurosurgeons, the most prestigious and highpaying specialization. In education, 81 percent of primary- and secondary-school teachers were women in 1974-1975, but only 31 percent of primary-school principals and 28 percent of secondary-school principals were women. It should be added that these figures have risen from 23 and 20 percent in 1960-1961, however (Dodge, 1977:218-22). Men still tend to get the better jobs even in those fields where women are and have for some time been active in large numbers. Third, Soviet working women, both professional and nonprofessional, bear a double burden of career and housekeeper. Soviet sociologists Leonid Gordon and E. Klopov (1975) point out that this inequality is related to and reinforces the inequalities mentioned above: "Working women devote from 2 to 2.5 times more of their time to housework than do the men, therefore they have less opportunity for rest, raising their professional skills, and cultural levels—in general, less opportunity for their own development" (73).

Soviet authorities and other East European leaders now openly recognize this inequality. Hilda Scott (1974) provides an excellent account of the current feminist debate in Czechoslovakia. In general, the system has been trying to deal with women's double burden through better daycare facilities for children, more labor-saving appliances, and better community laundering and shopping services. The system has been much more reluctant to pressure men to change their attitudes toward housework and childcare activity, although among younger and better-educated people there is some evidence of a generational attitude shift toward greater equality. In recent years, there have been signs that Soviet women are pressing for greater equality in job promotion, pay, and (especially) higher representation in the party leadership. The percentage of women among party membership has risen from 23 to 27 percent in the past decade, and nearly one-third of new members are women (Moses, 1986). For the first time since the early 1960s, a woman, Biryukova, was elevated to the Secretariat at the 27th Party Congress in 1986. Since the mid-1970s, women's issues have been voiced more openly, and women, both in and outside the party, have articulated a series of demands which demonstrate, according to Moses (1986:401), "the evident ability of Soviet women as a group to shape the direction of public policy discussions and decisions in the USSR in the past decade." Issues such as health care reform, population policy, divorce, crime, and labor productivity are now linked to solutions of women's problems in Soviet policy debates.

An Equality Summary

In each of the areas discussed in this chapter, communism has produced important and basic shifts toward greater equality. In equality of income (not to mention wealth) distribution, educational opportunity, leadership recruitment, and emancipation of women, the communist systems compare favorably with the liberal democracies, even if they have not reached and probably will not achieve full equality. The "politics of equality" in the communist systems is, if anything, more visible, since the party and state are more clearly and directly responsible for what happens in wage, educational, and occupational policy than under capitalism, where the economy and much of higher education, while open to government influence, remains basically in private hands. John Echols (1981), in a critical review of equality in communist nations, says that communist systems have made consistent gains toward reducing class inequalities. On the other hand, he argues, after an initial effort toward greater equality communist systems have not given the same priority to reducing ethnic, racial, regional, and sex inequalities. In some cases, the current evidence indicates either constant (e.g., black underrepresentation in Cuban political leadership) or even increasing (ethnic income differences in Yugoslavia) inequalities.

The main factors that have produced greater social equality under communism are: (1) the elimination of concentrated private wealth and (2) the elimination of mass unemployment. The abolition of private fortunes has both reduced income inequality and put greater stress on educational merit for getting ahead, since large-scale inheritance is not allowed. The end of mass unemployment has eliminated the subproletarian poverty culture that still characterizes some liberal democracies, including the affluent United States but also Britain and Italy. In a growing labor-scarce economy, women and Central Asian minorities have had greater chances for upward mobility without threatening the chances of males and Russian ethnics.

On the other hand, communist systems have, after some initial experimentation, decided not to radically reorganize the family structure. The persistence of the conventional family environment continues to produce educational advantages for children of well-educated parents and a double burden for working women. Additionally, communist systems continue to regard wage and salary differentials as necessary for economic growth, so there are limits to the reduction of income inequalities that have characterized the post-Stalin period. In post-Mao China and some other underdeveloped communist economies, greater wage differentials may be introduced as part of the initial industrialization effort, as they were under Stalin. What the more advanced communist nations have shown is that the level of social inequality is not immutable, that gross levels of inequality can be done away with, and that greater opportunities can be opened up to the lower classes, to women, and to ethnic minorities at an earlier stage of economic development than has been achieved in capitalist nations.

Chapter 10

Liberty—Failures in Personal Freedom

A MOST UNPLEASANT TASK FOR A SOCIALIST is to describe the state of personal freedom in the communist nations. That is undoubtedly why most official descriptions made by the ruling communist parties are evasive or full of half-truths. The fact is that compared with the liberal democracies, communist systems provide almost none of the basic personal liberties that are guaranteed in their own constitutions. This is a clear barrier to the development of the kind of society that Marx called communist, since Marx expressly stated that, in communism, "the free development of each is the condition for the free development of all" (Marx, Communist Manifesto of 1848). The suppression of personal liberty requires extensive effort by the ruling party to monopolize political discussion and decision making. To accomplish this, the state and its bureaucracy, rather than "withering away" as Marx had hoped, has grown larger and more obtrusive. This obstacle to the realization of communism is a direct result of the party's decision to suppress personal liberty. Thus, not only by liberal democratic but also by Marxist standards the current lack of personal liberty is a failing of the communist systems.

This condition applies currently across all communist systems, with some exceptions worth mentioning, mostly in the Yugoslavian system. In all communist systems, there is essentially no free choice in political elections at any level. Lists of officially supported candidates (part of the *nomenklatura* system) are presented to lower-level bodies for automatic approval. Noncommunist parties are either banned, as in the USSR, or, as in Poland, Czechoslovakia, and China, survive as docile vestiges of former opposition parties and groups. In Poland and Yugoslavia there is some choice of candidates for parliamentary elections, but only from among "approved" candidates. The same applies for Cuban trade unions and some other mass organization elections. The lack of suppression of independent noncommunist candidates seems to be a key criterion on which the Soviet leadership based its military intervention in Hungary in 1956 and in Czechoslovakia in 1968. It has tolerated an independent-minded Rumanian regime and did not intervene in Poland in 1956 because in both cases it was more confident that the local Rumanian and Polish communist parties, despite some policy differences with Moscow, were firmly in control and would continue to suppress independent political groups.

In all communist countries, there is censorship of press, radio, and television, in some cases by a separate censorship office, in other through self-censorship within publication or broadcast facilities. Dissident publications, for example the so-called *samizdat* (self-publishing) network of typewritten journals and newsletters in the Soviet Union, do exist, but their authors are frequently arrested on charges of "slandering the state." In all communist countries, there is a virtual ban on nonsponsored demonstrations, and violators may be arrested for "hooliganism" or "rowdyism."

In cultural affairs, there are limits on artistic freedom and religious practice in most communist nations. To be sure, the Soviet government has made its peace with a domesticated Russian Orthodox church, the Polish regime has followed a relatively relaxed policy in its dealings with the Roman Catholic church, and other communist parties now practice a kind of detente vis-à-vis the major organized religions in their countries. Yet activist or especially proselytizing behavior by Soviet Jews, Baptists, and Jehovah's Witnesses may still result in harassment and punishment, and some obstacles are still placed in the way of normal religious observances. In art, sculpture, and music, a doctrine of "socialist realism" stands as an official guide to channel artistic creation into the service of the party's goal of building socialism. Poetry, novels, painting, and composition are supposed to encourage and support communism, never to oppose or question it, and defiant artists soon lose their jobs if they persist in making basic criticisms of the existing order.

In all communist nations, the legal system is subservient to the party, and the right to a fair trial is by Western standards not enforced. Adequate legal counsel is not permitted. In general, the outcome of political cases rests on political considerations rather than on evidence and legal statute. There is evidence that psychiatric clinics and sanatoria are used to imprison political dissidents without trial or benefit of any legal proceedings.

In communist nations, although most workers are members of officially sponsored unions, there is no right to organize an independent trade union if workers are dissatisfied. Official trade unions, in practice, do not call for strikes. An exception is Yugoslavia, where strikes are sometimes called in the privately owned, small and medium-sized factories. Although it is claimed that there is no need for strike action since all major enterprises are publicly owned, worker support for the independent union Solidarity in Poland and occasional slowdowns and mass resignations at some plants in the Soviet Union to protest management policies indicate that there are occasions where workers feel strike action is called for.

Finally, only in Yugoslavia are people free to emigrate from the country. In the USSR, during the era of detente in the 1970s, large numbers of Soviet

Jews and lesser numbers of ethnic Germans and Armenians have been allowed to immigrate to Israel or to the West, but this is an exception to the general rule. People who apply for emigration visas are harassed, especially if they join in public protest or sign petitions about their desire to leave. In East Germany, Poland, and Czechoslovakia, thousands of ethnic Germans have been allowed to emigrate since West Germany established normal diplomatic relations and trade relations with its Eastern neighbors, giving up its claim to the old borders of the Third Reich, but the Berlin Wall remains to prevent escape to the West by East German citizens.

STALINISM, DESTALINIZATION, POST-DESTALINIZATION, AND GLASNOST

Although the current level of personal liberty in the communist systems is not high compared with that in the liberal democracies, there has been change since the death of Stalin in 1953, and this change has been in the direction of greater relaxation of restraints and less coercion. It is important to recognize the significant and qualitative progress that has been made in this area, even though this progress has in no case led to a lasting communist system that has effectively guaranteed rights of speech, press, political and union activity, religious belief, due process of law, and emigration.

The worst years for personal liberty in the communist systems came during the period of Stalin's one-man rule in the Soviet Union (1928–1953) and in the early postwar years of Eastern Europe (1945–1953). During this period the power of the secret police agencies grew enormously, so that in the 1930s the Soviet NKVD controlled not only internal and external intelligence activities but also border and internal convoy troops, highway patrol, civilian registry bureaus, and fire departments. The NKVD also oversaw a huge economic empire run by forced labor (the GULAG), which Stalin filled with his purge victims. The forced labor system may have included from 3 million to 20 million people, depending on who has been considered a forced laborer and whose estimates are used (see Fainsod, 1963). Besides the perhaps 3 million who were put into labor camps, there were many more who were exiled to remote one-industry towns, others who were forced to work at a particular job under constant secret police supervision, and still others whose wages were cut by 25 percent and more for political offenses. Those who served out their sentences or were released, often after the completion of some major GULAG project, frequently continued to suffer discrimination at the hands of the authorities. The NKVD operated whole mining towns, lumber camps, hydroelectric and canal construction projects. A few prominent purge victims, such as Zinoviev, Kamenev, Bukharin, and Rykov, went through elaborate "show trials" in which they confessed to crimes that they could not possibly have committed before they were sentenced to execution. Most of the people arrested simply disappeared from public view, their fates decided by secret courts run by the NKVD.

In the arts, the norm of "socialist realism" was dogmatically enforced by Stalin's associate Andrei Zhdanov. All thoughts of "art for art's sake" were denounced as bourgeois deviations, and nonrepresentational painting was treated as a mental aberration. Even in science, the agricultural biologist T. D. Lysenko was able to use the political support of Stalin to purge Soviet biology of its most talented geneticists. At the same time he built up his own theory of "vernalization" (see Z. Medvedev, 1969) from falsified or incompetent research, which set Soviet biology back several decades.

Even within the party hierarchy, Stalin ruthlessly punished any dissent or suspected opposition. From 1939 to 1952 no Party Congress was even held, and the Central Committee and Politburo, which in Lenin's time had been centers for debate and policymaking, were dormant. Stalin simply formed *ad hoc* groups of a few trusted people who carried out his directives. Between 1948 and 1952, after Tito's break with Stalin, new purges of suspected "Titoists" were ordered throughout Eastern Europe, and it is thought that Stalin was about to launch a new massive purge in the Soviet Union shortly before his death. During Stalin's one-man rule, the Soviet Union was in many ways a "mobilization" system that not only crushed opposition but also demanded rapid change of individual behavior, with obligatory displays of support and even enthusiasm for the goals of the regime.

Almost immediately after Stalin's death, a process of general relaxation of controls, a "thaw" in the frozen landscape of Stalinism, began to emerge. Without much fanfare, labor camp inmates were released, and the power of the secret police was dramatically downgraded. Stalin's last secret police chief, Lavrenti Beria, was executed. The military and economic functions of the secret police were turned over to the normal government ministries. In literature, books somewhat critical of the past and calling for a better future were published (e.g., Ehrenburg's *The Thaw*). This movement was accelerated in early 1956 when Nikita Khrushchev, first secretary of the CPSU, denounced Stalin for his crimes and his one-man dictatorship at the Twentieth Party Congress. Almost immediately, the release of millions from labor camps was ordered, and the process of their assimilation into Soviet society was aided by the Khrushchev regime (Medvedev, 1975). Khrushchev revealed the extent of Stalin's purges, his paranoia, and his mistakes as a leader that cost the Soviet people so much in World War II (see Khrushchev, Report to the Twentieth Congress of the CPSU, 1956), Khrushchev demolished the cult of Stalin as an infallible leader and launched a broad campaign to "destalinize" Soviet society.

Over the next six years, many purge victims were rehabilitated, reinstated in previous careers, and given some compensation for their losses. In the arts, critical voices like Solzhenitsyn and Yevtushenko were published; Khrushchev personally okayed the publication of *One Day in the Life of Ivan Denisovich*. In Soviet politics, a variety of interest groups began to lobby more openly and actively for influence over policy, without fear that Khrushchev would or could suppress such group participation as Stalin had (Skilling and Griffiths, 1971). We know now that Khrushchev never had the kind of one-man control that Stalin held, and that several of his favorite reforms in education, fertilizer production, and party organization were defeated by his opponents. At one point in 1957 Khrushchev was faced with a hostile majority in the Politburo calling for his ouster. After a two-day debate in the larger Central Committee Khrushchev was sustained in his office, and his opponents were forced to resign. However, his defeated opponents, Malenkov, Molotov, Voroshilov, Bulganin, and Kaganovich, were not executed or imprisoned; some even continued as party members and government officials, though demoted several levels. Soviet government had returned in some ways to the Leninist norms of a collective leadership, and a higher level of tolerance for party debate from the "loyal opposition" within party, state, military, trade union, educational, and cultural organizations had been re-established.

The limits of this destalinization or liberalization have been demonstrated many times over. In October 1956, Soviet troops marched into Budapest to arrest and later execute Imre Nagy, a liberal communist who had overstepped the bounds of acceptable destalinization by bringing noncommunists into high government posts and considering pulling Hungary out of the Warsaw Pact. In the Soviet Union, students rejected officially sponsored candidates for student offices in many universities in 1957 and wanted to put up their own candidates, but the party refused and simply appointed new officers. In literature, as writers demanded greater freedom and some, like Solzhenitsyn, became more strident in their rejection of Soviet society, their works ceased being published. Even at the high point of Khrushchev's populist destalinization campaign, the basic commitment to achieve communism, the basic structures of the economy, and the right of the party to dominate the political life of the nation could not be questioned.

Khrushchev's removal from office in 1964, by majority vote of both the Politburo and the Central Committee, led to the formation of the Brezhnev-Kosygin collective leadership (see Tatu, 1969), in which from the start Brezhnev and Kosygin had to build working majorities on various policy issues. We know that there were hawks and doves on detente, consumerists and "steel-eaters," decentralizers and central planning die-hards in the top ranks of leadership. These seem to have agreed to disagree, without resorting to nasty means of getting their own way or eliminating their opponents. In this post-Khrushchev period, a cautious pragmatism toward dissent and dissenters outside the party emerged. On the one hand, the reins were tightened in literature and the arts, and dissident writers Daniel and Sinyavsky and Andrei Amalrik were brought to public trial for "slander." On the other hand, as part of detente with the West, the Brezhnev regime permitted large-scale emigration of Soviet Jews to Israel and Germans to West Germany. And in the social sciences, a new Soviet sociology emerged that was more honest and open in its investigations of such social ills as alcoholism, crime, delinquency, and discrimination against women in Soviet society. Rather than arresting or imprisoning many leading dissidents, the Brezhnev regime forced people like Solzhenitsyn, Medvedev, and human rights activist Chkaidze to leave the country. Apparently the judgment was that there was little popular support for the dissenters. Most Western observers put the number of active supporters at somewhere between several hundred and perhaps three thousand people (Barry and Barner-Barry, 1978:227). Pressure from bad publicity abroad has played a role in the more prominent cases and in the issue of Jewish emigration, but more important is probably the quite limited appeal of the dissident groups, who are divided among themselves and prone to cliquish infighting.

Other dissidents, such as Jewish activist Sharansky and the physicist Sakharov, were either imprisoned or sent into internal exile. Still, Sakharov, from his exile in the city of Gorky, continued to protest against a variety of Soviet policies and went on hunger strikes to gain the right for his wife, Yelena Bonner, to travel to the West for medical treatment. Even in the worst years of the conservative Brezhnev era, dissidents were not terrorized into silence, as would have been the case under Stalin. Former Communists like Robert Haveman in East Germany and Vaclav Havel in Czechoslovakia continued their outspoken opposition. Ivan Szelenyi, commenting on dissent in Eastern Europe in the 1970s, wrote: "Few political trials have been staged against intellectuals, and most of them get away with relatively mild, sometimes suspended, sentences. Nowadays, the lives of dissenting intellectuals are not threatened anymore and the worst that they can expect is a few years in jail or probably just a one-way ticket to West Germany or England" (1979:189). The Brezhnev regime, while stopping the process of destalinization, did not return to the use of mass terror or blood purge to intimidate political, cultural, or religious dissenters. Rather, it tried to use a wide variety of lesser punishments to discourage open opposition to regime policies or to the system itself.

At the end of the Brezhnev era, there were, by CIA and U.S. State Department estimates, somewhere between 1 million and 2.5 million citizens in prisons and labor camps in the Soviet Union, of whom as many as 10,000 could be described as political prisoners (*New York Times,* Nov. 7, 1982). The CIA has stated that in the mid-1970s approximately 85 percent of those "confined" were in labor camps, with the remaining 15 percent in prisons.

Vadim Medish (1987:286) has recently estimated that there are currently 1 million criminals in prisons and labor camps. For comparison, the United States in 1986 had 820,000 inmates in federal, state, and local prisons (see chapter 6).

In 1985, after the deaths of Brezhnev and his short-term successors Andropov and Chernenko, a new leadership team under Mikhail Gorbachev began to steer the Soviet Union on a new course of openness and democratization, termed "glasnost." The Soviet media are now reporting on such issues as drug abuse, official abuse of power, corruption, crime, and natural disasters, which were formerly out of bounds for normal reportage. Even subjects such as abuses of Soviet psychiatry and the war in Afghanistan have been given more detailed and honest treatment in Soviet newspapers and journals; however, attempts to form nonofficial publishing cooperatives have been rejected, and this represents a clear barrier to still wider and more free press reporting. Some new unofficial journals, one named *Glasnost,* must still operate in a shifting gray zone of relaxed suppression but continuing illegality. In early 1987, more than one hundred political prisoners were released, and Andrei Sakharov was allowed to return from exile in Gorky. Sakharov even became a cautious supporter of *glasnost,* though he continued to criticize Soviet policy in Afghanistan. In film and literature especially, formerly censored works are now being released, and new works are breaking down old barriers of censorship. There is an excitement again among Soviet intellectuals and reformers and a spirit of hope for greater freedom of expression. In the 1987 local elections in the Soviet Union, in about 5 percent of districts limited candidate competition was introduced, although only among party-approved candidates. In the spring and summer of 1988, the Soviet media began to expand coverage of controversial issues, including ethnic tensions over the Nagorno-Karabakh region between Armenians and Azeris, calls for a noncommunist popular front to offer some sort of alternative to the CPSU, and even criticism of Lenin for his responsibility for secret police terror in the early years of the Bolshevik regime. This Moscow spring of 1988 culminated with the week-long meeting of the 19th Party Conference, which offered Soviet citizens live television debates between party leaders and, for the first time since the 1920s, an intra-party pluralism of ideas and leadership positions. By mid-1988, the Soviet public and mass media were also involved to an unprecedented degree in open and freewheeling discussion of the future course of Soviet socialism. As many in the West have cautioned, it is not clear how much of this new openness and pluralism will be institutionalized or, as Mr. Gorbachev said at the 1988 Party Conference, made irreversible. But there is no longer any doubt of the momentous nature of this reform undertaking in the weakest performance of the Soviet system.

Yugoslavian Workers' Self-Management

Since its break with Stalin in 1948, Yugoslavia has followed along a path different from that of the USSR and has been characterized as a more liberal type of communism. Its market socialism is relevant to personal liberty in several respects. First of all, Yugoslavia is the only communist system that upholds the basic right of citizens to emigrate. Second, through the development of workers' councils in the state-owned industries, about half the working population participates in an economic decision-making process that is unique to both communist and noncommunist systems. Yugoslav self-management, providing for election of workers' councils, gives blue-collar, white-collar, and managerial personnel opportunities to share in the running of the enterprise and its profits (or losses). Although this system has had its setbacks over the more than three decades of its evolution and faces some difficult future problems, it represents a qualitative advance in the rights of ordinary citizens to freely express grievances, put forward their own ideas, and in general vote on issues that affect their daily lives. Bogdan Denitch (1976:273) in his extensive studies of this system concludes that "the norm of participation is now firmly rooted; and given the system of rotation which is used in electing representatives to self-managing bodies, this means that a major part of the working population at one point or another participates in running its own institutions."

Press censorship in Yugoslavia is also more liberal but remains censorship just the same. In general, critical articles do appear in print, and if they have gone too far, a censorship is placed on further publications either by the same author or by the journal involved. This is a sort of after-the-fact censorship, as opposed to the pre-publication censorship that exists in most other communist nations. Critics of Yugoslav socialism from Djilas in the 1950s to professors Mihajlov in the 1960s and Stojanovic in the 1970s have been treated with relative leniency, yet they have been fired from their jobs and party positions and, in the cases of Djilas and Mihajlov, they have been in and out of jail a number of times.

The Yugoslav parliament is one of the few relatively active communist legislatures. Noncommunist candidates can run for office, and voters have some choice, but noncommunist candidates must be acceptable to the Yugoslav League of Communists. Trade unions are also more active and occasionally capable of independent action. In early 1987, a wave of strikes swept across Yugoslavia to protest government austerity policies and to agitate for higher wages. And critical, even self-critical, debate among Yugoslav leaders is far more free-wheeling and public than elsewhere in Eastern Europe. In general, the League of Communists is a far less obtrusive fact of life than similar organizations in other communist systems. Yet there are also numerous indications, including the relative retrogression of ideological norms in the universities in the early 1970s and the banning of the critical journal *Praxis,* that the party has the capacity and will to tighten controls a notch or two if it believes events are getting out of hand. Canadian political scientist Skilling nevertheless refers to the Yugoslav system as a "democratizing and pluralistic authoritarian" regime (1971:222–28).

TWO-LINE STRUGGLE IN CHINA

The status of personal liberty in the People's Republic is difficult for outsiders to judge. By Western standards, freedom of speech, emigration, voting choice, protest, fair trial, political association, and especially privacy are nonexistent in China. Many times the West has heard of examples of Chinese self-criticism, where citizens are put under great social pressure to confess the error of their ways, to repent, and to humble themselves before the will of the party. Sometimes this process of public self-criticism has been called "brainwashing," although that term is certainly used too freely.

Yet there are also times when Chinese citizens have been much more active in their criticism and even punishment of high government officials than has been the case in other communist systems. In 1966 to 1968, informally organized (one might say self-appointed) Red Guards went through villages and cities to denounce government, educational, managerial, party, and even military leaders for their elitism, bureaucratism, and "betrayal" of socialism. Wall posters and impromptu Red Guard newspapers appeared to rally people against the "capitalist roaders" in positions of power. Liu Shaoqi, the president of the People's Republic, and Deng Xiaoping, deputy premier under Zhou Enlai, were among the most prominent targets. Intellectuals, educators, and state bureaucrats were often sent into the countryside to help the peasants with the harvest and learn from the daily life of the masses. Though the Great Proletarian Cultural Revolution did not turn into the kind of blood purge that Stalin had conducted in the 1930s in Soviet Russia, it was indeed a pretty rough time for many Chinese who had held top posts in many fields. The Cultural Revolution would seem to indicate that ordinary citizens have at least at times directly exercised freedom to criticize and protest, even to "throw the rascals out."

To understand some of these seemingly contradictory impressions, we must set the Chinese experience in the context of Mao and his opponents within the Chinese Communist party. Mao, as indicated in chapter 8, believed that even after the revolution had won political power, a class struggle would continue in China. There would be a tendency for the new governmental and highly educated strata to set themselves apart from the masses of workers and peasants and return to the "capitalist road" of development to become a new bourgeoisie. Mao believed that this had happened in the Soviet Union under Khrushchev and that destalinization was a betrayal of socialism. In China there has been no grand denunciation of Stalin, but rather a back and forth struggle between two major party factions, the Maoists (or radicals) and anti-Maoists (or moderates), of whom Zhou Enlai was often taken as spiritual leader.

In the spring of 1957, Mao had invited the intellectuals to criticize the communist system of the People's Republic—a "Hundred Flowers" to bloom and contend. When the criticisms turned out to be harsh and far reaching, Mao declared them to be weeds instead of flowers and launched his Great Leap Forward campaign. This decentralized the economy and put strong faith in local initiatives and efforts to build commune planned and run industries, including production facilities for machine tools, iron, and steel. The Great Leap Forward reflected Mao's break with the Soviet pattern of central planning and urban-based, technocrat-managed industrialization. It also signalled his split with Liu Shaoqi and Zhou Enlai, who apparently wanted to follow the more proven path of economic modernization that had already been introduced in the first Five Year Plan, 1952–1956. The Maoists stressed the necessity for "politics in command," meaning the priority of antielitism and antibureaucratism, even at the price of slower industrial growth. The moderates stressed priority of economic modernization, with greater power for those technically trained and competent to build and manage the new factories and enterprises.

The Great Leap Forward achieved some early successes, but many failures occurred as well, especially in the backyard iron and steel foundries. By the early 1960s Mao's power was on the wane, with Liu Shaoqi, in particular, appearing to take over general responsibility for the course of government policy and a "normalization" of economic development. Mao seemed to go along with this arrangement, and it was widely assumed in the West that the aging Mao would gradually fade from active political life. The Cultural Revolution, initiated by Mao's call for formation of Red Guard groups to attack Liu's policies, was a comeback attempt by the Maoist faction. Again Mao pinned his hopes on mass support, mobilized by the Red Guards, to oust his opponents from power. As Michael Oksenberg (1976) has noted, however, the Red Guard campaign rather quickly got out of hand, and even the People's Liberation Army (PLA) leadership, whom Mao counted on as allies, were by early 1968 calling for a return to normalcy and the reestablishment of control over China's rampant youth. By the early 1970s, Deng Xiaoping had been restored to his position, although Liu Shaoqi was still reported to be under house arrest. A group of Politburo radicals, including Mao's wife, Jiang Qing, continued to do battle with Deng and Zhou. After the death of Zhou in 1976, Deng was ousted from office in disgrace for a second time. After the death of Mao later in 1976, however, Deng made a remarkable second comeback, and the radical "Gang of Four" was purged and arrested. It is still too soon to tell what course the "two-line struggle" will take after the 1980s. What is clear is that the Chinese Communist party was not à monolithic organization that did an about-face at the whim of Mao Zedong. The great programmatic differences that existed (and presumably still exist) within the party were never crushed by blood purge, so that each side has been able to make several political comebacks.

The Chinese system never experienced full-blown Stalinism and therefore has had no need for East European-type destalinization. At those times when the Maoist faction had the upper hand, a greater emphasis was put on grassroots participation in politics, including criticism of authority figures. When the moderates or anti-Maoists were in power, the better educated and technically trained were given more authority and greater freedom to pursue their specialized work. The question of personal liberty must always ask "for whom" in any system, and in China the swings of the political pendulum have produced periods of alternating relaxation and pressure on different groups in the society. The trend has been more cyclical in nature, unlike the rather steady progression of change in the Soviet Union and Yugoslavia. Since the deaths of Zhou and Mao, we can be even less sure of the future course of personal liberty in China. The post-Mao leadership around Deng, after an early period of open and public contention of views through "wall newspapers" in Peking, once again tightened cultural and ideological controls for most citizens, while expanding the authority and autonomy of economic managers and educational and scientific specialists.

In late 1986, after a series of demonstrations by university students demanding more democracy and Western-style personal liberty, the Deng leadership, under pressure from more conservative elements still in the party, again tightened controls over public debate, and several more reformist leaders, including the top party secretary, Hu Yaobang, were criticized and demoted, although Hu still remained a member of the Politburo. On the other hand, at the Chinese Party Congress in 1987, the economic reformers made a modest comeback, and many aged party hardliners were retired from office, though not disgraced. Those Western observers who have asserted that economic liberalization must also produce personal liberty in lockstep or of economic necessity have been mistaken. The link between the two is far more problematic, as both the Chinese and Soviet experience have shown.

CAUSES FOR OPTIMISM, WITH LIMITS

At least with respect to the Soviet Union, Yugoslavia, and the East European communist nations, there is some reason to believe that the relative gains since Stalin's death will not be destroyed in a massive restalinization and that further partial gains in personal liberty will appear. First of all, the communist nations are no longer industrially and militarily weak and surrounded by openly hostile capitalist nations as the Soviet Union was in the interwar period. Their economies are now relatively advanced, the Soviet Union is a world superpower on a parity with the United States, and detente has lessened (even with its setbacks in the 1980s) the hostility levels of the Cold War. Under these circumstances, communist regimes should feel more secure in permitting personal liberties to expand without fear that the West will immediately try to use dissent for counterrevolution (as the Voice of America did in Hungary in 1956) or to destabilize the system. The passage of a generation since the founding of most communist systems has given them a certain maturity. The old mainstays of anticommunism—the land-holding aristocracy, the industrialist class, and the old intelligentsia—have now largely passed from the scene. Die-hard émigré groups no longer pose any counterrevolutionary threat, since they have largely lost touch with their native societies and are hardly credible alternatives to the communist system. Even the Catholic church has made its own detente with political reality and no longer preaches insurrection against the system. Continuation of detente helps to produce a climate in which greater personal liberty is not particularly threatening, even if it is occasionally bothersome to the regime. This continuation of detente depends upon the West's attitudes as well, but there is every indication that the USSR and its East European neighbors are strongly supportive of detente policy.

Second, the initial period of rapid and forced industrialization and collectivization of agriculture has passed in Eastern Europe, and there has been a steadily growing reliance on material incentives and personal choice in economies that are now supplying consumer goods, appliances, cars, and even leisure items in ever greater quantities. In the industrial economies of East Germany, Czechoslovakia, the Soviet Union, Hungary, and Poland, and in others somewhat further behind, the drastic choices of Stalin's time are not on the agenda, and the coercion deemed necessary to industrialize these economies would only be counterproductive now.

The serious difficulties of the Polish economy in the early 1980s and the slowdown of growth in the rest of Eastern Europe and the USSR are cause for alarm among communist leaders. These issues have not yet been satisfactorily addressed by the Soviet leadership. Yet despite the blossoming of Solidarity in Poland as an expression of both consumer dissatisfaction and the desire for personal liberty, top communist leaders have shown little sign of returning to Stalin's methods of mass terror to eliminate dissent. Some claim that the younger generation of well-educated and comfortable Soviet and East European citizens would not accept a return to Stalinism, that they particularly desire greater personal liberty now that basic material needs have been largely taken care of.

Third, Stalinism seems, with every passing year, to have been a deviation from the norms of Marxism-Leninism, not its logical extension. Western experts now foresee a continued collective leadership more tolerant of intra-party and interest group debate on policy and perhaps even the institutional-ization of debate within the bounds of official party versus the "loyal oppo-sition" within the party. There are signs that local councils, courts, parliamentary committees, and even trade unions are slowly becoming more effective and more active in response to citizen demands (Hough, 1977). Certainly the glasnost policies of the Gorbachev leadership give hope for progress in the extension of freedom of expression and political debate within the Soviet Union.

It would be best, however, to conclude this chapter with several cautions against overblown optimism in this area. While there had been some growth of personal liberty and there may well be more, there are also some inherent conflicts between liberty and other values in the areas of economic develop-ment, equality, and quality of life (see chapter 11). Even though extreme coercion may no longer be necessary or desirable for generating forced savings and industrial investment and even though planning can be decen-tralized somewhat, it is still probable that liberty to emigrate for all citizens would complicate economic development. As in East Germany before the Berlin Wall, those most likely to emigrate would be the highly educated professionals and scientists who could make a lot more money and live a much more plush life in the West. This would create "brain drain" milder but similar to that which robs the Third World countries of their best educated, those on whom development heavily depends. Unless the communist nations sacrifice the priority of social equality, so that their technical intelligentsia can live in luxury comparable to the West, a free emigration policy runs some risk of damaging the economy.

Policies on personal liberty that are most liberalized in Yugoslavia are directly associated with the growth of inequality there, though this does not reach the levels of most capitalist societies. Freedom of organization and even participation may be more effectively used by those already out in front economically and educationally, thus increasing social inequality. Surveys in Poland and Czechoslovakia indicate that the more highly educated are more likely to favor inequality in income than blue-collar workers. Greater liberty for the intelligentsia might well result in increased inequality in income, educational opportunities, and leadership recruitment in favor of upper strata groups.

Finally, communist systems have been relatively successful in holding down crime, drug abuse, pornography, and chronic unemployment (see chapter 11). These quality-of-life gains have been possible in part because of limitations on personal liberty. For example, elimination of organized crime is no doubt facilitated by the absence of extensive safeguards of the rights of the accused and rights of privacy that Mafia dons and their high-priced lawyers enjoy in the West, especially the United States. Suppression of drug trafficking would be made much more difficult if protection against search and seizure and wiretapping and the proof of transaction necessary in Western courts had to be upheld. Extension of freedoms of the press and speech would probably also lead to large-scale commercial pornography, as has happened in the Western democracies.

Some observers, like Ted Gurr (see chapter 6), state that high criminality is one price the West pays for its guarantees of personal liberty, and that we must realize this trade-off. But how far can the concept of individual liberty be carried before society ends up the victim of vicious street crime, organized drug syndicates, and the crudest exploitation of women for pornography and prostitution? These are questions that are troubling to modern liberal democracies, where the priority of personal liberty is ranked much higher than in the collectivist-oriented political cultures of the communist societies. It seems fairly clear that as long as the Soviet and East European systems give high priority to these quality-of-life issues, there will be considerable limits to the expansion of personal liberty. In Yugoslavia, the one communist system that has severely reduced the power of central planning authorities in favor of local workers' councils, the price has been a 10 to 15 percent unemployment rate. With all of the demoralization and degradation that goes with being told that one's skills and talents, whatever they are, are useless or even a drain on society, that is a considerable price indeed.

Personal liberty, as protected by the Western liberal democracies, has its costs as well as its benefits. It interacts with the values and goals of individuals as well as groups and not necessarily in a mutually reinforcing way. There is no particular reason to give top priority to personal liberty at whatever the cost. A study of political culture in the Soviet Union (Brown and Gray, 1977) concludes that public values there are in fact broadly collectivist and supportive of the present system and that they provide little support for Western-style liberties. If that is the case, there is little popular pressure to sacrifice other priorities for greater personal liberty. Given the low priority especially that collectivist societies have given to individual rights and individualism, it appears likely that there will be tension between personal liberty on the one hand and economic development, equality, and quality of life on the other. Personal liberty in communist societies remains low by current Western standards, and the prospects for the future are for limited reforms, not major breakthroughs. On the other hand, the momentum that has been built up in the Soviet Union (and now in other parts of Eastern Europe as well) behind glasnost and democratization may have more far-reaching effects than either Western "experts" or Soviet leaders themselves imagine. A breakthrough to a durable, sustained higher level of personal liberty would create an entirely new priority constellation or performance syndrome associated with communist systems.

Chapter 11

Quality of Life—Security and Alienation

THE QUALITY-OF-LIFE AREA OF SYSTEM performance is a relatively favorable one for communist societies since it shows improvements over prerevolutionary conditions and in some areas over those in the advanced liberal democracies as well. But it also contains some problems and failings common to both advanced capitalist and communist systems. The gains made on certain social ills, such as criminality, drug abuse, pornography, and unemployment, have often been at the expense of personal liberty, illustrating again the competing claims made on a political system's capacities by a variety of goals or values.

CRIMINALITY IN COMMUNIST SYSTEMS

During Stalin's reign, the Soviet Union claimed that communist society was free from crime and that any criminal activity was the result of counterrevolutionary terrorists and economic saboteurs. Virtually no reliable data on the frequency of criminal behavior of any type is available from the Stalinist era. In the post-Stalinist "thaw" and early destalinization period, however, Soviet authorities began to admit the persistence of common criminal behavior that was not part of some counterrevolutionary plot, although they claimed that such behavior was a cultural throwback to the tsarist society and would eventually die out as the socialization of the new Soviet citizen became more effective. Only in the mid-1960s did the newly born field of Soviet criminology introduce the idea that some criminal behavior was not a holdover from the prerevolutionary order, but was in fact produced by modern Soviet society. In the post-destalinization period, Soviet, East European, and some Western social scientists are producing more frank and reliable studies of both criminal and deviant behavior in communist systems (with the important exceptions of China, North Korea, Albania, and Vietnam, where we must still rely on impressionistic evidence).

There is agreement among most observers that in fighting or preventing certain types of crime, communist systems have produced tangible results. Organized crime, violent crime, and high-level corruption have been markedly reduced in virtually all communist systems. In these areas, communism

191

has meant an advance over prerevolutionary society. Comparisons with similar criminal activity levels in the Western democracies are on balance favorable to the communist systems.

With respect to organized crime, communist systems have been able to largely eliminate the type of crime syndicate that controlled much of the drug traffic, gambling, prostitution, and "protection" extortion from small businesses. Greater leeway for legal authorities, harsh penalties for ringleaders, the relative inability of organized crime to corrupt the regime, and mobilized popular support characterize the campaigns against organized crime by revolutionary communist regimes. There are several outstanding examples that illustrate this success. The Cuban revolutionary regime has driven the Mafia out of its once-lucrative Havana business in gambling, drugs, and prostitution. The Mafia (supported by the American CIA) tried to assassinate Fidel Castro several times because the Cuban revolution had effectively closed down its Havana operation. The People's Republic of China, in its first years in power, broke the back of drug trafficking to what was at that time the largest addict population in the world, ended prostitution and concubinage, and abolished the banditry and local warlordism that extracted "protection" tribute from the people.

This does not mean that there is no drug traffic, no illegal gambling, or no prostitution in the communist nations (cf. Barry and Barner-Barry, 1978:263-64). There is some pot smoking, probably more in Cuba and Eastern Europe than in China or North Korea, but this is by Western standards small-scale and not part of a hard-drug subculture. In the Soviet Union, the new glasnost (openness) has revealed significant drug trafficking associated in part with the Soviet occupation of Afghanistan. It is also clear that prostitution still exists and has perhaps even increased recently in Soviet urban areas. Yet, by nearly all accounts, prostitution no longer exists as a major business that pervades whole sections of the central city, as it does in any Western metropolis.

Violent crime and especially street crime are also rarer in the communist countries than in the liberal democracies. Rates of homicide, serious assaults, and rape are far below American frequencies, though not so different from rates in Japan or Sweden. There, effective gun control has played a significant role, but one should not overlook the system's ability to mobilize people to aid police in crime prevention. In the Soviet Union, for example, the *druzhiny,* a nonpaid volunteer group that is sometimes derided for "vigilante" tendencies, helps to patrol parks, streets, and other public places and events; they assist drunks to sobering-up stations, break up fistfights, and generally add to public confidence that if any trouble occurs, a yell for help will actually bring help. Donald Barry and Carole Barner-Barry, two thoroughgoing critics of the Soviet system who have lived in the USSR on research stays for several years, admit that "the Soviet people certainly seem to feel safer in their parks and on their streets than do Americans, though much of this atmosphere of security may be created by the failure of the media to report much in the way of crime news. But, given the efficiency with which news seems to spread by word of mouth, the safer feeling may also not entirely result from delusions on the part of the public" (1978:270).

In Cuba, the revolutionary regime inherited a society that had quite high rates of homicide and rape. Voluntary militia groups, called Committees for the Defense of the Revolution (CDR), were set up to patrol neighborhoods and look for crime and counterrevolutionary activity. The CDRs were instrumental in defeating the CIA-financed Bay of Pigs invasion in 1961, but they were also effective as a crime-fighting factor. Between 1959 and 1974, the murder rate dropped by more than 75 percent; the rate of violent crime fell by 77 percent between 1959 and 1968; and rape declined by 61 percent between 1960 and 1977 (Salas, 1979). Drug arrests declined from 1,464 in 1959 to 257 in 1968 (*Granma*, May 11, 1969), and common property crimes declined by 63 percent from 1959 to 1969. However, property crime rose again in the 1970s and by 1977 was 12 percent higher than in 1959; drug arrests also rose in the 1970s, though by 1977 they were still less than half the 1959 figure (Salas, 1979:52). In revolutionary Cuba, the gains made against organized crime, drug trafficking, elite corruption, and violent crime have been maintained even as Cuban common criminal behavior has gradually returned. After 1970, the regime has generally taken a more modest view of the possibilities of reshaping citizen values and behavior. The sociology of Cuban criminals, mostly male, young, and poorly educated, is similar to the prerevolutionary pattern and to most other nations. The Cuban experience indicates both the achievements and the limitations in crime fighting for a revolutionary regime.

Still a third crime area in which communist regimes have relatively good records is that of high-level government or elite corruption. Especially in China, the Soviet Union, Vietnam, and Cuba, communist systems replaced governmental systems infamous for the extent of corruption. In the late tsarist period, under the weak-willed Tsar Nicholas II, high political offices were commonly bought and sold, and the bureaucracy was noted not only for its inefficiency but also for its susceptibility to graft, bribery, and outright theft of public funds. The culmination of this was represented by the monk Rasputin, who directed the most scandalous transactions from inside the circle of the imperial family until his assassination in 1916. While it is no secret that lower-level pilfering and corruption are quite common in the Soviet system, there can be no doubt that the Soviet system has now weathered more than a half-century without building up a similar reputation.

In the more recent postwar period, communist revolutions in less-developed nations such as Cuba, China, and Vietnam have illustrated the ability of the new system to reform political cultures seemingly anchored in corruption. In pre-Castro Cuba, Havana was the "sin capital" of the Caribbean, and massive corruption of the tax system enabled the wealthy to shift the burden of government onto the less fortunate (Groth, 1971:77). Maurice Zeitlin's public opinion surveys in Cuba in the early 1960s found that the Cuban revolution was given high marks for honesty, and Havana is no longer a crime capital or the seat of a corrupt government.

The classic case must be that of Vietnam, however. One analysis of political corruption (although it fails to analyze the impact of communist revolutions on corruption in any systematic way) cannot help but note the contrast between the American-supported Saigon regime and the communist N.L.F.:

> To take the most striking example, the cadre of the National Liberation Front of South Vietnam and the local officials of the Saigon regime are drawn from the same cultural milieu and operate within the same society. From all accounts, however, N.L.F. cadre administer the villages they control with scrupulous attention to N.L.F. regulations, whereas even Saigon's partisans concede that the South Vietnamese administration is generally characterized by dishonesty, malfeasance, and a rapacious attitude toward the local populace. (Scott, 1972:ix)

One might also note in this respect that those cities and states in India (Kerala, West Bengal) and in Italy (Bologna, Turin) where communist governments are in power maintain a reputation for honesty and incorruptibility unusual for the political system as a whole. The uniformity of pattern is such that one might suspect that communist revolution is in part an alternative to political corruption. James Scott (1972) and Sam Huntington (1968) have argued that corruption is basically conservative and system-supportive, being a way in which wealthy elites influence politics in the absence of legitimate and institutionalized channels. For those without financial resources, violence and ultimately revolution are major ways of influencing policy or changing the government priorities.

These analyses do not explain how communist systems like those in the Soviet Union, China, and Cuba, which have now been in power for some time, have managed to keep corruption from reasserting itself at top government levels. Many noncommunist revolutions, such as those in Mexico (1910), Indonesia (1965), and Egypt (1952), while originally directed against the corruption of the previous regime, succumbed in a relatively short time to the development of new and widespread corrupt practices.

More important in keeping the levels of social inequality low in communist systems are: (1) the absence of great private wealth that could be used for high-level bribery; (2) the inability to enjoy the fruits of bribery and graft for conspicuous or luxury consumption; (3) a strong and disciplined party organization; and (4) Marxist-Leninist emphasis on collective well-being and effort rather than on individual self-seeking or egoism. It would appear that this combination of characteristics of communist systems is responsible in large measure for their achievements in fighting high-level government corruption.

No one would seriously argue that communist nations have eliminated all types of crime. Since the rebirth of criminology in Eastern Europe as part of the post-Stalin evolution, we are able to see that many of the patterns and background factors associated with juvenile delinquency, theft, larceny, and more serious offenses are quite similar to those in the liberal democracies. As in the West, the convicted criminal is likely to be male, young, poorly educated, unskilled, and may also be prone to excessive drinking. Juvenile delinquents are overwhelmingly male, poor students or dropouts, and often products of disturbed family environments. Soviet sociology points to problems in the family—alcohol abuse, fighting among family members, financial difficulties, negligence, physical abuse—as common correlates of delinquency, vandalism, and hooliganism. In these areas Eastern Europe would seem to face social problems common to urban, industrial, mobile, and stratified societies generally.

Additionally, under the post-Mao "four modernizations" program, criminal behavior has apparently increased significantly, including theft, smuggling, gang violence, rape, murder, and banditry. In 1983 the Chinese party leadership began a major anticrime campaign that included numerous mass executions of criminals, perhaps a total of 1,000 to 2,000 (see Schell, 1984:64). Chinese officials have claimed that this campaign had reduced the crime rate by some 40 percent by the end of 1983 as compared with 1982, but it seems clear that the new consumerism in Chinese society is associated with a new level of criminal behavior not seen during Mao's time.

Some statistics point to differences in criminal rehabilitation. Both Connor and Chalidze estimate that fewer Soviet criminals become "repeaters," that is, return to criminal behavior after serving their sentences, than is the case in the United States. This lower rate of "recidivism" in the USSR can be interpreted in different ways. Soviet authorities put greater effort into reassimilating young offenders into law-abiding society, with the factory collective taking the young parolees under watchful guidance. In Soviet rehabilitative practice, there is a strong emphasis on work, education, and raised political consciousness; at least with respect to finding work for parolees, the Soviet system probably does a better job than is the case in the West. Chalidze (1977:214), on the other hand, suggests that both socially and geographically, crime in the USSR is less concentrated. The communist systems have no urban ghettos of racial and ethnic minorities where massive unemployment, social segregation, and social despair make rehabilitation unlikely. While communist nations of Eastern Europe still have to deal with many of the factors associated with common crime, the rehabilitation process may not be faced with the same ghetto complex of barriers that exists in many of the liberal democracies.

Changes and Problems in Family Life

The family has undergone a number of profound changes in the communist nations, as has government policy toward the family. Some of these changes, such as the transition from the extended family structure to the smaller nuclear family (parents and minor children), the dropping of legal and religious barriers to divorce and abortion, the influx of women into the workforce, and greater geographical and social mobility for the individual, are common to Western societies as well over the past half-century. These trends were greatly accelerated in many cases by the communist revolution, with the result that the transformation of family life and child-rearing practices has been compressed into a shorter time span and has in many ways gone further than the more gradual trend in the West.

Marx was very critical of the bourgeois model of marriage, especially the domination of husband over wife and the double standard of fidelity for men and women. In the earliest years of the Bolshevik Revolution, the family was seen as a holdover from the past order and a source of reactionary and religious values. Alexandra Kollontai called for a new communist family, "a union of affection and comradeship, a union of two equal members of the communist society, both of them free, both of them independent, both of them workers. No more domestic servitude for the women. No more inequality within the family" (cited in Lane: 1971:375).

Kollontai also advocated extensive child-care services, to be provided by the state, to encourage a more communal style of raising children. In the early days of the Soviet experience and that of other communist systems, the power of the family over private property was sharply reduced. Divorce and abortion were legalized and made readily available. Children born out of wedlock were given equal standing with children born in wedlock. The paralegal powers of the church over matters of marriage and divorce were curtailed. By the mid-1930s, however, in the midst of the industrialization drive in the USSR, and especially since the end of World War II, Soviet policy has attempted to strengthen the family and encourage parenthood. This turnabout in family policy can be seen as a response to two factors. One is the recognition of the family in communist society as a vehicle of support for the system. Most adults in the USSR now were born and raised under communism, have assimilated its norms, and can be expected to pass them on to their children. That generation of parents who had been socialized under the tsarist regime has now greatly declined in importance. What was once seen as an institution for preserving reactionary values could now be enlisted to preserve communist values. Second is the need for public support of child rearing to ensure a sufficient workforce in an economy short of

manpower. (Two exceptions here are China and Yugoslavia. China instituted programs for population control in the 1960s because of the strain of its
one billion population on its economic capacity; Yugoslavia has a severe
unemployment problem due to the scrapping of central planning.) In all the
centrally planned economies of Eastern Europe there is a need for more
workers, engineers, technicians, and office personnel. Every attempt is made
to entice mothers and retired persons into employment, and despite the
continuing availability of abortion (except in Rumania), government policy
has been pronatalist, in favor of childbearing.

But those trends that have produced higher rates of family breakup and
declining birthrates in the West (see chapter 6) have also affected communist
society in Eastern Europe. Since the 1950s, divorce rates have climbed
steadily in all these systems, and birthrates have fallen off sharply.

Divorce is now about as common in the USSR as in Britain or the United
States; birthrates are as low in East as in West Germany. To be sure, the
special problem of alcoholism in the USSR exacerbates the divorce rate;
according to Mandel (1975:247) about 40 percent of Soviet divorces are
caused by alcoholism, almost always on the husband's part. The full-time
careers of most Soviet women especially have made them more economically
independent of their husbands, making divorce less difficult financially. On
the other hand, some evidence (Moses, 1987:400) indicates a growing poverty problem for single-parent female-headed households with minor children, as has occurred in the United States. The trend is quite similar across
national borders and ideological system-types. In both Eastern and Western
Europe, family breakup and declining birthrates pose social problems of
roughly similar magnitude. As in the West, the modern family is an institution in transition, without a clear image of its future. This transition has
some disturbing consequences for the quality of life in the world's most
successful economic systems.

Table 11.1 Divorce Rates in Communist Nations *(per thousand population)*

	1957	*1967*	*1975*	*1984*
Bulgaria	0.90	1.16	1.27	1.48
Czechoslovakia	1.07	1.39	2.18	2.42
East Germany	1.33	1.66	2.47	3.02
Hungary	1.81	2.06	2.46	2.69
Poland	0.55	0.85	1.21	1.43
USSR	1.27[a]	2.74	3.08	3.39
Yugoslavia	1.14	1.05	1.18	0.92
Cuba	—	1.14[b]	2.45	2.89

a. 1961
b. 1965

Source: *UN Demographic Yearbook,* 1976, 1982, 1986.

Elimination of Mass Unemployment

One of the achievements of the communist systems in the quality-of-life area is the ending of massive and chronic joblessness and with it the social despair and personal degradation that it breeds. Until the establishment of the strong central planning agency (GOSPLAN) in the first Five-Year Plan (1928-1932), the Soviet Union during the NEP period experienced considerable unemployment (about 1.5 million registered unemployed persons in 1927). Planned economic growth since the 1920s, however, has generated employment at a pace that has kept up with the numbers of job seekers. The number of unemployed in the USSR declined to 1.1 million by 1930 and to only 200,000 by 1931. Since 1931 there has been no official record of unemployment in the Soviet Union. Canadian economist Alan Abouchar (1979:10-12), in a summary of Soviet performance, estimates that Soviet central planning since the late 1920s has largely eliminated longer term secular unemployment and short-term cyclical unemployment associated in capitalist economies with the business cycle of expansion and recession. If anything, the labor situation in the USSR, and also in some other East European systems, is one of scarcity of people to fill available positions. As pointed out above, lack of population growth, rather than overpopulation, would seem to be a problem. Soviet economist Efim Manevich, in his short book summarizing how central planning provides for full employment, definitely views this as a quality of life achievement:

> THE elimination of unemployment was a great attainment of the Soviet people. It meant, first and foremost, that each citizen's most important right—the right to work—had been put into practice. Doing away with unemployment gave working people confidence in the future and encouraged them to develop their abilities and talents. (Manevich, 1968: 16-17)

Of course, there is some unemployment in the USSR and Eastern Europe. There is frictional unemployment, which includes people who are in the process of changing jobs. Abouchar (1979:11) estimates this frictional unemployment at less than 1 percent. There are a few "social parasites," adults who sponge off their parents or friends or engage in only occasional and sometimes shady work. There are the cases of people who cannot find the kind of employment they prefer or were trained for because of planning errors or geographical preferences. It is, for example, particularly difficult for Soviet planners to get highly trained people to accept employment in the frigid climate and barren landscape of the Far North, even with hardship pay incentives. Yet despite these and other facts about unemployment, what is irrefutable is that central planning has eliminated mass chronic unemployment as a social problem. In the USSR and its East European neighbors there are no ghettoes of the jobless, nothing comparable to Watts, Hough, the South Bronx, Belfast, Liverpool, London's East End, Amsterdam, Rome, and Naples, where, in the poor working-class districts, jobless men line the sidewalks, hanging out in winter and summer, in good years and bad, a constant feature of the social landscape.

A few of the liberal democracies—West Germany, Japan, and Sweden—have in their best boom years been able to reduce unemployment to levels comparable to those in the USSR, but none for such a prolonged period. In a relatively rare display of candor for a Western analyst, Keith Bush compares unemployment in four liberal democracies (the United States, Britain, West Germany, and France) with the situation in the Soviet Union:

> AT the time of writing, over 10 million persons and their families in the four Western countries cited are undergoing the trauma and misery of unemployment; this is alleviated but not expiated by the various forms of unemployment compensation. Others are on short time. In this respect, the Soviet citizen is, generally speaking, appreciably better off. (Bush, 1975:51)

If one wants to find a communist system in which joblessness is a problem, then one must take the case of Yugoslavia, which scrapped central planning of its economy in the 1950s. As Yugoslavia began to substitute market mechanisms for central planning, it experienced a ballooning of unemployment, from 2.3 percent in 1953 to 5 percent in 1963, and upwards of 10 percent in the 1970s. This figure would be even higher if it were not for the migration of hundreds of thousands of Yugoslav workers to West Germany, Switzerland, and Sweden in search of jobs. And there is no doubt about which social strata and regions bear the brunt of joblessness in Yugoslavia. Parkin (1971:175) shows that it is overwhelmingly the unskilled working class (87 percent of all jobless) and the poorest regions that are most affected, thus increasing the already present inequalities among social strata and ethnic groups of the country. Enthusiasts of Yugoslav market socialism must consider that the return of large-scale unemployment is one price for dropping a central planning capacity of the political system.

We should also note that China, which dismantled much of its industrial planning mechanism in 1978 and initiated decentralized "responsibility systems" for investment and production decisions, has also experienced a rebirth (though not accurately measured in extent) of chronic and large-scale joblessness. The Gorbachev leadership has recognized that any decentralization reform involving a qualitative weakening of central planning will produce considerable joblessness in the Soviet Union; yet the Soviet leader seems prepared to accept this trade-off for greater efficiency and innovation in production. Should Gorbachev's reforms be fully implemented, it is certain that chronic unemployment would return to the Soviet economy.

POLLUTION AND THE ENVIRONMENT

Pollution and damage to the natural environment caused by industrial growth and mass consumer behavior is not confined to the capitalist democracies. Indeed, the pollution of Lake Baikal in the USSR became in the 1970s an international environmental scandal. Large state-owned cellulose plants had for years dumped wastes into the world's largest fresh-water lake. Pressure from a loose coalition of Soviet scientists, local residents, and international ecologists forced some government action to reduce the polluting activity, but it is not yet clear if this has been sufficient to reverse the environmental decay. There have been other reports in the Soviet press of oil spills in the Caspian Sea and of air and water pollution in different localities, without any corresponding vigorous response by the government to remedy the situation. Studies of Soviet environmental policies (Goldman, 1972; Enloe, 1975; Kelley, Stunkel, and Wescott, 1976) recognize that pollution is a problem in both the Soviet Union and Eastern Europe.

Some differences occur in the kinds of pollution that affect Soviet society compared with those that affect the Western democracies. Auto emissions are still a much smaller factor in Russian urban air pollution, although this will likely increase with the growing "automobilization" of the USSR. Noise pollution is generally a greater urban problem, especially where industrial activity and residential units are in close proximity. Both in factory and in residential construction, noise considerations are not weighed very heavily in planning, and noise levels are considerably higher than in most Western factories and urban homes.

On the whole, the emergence of pollution as a political issue in the Soviet Union in the 1970s seems to add strength to the notion of a certain "convergence" of communist and capitalist industrial societies. Goldman and Kelley argue that despite (1) public ownership of industrial plants; (2) central planning that should aid effective enforcement of environmental standards; and (3) the lack of a private profit motive antagonistic to ecological concerns, the Soviet record on pollution is no better than that of the United States or of any other industrial society. Soviet regulations concerning land development, public health, air emissions, and water purity were tightened in the late 1960s, and Enloe (1975:194) points out that environmentalism was given official backing in the ninth Five-Year Plan (1971-1975), but it is clear that a number of factors have hindered the fight against pollution.

Most important is the high priority given to increased productivity in heavy industry, consumer goods, and agricultural production. Within state-run factories, mills, and farms, those responsible for enforcing waste disposal and emissions regulations generally have less bureaucratic clout than those responsible for meeting production quotas. Second, although citizen complaints about pollution do appear in Soviet newspapers, there is little opportunity for independent citizen groups to intervene against polluters via court action or public hearings. Third, even when fines are imposed on polluters, they are often small and are thus (as in the West) simply written off as another cost of production, a cost that does not achieve the goal of reducing antienvironmental behavior. Cynthia Enloe summarizes the dilemma of environmentalism in industrial communism as follows:

> THE production ethic has elevated to top political posts men and women whose training and career aspirations bias them against policies that would restrict industrial output for the sake of public-health protection of nature. Likewise, those central ministries responsible for heavy industry have superior 'clout' in policy discussions and can frustrate the operations of agencies assigned to implement environmental laws. (1975:220)

Enloe concludes that the theoretical advantages that a centrally planned and state-owned economy should have in combating pollution and enforcing environmental conservation will not be realized unless and until industrial growth is lowered in priority. On the other hand, it can be argued that the Soviet ecology movement now has some institutional recognition, and at those points where pollution threatens production or workers' efficiency, Soviet authorities have the capacity and motivation to take action.

Perhaps the worst problems of environmental decay are found in East Germany, which is the most industrialized and urbanized communist society and which relies heavily on brown coal for heating and industry. Air pollution from brown coal is immediately noticeable in East German cities, as are the deterioration of building facades and the dying of forests from industrial and urban air pollution.

One exception to this general picture may be the People's Republic of China. William Ophuls (1977), in his discussion of ecology in the less-developed nations, singles out China for some praise. The Maoist strategy for development was far more favorable to the environment because of its emphasis on "decentralized, local self-sufficiency, 'appropriate technology' that is cheap and suitable for small-scale use, cadres with practical technical skills instead of highly specialized and expensive training, labor-intensive instead of capital-intensive modes of production, careful husbandry of resources and fanatical vigilance against waste, and some degree of ecological restoration (for example reforestation of mountains denuded since ancient times)" (207-8). While the Maoist strategy was probably less harsh on the environment, it was also less successful in modernizing the economy, although it may have helped build the basic infrastructure for development. Ophuls himself predicts that Chinese determination to modernize and expand production will now overrule the environmental achievements of the Maoist period. In just the past decade, with Deng Xiaoping as leader of a new economic modernization drive, we are witnessing this shift in priorities to the detriment of environmentalism.

ALIENATION AND ALCOHOLISM

In chapter 6, I discussed the rise in the affluent democracies of social problems having to do with feelings of alienation and loss of community morale. Sometimes these problems appear in the forms of drug abuse, alcoholism, and the growth of exotic cults or sects. Communist societies have generally been successful in preventing widespread drug abuse, and there is little evidence of the cultism now found in the West. Clearly, communist governments have greater power to prevent the free proselytizing and public appearances of sects like the Moonies, the People's Temple, or the Hari Krishna. The personal liberty of the individual to form or join a sect, even if harmful to the individual, is protected in the liberal democracies, but not in the communist nations, where the collective well-being of the society, for which the ruling communist party claims responsibility, is given higher priority.

The major social problem facing the Soviet Union, and to a somewhat lesser extent Poland, Hungary, and Czechoslovakia, is alcoholism and alcohol abuse. Alcoholism and drunkenness are recognized by Soviet authorities as the greatest factors in family breakup, criminality, home and automobile accidents, and production losses due to absenteeism or poor workmanship. Barry and Barner-Barry (1978:258) report that in the Soviet Union about 90 percent of hooliganism, 84 percent of assaults with intent to rob, 82 percent of open stealing, and 60 percent of thefts are committed by people under the influence of alcohol. Nearly 30 percent of all intentional homicides are committed by intoxicated persons.

One might expect that, since the Soviet government has direct control over state-owned distilleries, it could effectively dry up the source of alcoholism by turning off the vodka spigot. However, there are two difficulties that the government faces. First is the widespread practice of home brewing liquor (samogon), which is estimated to account for more than half of all vodka produced. Unless Soviet authorities take much stronger measures against this, a decrease in legal vodka production will simply be offset by increased illegal samogon distilling. A second limiting factor is the tax revenue that the government gets from legal liquor sales, which accounts, according to one estimate, for 10 to 12 percent of all government revenue (Treml, cited in Barry and Barner-Barry, 1978:261).

The Soviet government turned in the 1970s to public campaigns, peer group pressure, limits on hours of vodka sales, and price increases to try to moderate Soviet (and especially Russian) drinking habits. There were, in the opinion of Walter Connor (1972:71ff.), several problems with the government's antialcoholism effort. First, there is a long tradition in Russian culture of heavy drinking as a positive male attribute. Second, the campaign against alcoholism is often inconsistent, portraying alcohol abuse as a terrible evil but recommending only moderation in drinking. Third, problem drinkers are often those at the bottom of Soviet society, for whom alcoholism (and crime) are signs of a deeper alienation. We might also add a fourth factor, namely that alcoholism is overwhelmingly a problem of a male macho subculture, and the political leadership in the USSR (and Eastern Europe as well) is a male-dominated elite. Only in the 1980s, first under Andropov in 1983 and under Gorbachev since 1985, have Soviet authorities launched antialcoholism programs with real muscle. Alcohol abusers have been forced into treatment programs and face loss of jobs or severe demotion. Public intoxication is now unacceptable to law enforcement, and raids on illegal brewers have increased. Some initial gains have been made; public drunkenness in Soviet cities has decreased, and alcohol consumption has dropped. But the Soviet struggle with alcohol abuse has only begun, and it remains to be seen whether the current campaign will succeed over the long run.

Marx had hoped that socialism would create a society without social alienation, a society in which people would be able to combine both mental and manual talents in their daily work. As Marx saw it, one of the most pressing problems of capitalism was its division of labor into segmented, tedious, and unchallenging occupational slots, which, combined with the exploitation of the worker's labor by the capitalist, produced alienation of the worker from his work. Soviet theorists and sociologists have argued that since the elimination of the bourgeoisie, work in the USSR has ceased to be a source of alienation:

> SOCIALISM, while possessing the same productive systems as capitalism, fundamentally changes the conditions of its utilization. The separation of labour from property is done away with. . . . That is why any labour, no matter how arduous and unpleasant, takes on a totally new quality under socialism, making it possible for the worker to work for himself. The alienation of man from the conditions of his existence is ended. For the first time in history work becomes a matter of honour, valour, and heroism. (Blyakman and Shkaratan, 1977:32)

This approach forgets that Marx pinpointed the nature of the work process, the lack of creativity and autonomy allowed to the worker, as well as the capitalist exploitation of the work process, as a source of alienation. There is much evidence that assembly line work and unskilled manual labor in general is just as tedious, uninteresting, and alienating in Soviet factories as in the capitalist West. Soviet sociologists Zdravomyslov and Yadov (1966), in a survey of attitudes among young workers in Leningrad, have traced highest job dissatisfaction (they avoid the term "alienation") to the unskilled manual occupations and to the elements of monotony and lack of opportunity to use ingenuity in other occupational roles as well. In practice, then, Soviet sociology does acknowledge the continuing problem of providing not just work, but satisfying work opportunities for Soviet citizens. The Soviet leadership places great hope in automated systems to eliminate hard manual labor and job tedium: "As the current revolution in production develops it will eventually relieve the worker of various noncreative operations involved in the production process and of the need to spend a large part of his active life on the performance of monotonous, mechanical operations" (Blyakman and Shkaratan, 1977:35). Nevertheless, it is clear that this is, for the Soviet and East European economies, still a distant goal, and it is among the unskilled manual workers that other signs of social alienation, such as alcoholism, delinquency, and petty criminality, are most frequently found.

Chapter 12

The Third World, Imperialism, and Dependency

THE COLLECTION OF NATIONS KNOWN AS the Third World includes a majority of the world's population and over one hundred countries with an immense diversity of geography, cultures, economic development, natural resources, political institutions, and system origins. Third World government is appropriately the last system-type to be discussed, because it is the most recent type to emerge and to be recognized in comparative studies.

To some, there is considerable doubt as to whether the category of Third World nations is at all useful (see Sartori, Brogan, and Verney). Many people use the term only to identify those nations that are neither industrially advanced liberal democracies nor communist systems. Certainly the Third World category is much more diverse than the relatively well-defined liberal democracies category and is somewhat more diverse than the collection of communist systems, although the boundary line between the Third World and the communist systems is becoming blurred by Ethiopia, South Yemen, and Afghanistan. This negative definition of the Third World tells us little about what these nations have in common. A superficial survey of these systems could well conclude that there is little in common.

THE SCOPE OF DIVERSITY

The geographic scope of the Third World covers most of Latin America, Africa, the Middle East, and noncommunist Asia. Some Third World nations are predominantly Roman Catholic (Latin America, the Philippines), others are Moslem (North Africa, the Middle East, Iran, Pakistan, Bangladesh, Indonesia), Hindu (most of India), Buddhist (Burma, Thailand, South Korea, Taiwan), or pagan-animist (much of sub-Saharan Africa). Ethnic diversity within some nations, like India, Nigeria, Zaire, or Iran, is great. In Latin America, where Catholicism and a Spanish/Portuguese colonial heritage are common factors, individual nations have cleavages between Spanish, Creole, Mestizo, Mulatto, Negro, and Indian elements, depending on their mix in the population.

Economic development levels (to be discussed in the following chapter) range from semiwealthy and rather urbanized countries, like Argentina,

Uruguay, and Venezuela, to the still very poor and predominantly rural economies of India, Bangladesh, Chad, Somalia, Honduras, and Paraguay. Brazil, Mexico, South Korea, and Singapore have achieved considerable industrial and commercial development in the postwar years, while in Pakistan, Tanzania, and Indonesia the great majority of the population is still engaged in subsistence-type production.

Natural resources are unequally distributed among Third World nations. The oil-rich nations of OPEC (Organization of Petroleum Exporting Countries) are the most outstanding example of relatively underdeveloped economies that nevertheless possess valuable resources that can command large prices on the world market and are also crucial for internal development. Some OPEC nations (Kuwait, Abu Dabi, United Arab Emirates) have the highest GNP/capita levels in the world and can generate great trade earnings through the relatively simple exploitation of a single commodity. Other Third World nations, like Brazil, Zaire, Zimbabwe, Peru, Zambia, and Mexico, also possess considerable natural wealth in minerals, rich agricultural lands, or both. But quite a few of the poorest nations in Africa, Asia, and Latin America have few known mineral, oil, or gas deposits and are not well endowed in arable land relative to population size. Bangladesh, Pakistan, Tanzania, and some of the drought-plagued nations of the African Sahel (Saharan desert region) fall into this category. Some economists have referred to these nations where prospects for development seem most bleak as the Fourth World.

The political institutions of Third World governments are notable for their instability relative to the advanced liberal democracies or the communist systems. There are fairly few Third World nations with a long-term history of even a generation of stability in their political structures. Since the 1940s in South Asia and Southeast Asia, and since the 1960s in Africa, most nations in these regions have experienced political upheavals, predominantly military coups d'etat but also civilian seizures of power, civil wars, and popular rebellions that have changed the official description of the political system. In Latin America during the 1960s and 1970s, most nations, including Brazil, Argentina, Chile, Peru, Ecuador, Uruguay, El Salvador, Honduras, Guatemala, Panama, Bolivia, and Paraguay, experienced military dictatorships. Some, as with the twenty-year Brazilian junta, developed a civilian political party (the ARENA party) to serve as a civilian front for the military. Others, as in Argentina and Chile, suppressed all civilian parties and ruled through the widespread use of military and paramilitary terror. In the 1980s, many of these military regimes have again been replaced by civilian, elected governments, often after disastrous economic and foreign debt crises or, as in the case of Argentina, the humiliation of losing the Falklands (Malvinas) war with Great Britain. Yet, even as they returned to the barracks in many of these nations, the military remained above the law and protected from criminal prosecution for their use of torture and terror. Thus, in Brazil,

El Salvador, Guatemala, Panama, Honduras, Uruguay, and with a few exceptions also in Argentina, the civilian regimes which replaced the military juntas have been too weak to bring the military within the law and to bring to justice military officers who were responsible for even the most gruesome human rights abuses only a few years ago. In 1987, the Argentine military refused to turn over accused officers to the civilian court system and forced the Alfonsin government to pass a general amnesty for officers who participated in the killings of some 20,000 Argentinians during the 1970s campaign against leftist "subversives."

The majority of African governments are also military dictatorships, as are the important states of Pakistan, Bangladesh, Burma, Thailand, and Indonesia in Asia. As one of the best-organized, and certainly the best-armed, groups in these systems, long on problems and generally short on legitimacy, the military has become a natural and favored contender for political power, superseding in most cases the political movement, party, or leader who led the first independence government. One might ask why there are some military establishments that have not reached for political power, since by now the demonstration effect of how to execute a military coup is universal.

In some nations, however, the party of the independence movement, or its top leader, has managed to hold the reins of government, usually in a one-party system. Jomo Kenyatta and his KANU party in Kenya, Julius Nyerere and his TANU party in Tanzania, Kenneth Kaunda in Zambia, Habib Bourguiba and his Neo-Destour party in Tunisia, and Houphuët Boigny in the Ivory Coast managed for a decade or more to maintain their authority, preventing both military coups and at the same time, especially in the cases of KANU, TANU, and Neo-Destour, building up a degree of civilian political organization. The Mexican PRI belongs in this category as well, since it dominates the Mexican political system and has a half-century record of civilian government under the basic organization of the PRI's different social sectors. However, the PRI, getting 80 to 90 percent of the vote in a rigged electoral process allows some minor opposition parties to exist as long as they don't challenge PRI hegemony.

In the African ex-colonies, which have a short history of modern independence, there has scarcely been time for civilian parties to establish deep roots. Kwame Nkrumah and his CPP in Ghana at one time seemed to have built up a considerable and powerful party organization, until he was suddenly dumped by the Ghanaian military in 1966. In many Third World political systems, external appearance of strength and stability can be deceiving. Organizations that look solid on paper, popular demonstrations of support, and public declarations of loyalty by various allies can disappear in quick order. In some cases, like the Shah's regime in Iran or Emperor Haile Selassie's in Ethiopia, elaborate structures fall apart like a house of cards.

A small but significant number of Third World systems are still governed by monarchies or feudal oligarchies (Morocco, Saudi Arabia, Jordan, North Yemen, Oman, the United Arab Emirates, and Kuwait). Until recently this category would also have included Iran, Ethiopia, and Afghanistan. It would appear that feudal-monarchial regimes have become steadily less viable in the last decade, although the oil wealth of the Arabian states has heightened Western interest in the types of systems that might follow in the wake of the feudal aristocracies.

Finally, a number of Third World systems currently have multiparty political systems incorporating varying but significant levels of political liberties usually found in the advanced capitalist systems. India, Sri Lanka, Venezuela, Colombia, Guyana, and Jamaica, despite some crisis points, considerable violence, and some blatant breaches of democratic ethics, are still characterized by electoral competition among political elites for government office. Guyana and Jamaica have basically two-party systems, Colombia and Venezuela have three-party systems, India and Sri Lanka have a multiplicity of parties formed into shifting governing and oppositional coalitions. Each system mentioned has experienced a change of governing party without a great deal of bloodshed. (The civil war between minority Tamils and majority Sinhalese in Sri Lanka is largely outside the party system.)

The origins of the Third World nations are mixed. A few, such as Ethiopia, Iran, Turkey, and Thailand, are modern successors to ancient kingdoms or empires with histories of sovereignty going back thousands of years. These nations were never completely conquered and colonized (Ethiopia was briefly conquered by Mussolini's Italian fascist regime in the 1930s) as were most of Africa and Asia. In one sense, these nations have a political order and cultural heritage of their own making.

Most of the countries of the Third World, however, were for a considerable period colonial possessions of one of the nations of Europe or North America. Until the 1820s, all of Latin America was a colonial domain of Spain and Portugal. The British, French, and Dutch also held some colonial possessions in the Caribbean. Since the wars of independence (1810-1826) against the Spanish crown and Brazil's secession from Portugal at about the same time, these nations have been independent, though their sovereignty often has been battered by the gunboat diplomacy of the Great Powers. Their boundaries as nations were in large measure determined by the economic, military, and diplomatic policies of the Spanish and Portuguese monarchies during the era of colonialism. This is also the case with the more recently decolonized areas of Africa, Asia, and the Middle East. Especially in black Africa, European imperial domains were carved out with little regard for tribal boundaries and even less regard for the requisites of a viable nation-state. Great tribes such as the Bakongo were split by the division of their land into the Belgian Congo and Portuguese Angola. The Somalis were divided five ways, into colonies of the French, Italians, British (two separate colonies), and parts of Ethiopia. Independent Somalia is a union of the former Italian and British Somalilands, but its national flag has five stars, one for each of the five regions inhabited by Somali peoples. Thus the nation of Somalia was born with adamant claims on the territory of three of its neighbors, a continuing effect of Western imperial conquests of the past century.

On the other hand, Western imperialism enclosed peoples of different religions, languages, and levels of development into colonies, which later became independent nations. The British colony of Nigeria, for example, included the Moslem Hausa-Fulani of the North, the paganist Yoruba in the West, the Christianized Ibo to the Southwest, and literally hundreds of smaller tribes in between, most with their own languages. Within the first years of independence, Nigeria fought a bloody civil war to prevent the Ibo, whose region held most of Nigeria's oil wealth, from breaking away to form an independent Biafra. In the liberal democracies we know that language, ethnic, and religious differences can cause tremendous problems for a political system, as with the French-English split in Canada, the Flemish-Walloon split in Belgium, or the Protestant-Catholic conflict in Northern Ireland. In Third World nations, the national governments generally have far fewer resources to try to reconcile antagonistic groups; thus these tribal/ethnic/ linguistic/religious cleavages, often consciously used as part of a divide-and-rule strategy by the Western colonial powers, continue to plague the postindependence political systems. Such contradictions have led to: the secession of Bangladesh from Pakistan and of Singapore from Malaysia; the attempted secession of Katanga (Shaba) from Zaire, Eritrea from Ethiopia, the Tamils from Sri Lanka, the Sikhs from India, and the Kurds from Iraq, Turkey, and Iran; Moslem/black civil wars in the Sudan and Chad; and a series of wars between India and Pakistan over Kashmir.

Considering all the variety found in the Third World, which I have only touched upon here, what basis do we have for treating these nations as a political system-type?

HISTORY OF A CONCEPT

One reason for grouping together more than one hundred nations with the divergences mentioned is that these nations' political leaders have gradually come to see themselves more and more as a group. The concept of a Third World of nations has developed through two broad but distinct stages thus far: first, a foreign policy or strategic diplomacy period in the 1950s and 1960s; and second, an economic policy period begun in the 1960s and continuing today. Each stage has contributed to the growth of a self-perception among Third World leaders and to a delineation of interests between the Third World and the industrialized capitalist systems of the West. (The industrialized communist systems of Europe have played a relatively minor role in this development.)

In the first stage, a group of prominent leaders of the emerging states, including Prime Minister Jawaharlal Nehru of India, President Achmed Sukarno of Indonesia, Marshal Tito of Yugoslavia, and President Kwame Nkrumah of Ghana, developed and elaborated a position of nonalignment with either the American-led capitalist West or the Soviet-led communist nations. With the breakdown of the World War II U.S.-Soviet alliance in the latter 1940s, both the United States and the Soviet Union began to develop military alliances or blocs that, for example, partitioned Europe into the NATO nations of the West and the Warsaw Pact nations of the East. Stalin had sought to integrate Yugoslavia into the Warsaw Pact as well, but Tito and his League of Yugoslav Communists resisted and effectively demonstrated their independence of Moscow. The United States in the 1950s, by far the stronger superpower, pressed for formation of additional regional military pacts in the Middle East (CENTO, now defunct, with Pakistan, Iran, Iraq, and Turkey as members), in Southeast Asia (SEATO, now defunct, with the Philippines, Thailand, and Malaysia originally as members), and in the South Pacific (ANZUS—Australia and New Zealand). Separate defense arrangements were concluded between the United States and Japan, South Korea, and Taiwan. In Latin America, the Organization of American States (OAS), while not a military pact, became the key organizational forum for the policing of South America and Central America against communism. During this heightened Cold War diplomacy, U.S. Secretary of State John Foster Dulles considered nonalignment or neutralism to be both immoral and antagonistic to the interests of the free world, of which the United States was the recognized leader.

The Bandung Conference, held in Indonesia in April 1955, represented a first attempt both to oppose pressures to join in Cold War military alliances and to develop a grouping of less-developed nations of Asia and Africa to represent their interests in the world community. Twenty-nine nations participated, including communist China and capitalist Japan. While President Sukarno hosted the conference, the main speeches were delivered by India's Nehru and China's Zhou Enlai. No Latin American states were represented or even sent observers. At this time Latin American countries generally followed the lead of the United States in international affairs. The Bandung Conference did not set up any institutional structures, but did approve a set of principles, including:

1. support for national sovereignty;
2. noninterference in another state's internal affairs;
3. recognition of racial equality;
4. nonaggression;

5. recognition of equality of nations;
6. abstention from joining in military pacts headed by the major powers;
7. abstention from damaging the economic interests of other nations;
8. peaceful settlement of international disputes;
9. promotion of mutual interests;
10. respect for justice.

While these principles were quite general, they were clearly aimed at the attempts of the United States to force the emerging nations to accept anti-communist military alliances. At the same time there was, despite China's presence at the conference, no attempt to forge ties with the communist nations either. The Bandung principles were also directed against the colonialism of Britain, France, Portugal, Spain, and Belgium, which in the mid-1950s still held most of Africa and parts of Asia as colonial domains or semicolonies. The Bandung nations, many of them only recently independent, demanded swift decolonization in Africa and Asia.

It is important to remember that, in the early 1950s, the independent nations of Africa and Asia were a distinct minority within the United Nations membership. In 1945, only a dozen of the original fifty-one U.N. member-states were Asian or African (not counting the Union of South Africa). By 1960, however, with the decolonization of much of British, French, and Belgian Africa, nearly half (forty-five out of ninety-nine) of the U.N. membership was composed of Afro-Asian states. Today, if we include the nations of Latin America, most of which were charter U.N. members, and the additional decolonized states of Africa and Asia in the 1960s and 1970s, the Third World nations hold better than a two-thirds majority on all U.N. bodies, except for the key Security Council, where the veto power of the United States, France, Britain, China, and the Soviet Union blocks majority rule. The Third World (even with its divisions) within the United Nations has considerably changed U.N. policy and initiatives, as is evidenced by growing American dissatisfaction with recent U.N. performance, the growth of Western vetoes in the Security Council, and suspension of the United States share of payments for certain U.N. activities. (The United States temporarily pulled out of the U.N.'s labor organization, the ILO.) This is in sharp contrast to the early history of the United Nations, when Security Council vetoes were cast mainly by the Soviet Union.

By the 1970s, we witnessed the culmination of the Bandung Conference trend, which sought to build a Third World of independent, less-developed states in international affairs, nonaligned with any of the great powers, avoiding and perhaps moderating, it was hoped, the East-West Cold War conflict. Though the main leaders (Nehru, Sukarno, Nkrumah, Nasser) of this first phase in the evolution of Third Worldism have passed from the scene, the trend that they represented has continued. And in the wake of

America's defeat in Southeast Asia and the overthrow of the Shah of Iran in 1979, the SEATO and CENTO military alliances headed by the United States have crumbled. In Latin America as well, the OAS is no longer the pliant tool of U.S. foreign policy that it once was.

With decolonization largely achieved and with neutralism internationally accepted by the mid-1960s, the second phase of development for the concept of a Third World focused on economic matters. One of the first organizational results of the Third World majority in the U.N. was the founding, in 1964, of the Conference on Trade and Development (UNCTAD), under the initial leadership of Latin American economist Raul Prebisch. At the first UNCTAD assembly at Geneva in March 1964, Prebisch put the international spotlight on a series of economic issues that have now come to be known as the North-South dialogue (really two monologues up to now). The UNC-TAD meetings (UNCTAD II was held in Delhi in 1968, UNCTAD III in Santiago in 1972, and UNCTAD IV in Nairobi in 1976) have served to significantly shift U.N. activities and the debate from East-West tensions to the economic gap between the rich, developed nations of the Northern Hemisphere and the poorer, underdeveloped nations of Latin America, Africa, and Asia.

The North-South debate has until now largely excluded the industrialized and well-to-do European communist states for two reasons. One is that of the total trade with the Third World, 75 percent is consumed by the rich Western nations, 20 percent by other Third World nations, and only 5 percent by the communist states. There are no Soviet or Chinese multinational corporations dominating trade or industrial development in the Third World. Therefore, the debate over the terms of trade between the rich and poor nations will for the foreseeable future only marginally touch on the communist economies. Second, the communist nations, while generally supporting Third World demands, are neither former colonial powers with bad consciences nor even members of the General Agreements on Trade and Tariffs (GATT), the World Bank, or the International Monetary Fund (IMF), whose trade, loan, and aid policies lie at the heart of the North-South conflict. Prebisch and UNCTAD have in effect put on the U.N. agenda the problems that impede the economic development of the Third World: unfavorable terms of international trade, dependence on special commodity exports, trade barriers by the "have" nations against Third World manufactures, financial dependency on a Western-controlled international monetary system, and a mounting debt burden. The Third World nations have pressed for the establishment of a New International Economic Order (NIEO), which would redress these problems in favor of the less-developed nations. It should be added that through UNCTAD (and Prebisch) the Latin American states have become more closely identified with the concept of the Third World than in the 1950s, when Afro-Asian leaders took the initiative and Latin American leaders were reluctant to join their efforts.

With the foundation and development of UNCTAD has come the evolution of two other centers for Third World activities, the Group of 77 and the Non-Aligned. The Non-Aligned grouping is a direct continuation of the Bandung Conference of 1955. Further conferences were held in Belgrade (1961), Cairo (1964), Lusaka (1970), and Algiers (1973), publicizing the mutual interests and desires of these nations to enhance their development without joining the military blocs of either superpower. With an enlarged membership of about eighty nations, the Non-Aligned greatly expanded its organizational capacity over the previous two decades, including a Non-Aligned Coordinating Council, which under the chairmanship of Algerian President Boumedienne was particularly active from 1973 to 1976. The Group of 77 was originally made up of the seventy-seven states participating in UNCTAD I in Geneva and now has grown to about one hundred member-states, including many of the Latin American States not affiliated with the Non-Aligned. Over the past twenty years UNCTAD and the Group of 77 have developed a sort of mutually reinforcing momentum for greater Third World unity and for the building of NIEO. With all the diversity that exists within the Third World, and despite efforts by the richer nations of the West to divide and fragment Third World leadership, the Group of 77 has shown a surprising level of organizational integrity, strengthening the concept of this set of nations as a political system-type.

To further explain why this heterogeneous set of cultures, levels of development, political institutions, and national origins has come to be identified generally as the Third World, we must examine two theories that form a common linkage for these systems. These theories are the theory of imperialism and the theory of dependency. They have emerged as explanations for the behavior and dynamics of Third World politics, and although both theories raise considerable controversy, their use and acceptance has grown steadily.

THE THEORY OF IMPERIALISM

Any attempt to study the political systems of the less-developed nations must recognize the realities of Western intervention in these societies. As noted in the descriptions of economic development in the liberal democracies, the industrialization of the West (and Japan) enabled these states both to raise their own productivity and to subjugate the nonindustrialized societies of Latin America, Africa, and Asia.

Modern imperialism is in part a continuation of the expansion of the West begun by the age of exploration and colonization. Already in the 1500s, Spain and Portugal, then England, the Netherlands, France, and Sweden were finding new trading routes to the New World and the Far East and implanting colonial rule over native populations in South America, North America, and some coastal parts of Africa and South and Southeast

Asia. Much of the early exploitation of the Third World was through slave or semislave labor, used for the mining of gold and silver and on large plantations. The Spanish and Portuguese colonies represented a sort of feudal colonialism that transplanted a landed aristocracy to Latin America and parts of Africa. The British, Dutch, and French colonies represented expansive mercantile capitalist states that vied with each other for exclusive trading rights in the Caribbean, North America, South Asia, and on the China coast. By the early nineteenth century, these forms of Western colonial presence in the Third World were in decline. First in North America (1776-1781) and then in Latin America (1810-1826), British, Spanish, and Portuguese settlers rebelled against the mother country and won their independence. The greatest sea power of the nineteenth century, Britain, adopted a Little England policy of gradually granting self-rule to Canada, Australia, and New Zealand. The European powers seemed to have lost interest in conquering imperial domains, and former colonies were on the road to nationhood.

In the last quarter of the nineteenth century, a new imperialism was born. From 1878 (the Congress of Berlin) to 1914 (the beginning of World War I), the major industrial nations, including Germany, the United States, Italy, and Japan, as well as Britain and France, partitioned the Third World into colonies or semicolonies (protectorates or spheres of influence). The extent of this new industrial-power imperialism went much further than that of the previous colonialism. In Africa nearly every piece of land was gobbled up. Only tiny Liberia escaped conquest. The British expanded their holdings in the Gold Coast and Nigeria, and they carved out a string of possessions from the Cape of Good Hope to Cairo (including eventually the Union of South Africa, Rhodesia, Nyasaland, Uganda, Zambia, Kenya, the Sudan, and Egypt). The French took Morocco, Algeria, Tunisia, Mauretania, Senegal, Guinea, the Ivory Coast, Equatorial Africa, Dahomey, French Somaliland, and Madagascar. The new German empire, seeking its "place in the sun," conquered Southwest Africa, Tanganyika, German Cameroun, and Togoland. Italy seized Libya and Italian Somaliland (and later Eritrea and Ethiopia). Even tiny Belgium annexed the huge Congo State in the heart of black Africa.

The picture in Asia was similar. Even the great Ottoman empire (Turkey), Persia, and China were divided into spheres of influence by the different Western powers. Britain, on whose empire "the sun never set," enlarged its holdings in Asia to include all of India, Pakistan, Bangladesh, Sri Lanka, Burma, and Malaysia, while the French took over Indochina (Laos, Cambodia, and Vietnam). The United States, after achieving its continental "Manifest Destiny" at the expense of native Indians and Mexico, also laid claim to the Hawaiian Islands, and, in the Spanish-American War of 1898, seized Puerto Rico, Cuba, and the Philippines from Spain.

This land-grabbing by the industrial powers was not without bloodshed. The Dervishes in the Sudan against Lord Kitchener's campaign, various ethnic groups in India against British expansion, the Watusi in southern Africa against both Dutch and British, the Hereros in southwest Africa against the Germans, and the Filipinos in the Philippines against the Americans all fought to defend their independence and avoid inclusion in Western imperial domains. But the industrial nations, with the aid of nineteenth-century technology, in particular the machine gun, the telegraph, and the railroad, were able to conquer and effectively administer huge empires at modest cost and with minimal personnel.

Many theories have been advanced to account for this burst of Western imperialism. Political theorist Hannah Arendt and historian Carleton Hayes blamed it on a new supernationalism of the West, fueled by the challenge of Germany to both Britain and France. Economist Joseph Schumpeter attributed it to a militaristic aristocracy that, in the capitalist societies of the West, still dominated the officer corps of Britain, France, and Germany. This aristocratic social throwback to feudalism (a social atavism) was pictured by Schumpeter as trying to regain its former glory through imperial conquest. Still others saw the new imperialism as an outgrowth of earlier explorations combined with new Western technology and a prolonged period of peace in Europe.

These noneconomic interpretations, however, have been overshadowed by the development of theories that attribute imperialism to the workings of industrial capitalism on a world scale. Lenin's 1916 work, *Imperialism: The Highest Stage of Capitalism*, has dominated the discussion of imperialism in this century, but Lenin was not by any means the only, or the first, to link industrial capitalism with Western imperialism in the Third World. British economist J. A. Hobson, a left-liberal publicist, had presented elaborate evidence in his 1902 book *Imperialism: A Study* for the thesis that modern finance and investor groups were the main beneficiaries of imperialism. Hobson, concentrating mainly on the British case, argued that these finance and investor groups were instrumental in pushing government policy in the direction of securing new Third World areas for their exploitation, and that even though imperialism did not bring much economic benefit to the average Englander (according to Hobson), it was increasingly profitable for the wealthy investor class. Hobson criticized the new imperialism as bad business for the nation, but did not outline a strategy for overcoming imperialism. Hobson's theory of imperialism is not based solely on economic interests, either, since he gives considerable attention to the forces of nationalism and racism in the conquest of nonwhite Third World peoples by the white Christian European powers.

Lenin's theory of imperialism, using much data collected by Hobson and by Hilferding, a German Social Democrat, focuses more exclusively on the economic causes of imperialism and also provides both a prediction of and prescription for the defeat of imperialism. Hobson had tied his definition of imperialism to the conquest of new Third World territories by the great powers. Lenin included in his analysis the independent nations of Latin America as economic dependencies of the West, because their finances and their economies were so heavily penetrated and dominated by foreign (Western) capital. He also regarded tsarist Russia and imperial China as new targets of Western imperialism, despite the fact that in some areas (e.g., Korea, Tibet) these two systems themselves acted as imperial powers.

Lenin's theory is, therefore, not limited to situations where the Western powers had formally subjugated Third World peoples in colonies, because the key aspect of imperialism was its economic exploitation of less-developed nations, regardless of formal status. Leninists argue that the post-World War II decolonization of Third World countries did not liberate them from Western imperialism. Even though it created independent governments with flags, national anthems, and political leaders, the governments have just about as little control over their nations' resources as before decolonization. The overriding factor that hinders Third World nations from taking a path of self-reliant development that would benefit their own peoples is the economic control exercised by Western corporate and finance groups.

Lenin describes this new imperialism as the latest stage in the development of capitalism. This stage is quite different from Adam Smith's laissez faire model:

1. The concentration of production and capital developed to such a high stage that it created monopolies which play a decisive role in economic life.
2. The merging of bank capital with industrial capital, and the creation, on the basis of this "finance capital," of a "financial oligarchy."
3. The export of capital, which has become extremely important, as distinguished from the export of commodities.
4. The formation of international capitalist monopolies which share the world among themselves.
5. The territorial division of the whole world among the greatest capitalist powers is completed. (Lenin, 1916:89)

Lenin saw that imperialism was able, through the exploitation of Third World labor and natural resources, to generate higher profits for the large monopoly corporations (now generally called multinational corporations or MNCs). A part of these superprofits could be used to raise the standard of living of the most organized workers (usually the skilled union members) in the industrialized West. This "labor aristocracy," as Lenin called it, which had been quite militant in the nineteenth-century capitalist systems, could be bought off in this way and could even be enlisted in support of British, American, German, or French imperialism, since they too benefited from it.

If this labor aristocracy could be bought off, then well-paid British workers would support British imperialism in India, American workers would support American seizure of Hawaii, Puerto Rico, and the Philippines, as they in fact often did, marching under the banner of patriotic nationalism. For the time being, Lenin predicted, imperialism would be able to defuse the class struggle in the already industrialized nations of the West, where Marx had predicted socialist revolution.

Lenin went beyond Hobson's analysis in predicting that monopoly finance capitalism, while staving off proletarian revolution in the West through imperialism, would rouse Third World peoples to struggle for liberation of their countries from the worldwide chain of imperialism. Lenin also predicted that imperialism would retard the progress of the less-developed nations and increase the gap between the rich and poor countries of the world. This uneven development among the world's nations would set the stage for the class struggle to be displaced from the industrially developed West to the less-developed nations of Asia, Africa, and Latin America; this struggle would for the first time take place on a worldwide scale.

The struggles of Third World peoples, which Lenin termed wars of national liberation, would be led by a popular alliance of workers and peasants and could include even the native bourgeoisie of a Third World country, which also was limited in its development by Western financial power. Wars of national liberation, starting at the weakest links in the worldwide chain of imperialism, would deny to the capitalist powers the opportunity of extracting superprofits from the less-developed lands, and this in turn would lead to the reintensification of the class struggle within the industrial West. Lenin viewed the Russian Revolution as a first step in this process and had hopes that it would be the spark that would ignite revolution in other areas. Other revolutionary uprisings at the end of World War I were defeated, however, and the Soviet Union (see chapter 7) was forced to develop its economy and socialist system in isolation and in a hostile world environment. Yet, Leninists view the Chinese, Cuban, Vietnamese, and Angolan revolutions as part of the continuing anti-imperialist struggle. Soviet support for liberation movements in the Third World, while selective, is based on Lenin's theory, which is probably the most important addition to Marxism made in this century. Che Guevara's call for creating "two, three, many Vietnams" in a tricontinental uprising against imperialism and for Cuban involvement in Bolivia, Angola, Ethiopia, and elsewhere is a continuation of the vision of a worldwide struggle to overthrow imperialism.

Since Lenin's time (he died in 1924) there have been changes in the relationship of Western capitalism to the Third World that have produced some important adaptations of his original theory to current conditions. Some reinterpretations of the economic data from Lenin's own time have been reincorporated into what might be called a neo-Leninist theory of imperialism. The most important change is perhaps the rise of the United States after World War II as the leading and coordinating defender of Western interests in the Third World and the leading single investor abroad. United States dominance supersedes the Pax Britannica of the late nineteenth century and the clash of capitalist interests that led to both world wars. While there are definite signs in the 1980s that the Pax Americana within the capitalist world is fading somewhat, there is yet no clear alternative on the horizon, and only the United States is in a position to act militarily on behalf of the West on a global scale. Within the framework of American postwar leadership of the West, the basic outlines of contemporary imperialism have been nicely summarized by James O'Connor:

1. The further concentration and centralization of capital, and the integration of the world capitalist economy into the structures of the giant United States-based multinational corporations, or integrated conglomerate monopolistic enterprises; and the acceleration of technological change under the auspices of these corporations.
2. The abandonment of the "free" international market, and the substitution of administered prices in commodity trade and investment; and the determination of profit margins through adjustments in the internal accounting schemes of the multinational corporations.
3. The active participation of state capital in international investment; subsidies and guarantees to private investment; and a global foreign policy which corresponds to the global interests and perspective of the multinational corporation.
4. The consolidation of an international ruling class constituted on the basis of ownership and control of the multinational corporations, and the concomitant decline of national rivalries by the national power elites in the advanced capitalist countries; and the internationalization of the world capital market by the World Bank and other agencies of the international ruling class.
5. The intensification of all of these tendencies arising from the threat of world socialism to the world capitalist system. (1971:121)

In the light of most recent experience, after the collapse of American Vietnam policy and the victory of the MPLA in the Angolan revolution, greater stress should perhaps be put on O'Connor's fifth point. The military power of the United States (and its allies) is no longer superior to that of the Soviet Union (and its allies); there is instead a rough superpower parity. Within the Third World, currently, national liberation movements in smaller countries like Cuba, Vietnam, and Angola are able to get significant military aid from the industrial communist nations of Eastern Europe in their struggles. Despite some basic differences of opinion between Third World revolutionary leaders (Castro, Ho Chi Minh, and Neto) and the Soviet Union on the appropriate model of communism, the USSR and the Warsaw Pact nations have been willing to offer considerable aid. On the other hand, anti-

In every society, people's lives revolve mostly around their work. Most Third World societies, in contrast to both the industrial democracies and the communist systems, suffer from large-scale unemployment and especially underemployment of their human resources. Work is often physically strenuous because of a lack of machine power for transportation, fabrication of materials, agricultural production, communications, and marketing of goods. In the following photos, notice the tools available, the physical content of the work, and the marketing system for the products.

Top: Indian market women in Quito, Ecuador (photo by Ron McDonald). Bottom: A Kenyan market center (photo by Jim Newman).

Left: A village bicycle mechanic in India. Below: Working at a cook stove in rural India. (Photos by Sue Wadley.)

Above: Street vendors in urban India (photo by Barbara Miller). Left: Making rope in a Tanzanian village (photo by Jim Newman).

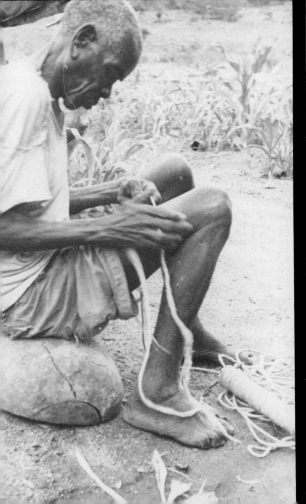

Top: A Kenyan village market (photo by Jim Newman). Bottom: An open-air market in Mexico (photo by Ron McDonald).

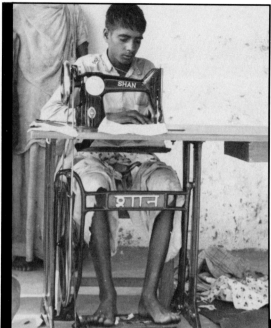

Right: A village tailor in India (photo by Sue Wadley). Below: Making rice flour at home in Luzon, Philippines (photo by John Tyo).

Right: Grinding
betel nut in Luzon,
Philippines (photo
by John Tyo).
Below: Indian
laborers at grain
harvest (photo by
Sue Wadley).

In most societies, housing conditions are a strong indicator of the material standard of living. In the Third World, massive urban slums, homeless people, and impoverished rural areas contrast with the houses of a small middle class and the country estates and luxury city homes of a tiny elite. Compare the following photos with the standards of housing of American society.

Above: Hillside slums overlooking Rio de Janeiro, Brazil. Below: Lower-class housing in Guayaquil, Ecuador. (Photos by Ron McDonald)

Top: Upper-class estate in Nairobi, Kenya. Bottom: Middle-class project housing in Nairobi, Kenya. (Photos by Jim Newman) Facing page, top: Poor peasant housing in rural Mexico (photo by Ron McDonald). Facing page, bottom: Village housing on stilts, Benin, West Africa (photo by Deborah Pellow).

Top: Company-town housing for workers in Recife, Brazil. Bottom: Slums of Rio de Janeiro, Brazil. (Photos by Ron McDonald) Facing page, top: Middle-class housing in Ahmedabad, India (photo by Barbara Miller). Facing page, bottom: Mud, brick, and thatch rural housing in India (photo by Sue Wadley).

The quality of life for Third World peoples depends on factors such as access to clean water, disposal of urban garbage and sewage, protection from criminal and social violence, and the physical possibility of maintaining family life. Rapid population and urban growth, combined with the inequalities of economic development, degrade the environment for large sections of the population.

Top: Trying to overcome cultural and social cleavages in India (photo by Robert Kearney). Bottom: A mountain of garbage creates a serious health hazard for local residents of Jakarta, Indonesia (photo by John Tyo). Facing page, top: Fresh water supply in a Kenyan small town (photo by Jim Newman). Facing page, middle: Population control is a major issue in India and many poor nations (photo by Sue Wadley and Bruce Derr). Facing page, bottom: Homeless children in Bogotá, Colombia. An estimated 150,000 homeless children live in Bogotá alone (photo by Ron McDonald).

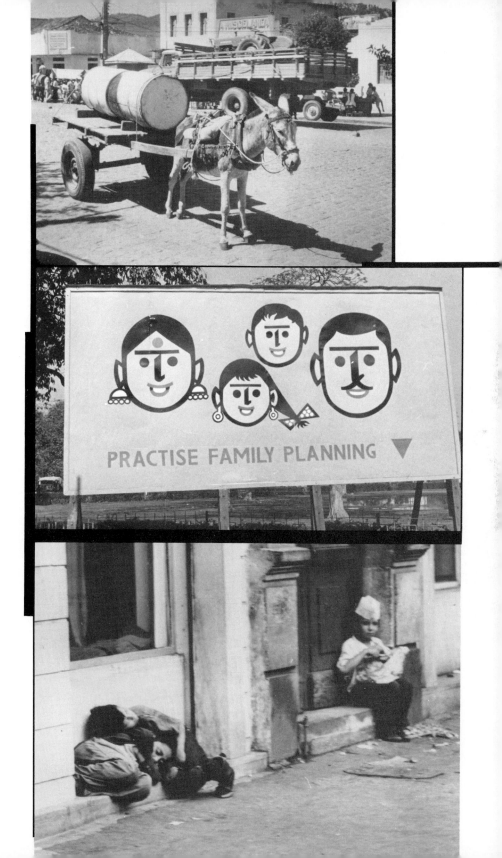

PRACTISE FAMILY PLANNING

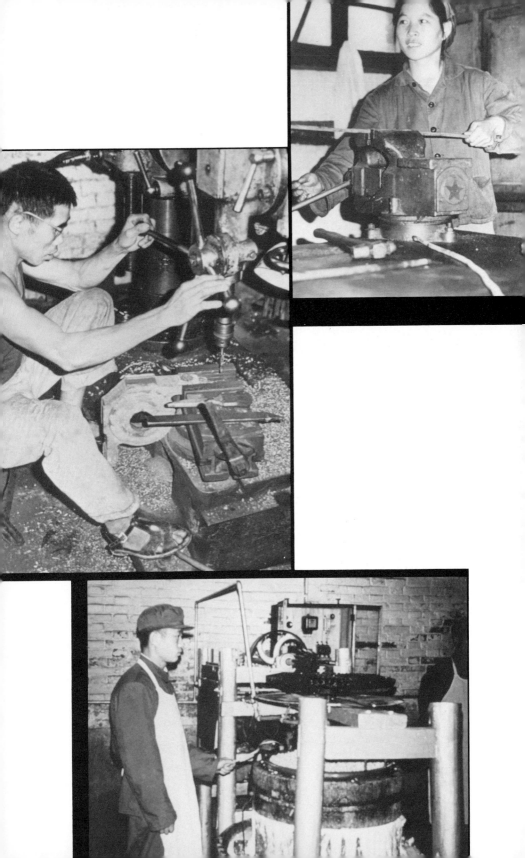

The Chinese system during Mao's period of leadership combined distinctive features of a rural commune-centered economic development strategy with mass propaganda campaigns to change individual behavior and a health care system provided by a corps of village "barefoot doctors" who used a mixture of traditional and Western medicine. These photos by Sari and Doug Biklen provide a look at aspects of the Maoist model.

Above: "Save the Rice Crop": propaganda as a means for social transformation. Facing page, top: A factory apprentice on a rural commune. Facing page, middle: A machine-tool worker on a rural commune. Facing page, bottom: A Chinese army soldier working in a bean curd plant.

Left: A day-care center at the workplace in China. Below: Acupuncture treatment for a deaf Chinese girl.

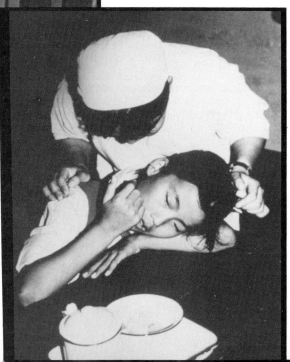

imperialist movements, if they are to resist overt or covert intervention by Western forces (as in Chile in 1973, Guatemala in 1954, Iran in 1952, Angola in 1975, Bay of Pigs in 1961, Dominican Republic in 1965), must generally turn to the USSR for political and military support and perhaps in the longer run for organizational and ideological models as well.

Observers of the current stage of imperialism have noted several modifications in its pattern of economic exploitation. Paul Sweezy, Harry Magdoff, David Horowitz, and James O'Connor have noted: (1) growing investment in manufacturing as opposed to mining and agriculture; (2) a growing role for government loans and international bank credits as opposed to private investment; (3) growing collaboration of the Third World bourgeoisie with Western capital, as opposed to its potential competition with Western capital; (4) growth of self-financing from internal funds for expansion abroad by the major MNCs; and (5) growth of foreign arms sales and the U.S. armaments industry generally as a necessary component of a healthy U.S. economy. Magdoff in particular stresses the connection between imperialism and the armaments industry in providing employment in the United States, maintaining a favorable balance of trade, and for support of client regimes with pro-Western policies.

THE SPECIAL ROLE OF THE MULTINATIONAL CORPORATION

The role of the MNCs has assumed special importance in recent analyses of imperialism, although its development was already forecast at an early date by Lenin and others. O'Connor has stated that for the world capitalist system, "the multinational corporation has become the instrument for the creation and consolidation of an international ruling class, the only hope for reconciling the antagonisms between national and international interests" (1971:141). The MNCs are the main connecting link between the developed, rich nations and the Third World nations.

There is much debate over the effects of MNCs on the development of Third World nations. Defenders of the MNCs say that the multinationals are the best hope for economic progress in the poorer countries. They argue that perhaps only the MNCs have the capital capacity, management, marketing, and technology resources that the less-developed nations require for the economic growth that has already taken place in the rich nations of the north. MNCs are the most viable mechanism for immediate investment and job creation in the less-developed countries (LDCs) and also for the transfer of business skills and production know-how to Third World employees. What the large corporations made possible in the already developed nations, they should also be capable of in the LDCs, given sufficient freedom of operation and a favorable investment climate. Economics professor Harry

Johnson, one of the enthusiasts of the MNCs, sees them as the most potent agent for the economic transformation of the Third World, the most efficient economic decision makers on a global scale, and indeed the best hope for overcoming national conflicts and narrow interests in the development of a single global system, integrated both politically and economically (Johnson, 1971:242-52).

Even the most die-hard supporters of multinationals now realize that there are growing doubts about the benefits that the MNCs may bring. There are serious arguments that development that benefits Third World peoples can *never* be expected from a system dominated by foreign-owned corporations. Magdoff and Sweezy (1971) point out first that the MNCs are not multinational in ownership or control. For all practical purposes, MNCs are owned and led by a single national group, whether American, British, Japanese, German, or Dutch. (There are two exceptions: Royal Dutch/Shell and Unilever, which are genuine British-Dutch partnerships in ownership.) Sweezy and Magdoff argue that, given the overriding interest of Western investors in high profits, foreign corporate domination of Third World economies can damage their development prospects and undermine newly achieved national independence. In particular, Third World nations have real fears about the record of MNC behavior:

1. Fear that the international corporation will take too much and leave too little. The fear is often expressed that the big foreign corporation will take away the national resources (oil, iron ore, foodstuffs, etc.), all the profits, the most able local people (hence the brain drain), and leave only the crumbs in the form of low wages, low compared to the wages the same corporations pay at home.
2. Fear that the international corporation will crush local competition and quickly achieve a monopolistic dominance of the local market if not the local economy. "Who can compete with the enormous technical resources of a giant corporation whose annual sales are more than the French national budget?"
3. Fear of becoming dependent on foreign sources for modern technology needed for national defense, and for being competitive in world markets.
4. Fear that the international corporation's local subsidiary will be used as an instrument of foreign policy by the government of the parent company. For example, in the case of a U.S. subsidiary, fear that the U.S. government will prohibit sales to certain markets (Red China, Cuba, North Korea, North Vietnam, etc.); or that the U.S. government will prohibit the parent from sending certain technology to the subsidiary which technology would be useful locally for national defense or for other purposes; or fear that the U.S. government will prevent the U.S. parent from sending new capital to the local subsidiary, and will require the local subsidiary to remit virtually all of its earnings home, thus damaging the balance of payments of the local government.
5. Fear that the good jobs will be given to nationals of the parent company and not to local nationals.

6. Fear that decisions will be taken by the parent company in callous disregard for their impact on the local town, province, or even on the national economy. For example—a decision to close down a factory and put thousands of workers out of jobs. (Magdoff and Sweezy, 1971:109)

These fears grow out of bitter experience, not fancy, and lead to the conclusion that an MNC-dominated economy would not produce benefits for the average citizen; rather it would produce a modern underdevelopment, with extremely skewed benefits and costs. Further, it is all too clear that the MNCs, and not only the American MNCs, are not simply the helpless and peaceful businessmen they picture themselves to be. Harry Magdoff and James Petras in particular have highlighted the intimate relationship between U.S. foreign and military policy and the interests of the U.S. multinationals. In any number of case studies, of which United States intervention against the elected Chilean government of Salvador Allende from 1970 to 1973 is only a recent well-publicized example, U.S. MNCs have attempted, through privileged links to the State Department, the CIA, and the Pentagon, to undermine policies and overthrow regimes that threaten their interests (to make and repatriate profits to shareholders). The MNC would of course prefer not to have to "get tough" in order to assure a favorable investment climate; but in fact it does get tough when its profit margins are at stake, and it can call in some pretty powerful friends to help it get its way.

DEPENDENCY: THE DEVELOPMENT OF UNDERDEVELOPMENT

In the eyes of Western leaders and most Western economists, the tasks of economic, social, and political development in the Third World have been seen as the duplication, with perhaps some complicating factors, of the West's transition from essentially feudal, agrarian systems to modern, urban-dominated systems. In this view, development in the Third World is a continuation through diffusion of the Western pattern begun at an earlier point in time. The diffusion perspective treats the growth of foreign commerce with the West and the penetration of Western capital, technology, and MNCs as positive signs of development which challenge the feudal/traditional and less productive institutions of Third World societies. These agents of change, in this view, strengthen new and growing urban business elites and foster the growth of Western middle-class life-styles, including consumer desires and social attitudes (see Chilcote and Edelstein, 1974, for a good summary and critique).

From the cities, the forces of modernization challenge rural landowning oligarchs and create conditions of a "dual society" in transition, part modern and part feudal. Most important from the Western diffusionist perspective is support for local pro-Western groups, mainly friendly governments, business elites, and military leaders, who permit and encourage Western finance and corporate involvement in their society and support the international change agents, primarily Western banking and business organizations. Until the 1960s, the Western diffusionist view was the dominant perspective on the prospects for Third World development.

Seen from the vantage point of the Third World nations, the theory of imperialism and the special role of the MNC have given rise, in more recent years, to a new explanation for the growing gap between rich and poor nations and for the inability of even the best-suited candidates for development (mainly in Latin America) to produce anything like the healthy industrial growth pattern of the Western powers in an earlier era. Special hopes and much publicity had been given to the Alliance for Progress, a United States-sponsored investment and aid program of the 1960s, the goal of which was to achieve a breakthrough to sustained and independent economic development for at least several Latin American nations. The spectacular failure of the Alliance (judged by both friends and critics) led to a thorough critique of conventional Western models (Rostow, Kuznets) of economic development, which spelled out a general "do it like we did it" approach. This critique in turn led to a new theory of dependency, which accounted for the failure of Western-style development to appear in Latin America and also predicted that real development would not appear as long as the dependency syndrome lasted. Begun originally with special focus on the Alliance for Progress by a group of Latin American economists (Dos Santos, Sunkel, Cardoso, Gonzalez Casanova, and later especially Andre Gunder Frank), the main thrust of the dependency theory has now been extended to African and Asian regions of the Third World by analysts like Samir Amin, Giovanni Arrighi, and Pierre Jalee. While there are many differences of emphasis among dependency theorists and of opinions about the best future course for the Third World, there is agreement on one fundamental point, which contradicts the previously held (Western) model for development. That point is that the problems of Third World systems cannot be solved under conditions of Western corporate and financial domination over their natural and human resources.

Dependency theorists point out that during the nineteenth-century industrialization of the West, there were no already developed nations whose economic power could effectively control or manipulate the paths of development. None of the now-wealthy nations of the West were industrialized primarily or even substantially by foreign corporations. While there was some German investment in France, some British investment in the United States, and so forth, the modernization of each economy was financed and managed overwhelmingly by the industrial capitalist class of each individual nation. Japan, the one Asian nation that successfully industrialized in the late nineteenth century, did so by first fighting off Western imperialism and by prohibiting foreign investment from coming into Japan; in current jargon, it "delinked" itself from the world capitalist system in order to independently develop its economy from internal sources and under the leadership of a native entrepreneurial class. Only then did Japan join the European powers in imperialist exploitation of China and Southeast Asia. In the twentieth century, the Soviet Union is the other example of a latecomer nation that has successfully industrialized itself, and in this case too it was by "delinking" or isolating itself from the world capitalist system, although not under the leadership of a classic industrial bourgeoisie but of a domestic communist vanguard party. Delinking the economies of the Third World nations from the world capitalist system, rather than simply improving the terms of trade, is now viewed by many dependency theorists as the best way for these nations to get a development process in motion that is directed to the needs of their own peoples. Delinking of a Third World economy from the world capitalist system in all probability will mean kicking out the MNCs and foreign military bases and resisting the temptation to import many Western-style consumer goods that the well-to-do economic elite strata want.

Dependency in the Third World nations means that the major economic changes will be geared not to needs of local citizens but to the needs of the great consumer societies of the Western democracies and to those of the great corporations that market their products in these wealthy societies. This dependency syndrome has not decreased but increased since formal decolonization in Africa, Asia, and parts of Latin America since World War II. If partial industrialization in the Third World does occur under such conditions, it is increasingly dominated by foreign ownership, either directly or indirectly through foreign financing of government projects and government industries. This control includes control over actual production, marketing, technology, and, of course, profits for reinvestment. The MNCs increasingly have the advantage over domestically owned and smaller corporations; indeed, the top multinationals' total annual sales are greater than the gross national products of most Third World nations, and they employ more skilled workers, highly trained technicians, and researchers than are available to entire Third World countries. One result of MNC takeovers or control of formerly nationally owned firms is that profits from their operations flow abroad to Western investors. In fact, by several estimates the flow of profits from the Third World to the West is considerably greater than new investment by the West in the economies of the Third World. Dos Santos (1971:232) estimates that between 1946 and 1967, for every dollar that U.S. companies invested in Latin America, 2.73 dollars were taken out of Latin America by U.S. companies. Baran and Sweezy (1971:77) have calculated that, between 1950 and 1961, U.S. firms brought back to U.S. stockholders $9.5 billion *more* than they sent out as new investment abroad. In effect, the poorer nations, primarily through the activities of the multinationals, have been giving aid to the rich nations by allowing their economic wealth to be drained by external forces. And at the same time that the MNCs are draining more from the Third World than they are investing, Third World governments are forced to borrow from Western governments and international banks to pay for imports. The LDCs are increasingly becoming the world's debtor nations, and several are currently on the verge of default on their debts. For the non-OPEC Third World nations, additional annual debts mounted from $9 billion in 1973 to $28 billion in 1974 and $38 billion in 1975; total indebtedness of the Third World to governments, international and national banks, and private lenders was estimated in 1975 at between $150 and $200 billion (Payer, 1976:5) and at more than $700 billion by 1985 (World Bank, 1986).

Dependent economic development is tied to social and political dependency, the creation of clientele or comprador social elites whose affluence comes from serving powerful foreign interests. This comprador stratum includes the local bourgeoisie, too weak to compete with the MNCs but able to act as a junior partner in middleman or service roles. It includes the government higher bureaucracy, which allows for multinational activity, suppresses local dissent and militant union activity, and provides a tiny island of luxury consumption through the pilfering of state funds and bribes from the multinationals. These islands of affluence can be seen in nearly every Third World capital city, rising up out of the cardboard and tin-can shantytowns that surround the capital. And it includes the military elite, whose weapons, training, and often command come from United States, British, and French sources. Third World military establishments supported by the West have the primary mission of suppressing internal rebellion and only secondarily the defense of the nation's borders.

Once again, this pattern of social and political dependency is radically different from that of the growth of the business class, of the modern state bureaucracy, and of the professional military in the West. In the United States, Britain, France, Germany, and Japan, and in the smaller capitalist nations as well, the industrial bourgeoisie fulfilled a vital role in the industrialization process, a role that the comprador middle classes of the Third World nations are less and less able to do. Frantz Fanon has poignantly summarized this situation in the African nations:

> THE national bourgeoisie will be quite content with the role of the Western bourgeoisie's business agent, and it will play its part without any complexes in a most dignified manner. But this same lucrative role, this cheapjack's function, this meanness of outlook, and this absence of ambition symbolize the incapability of the national middle class to fulfill its historic role of the bourgeoisie. Here, the dynamic pioneer aspect, the characteristics of the inventor and of the discoverer of new worlds which are found in all national bourgeoisies, is lamentably absent. In

the colonial countries, the spirit of indulgence is dominant at the core of the bourgeoisie; and this is because the national bourgeoisie identifies itself with the Western bourgeoisie along its path of negation and decadence without ever having emulated it in its first stages of exploration and invention. . . . In its beginnings, the national bourgeoisie of the colonial countries identifies itself with the decadence of the bourgeoisie of the West. We need not think it is jumping ahead; it is in fact beginning at the end. It is already senile before it has come to know the petulance, the fearlessness, or the will to succeed of youth. (1971:305-6)

James Cockcroft, Andre Gunder Frank, and Dale Johnson (1972) make much the same point about Latin America, emphasizing not only the inability of the national bourgeoisie in these countries, despite one hundred fifty years of formal political independence, to generate self-sustaining economic growth, but its declining prospects for ever doing so.

THE close correspondence between the interests of Latin America's bourgeoisies and those of foreign investors, their dependence upon international support for survival against the forces of nationalism and revolution, and the growing importance of the multinational corporation all testify to the impact of the metropolis upon the class structures of the satellites. The so-called "national" and "progressive" bourgeoisie in Latin America is neither nationalist nor progressive—it is a dependent, comprador bourgeoisie. Latin America's bourgeoisies have been the active agents of foreign economic penetration—and related phenomena such as increased militarization—over the past two decades. The masses, of course, continued to produce the wealth and pay the price for this ongoing misdevelopment. (P. xviii)

Dependency must be looked at in all of its many aspects, for it is a syndrome or system of dependency that shapes (or misshapes) the basic economic, social, political, and military developments in the Third World. Not democracy, or military dictatorship, or one-party rule, or monarchy, but rather dependency is the real system in these nations. The formal political system of most Third World nations, whether it is called a military junta, a civilian dictatorship, or a multiparty parliamentary democracy, is less important (though for other purposes not unimportant) to an understanding of the real consequences, the real economic and social outcomes of the society. The formal political systems of Third World nations may be viewed, in fact, as attempted responses to the dependency syndrome and to the real consequences of dependency.

THIRD WORLD POLITICS: REACTIONS TO DEPENDENCY

In the following chapters we will examine the widely perceived feeling that most Third World systems are unsuccessful in comparison with both the advanced capitalist democracies and the communist systems in providing "healthy" outcomes in material well-being, social equality, personal liberty, and quality of life for their citizens. This lack of success, perceived by increasingly wider groups of the population, lies at the heart of the political instability in the Third World, although this instability may be expressed in a great variety of ways. Political instability, as Robert Gamer (1976) has nicely expressed it, is also tied to the personal insecurity of the great majority of citizens living in these changing but relatively unsuccessful dependent systems:

> A healthy political system will provide a great many of its citizens with a basic human need—a stable personal environment. Developing nations once contained healthy political systems; since the introduction of extensive commerce they no longer do. This is because political systems once emerged from the societies in which indigenous people lived. Today, political systems are actually quite separate from indigenous social systems, and they will remain so until the structure of international trade changes. (P. viii)

Dependency as a system of misdevelopment does not fulfill basic human needs for many or even most of its citizens; one might well expect that such a system would breed discontent, revolt, and eventually revolution. Indeed, most of the readers of this text, on first thought, would surely find an average Third World standard of living and the social inequities tied to it totally unacceptable and would fight, rebel, or lead a struggle to improve matters. Or would they? Dependency and underdevelopment do breed discontent, frustration, and anger, but these feelings are not always channeled into opposition to the system. Misdevelopment also produces ignorance, despair, hopelessness, and fatalism (see chapter 16), which lead people (not only in the Third World, to be sure) to try to solve or avoid their problems through alcohol, drugs, gambling, crime, random violence, and otherworldly mysticism, including both established religions and newfound sects or cults. Migration to another land is always more practical than fighting to radically restructure one's own native country, so millions of dissatisfied or desperate Third Worlders choose emigration over social struggle.

Still, although thoroughgoing social revolution is relatively infrequent, there is enough political dissatisfaction generated within the dependency syndrome to cause frequent changes in government institutions, structures, and official programs in most Third World systems. There are several recurring political responses to dependency that characterize different Third World systems at given times. These regular or modal response patterns correspond to competing elites or would-be leaders within the society, and each pattern attempts in some way to establish the legitimacy of the regime. These patterns are: (1) nationalism, (2) socialism, (3) dependent capitalism, (4) democracy, and (5) communism.

Nationalist regimes, very often in the form of military or military-backed dictatorships or juntas, emphasize the unity of the people across all classes in the defense of the national interest. Real and concocted foreign threats and "alien" ethnic or ideological forces provide fertile soil for a nationalist elite to assume power. For societies whose independence is only a recent achievement and whose practical dependence is a demeaning of national pride, nationalism is a very powerful force indeed. The Peruvian military junta under Bermudez and the Videla regime in Argentina rallied nationalist support behind territorial claims to parts of Chile. Idi Amin aroused nationalist sentiment against "foreign" Indian and Pakistani merchants in Uganda. The Suharto-led junta in Indonesia utilized nationalism against an "alien" Chinese communist ideology. The Nigerian military regime stressed unity of the nation against a secessionist Ibo movement in the Biafran civil war. President Marcos of the Philippines was aided by Catholic nationalist sentiment in his struggle against an insurgent Moslem nationalist minority in the southern islands of his country.

Sometimes nationalists will call for tighter control over foreign-owned companies, the sale of foreign-owned firms to local businessmen, or nationalization of these businesses. Even the right-wing Chilean Nationalist party, despite its hatred for the socialist government of Salvador Allende, supported the expropriation of the American-owned copper companies in Chile. Nationalist regimes may try to stimulate the national bourgeoisie to greater activity and may give them help in competing against foreign firms. Nationalism seeks its legitimacy through attempts to restore a sense of patriotic pride in systems where dependency has damaged pride in country in so many ways.

Third World socialism as a patterned response to dependency builds an image of a more just society, a new path to socialism that is neither capitalist nor communist. Generally there is no comprehensive nationalization of foreign-owned companies or of the native bourgeoisie and no central planning of the economy, but in foreign policy there is a militant anti-imperialism that has placed several of these socialist systems in the vanguard of Third Worldism in the North-South confrontation. These non-Marxist socialisms seek their legitimacy in the priority given to popular welfare, eduation, and local development programs. Very often this type of socialism is tied to some strong traditional ethic that denies the necessity of class struggle. Thus, Julius Nyerere in Tanzania and Kwame Nkrumah in Ghana had pictured an African socialism based on the asserted classlessness of African traditional society. Tanzania's program, embodied in the Arusha Declaration, stressed economic self-reliance, local village development, and curtailment of Western-style consumer imports. President Chadli Bendjedid of Algeria, Colonel Quadaffi of Libya, and the ruling Baath parties of Syria and Iraq have based their programs on some concept of Arab socialism that attempts to combine pan-Arabist sentiment, some elements of Islamic tradition, and some elements of popular welfare. The common thread of Arab socialism would seem to rest with its denial of class concepts of society, both capitalist and Marxist. In Latin America, there are Christian socialist movements, both within the Catholic church and as political parties or factions, seeking to integrate Christian theology with popular desires for social justice. The legitimacy of Third World socialism depends on its popular association with social justice and welfare, while stressing anti-imperialism in its foreign policy.

Dependent capitalism (or comprador capitalism) in the Third World represents an acceptance of the dependent status of the economy within the world capitalist system and attempts to maximize its own market position within that system. Foreign investment is openly welcomed, encouraged, even given tax breaks denied to local businesses. Workers are not allowed to form independent labor unions, so that a tamed labor force is offered for foreign corporations to exploit. Local businessmen play assorted middleman roles for the MNCs, mainly in catering to the needs of Western personnel:

> THE national bourgeoisie organizes centers of rest and relaxation and pleasure resorts to meet the wishes of the Western bourgeoisie. Such activity is given the name of tourism, and for the occasion will be built up as a national industry. If proof is needed of the eventual transformation of certain elements of the ex-native bourgeoisie into the organizers of parties for their Western opposite numbers, it is worth while having a look at what has happened in Latin America. The casinos of Havana and of Mexico, the beaches of Rio, the little Brazilian and Mexican girls, the half-breed thirteen-year-olds, the ports of Acapulco and Copacabana—all these are the stigma of this depravation of the national middle class. Because it is bereft of ideas, because it lives to itself and cuts itself off from the people, undermined by its hereditary incapacity to think in terms of all the problems of the nation as seen from the point of view of the whole of that nation, the national middle class will have nothing better to do than to take on the role of manager for Western enterprise, and it will in practice set up its country as the brothel of Europe. (Fanon, 1971:306)

Nicaragua under the Somoza family dictatorship, South Korea under General Park Chung Hee, the Ivory Coast under President Houphuët-Boigny, Iran under the Shah's regime, Taiwan under Chiang Kai-shek, Zaire under Mobutu, and Mexico during the presidency of Miguel Alemán best characterize the strategy of compradorism. These systems are the most pro-Western in foreign policy, are often dependent on the United States, Britain, or France for extensive military aid and in general are less loyal to the Third World position in the North-South debate. Their own claim to political legitimacy rests upon economic growth and a Western-style level of consumption for a small but influential urban middle class.

Democracy deserves to be mentioned here as one of the major patterns, primarily because the most populous democracy, India, is a Third World nation. Other Third World democracies include Sri Lanka, Venezuela, Turkey, Colombia, and Jamaica. Chile before the 1973 fascist coup, the Philippines before Marcos's dictatorship in 1972, Brazil before the military coup in 1964, Uruguay before the creeping military takeover in the mid-1970s, and Lebanon before the 1970s civil war all had rather extensive experience in democracy, including freedom of speech and press, open party competition, and independent trade unionism. The list of casualties among Third World democracies indicates how difficult it is for this system-type to survive over an extended period in the LDCs; yet the example of India over the last thirty years indicates that even in a very poor nation, and in so many ways a very divided nation, personal liberty is also a valued goal. In 1975 and 1976, during the so-called emergency period of limited dictatorship by Prime Minister Indira Gandhi, it seemed as though Indian democracy was about to crumble. Yet Mrs. Gandhi did not, by most accounts, try to establish a full-blown dictatorship; rather she called for elections, which she lost, and after losing peacefully turned over the reins of government. Whatever the damage done to the personal liberty of both ordinary citizens and oppositional leaders during the eighteen-month emergency, the main point remains that the whole structure of Indian democracy did not collapse like a house of cards, as had been the case in many other countries. Third World democracies cannot afford to ignore the values of economic development and social welfare, but their main claim to legitimacy rests on a commitment to personal liberty. For many newly independent nations, where under colonial rule there was no right to vote, no right to free trade unionism, no free press, these liberties are not unimportant and will continue to express some desires of the peoples of the Third World. The return to democratic, elected government in Argentina, Brazil, Peru, Uruguay, and Ecuador in the 1980s, after extended periods of military rule, are further evidence of the legitimacy of democracy in the Third World.

A major systemic alternative for the Third World nations is, of course, communism, discussed in chapters 7 to 11. We have already noted the growing number of less-developed nations (China, North Korea, Cuba, Vietnam, Angola, Mozambique) that have undergone social revolutions leading to the establishment of communist systems, though with differing strategies for development. Communism in the Third World has an appeal based on its record of economic development, greater social equality, and successes in some quality of life areas (crime, unemployment, corruption). Communism also has the effect of significantly "delinking" a Third World economy from the world capitalist market, first through the expropriation of foreign and native-owned firms, and second through the economic boycott that the Western nations then placed on countries like China, Vietnam, North Korea, and Cuba. There is still no global socialist economic system comparable in scope to the world capitalist system, so that the economic embargoes on trade with China, Cuba, North Korea, and Vietnam have, for better or for worse, forced them to be much more self-reliant in their own paths to communism. This self-reliance often contains a strong appeal to nationalism and patriotism as well as a commitment to an international struggle against Western imperialism. In this sense, Third World communism blends both nationalist and internationalist appeals with its other commitments and achievements. As discussed in chapter 10, personal liberty is not one of the priorities of communism, and this does cost communism some support among Third World peoples. The fall of the Pol Pot regime in Cambodia in early 1979 at the hands of rebel Cambodians backed by powerful Vietnamese units may be the first example of a communist regime overthrown in no small measure due to its brutal suppression of the most basic personal liberties of its people.

We could have mentioned monarchy, populism, and fascism as Third World patterns that attempt to solve the riddle of political legitimacy under conditions of dependency. Monarchy, where it still exists, rests on traditional aristocracy, often with religious underpinnings ("divine right") for its legitimacy. Populism, as in Argentina under Juan Perón or in Mexico under Cardenas, is somewhat akin to Third World socialism but has generally lacked the longer-run vision of either socialism or communism and has, therefore, been more often associated with a particular charismatic leader. Third World fascism stresses an ultranationalist, violent, antisocialist, anticommunist, antidemocratic rhetoric, generally glorifies the role of the military, and often utilizes racist slogans and programs against ethnic groups or neighboring states. The Fatherland and Liberty Front in Chile, the Greek EOKA movement on the island of Cyprus, the semisecret Broederbond elite within the Nationalist party in South Africa, and the National Salvation party in Turkey are examples of this tendency.

In many if not most Third World nations, there is a considerable overlapping of many of these features. Socialist systems, dependent capitalist systems, and both democratic and communist systems may all use nationalist sentiment to strengthen their legitimacy. Democratic India certainly utilized nationalism in its annexation of Goa and in its border wars with Pakistan. The military regime of Juan Alvarado Velasco combined elements of socialism and nationalism in its agrarian reform and expropriations of some multinationals in Peru in the early 1970s. President Kenyatta used the term "African socialism" to describe his KANU system in Kenya, although it contained little concern for popular welfare and a lot of opportunity for foreign investment. Thailand's political system contains a still-active monarchy, a rapidly shifting degree of military-led nationalism, some stop-start attempts at parliamentary democracy, and a relatively constant degree of dependent capitalism, all in addition to an active communist insurgency in the northeast provinces. The Ethiopian military Derg led by Lieutenant Colonel Haile Mengistu Mariam has combined elements of communism without any local communist party, including thoroughgoing expropriation of the property of both feudal landowners and urban bourgeoisie, with strong nationalist appeals to prevent the secession of Eritrean- and Somali-populated provinces. This mixture replaced in a few short years the dynasty of Emperor Haile Selassie, a feudal monarchy closely allied with the West.

Some of the above comments indicate the variety and competition of goals and the pressing problems of the Third World. The shifting of priorities and the instability of many systems indicate the failures to provide what Gamer has called a "healthy" political system and increases the opportunities for ambitious contenders to take over in the *name* of some different approach. We should recognize that names like socialism, communism, democracy, nationalism, and capitalism are important symbols for different social groups, independent of whether actual policy outcomes are consistent with the legitimizing symbol. Without being overly cynical, one should question whether actual practice measures up to announced or official ideals. As a not-so-famous American attorney general once said about his own administration: "Watch what we do, not what we say." This rule of thumb applies to all systems, of course, but it is most important in those systems that are, on a global scale, least successful and therefore more dependent on symbolic manipulation to try to maintain legitimacy.

Chapter 13

Economic Development—
Growth and the Widening Gap

THIS CHAPTER PRESENTS DATA AND interpretations of economic development in the Third World nations. In some ways, the data on Third World growth and levels of economic welfare point up the wide disparities of development within the Third World, from an oil-rich Kuwait or Libya to an urban and semideveloped Argentina to the widespread poverty of Pakistan and India. Yet, despite this disparity among the nations included in the Third World category, the main points of this chapter remain those common factors that characterize economic development in the Third World generally and that separate this development from both the earlier capitalist industrialization of the West and the industrialization of the USSR and Eastern Europe. This pattern of Third World economic growth, even where it has produced high rates of GNP increase, has not created the same correlates in education, housing, health, and nutrition for the people as occurred in the liberal democracies or the communist systems. Urbanization and population growth do not correlate with industrialization and job creation, aggregate economic growth does not signify the emergence of either a native business class or a government bureaucracy capable of planning and promoting a self-sustaining industrialization. Rather, development has been dependent, to an increasing extent, on MNCs owned and managed by Western interests and on financial lending institutions (national and international) dominated by Western banks and governments.

ECONOMIC GROWTH AND POPULATION GROWTH

An initial point to be stressed in any discussion of Third World economic development is the rapid population growth that has complicated all attempts to raise standards of living for the people of these nations. A second point is that despite the tremendous increases in population, economic output (the total value of goods and services produced) has still managed some modest gains in GNP/capita for most, though not all, Third World nations. Unfortunately, the record is worst for the poorest of the poor, nations like Bangladesh, Somalia, Chad, Niger, and Afghanistan. Especially in comparison with both the liberal democracies and the communist systems, annual

233

rates of population growth (about 2.9 percent in Latin America, 2.5 percent in Africa, and 2.7 percent in Asia from 1950 to 1970) have been dramatically higher, which puts greater pressure on resources and requires higher levels of growth just to remain at the present standard of living. On the other hand, Third World nations have done fairly well (on average) in recent years in increasing national economic production (GNP), providing a real increase per person of 2.9 percent per year. This is no small achievement, and in some respects economic development should be regarded as the most favorable area of system performance.

Table 13.1 Third World Population and Economic Growth

	Population (millions 1984)	Annual Population Growth Rate 1965-73	Annual Population Growth Rate 1973-84	GNP/capita Growth Rate 1965-84
Mexico	76.8	3.3	2.9	2.9
Brazil	132.6	2.5	2.3	4.6
Nigeria	96.5	2.5	2.8	2.8
Kenya	19.6	3.8	4.0	2.1
Egypt	45.9	2.2	2.6	4.3
India	749.2	2.3	2.3	1.6
Indonesia	158.9	2.1	2.3	4.9
Averages:				
Third World		2.5	2.2	2.9
Liberal democracies		1.0	0.8	2.4
East European communist nations		0.8	0.8	4.0[a]

a. 1960-1975

Sources: World Bank, *World Bank Atlas*, 1977; World Bank, *World Development Report*, 1986.

The rapid population growth in Third World areas is a phenomenon of the post-World War II period and is unprecedented in human history. Prior to World War I, world population growth was about 0.6 percent per year. Population growth was somewhat higher in the more developed nations of Europe and North America than in the less developed regions. In the latter stages of Western colonialism, however, the more advanced medical practices of the West spread noticeably throughout the colonies and semi-colonies, producing a rapid drop in mortality (death) rates, while birthrates remained high. Between the 1940s and the 1960s, annual population growth rates doubled for the Third World, from about 1.2 percent to 2.4 percent. And although there is currently evidence that the increase in population growth rates peaked in the 1970s at about 2.7–2.8 percent, this is a high figure for poor nations struggling to modernize their economies and raise the level of general welfare, in many cases now at bare subsistence.

French economist Paul Bairoch notes that when the Western nations began their industrial revolutions in the eighteenth and nineteenth centuries, they too experienced an increase in population growth rates, but only a modest increase from about 0.5 percent to 0.7 percent (Bairoch, 1975:7–8). The Third World nations are in this respect, as in so many others, faced with an entirely different situation and are not likely to be able to duplicate or tolerate the pattern of development that typified the Western world one hundred and fifty to two hundred years ago.

Even if population planning were to make unexpected and radical advances toward lowering the birthrate, the effects of the population inflation of the past generation would continue to affect Third World prospects for development in the future, since the absolute number of women of child-bearing age has increased so dramatically. In the present situation, the extraordinarily high rate of population growth, along with considerably shorter life expectancy, has created a youthful age distribution in most Third World nations. Whereas in the developed countries only about 27 percent of the population is under fifteen years of age and 10 percent is over sixty-five, in the Third World 41 percent is under fifteen and only 3 percent is over sixty-five. This means that a smaller proportion of the Third World population (56 percent compared with 63 percent) is of working age (fifteen to sixty-five). The disparity is even greater when we take into account the greater proportion of people (mainly women) tied to child care and the higher proportion of physical infirmity and invalidism among working-age people in the Third World (Uri, 1976:28–29). This means that a smaller segment of the total population is working (or seeking work) to support dependents (children, the aged, or invalids). For every 100 people active in the workforce in the Third World, there are 162 dependents to support; the comparable number of dependents for the developed nations is 123. These figures indicate that the Third World working population has to increase productivity more to achieve a real per capita gain than is true for the developed nations. Once again, the Third World must run harder just to stay at current levels, run harder to keep from falling further behind, let alone close the gap between themselves and the rich nations.

DEVELOPMENT OF UNDERDEVELOPMENT: AGRICULTURE

Still, it would seem that in general the Third World has made some progress in raising per capita output (2.9 percent per year), even with the population inflation. This is comparable to the historical rates of per capita growth achieved in the period 1865–1950 by developed nations like the United States (2 percent), Sweden (2.5 percent), and Japan (2.4 percent), and better than nations like Germany (1.4 percent), France (1.3 percent), and Britain (1.2 percent) (Weiskopf et al., 1972:365). But this aggregate-level comparison is misleading, for it masks many crucial differences between what was taking place in the Western nations in the past century and what is happening to the Third World today.

At the time of the industrial revolution in the West, agriculture had already achieved a level of productivity capable of supporting a growing non-farm population without constant threat of famine or need for large-scale import of foodstuffs. While this is currently the case in parts of Latin America (especially Argentina, Brazil, and Chile) and parts of the Middle East, it is definitely not true in most of Asia and Africa. Worse yet, agricultural production per capita has shown virtually no growth and in some regions a decline between the 1930s and the 1970s.

Table 13.2 Growth Rates of Agricultural Production in the Third World

	1934/38 to 1968/72		1971 to 1980	
	Total	*Per Capita*	*Total*	*Per Capita*
Africa	2.4	0.1	1.7	−1.2
Asia	1.9	−0.1	3.5	1.0
Latin America	2.1	−0.3	3.9	1.2
Middle East	2.5	0.5	3.4	0.6
Third World	2.1	0.0	3.3	1.1

SOURCE: Bairoch, 1975; *World Almanac*, 1983.

Paul Bairoch (1975:17–19) points out that the rates of growth for total agricultural production are in most Third World nations quite good and compare favorably with those of most developed nations during their earlier period of industrialization. Only in the United States and Russia during the latter part of the nineteenth century were even higher rates of growth achieved, in large part due to the opening up of new frontiers to settlement and cultivation. This possibility is largely absent in the Third World today, especially in Asia and Saharan Africa, where the food supply is most precarious. The unprecedented population growth in the Third World has eaten up the gains in production and in some cases caused a net decline in per capita food production. The introduction of Western medicine and the rapid fall-off in death rates occurred before the Third World countries had achieved an agricultural revolution. In the West the development of modern medicine was part of an indigenous technology and one of the fruits of industrial modernity itself. By the time medical technology became available to further lower death rates in the West, birthrates had already begun to decline as families began to perceive that more children were surviving to adulthood. This demographic transition from high birthrates and high death rates to (first) lower death rates and (later) lower birthrates will probably take place in the Third World nations as well. A decline in birthrates has now begun. But the timing of this transition, introduced from outside the Third World societies, has brought with it a population explosion before the economic transition to modernity and especially before agricultural development has advanced enough to sustain both population growth and provide for real improvement in the standard of nutrition.

In the late 1960s and early 1970s there was a burst of optimism that a "Green Revolution" was about to transform agricultural production in the Third World. For many years, the Rockefeller Foundation had sponsored research to develop new wheat varieties (and later, in cooperation with the Ford Foundation, rice varieties) that were both high-yielding and resistant to stem rust (blight). A research team headed by Nobel Prize winner Dr. Norman Borlaug did develop several wheat types that were initially tested in Mexico, then in the Middle East, India, and Pakistan. In the small test cases, impressive increases in wheat yields per hectare (one hectare = 10,000 square meters = 2.471 acres) were recorded. A new rice strain (called IR-8) developed in the Philippines also gave much-improved yields and was named the "miracle rice." Introduced on a larger scale in the latter 1960s, these new advances in Western agricultural technology seemed to indicate that a Green Revolution in Third World agriculture was at hand, a revolution that would turn famine-prone nations into cash crop exporters. Lester Brown, in his 1973 book *Seeds of Change: The Green Revolution and International Development in the 1970s,* stated his belief that this agricultural revolution would in turn bolster investment in other sectors of the economy, provide rural employment, and counter the massive migration from countryside to the cities. In a 1970 international conference sponsored by Columbia University, Brown summarized his findings:

> Countries traditionally in food deficit are now using the new seeds and becoming self-sufficient, some actually generating exportable surpluses. The Philippines, the first country to use the new rices on a commercial basis, has ended half a century of dependence on rice imports, becoming a net exporter. Pakistan, as recently as 1968 the second-ranking recipient of United States food aid, has sharply reduced its dependence on food imports and is expected to be self-sufficient in both wheat and rice in 1970. Food imports into India are now less than one-half those of the food crisis years of 1966 and 1967.
>
> Gains in cereal production in countries where the new seeds have been successfully introduced are without precedent. Pakistan increased its wheat harvest 60% between 1967 and 1969. India upped its wheat harvest by one-half from 1965 to 1969. Ceylon's rice harvest increased 34% in two years. (Ward, Runnels, and D'Anjou, 1971:128)

In the 1970s, however, this early optimism was dampened by several factors. First, the increase in yields in India and Pakistan in 1967 and 1968 followed particularly poor harvests in 1965 and 1966; at least part of the early increases was due to favorable weather conditions and not to the new seed varieties. Over the longer period from 1967 to 1972, despite more extensive planting of new "miracle" wheat and rice, food production in the Third World increased by only 2.5 percent annually, which is less than the rate of increase in population (Bairoch, 1975:46). Over the period 1970–1972, Third World grain imports averaged 19.1 million metric tons; this inceased to 23.2 million in 1973 and to 30.3 million in 1974. Total world reserves of grain (including grain that could be produced from now-fallow United States farmland) that had slowly declined from 222 million metric tons in 1961 to 151 million in 1967 did rebound in the first several years of widespread use of the "miracle" seeds, reaching 217 million metric tons by 1970. But in the next four years world reserves shrank again to only 90 million metric tons by 1974 (Howe, 1975:244–45). Over the next decade, the Green Revolution did in fact increase grain production in India and Pakistan to the point where they no longer had to import basic cereals; rice production in the Philippines also expanded to the point where rice became an export commodity. But, while the new "miracle" seeds have made a sizeable impact in selected nations, the Green Revolution has not yet spread more generally through the Third World and has been notably absent in Africa.

Further, in order to produce higher yields, the new seed varieties require larger inputs of fertilizer and pesticides and better-controlled irrigation than the traditional varieties they replace. Pesticides and fertilizers are petroleum-based products, and the costs of these inputs have risen rapidly as the price of crude oil and its derivatives has escalated. Soviet analyst V. G. Rastyannikov, also a participant at the 1970 Columbia University conference, pointed out that only a small minority of big landowners in the poorer nations can afford to adopt the new grains. The poor peasantry are generally precluded from sharing in the potential gains of the Green Revolution, and their economic position may even deteriorate in relation to that of the rich farmers (Ward et al., 1971:127–31; also Bairoch, 1975:47; see also chapter 14). This social polarization in the countryside between a small minority of increasingly productive and wealthier farmers and a majority of poorer and less productive peasants who cannot afford the new agricultural technology erupted into violence in India in the latter 1970s. Unless there is a strong government program to assure equitable participation by poorer peasants, or adequate compensation for their deteriorating position, one unintended consequence of the Green Revolution could be class polarization and violence (as Lester Brown also admits; see Ward et al., 1971:134–35). Once again, as we shall show repeatedly, transplantation of Western technology and Western expertise may not produce the kind of development that can satisfy basic human needs in the Third World, even though it may seem promising (a technological "quick fix") on the basis of previous Western experience.

DEVELOPMENT OF UNDERDEVELOPMENT: EXTRACTIVE INDUSTRY

At first glance, Third World nations seem to have done better in the growth of industry than in the growth of agriculture. Here we must first make a distinction between extractive industry, which produces basic raw materials (minerals and fuels), and manufacturing industry, which processes materials into finished or semifinished goods.

The rapid growth in output from extractive industry in the Third World began in the early 1900s, when most of these nations were still colonies or semicolonies of the Western powers. Between 1900 and 1940, output of fuel and minerals grew at an annual rate of about 6 percent, quite high by historical standards. In the post-World War II period, however, annual rate of growth in Third World extractive industry has averaged an even higher 9 percent (1948–1970), with production of fuels increasing nearly seven-fold and that of minerals more than three-fold (Bairoch, 1975:52). These rates are much higher than the rates of population growth. In the Western nations, the growth of extractive industry went hand in hand with the early growth of the manufacturing sector; mining and drilling activities fed raw materials into local iron and steel mills, processing plants, and factories. In the Third World nations, fuel and mineral production does not go hand in hand with an organic or overall pattern of economic development:

> IT must be emphasized that the enormous increase in the output of the extractive industries in the developing countries was in no way due to the demands of local industry. Indeed local industry absorbed only a fraction of production. For proof of this it is only necessary to compare—either globally or country by country—output with exports of the products of mining and extraction. Thus, for countries like Brazil, Chile, Liberia, and Malaysia, exports of iron ore vary from 80 to 100 per cent of production. Further, while in 1970 the under-developed countries produced 39 per cent of world output of iron ore (excluding China and the USSR), the same countries produced slightly less than 5 per cent of the world's steel. Thus, some 90 per cent of the iron ore mined in the under-developed countries goes to feed the blast furnaces of the developed countries. (Bairoch, 1975:54)

The growth of extractive industry has in all probability actually retarded manufacturing industry in the Third World. This follows first from the fact that the rapid growth of oil and mineral exploitations has been not only directed toward export to the West (and Japan), but also has been financed and managed by Western-owned MNCs. The interests of the multinationals, such as Anaconda Copper, Union Miniere, Reynolds Aluminum, and the great oil corporations, are not the overall development of Third World economies, but payoffs for shareholders who live in the rich, developed nations. Economist Charles Rollins has illustrated the impact of MNC investment in extractive industries:

> The Bolivian tin-mining operations provide an excellent example of the importance that such a negative influence can attain. The tin mines were established in an economy very largely dominated by feudal agriculture. Within this economy they created a monetary sector (the cities and mines of the *altiplano*) whose chief interests were oriented toward the advanced Western nations where the tin was sold, and which remained to an extraordinary degree separated from the bulk of the populace, who continued in their old ways. (Rhodes, 1970:196)

Rollins argues that in some "new" countries, such as Canada and Australia, large-scale and rapid development of mineral resources has aided overall economic development. Here the institutional structures, including a strong and capable national government, plus the cultural, social, and economic prerequisites to capitalist development were present. This is to some degree also true for the nation of South Africa, where strong economic growth aided by gold and diamond mining has taken place, dominated by the European white minority. For the great majority of Third World nations that are not settler spin-offs from Europe (as Canada, Australia, and white South Africa are), these conditions are lacking. Most Third World governments are neither strong nor very capable. They are what Gunnar Myrdal (1968) called "soft states," easily penetrated by stronger outside or internal elite interests. Furthermore, the weakness of Third World governments may be one reason for investment interest by Western MNCs:

> If, prior to the consideration of a raw-material-exploitation possibility, there were in power a government willing and able to take the necessary measures to promote development, it is unlikely that large-scale investments would be made, for the country would be regarded as one in which a "hostile" investment climate prevailed. If such a government came to power after the scheme had begun, the companies involved could be expected to oppose the adoption of the necessary measures. (Rhodes, 1970:203)

Overall, there are fewer benefits to the Third World economies as a result of foreign (i.e., Western) exploitation of their mineral resources, and this situation will remain unless and until Third World governments are able to stand up to the MNCs and demand that resource exploitation be tied to a domestically controlled program of overall development. This in turn can succeed only if the MNCs cannot, through bribery, financing of coups, or calling in the Marines, topple the offending government (as in Guatemala,

Chile, Iran, and the Dominican Republic), and if the MNCs cannot find sufficient alternative and economically profitable mineral deposits.

The OPEC experience of the 1970s has been such a shocker primarily because of this unprecedented ability of a group of Third World nations to demand higher oil prices, to stick together as a group, and to resist being overthrown through overt or covert Western intervention.

In most Third World nations, the post-World War II growth of extractive industry has had few benefits, largely because these industries serve the needs of foreign developed markets, not local economies:

1. Machinery and equipment necessary for mining and drilling operations come almost exclusively from the developed countries, seldom from local producers.
2. Because Western "high" technology, which is capital-intensive and labor-saving, is employed, a relatively small workforce of skilled and unskilled workers is created, although these workers are often, by local standards, quite well paid. This tends to build small pockets of "labor aristocracy" among a much broader mass of poor and unemployed workers.
3. Management and technical employees are mainly drawn from the MNC home country, not from the local population. Modern technology is not being transferred socially to control by the host nation, but is only geographically present in the host nation. From the viewpoint of the MNC, it is to its best interest to retain control over technology, the better to avoid nationalization or expropriation. The few local nationals allowed to rise within the MNC structure must prove their loyalty to the company over country. Foreign management and technical personnel form small islands of conspicuous Western-style consumption in the midst of poverty (for example, the Belgian-French personnel in Kolwezi, Zaire, or the American personnel in Isfahan, Iran, before the overthrow of the Shah).
4. Profits from foreign-owned extractive industries (as well as from other MNC investments) are repatriated (taken out of the Third World nation) to the MNC home office to pay stockholder dividends. Only repatriation of a high proportion of profits will make foreign investment attractive, and repatriated profits are in general not reinvested in the host country but either consumed by the stockholder or reinvested elsewhere. Major diversification of MNC investment to manufacturing industries within one country, as part of an overall development plan, is in general not favored, since this might in fact force up local wages and might also make nationalization more practical in a company-government conflict. If the MNC spreads its facilities among many nations, nationalization of assets by one Third World government leaves the total operation still relatively intact and the nationalized assets useless without the extended network of manufacturing, transport, and marketing.

5. The growth of extractive industry output in the Third World is therefore not comparable to the earlier experience in the West, because it is so heavily controlled by and oriented toward the needs of foreign markets. There is the final danger, recognized by OPEC and now by UNCTAD, that the MNCs may exhaust irreplaceable natural resources so that when such resources are needed for domestic industry, they will no longer be available from local mines and wells. Indeed, with the postwar growing demand for raw materials from the rich nations, there is the danger that certain materials will either be too depleted to sustain new manufacturing development or too expensive for the poor nations (cf. Tanzer, 1980).

DEVELOPMENT OF UNDERDEVELOPMENT: MANUFACTURING INDUSTRY

Manufacturing industry has grown more slowly than extractive industry, but has made some progress in the postwar period. For the years 1950 to 1970, total output grew by 6.6 percent per year; if population growth is considered, the per capita gain was still a decent 4.1 percent annual average. According to Paul Bairoch (1975:66–69), this compares favorably with per capita rates of manufacturing growth in the West during the last two centuries, although it is definitely below the levels achieved by the USSR in its early Five-Year Plans (10.9 percent) and in Eastern Europe (9.5 percent) and the USSR (7.6 percent) for the same postwar period. It also falls short of the postwar achievements by the capitalist economies of Japan (14.8 percent) and Italy (7.3 percent). Several points need to be made about the pace of industrial manufacturing growth, and all of these points tend to diminish or qualify the achievements in this sector.

First and foremost, it must be recognized that high rates of growth are sometimes registered when the starting point of comparison is relatively low. This is a common problem in basic statistical analysis. For example, suppose that in 1950 production of steel is only ten thousand metric tons in a poor Third World country, versus 1 million metric tons in a developed nation. If each nation adds one extra steel mill with a production capacity of ten thousand tons annually, the Third World nation has increased steel manufacturing by 100 percent, while the developed nation has increased its steel manufacturing by only 1 percent. As the manufacturing sector grows somewhat beyond the minimum, it becomes more difficult to maintain the same high rates of increase. There are signs that Third World growth rates in manufacturing were somewhat lower for 1960–1970 than for 1950–1960, and this statistical factor may be part of the relative decline.

A second point relates to the distribution of manufacturing within the Third World. A few nations (Hong Kong, Singapore, South Korea, Taiwan, and Israel) have developed a thriving manufacturing export sector, but these nations are not typical of the Third World generally. Hong Kong and Singapore are city-states with special relationships and access to the British market; Taiwan and South Korea, firm military allies of the United States, have enjoyed extensive military and economic aid to help make them "showpieces" of Western-oriented development. Israel by most standards beyond geography does not belong in the Third World category at all. Hong Kong, Taiwan, South Korea, and Israel represent together only 3 percent of Third World population, but accounted in 1968 for 42 percent of manufactured goods exported from the Third World. As several observers have noted, it would be impossible for the Third World generally to copy the performance of these few small and favored states, if for no other reason than the lack of world market demand. Bairoch (1975:100) calculated that if all Third World nations relied on export of manufactures to the same extent as does Hong Kong, world imports of Third World manufactures would have to be nineteen times (that is, 1,900 percent) greater than it is.

A third point is that the growth of manufacturing output in the Third World has not created new industrial employment at the same pace. Here again lies a fundamental difference between the experience of the Western and Third World nations. The Western technology employed in many if not most large- or middle-sized manufacturing plants and factories in Third World nations is much more productive, in output per worker, than the nineteenth-century technology introduced into an industrializing England, Germany, France, and United States. In the West, manufacturing employment (among males) rose from around 10 to 15 percent at early "takeoff" to between 30 and 45 percent at its peak; more recently, in all of the affluent nations, this percentage has begun to slowly decline, with the service sector (government, office, sales, and professional-technical employees) becoming the most numerous broad category of employment. Roger Hansen (1974:20–23), an analyst of Mexican economic development since the late 1800s, notes that the percentage of the (male) workforce employed in manufacturing was already between 12 and 13 percent in 1895–1900. Although Mexico was widely regarded by orthodox Western economists until the 1980s as an "economic miracle" in the post-World War II period, the percentage of Mexican workers employed in manufacturing has increased only marginally over the last eighty years. British economist Robert Sutcliffe (1971) and Swedish economist Gunnar Myrdal (1968) both noted the failure of Third World manufacturing growth to create jobs on a major scale. Sutcliffe indicates that for the underdeveloped world as a whole, the proportion of the workforce in industry (both extractive and manufacturing) increased from only 8.4 percent in 1900 to 11.2 percent in 1960. Of course, there are important differences in the exceptional cases mentioned above and in certain regions; Latin America, for example, generally more advanced than Asia or Africa, has experienced a somewhat greater expansion of industrial employment. Myrdal has argued, however, that industrial employment may have actually fallen in some nations through the displacement of previous small-scale and more labor-intensive manufacturing by Western technology. Sutcliffe (1971:89–90) cites the particular cases of Argentina, Egypt, Cameroun, Kenya, Zambia, Malawi, Rhodesia, Tanzania, Uganda, and Nigeria, where manufacturing output grew while manufacturing employment fell. Yet this failure of recent manufacturing growth in the Third World to provide for expanded employment should not be used as a blanket argument against industrialization per se, as is sometimes heard: "Yet to oppose machines altogether, like Gandhi, or to argue that a long-run rise in the standard of living is possible without industrialization, are no more than forms of sentimentalism, especially when the condition of most of the population of the non-industrialized world is now both terrible and worsening" (Sutcliffe, 1971:106).

The reason for the failure of industrial growth to provide large-scale employment is fairly clear; the importation of "advanced" labor-saving technology from the West tends to destroy competing but more labor-intensive local firms. The labor recruited to the new facilities using "high" technology is in large measure simply a regrouping within the manufacturing sector's existing workforce and not an expansion of this category of employment. Therefore, despite annual per capita growth rates generally higher than those found in the nineteenth-century Western nations, employment in manufacturing has not grown proportionately and has not been able to absorb the rapidly growing population into the workforce. The question as to why modern Western technology has been so widely employed leads to consideration of the final markets for which Third World manufactures are intended and of who controls the choice of both markets and technology.

The International Labor Office (ILO) in Geneva in a 1976 report titled *Employment, Growth and Basic Needs* and Robert Sutcliffe in his study *Industrialization and Underdevelopment* (1971:ch. 6) outline the arguments for and against application of the latest "high" technology in Third World development. The arguments in favor include: (1) greater efficiency in use of materials, labor, and scarce managerial skills; (2) a more rapid closing of the technology gap between rich and poor nations; (3) capital savings for possible reinvestment; and (4) product standards necessary for competition in international markets. These are important claims, but notice that they are mainly directed toward viable corporate development for export markets. And the point about closing the technology gap not only assumes that Western high technology is the natural goal for all developing nations but also says nothing about who actually controls the new technologies used in Third World manufacturing.

The arguments for more labor-intensive technologies include: (1) production better adapted to developing-country availability of labor and relative scarcity of capital; (2) ability to utilize labor-intensive technologies in smaller-scale production with available domestic (i.e., nonimported) worker and managerial skills; (3) greater utility of labor-intensive technologies in an integrated development strategy that combines growth with social equity; and (4) the small proportion of workers who are employed from Western "high" technology, creating further burdens on the government in caring for the unemployed and underemployed. Unlike the previous arguments in favor of high technology imported "off the shelf," that is, unadapted to Third World conditions, these points are directed toward economic development of the society rather than the corporation, especially the Western-controlled multinational corporation. Do Third World governments have the capacity and the will to give priority to domestic social needs as opposed to the investment and profit needs of the large MNCs that dominate the industrial sector and the export markets? This is a question of "who's in charge here?" or who dominates the system and who is subordinate or dependent. The ILO report concludes:

> BUT of course the existing constellation of forces affecting technological policy and investment decisions is not neutral. For a variety of reasons, it is generally leaning heavily in favour of the transfer of unadapted capital-intensive technology, at least in those large-scale public sector projects included in development plans or sponsored by foreign aid programs, in private investment by multinationals and activities supported by major financial institutions. (ILO, 1976:143)

This type of dependent industrial growth in both extractive and manufacturing industries has led to a twisted form of underdevelopment that should not be confused, despite increases in aggregate production, with overall economic development. Sociologist Dale Johnson, in his studies of dependency and underdevelopment in Latin America, has emphasized:

> LATIN America is not *un*developed. The region has been underdeveloping for several centuries. The concept of "developing countries" is misleading to the degree that it implies a self-sustained process of industrialization or a process of economic and social development similar to Europe and North America in the nineteenth and twentieth centuries. (Cockcroft, Frank, and Johnson, 1972:72)

CONTROL OF TRADE, FINANCE, AND TECHNOLOGY

The economic growth in the Third World has not produced an overall modernization of the economy but rather small enclaves of high Western technology that only increase social inequality and that may actually retard a broader transformation, as occurred in both the earlier capitalist and later communist industrial revolutions. Third World development has been and is still a dependent form of growth, dependent on decisions made in the rich Western nations, over which (at least until the OPEC shock of the 1970s) Third World nations had little influence. Two important aspects of dependency still to be discussed are control of international trade and finance and of technology.

Most Third World trade with the major blocs of nations (liberal democracies, communist systems, and the Third World) takes place between the Third World and the rich Western nations. In the early 1970s, only 5 to 10 percent of all Third World import and export trade was with the communist world, despite a steady expansion of communist trade since Stalin's death. And less than 25 percent of Third World trade is with other Third World nations. Between 70 and 75 percent of Third World trade is, therefore, with the developed Western nations (Bairoch, 1975:102; Sewell, 1978:206–7). This in itself is unusual, since both the liberal democracies (70–75 percent) and the communist nations (55–60 percent) do most of their trading with other members of their own blocs. A major point here is that the communist world still plays a small role in the Third World trade picture; the main relationship is between the former colonial powers and the former colonies. Thus, while there is much discussion of a so-called Soviet imperialism in relation to smaller countries (Cuba, Angola), in terms of international trade and overseas investments the USSR is just not comparable to the widespread MNC interests and much larger trading interests of the West.

The Third World nations export mainly raw materials and fuels to the West, while they import mainly manufactured goods from the West. Between 80 and 85 percent of Third World exports are raw materials and fuels (primary products), whereas 65 to 70 percent of Third World imports are manufactured products. This international division of labor has changed little since the 1950s, despite economic growth in the Third World. This represents a neocolonial continuation of Third World trade as complementary to the needs of the developed West for raw materials. The West certainly needs the minerals, gas, and oil wealth of the Third World to help maintain its high standards of consumption.

While the United States, with its own extensive mineral riches, is less obliged to scour the Third World for mineral and fuels than are Western Europe and Japan, there is a growing reliance on the Third World nations for adequate supplies at the "right" price. These figures might indicate that the Third World nations should be able to demand favorable terms of trade for their raw materials so clearly in demand in the West. And yet the terms of trade between primary goods of the Third World and the manufactured goods of the industrial Western nations have actually deteriorated since the early 1950s. Bairoch (1975) calculates that, except for the brief rise in prices for most minerals in 1951, which was fed by the Korean War, there was a deterioration in the terms of trade for primary products versus manufactured goods of about 18 percent between 1952 and 1970. In the early 1970s, the Third World nations exported fully 11 percent of their total GNP to the West; in return the West exported 2 percent of its GNP to the Third World. Export trade is a matter of life or death for most Third World nations, since without sufficient exports to the West they cannot pay for Western imports of machinery and manufactured goods. Most Third World nations (with the exception of some OPEC states) are in fact not able to pay for imports with export earnings and are forced to borrow money from Western governments, Western banks, and Western-dominated international funds. Even the supposed success stories of Third World development, like Mexico and Brazil, are deeply in debt (see Hansen, 1974, and Hellman, 1983, for an excellent summary of Mexican development).

Table 13.3 Western Imports of Raw Materials (1974)

| | UNITED STATES | | EUROPEAN COMMUNITY | JAPAN |
	Total Imports Percentage	*Imports from Third World Percentage*	*Total Imports Percentage*	*Total Imports Percentage*
Aluminum	88	63	31	93
Chromium	90	29	100	90
Cobalt	99	50	100	100
Copper	20	10	76	93
Iron	17	9	59	100
Lead	19	11	70	67
Manganese	98	48	99	87
Nickel	72	6	100	100
Phosphates	6	—	100	100
Tin	84	73	87	90
Tungsten	64	35	100	100
Zinc	59	14	73	74
Petroleum (1973)	37	n.a.	98	100

SOURCES: Sewell, 1977; Hansen, 1976:163, International Economic Report of the President (U.S. Government Printing Office, 1975).

Since the early 1970s, the foreign debt (public and private) of Third World nations has grown in alarming proportions (see figure 13.1). In the 1980s, it has become clear that many of the most indebted Third World countries are unable to keep up with their debt servicing, payments of interest and principal, to their Western creditors. Inceasingly, more repayments were going just for interest and less for reducing the outstanding principal of the debt. For Latin America, in 1976, 21 percent of foreign debt

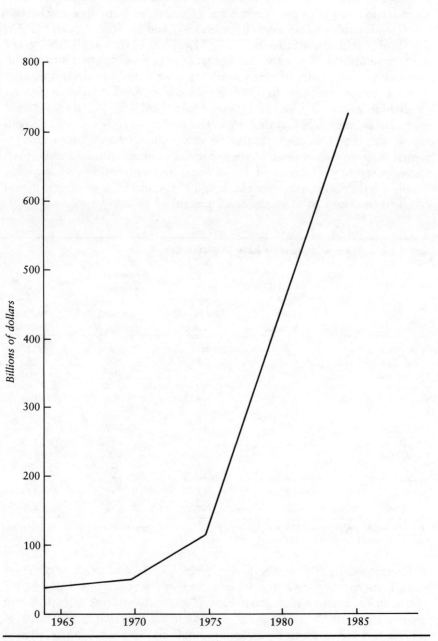

Figure 13.1 Debt Burden of Non-OPEC Developing Nations

SOURCES: Sewell, 1977; World Bank, *World Development Report*, 1986.

servicing went to interest payments, but by 1983 this rose to 79 percent. In this situation, debtor nations would remain permanently in debt, never able to repay the loan principal. The extent of the debt crisis was heightened in August of 1982 when Mexico announced that it was bankrupt and unable to continue its debt servicing without major new financial aid. While this situation had occurred before for smaller debtor nations, and periodically occurs in the troubled financial life of many Third World nations, Mexico was one of the largest debtor nations. Western banks have a large stake in Mexico's foreign debt, which in the latter 1980s stood at about $110 billion. When a Third World debtor nation finds itself unable to keep up its debt repayment schedule, it has generally sought additional loans and a rescheduling of existing loans over a longer payback period. In the 1950s and 1960s, these debt reschedulings were handled by a variety of international financial groupings of the wealthy Western powers, such as the so-called Paris Club, the Hague Club, and the OECD Donor Consortium (cf. Payer, 1985). In more recent times, the Western democracies have designated the International Monetary Fund (IMF) to handle the bulk of international debt problems for Third World nations and to discipline the debtor nations (Payer, 1974, 1982).

In the 1980s, Mexico, Argentina, Brazil, Peru, Chile, the Philippines, Egypt, Nigeria, Zaire, Sudan, Jamaica, and many other Third World debtor nations have had to submit to IMF "austerity plans" drawn up by IMF officials in order to receive debt relief and to avoid complete default (a drastic but increasingly considered alternative). The IMF austerity plans include an array of measures to increase exports, reduce imports, and in general to increase the ability of the debtor nation to generate a foreign trade surplus to be used to satisfy its Western creditors. Such measures often include: cuts in government spending (on health, education and social services); cuts in government subsidies on basic essentials like bread or flour, cooking oil, and bus fares; devaluation of the local currency to make exports cheaper and imports more expensive; an opening of the country to more Western investment and abolition of controls on profits from operations in the debtor nation; and monetary and banking controls monitored by the IMF. In short, many Third World debtors are faced with either default or giving up control (sovereignty) over substantial economic and social policy areas to an international agency, which is funded by the affluent Western democracies and widely perceived as their agent in maintaining Third World debtor discipline. IMF officials are seen as the real governors, or imperial "proconsuls," of the economic fate of the peoples of the debtor nations (Editors, 1984).

Perhaps no other agency or nation is as widely hated in the Third World as the IMF, because the burden of IMF austerity plans is borne by the poor in those nations. Agreements to IMF austerity plans have sparked food riots, looting of stores, strikes, and spontaneous uprisings in Brazil, Sudan, Morocco, and Tunisia in recent years. Third World leaders are caught between the prospects of social unrest if they agree to IMF controls and default if they resist. In Latin America, which has the largest concentration of big debtors (Mexico, Brazil, Argentina, Venezuela, Chile, and Peru), there is a continuing debate over the formation of a "debtors' cartel," with the aim of changing through collective negotiation with the IMF the terms of debt rescheduling and austerity policies, and some individual nations, notably Peru under President Garcia, have announced unilateral limitations on the rate of debt servicing. Yet, most Third World leaders, after denouncing the IMF loudly for its policies, still eventually submit to IMF requirements to remain credit worthy.

The OPEC nations, on the other hand, have since 1973 been able to build up their export earnings by changing the terms of trade for oil dramatically. They were able in 1973 to quadruple the price of oil because: (1) they organized the oil-producing nations into a common bloc (cartel), which the West, despite its obvious dissatisfaction, has not yet been able to undermine; and (2) they took the price-setting power for oil away from the Western-owned oil MNCs. Oil is, of course, a special commodity; it is by no means clear that Third World producers could do so well with OPEC-type organizations for other raw materials. Nor is it clear that the OPEC nations are now headed down a path of self-sustained development merely because of their recent financial gains. In many areas they are still just as dependent on Western manufactures, technology, and investment outlets for their newly acquired wealth, and for military supplies as well, as they were before 1973. Breaking the syndrome of Third World dependency on the West requires much more than getting a higher price for oil exports.

Yet, it is probably correct that the Third World struggle against Western dominance will be based to some extent on these two outstanding features of OPEC. Except for a few Third World giants like Brazil and perhaps Nigeria, most Third World nations are too small and resource-poor to attempt the self-sufficient (go-it-alone) economic development that the Soviet Union undertook from 1928 to 1940 and that China tried in the 1960s. In some form or another, the smaller and weaker nations of the Third World will have to organize their economic interests, cooperate amongst themselves, and not allow themselves to be played off against each other by the rich nations (the old "divide and conquer" tactic). And they will have to divest the MNCs (whose economic power often exceeds that of entire Third World nations—see the following chapter) of their power to make crucial decisions on investment, technology, marketing, and repatriation of profits. These decisions must come to be made by competent local governments as part of an overall strategy for development.

A major weakness of the OPEC strategy, taken in isolation from a whole array of transformations, is that control of technology still remains in Western hands. Indeed, this weakness may be one reason that the West's response to OPEC has not been more hostile or overtly military. One of the main characteristics of dependent economic growth in the Third World is the lack of local control over technology and its applications. More often now, observers of the Third World are concluding that without the independent development of technologies adapted to local conditions and needs, economic growth that would benefit the great majority, the masses of the poor, is exceedingly unlikely. Despite the increasing penetration of Third World economies by the MNCs, despite the drawing in of their resources to the world market, it cannot be said that the Third World is learning to master Western technology, but rather the reverse is true:

> No caricature is involved in describing modern science as a European invention which enabled the white nations to achieve military, economic and cultural domination over the rest of the world, and to make themselves prosperous while leaving the natives of the poor countries to progress very much more slowly. No injustice is done to say that most research workers and technologists have unthinkingly connived in these uses of science which are, at bottom, racist. Declarations about using science to feed the world's hungry have not stopped the prosperity gap growing wider; nor can they alter the fact that the intellectual interests of the great majority of research workers are far removed from any such program and that the preoccupation of technologists is with machines that enrich the rich. (Calder, 1970:252)

Calder's harsh judgment is shared also by Sutcliffe (1971), Sachs (1978), Bairoch (1975), and, in far more diplomatic language, the 1976 ILO report. Sachs, a keen observer of the Third World for many years, states in fact that, in terms of practical application, the Third World still has no "indigenous science" (Sachs, 1978:84). Research and development (R&D) represents only 0.2 percent of GNP for the Third World nations, less than 1 percent of the R&D (per capita) spent by the rich Western nations. Further, less than 1 percent of Western R&D is for adaptation of Western science and technology to Third World problems. Even the MNCs with considerable investment and profit stakes in the Third World spend less than 5 percent of their large R&D funds in the Third World (Apter and Goodman, 1976:109). For example, U.S.-owned multinationals in 1966 spent 97 percent of their global research and development funds in the United States (Erb and Kallab, 1975:87). Only in a few cases, notably South Korea, has Western control over technological development been effectively challenged by the national entrepreneurial class.

This Western dominance over production technology is mirrored by underemphasis on science and technology within higher education in the Third World itself. According to Bairoch's figures for 101 Third World nations, in 1966–1968 only 36 percent of students were in the fields of science, engineering, medicine, and agronomy, compared with 45 percent in Western Europe and 65 percent in communist Eastern Europe. Even worse is the "brain drain" of Third World specialists to the rich nations caused by lack of demand in the local economies and, by comparison, the glittering opportunities for the highly trained in the West (see chapter 15). As a result, "technology transfer" to the Third World from the West is largely fictitious and represents merely the continuation of the Western monopoly through patent and licensing rights. By the early 1960s, over 90 percent of new patents granted in most Third World nations were granted to (and therefore controlled by) foreigners, overwhelmingly Westerners. Foreign-controlled patents for the years 1957–1961 made up 89 percent of all new patents in India, 92 percent in Turkey, 93 percent in Egypt, 96 percent in Pakistan, and 91 percent in Chile (Wilbur, 1973:127). Indian political scientist Jyoti Singh (1977:79) reports that, according to UNCTAD estimates, the cost to the Third World for the use of Western patents, licenses, and trademarks was nearing $10 billion annually by the latter 1970s.

One heavily advertised strategy for industrialization in the Third World, and especially in Latin America, is called import-substitution. This calls for gradual replacement of imported Western manufactures with locally produced manufactured goods. While import-substitution seemed earlier to be making some progress in Latin America, it faltered in the 1960s and 1970s. Now import-substitution strategies have come under criticism for their failure to come to grips with the need to develop an independent technological foundation for growth that would reach out beyond a few modern industries. Sutcliffe points out that the late industrializers like Japan and the Soviet Union were able to develop technical capacities adapted to society-wide conditions.

> BY contrast, most underdeveloped countries, partly through government policy, partly because of the role of foreign industrial capital in these countries, have followed a pattern of more wholesale adoption of the more advanced Western industrial techniques. The result has been that, as import substitution possibilities come to an end, industrial progress has tended to grind to a premature halt; and one of the major reasons for this has been not the failure to assimilate technology but the absence of the technological dynamism which further industrial growth would need. (Sutcliffe, 1971:336; see also ILO, 1976:164 and Sachs, 1978:ch. 2.)

As long as the Third World, in technology as in trade and finance, cannot in Mao's words "walk on two legs," it will be dependent on strong external forces whose interests are primarily bound up with profit-making for Western stockholders.

CORRELATES OF UNDERDEVELOPMENT

Although the syndrome of dependency is common to the Third World generally, there is a great deal of differentiation in the aggregate levels of consumption, education, health and nutrition, housing, and welfare spending between regions and individual nations. Within the Third World there are a few OPEC states with small populations, like Kuwait, Libya, and Saudi Arabia, whose per capita GNP figures are among the world's highest. This is an anomaly that does not (yet) correlate with high literacy and low infant mortality in these nations. Next in per capita GNP comes Latin America as a region, with nations like Brazil and Mexico representing middle-income nations globally. Note that Brazil and Mexico both have higher per capita levels of car ownership than the USSR, despite GNP/capita levels half that of the Soviet Union. Next come the nations of Asia and Africa, which have standards of living well below the average for Latin America, a fact that is reflected in very low distribution of consumer durables (in this age of cheap transistor radios, radio ownership is only a minimal indicator of consumer affluence).

Table 13.4 Levels of Material Consumption in the Third World (1983)

	GNP/Capita (1983 dollars)	TVs/1,000 Population	Radios/1,000 Population	Autos/1,000 Population
Mexico	1,997	111	292	63
Brazil	1,987	122	355	77
Nigeria	782	6	80	7
Kenya	339	4	34	6
Egypt	674	41	157	19
India	248	3	56	1
Indonesia	541	23	131	1
Kuwait	16,720	257	286	305
For comparison:				
United States	13,492	646	2,133	535
Soviet Union	6,490	307	504	35

SOURCES: UN *Statistical Yearbook*, 1983/84; *Statistical Abstract of the United States*, 1987.

Educational opportunities in the Third World have grown considerably since World War II. Bairoch (1975:137–41) estimates that illiteracy in the Third World was about 80 percent at the turn of the century and was still about 74 percent in 1950. This figure was reduced by 1970 to 56 percent, ranging from 76 percent in Africa to 50 percent in Asia and 24 percent in Latin America. In secondary education and college-level (higher) education as well, considerable gains in enrollments were achieved between 1950 and 1970. In fact, by 1970 secondary-school enrollments were reaching levels (in per capita terms) attained by the developed nations in the 1930–1950 period, well after industrialization and economic modernization had taken place. In 1970, there were some 5.6 million college-level students in the Third World, compared with only nine hundred thousand in 1950, and compared with 5.4 million college-level students in the developed nations as of 1950.

Table 13.5 Educational Attainment in the Third World

	LITERACY PERCENTAGE	PERCENT GNP SPENT ON EDUCATION		STUDENTS PER MILLION OF POPULATION	
		1965	1984	1965	1984
Mexico	83	1.9	2.8	3,120	14,250
Brazil	74	1.7	3.3	1,890	11,400
Nigeria	25-35	1.7	2.2	160	2,040
Kenya	20-25	4.1	5.6	300	750
Egypt	38	5.4	4.1	5,980	19,570
India	41	2.0	3.2	2,840	7,760
Indonesia	67	0.9	2.2	950	6,000
Kuwait	67	3.0	4.2	8,040[a]	12,870
For comparison:					
United States	99	6.6	6.7	28,400	52,810
Soviet Union	100	7.6	6.6	16,740	19,180

a. 1975

SOURCES: Sewell, 1977; *UN Statistical Yearbook*, 1977; *UNESCO Statistical Yearbook*, 1986.

These impressive gains, however, have had limited impact on economic development in the Third World for several reasons. First, the facilities and staffing of educational institutions is in general quite inadequate, and most Third World nations spend a smaller portion of GNP on education than do the liberal democracies or the communist nations. Mexico and Brazil, often referred to as showplaces of capitalist-style development, are among the less generous when it comes to educational financing. Thus, even though more children are going to school, the schools are often too overcrowded and too poorly equipped to actually achieve educational goals. Second, school equipment, especially texts and curricula, often follows Western models and is not adapted to local circumstances. This is in part a continuation of the Western models of education introduced during the colonial period and constitutes a still-present cultural penetration in the postindependence period. This contributes to a third factor, which is the migration of highly educated citizens from the Third World where their talents are most needed to the developed

West, where the financial rewards and secure consumer life-style are most attractive. This is in many respects the natural outcome of higher education in the Third World, since in many ways it is dominated by Western standards and therefore trains people for positions and careers that exist (in sufficiently large numbers) only in the developed West. As in so many other areas, educational growth is out of synchronization with overall economic growth, ensuring that many college-educated will be able to pursue stable and financially rewarding careers only outside their homelands. Educational growth, especially higher education, was a correlate of an organic pattern of development in the West and even more so in the European communist nations. In the Third World, educational growth has outpaced job creation for the highly educated, and the areas of higher education emphasized (liberal arts, law) are not those needed for industrialization and technical progress.

As indicated in the beginning of this chapter, a rapidly declining death rate, beginning in the 1930–1950 period, has produced a rapid population growth in the Third World that has helped to increase life expectancy even in very poor nations like India and Egypt. Infant mortality rates, while still much higher than in the liberal democracies or communist systems, have declined from pre-World War II levels. Life expectancy, while still considerably lower than in the developed nations, has also increased, with relatively higher levels in Latin America and lower levels in Africa. This does not mean that the relative health and nutrition levels have also risen. Medical care, especially in rural areas and for the urban poor, remains at low levels, and medical personnel, both inadequate and unequally distributed in most Third World countries, are unable to meet basic health needs of the population. Nutritional standards may even have declined (Gamer, 1976) in many Third World nations, despite officially recorded increases in the value of agricultural production per capita. In some nations, where agriculture has converted from growing basic diet foods to growing commercial crops for export or for middle-class consumption, nutritional levels of the average citizen's diet have suffered. Agriculture in northern Mexico, now specializing in tomatoes and lettuce for the U.S. market rather than in beans and maize for basic local needs, is an example. In many Third World countries, average daily calorie intake is well below the 2,750 calories recommended by the World Health Organization (WHO). Protein intake often falls below the minimum eighty grams a day necessary to support normal mental and physical development. Under conditions of constant undernourishment, life may be sustained, but with marked mental and physical retardation. Past a certain age in children, this retardation becomes irreversible, even with later improved diet. In the West, population growth and increased life expectancy corresponded to an improved diet with higher nutritional content (see chapter 3) and to the improved physical and mental development of a large portion of the population. The impaired health of a large portion of the Third World population, on the other hand, creates a further hindrance to economic development, reducing the numbers of capable, able-bodied workers and increasing the ratio of dependents to workers.

Table 13.6 Health Care and Nutrition in the Third World

	POPULATION BELOW CRITICAL CALORIC INTAKE (percent)	LIFE EXPECTANCY AT BIRTH	INFANT MORTALITY RATE	POPULATION PER PHYSICIAN	ACCESS TO COMMUNITY WATER SUPPLY (PERCENT) urban	rural
GDP/capita (1970)						
Less than $200	35	44	119	19,000	69	15
$200-$400	20	52	76	3,700	88	18
$400-$1000	15	61	51	2,000	91	55
By comparison Market economies with GDP/capita over $1000	–	71	19	670	(a)	(a)
USSR/East Europe	–	70	33	520	(a)	(a)

a. not given

SOURCE: World Health Organization, *Nutritional Surveillance* (1984).

One of the main features of economic development in the West was the growth of cities as centers of manufacturing and trade. The housing conditions of early capitalistic societies have already been described. Third World urbanization differs from the Western pattern in several fundamentals. First, the growth of cities in the Third World is not related to the growth of industry and industrial employment in the cities (Weitz, 1973:5; Sinclair, 1978; Goldthorpe, 1975: 112–127), for reasons cited above. Although possibilities for employment in urban culture do attract peasants to the cities, many are driven from the land by the decline of employment and subsistence agriculture. The uncontrolled growth of the Third World cities is therefore a combination, well described by Stuart Sinclair (1978), of "push" and "pull" factors. Second, urbanization is proceeding at a much faster pace than was the case in the West, overwhelming the capacities of relatively weak and inexperienced municipal governments to supply essential water, sewage, garbage, power, and health services. By 1980, nearly one-fourth of the Third World population lived in cities of over twenty thousand, compared with less than 10 percent in 1940. Much of this urban growth has taken the form of slum and squatter settlements around the periphery of the core city. By recent estimates, one-third to two-thirds of the urban population live in slum and squatter (self-built) housing.

Lagos, with a population of perhaps 3.3 million in the early 1970s, is the capital of Nigeria and Africa's fastest-growing city. By some accounts it is the best example of the ills of Third World urbanization: "It now chokes on bad housing, traffic jams, and cement pile-ups. Whole streets are littered with compost, broken bottles, pieces of furniture, empty cans. The stench is intolerable during the dry season and worse when it rains. Then, over half the streets are flooded." The results are that "85 percent of Lagos school children have either hook-worm or round-worm; and that 10 percent of deaths are attributable to dysentery or diarrhoea" (Sinclair, 1978:20).

On the other hand, Mexican economist Eduardo Flores offers the following commentary from a visit to Calcutta, India:

> Calcutta affords the opportunity to see large-scale misery in its full harshness. At night its broad sidewalks become public dormitories, heaped with more than 600,000 emaciated men, women, old people, and children. . . . The poor of Calcutta lack the most elementary belongings, owning neither pillow, mattress, nor blanket; their bodies stink and are covered by soiled rags. At dawn, before the city awakens, carts collect the corpses of those who have died in the night.
>
> I, at once, realized that the misery of Calcutta was quite familiar to me. Hungry, ragged human beings were no novelty, since they are a standard part of the rural and urban landscape in Mexico, Bolivia, Peru and Brazil, countries I know well. What moved me in Calcutta was the overwhelming proportions of its misery. (Weitz, 1973:95)

These descriptions could be repeated over and over again, with some changes for climate, natural factors, and culture, for most major cities in Africa, Latin America, and Asia. Calcutta and Lagos are perhaps more striking examples of urban problems, but the general features are well known and common to the Third World pattern of dependent development.

Another effect of Third World urbanization combined with desperate conditions for the poorest strata is the growing numbers of homeless children, thrown out of their families or fleeing abuse from their parents. These children, often grouping together in gangs for protection, survive on the streets through peddling, washing cars or windshields, shining shoes, picking pockets, pimping, running numbers and sometimes drugs, and child prostitution. In Brazil, the state-run Foundation for the Welfare of Minors (FUNABEM) estimates that there are some 7 million homeless children in that nation, mostly in big cities like Rio de Janeiro and Sao Paulo. They attribute the disintegration of poor families to inadequate housing and massive unemployment among the urban lower classes. One consequence of this family disintegration is that 47 percent of Brazilian children never go beyond the first grade, because they must either work to support a single parent or must fend for themselves outside the family. This problem of homeless children and the disintegration of family life among the poor is not peculiar to Brazil. Any visitor to a big city in the Third World can see the large numbers of small children engaged in the wide range of activities, legal and illegal, made necessary by desperate circumstances.

Table 13.7 Slum and Squatter Populations

City	Percentage of Population in Slums and Squatter Housing
Latin America	
Mexico City	46
Rio de Janeiro	30
Lima	40
Bogota	60
Caracas	40
Asia	
Calcutta	67
Djakarta	26
Colombo	43
Seoul	30
Bombay	45
Manila	35
Africa	
Kinshasa	60
Ibadan	75
Accra	53
Casablanca	70
Nairobi	33
Addis Ababa	90

Sources: Ward, 1976:193; Sinclair, 1978:16.

Both the liberal democracies and the European communist nations have expanded government welfare systems and spending levels in the postwar years to the point where a national welfare system of social security, old age and disability benefits, unemployment compensation, health care, public housing, and family assistance characterizes most of the advanced industrial nations (with the partial exceptions noted in chapter 3). In the case of the liberal democracies, the development of the welfare system is an explicit commitment to basic human needs and an implicit guarantee that the suffering of the Great Depression will not return. In the European communist systems, it represents the fulfillment of regime ideology to satisfy human needs as an integral part of building socialism. In the Third World, basic human needs are not met for the average citizen, either through the private market or through governmentally sponsored programs. As a percentage of Gross Domestic Product (GDP), welfare spending remains quite low, welfare programs generally cover only a small fraction of the population (often privileged government and skilled union-organized workers), and welfare payments are generally insufficient to provide a sense or expectation of economic security. Some Third World systems that are touted as good examples of economic growth, such as Mexico, Brazil, or oil-rich Nigeria, increased welfare spending (as proportion of GDP) only marginally in the 1960s and 1970s, reflecting the relatively low priority placed on this area of government activity.

Table 13.8 **Welfare Expenditures in the Third World as Percentage of Gross Domestic Product (GDP), 1960-1980**

	1960	1970	1980
Mexico	1.6	3.0	–
Venezuela	2.5	3.1	1.3
Brazil	4.7	5.7	6.2[a]
Colombia	1.5	2.6	2.8
Kenya	–	1.9	1.6[a]
Nigeria	0.7	0.8	–
India	1.4	1.9	2.4[b]
Philippines	1.1	1.1	0.6
Malaysia	3.0	2.9	1.0
For comparison:			
United States	6.8	9.6	12.7
Soviet Union	10.2	11.9	14.1

a. 1977
b. 1976

SOURCES: ILO, *Cost of Social Security,* 1975-77, 1978-80.

SUMMARY

This chapter has stressed the great differences between the economic development of the West and the dependent economic growth that is taking place in the Third World today. Despite considerable variation in levels of development among regions and individual nations, the syndrome of dependency can be outlined as a general pattern. It includes the following factors:

1. A relatively weak national bourgeoisie that is not capable of leading the agricultural and industrial modernization of the economy. In areas such as Argentina or Brazil or Chile, where the national bourgeoisie was once a vigorous force, it has become weaker and more dependent on outside financing and skills as a result of economic growth.

2. The presence of strong Western entrepreneurship, operating through multinational corporations with strong and growing profit motives in the Third World. Progressively, the leading sectors of the Third World economies are organized according to the needs of the MNCs in a world capitalist market.

3. Control of export trade, international finance, and technology by the West. Local and independent development of a Third World technology or set of adapted technologies for modernization is largely absent.

4. Third World governments are not strong enough (even if dictatorial in relationship to their own citizens) or motivated to resist foreign investor control over key economic sectors, nor are they capable enough to undertake comprehensive economic planning for development.

5. Third World governments are what Myrdal (1968) has called "soft states," states in which government is easily penetrated by stronger interests, both domestic and foreign. This softness of the political system is much more important a consideration than whether it calls itself a democracy, a military junta, a personal dictatorship, or some sort of "socialist" regime (see Chaliand, 1978; Chirot, 1977).

Chapter 14

Inequality—Failures in
Social Justice

DISCUSSION OF THE DIMENSIONS OF SOCIAL inequality in the Third World must include the various inequalities between Third World nations and the rich, developed nations (and their extensions, the multinational corporations). These international dimensions of inequality in wealth, power, and control over both human and material resources are intimately linked to the development of internal inequalities within individual Third World nations. Indeed, the dependency syndrome arises from a combination of transnational inequalities that create the preconditions for dependency and is at the same time a process that adds to both international and internal inequalities. Dependency cannot be understood without reference to both types of inequality. Of course, no single nation is completely self-sufficient, and every nation is therefore somewhat limited in its relations with other nations whose products and services it wants to use. Yet, for the Third World, relationships with the rich nations of the West are on such an unequal basis of wealth, power, and resource control that they are the basis for a system of dominance rather than mutually useful relationships among relative equals.

TRANSNATIONAL INEQUALITY—INCOME

While it is difficult to measure the extent of world income inequality for years prior to 1900 and for agrarian societies in which cash income did not play a major role for most people, Dutch economist L. J. Zimmerman (1965) has estimated income levels for the developed and underdeveloped areas of the world for the years 1860, 1913, and 1960. During this period, only a few nations, most importantly Japan and the Soviet Union, have made the transition from the poor to the rich category. To these figures we can add estimates for income levels for the year 2000 developed by Indian economist Jagdish Bhagwati (1972) and develop a time-series of Lorenz curves for world income inequality from 1960 to 2000.

While we may dispute some figures in these global estimates, and while there is of course uncertainty in the projections to the year 2000, the trend is clearly toward greater global income inequality. In 1860, the richest 25 percent of the world's population received nearly 58 percent of world in-

261

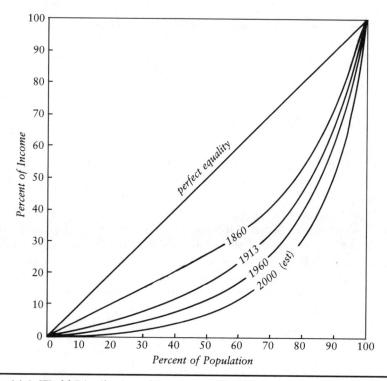

Figure 14.1 World Distribution of Income, 1860-2000: Inequality Becoming More Pronounced over Time

SOURCES: Adapted from Zimmerman, 1965: 34-40, and Bhagwati, 1972: 28.

come. In 1913, this top 25 percent got 69 percent; in 1960, it controlled 72 percent. Meanwhile, the share of world income going to the poorest half declined from less than 27 percent in 1860 to about 14 percent in 1913 and only 10 percent in 1960 (Zimmerman, 1965:38). If the Bhagwati estimates are accurate, the richest quarter of the world population will control about 75 percent of world income by the year 2000, and the bottom half will be left with about 7 percent. The gap between the rich and poor nations has increased from about a 2 to 1 ratio in the early 1800s to 20 to 1 in recent times (Hansen, 1975), despite the growth of GNP in the underdeveloped nations described in the previous chapter.

In the comparison between the rich and poor nations, "equal pay for equal work" does not exist. Barnett and Muller (1974), in their analysis of MNC penetration of the Third World, compared industrial wage rates for comparable jobs and skill levels between the United States and several underdeveloped nations. Not surprisingly, workers in the United States are paid generally five to ten times as much per hour for the same work that a Third World worker performs. And this fails to include the fringe benefits and Social Security accorded to American workers, which are seldom paid out for Third World workers. In some cases the differentials are even greater, as between Taiwan and the United States in consumer electronics products. As part of an adequate education in comparative politics, American students should be required to go to Sears, J. C. Penney, Montgomery Ward, or nearly any sporting goods or toy shop, to name only a few possibilities, and look at the labels that tell where the product was made (or assembled or sewn). Why are all these electronic calculators, digital games, Winnie-the-Pooh dolls, tennis racquets, running shoes, jackets, hardware items, and so much else being produced by Third World labor? What would they cost to American consumers if "equal pay for equal work" applied on a global scale? Why don't workers in Taiwan, South Korea, Mexico, Costa Rica, India, Pakistan, Haiti, and elsewhere demand higher wages? In some countries, like South Korea, the Philippines, Guatemala, Chile (since 1973), labor union organizations are violently suppressed. Union organizers are literally butchered by the regime and its assassination squads. Those unions that are permitted are paper tigers, docile and uncomplaining collaborators with the companies and the political system. In countries like India, Sri Lanka, Chile (before 1973), and Venezuela, real unions do exist, often under quite militant leadership. But here the MNC has the option of pulling up stakes and setting up its operations elsewhere, where the investment climate is more favorable. As long as there are enough countries with repressive regimes, this tactic remains a powerful hindrance to Third World workers. A docile and disciplined labor force is a vital ingredient of a favorable investment climate, and this factor explains why so much Western investment has gone to the worst dictatorships, rather than to the most democratic or progressive nations in the Third World. Thus, while U.S. foreign policy may verbally disagree with racist apartheid in South Africa, the atrocities of the Shah's SAVAK, the "disappearance" and murder of labor leaders in Chile, Argentina, and Brazil, and the suppression of human rights in South Korea, Taiwan, the Philippines, and Indonesia, U.S. and other Western MNCs are eager to exploit a tamed and defenseless workforce in these nations. U.S. presidents may proclaim their support for human rights, but MNCs owned and operated by American citizens both benefit from oppressive Third World regimes and provide a rationale (and often financial aid) for right-wing regimes and local collaborators with Western corporate interests. This may sound like a paradox, but it is not. It is a basic feature of the exploitation of Third World workers by Western multinationals, with higher profits going to Western stockholders and some benefits going to consumers in the rich nations (shoppers in Sears, Penney's, and so on).

Table 14.1 Differential Hourly Wage Rates[a] in Selected Industries: Underdeveloped Nations vs. the United States

Product	A Underdeveloped Nations	B United States	B ÷ A Ratio of Wage Rates
Consumer electronic products			
Hong Kong	U.S.$ 0.27	U.S.$ 3.13	11.6
Mexico	0.53	2.31	4.4
Taiwan	0.14	2.56	18.3
Office-machine parts			
Hong Kong	0.30	2.92	9.7
Taiwan	0.38	3.67	9.7
Mexico	0.48	2.97	6.2
Semiconductors			
Korea	0.33	3.32	10.1
Singapore	0.29	3.36	11.6
Jamaica	0.30	2.23	7.4
Wearing apparel			
Mexico	0.53	2.29	4.3
British Honduras	0.28	2.11	7.5
Costa Rica	0.34	2.28	6.7
Honduras	0.45	2.27	5.0
Trinidad	0.40	2.49	6.2

a. Hourly wage rates for a given country and the United States are for comparable skill levels.

Source: Adapted from Barnett and Muller, 1974: 127.

Transnational Inequality—Power

Inequalities in power between rich and poor nations are apparent in military terms. Even after formal decolonization in Africa and Asia, the Western powers have intervened militarily with some regularity in the Third World. The Soviet Union in recent years has also begun to intervene with military forces in places like Angola and Ethiopia as well, much to the dismay of the Western powers. But it was Britain and France (and Israel) that invaded Egypt in 1956, the United States that sent troops to Lebanon in 1958, to Vietnam from 1958 to 1973, and to the Dominican Republic in 1965. It was France and Belgium that sent paratroopers to prop up the corrupt Mobutu regime in Zaire in 1977, and France that sent troops to aid its client regimes in Chad and the Central African Republic. (More will be said of this with respect to political liberty in the Third World in chapter 15.)

The military and police forces of many Third World nations are dependent on the developed nations for their armaments, training, and leadership. The United States for years trained several thousand Latin American officers in antiguerrilla warfare at Fort Gulick in the Panama Canal Zone. Somoza's national guard was organized, equipped, and trained by the U.S. Marines. The Shah's SAVAK was organized and equipped by the CIA and the Israelis. Over twenty thousand U.S. military advisors were stationed in Iran during the Shah's reign to outfit, train, and even lead the army and air force. (Britain played a similar role for the Shah's navy.) The CIA and the Office of Public Safety (OPS) have given extensive training in interrogation techniques to police, secret police, and military forces in many nations. The OPS gave special aid to the Uruguayan military, which used torture and assassination in its battle against the Tupamaros in the late 1960s and early 1970s (Langguth, 1979). More recently, the CIA, along with Argentine and Chilean trainers, helped the Honduran military in kidnapping, torture, interrogation, and "elimination" techniques (LeMoyne, 1987). While it is claimed that American advisors do not actually participate in the use of torture and assassination, recent evidence indicates that they are aware of the murders of political prisoners and have still continued to provide their expertise.

The USSR and its Warsaw Pact allies (East Germany, Poland, and Czechoslovakia) have also been playing an active role in arming, advising, and leading certain Third World military forces (Angola, Ethiopia, South Yemen, Syria, Iraq, Afghanistan, and Nicaragua). While such military aid ties have on occasion backfired (Iran kicked out U.S. advisors in 1979, Egypt kicked out Soviet advisors in 1972), Third World nations remain the "arms junkies" of the developed world, although they may be able to choose an arms "pusher," either the West or the communist nations. The United States and the Soviet Union have each played major roles in the militarization of the Third World. From 1963 to 1983, arms exports to the Third World totaled some $223 billion, about half coming from NATO countries and 36 percent from Warsaw Pact nations. The United States alone accounted for 28 percent of the total and the Soviet Union for 33 percent (Sivard, 1986: 12). In just the decade from 1972 to 1981, Third World expenditures on military armaments increased from 7.9 percent of world armament expenditures to 15.6 percent (Castro, 1983:202), despite the desperate financial squeeze being put on social and welfare expenditures in many of these nations. This Third World arms race has been a direct and growing channel of influence for both the industrial democracies and the industrial communist states in the affairs of the less developed nations.

Still another aspect of the transnational power inequalities is illustrated by Lester Brown (1972:214-15) in a simple listing of gross national products for nations and annual sales for the largest MNCs. In the top one hundred on his list, there are fifty-nine nations and forty-one MNCs. In the top twenty, there are no corporations, but ten liberal democracies, six communist nations, plus India, Brazil, Mexico, and Spain. Of the bottom eighty, a majority (forty-one out of eighty) are not nations but MNCs, including twenty-five that are American in stock ownership, six West German, four British, two Japanese, one Italian, one Dutch, and two British-Dutch. This ordering changed somewhat in the latter 1970s, with the oil multinationals and the Arab OPEC states moving up considerably on the list (Exxon replaced General Motors as the top MNC), but the basic point remains: as economic concentrations, each large MNC has more clout than most individual Third World nations and can direct that economic power far more freely and rapidly than most Third World governments. In trying to regulate or discipline the behavior of MNCs with investments in its territory, a Third World government is, even without considering the possibility of retaliation by Western governments or the possibility of military intervention, challenging an economic power larger than itself. If should not be surprising that Third World governments, those that desire and attempt to challenge the multinationals (Allende in Chile, Manley in Jamaica, Velasco in Peru, Quadaffi in Libya, Mossadegh in Iran) for control of the nation's resources, have found great hindrances requiring a strong government and strong, organized popular support, and even this may not be enough. It will probably be necessary for Third World governments to form effective coalitions, to combine their strengths, in order to shift the balance of power against the MNCs. Otherwise the multinationals can play off individual nations against each other, making it nearly impossible for any one nation to regulate MNC behavior in the interests of a coordinated program of development.

TRANSNATIONAL INEQUALITY—RESOURCE CONSUMPTION

In the 1970s it became ever more apparent that global natural resources are not infinite in supply and that several key resources may in fact be largely depleted within a few decades. The Club of Rome (an association of prominent Western business and intellectual leaders) has sponsored two reports, *The Limits of Growth* (1972) and *Mankind at the Turning Point* (1974), that have made the more educated public aware of a resource crunch in the last decades of this century. Both reports utilize complex computer simulations of the global economy to predict the consequences of current patterns of growth and of various alternatives to the present pattern. Both reports have been challenged on methodological grounds, for political bias, and for lack of solid political analysis. Yet the questions they raised are now on the agenda of the U.N. (through UNCTAD) and will not go away.

In short, the developed nations, and especially the most affluent consumer societies of the West, use a disproportionately large share of global natural resources, and this has now reached such high levels that through Western overconsumption these resources may not be available for development of Third World nations. Oil is, of course, the single resource that has attracted most attention. According to estimates made by the U.S. Bureau of Mines and Geological Survey and used by Dennis Meadows et al. in the *Dynamics of Growth in a Finite World* (1974), world petroleum supplies would be exhausted in the next twenty-three to forty-three years if present patterns of growth in demand continue. And there is no question that the United States is by far the biggest consumer of oil, both in total usage and on a per capita basis.

On a per capita basis, the United States was already leading in energy consumption in the early 1950s; by the early 1970s oil consumption had increased in all regions of the world, and the economies of Japan, the USSR, and Eastern Europe had especially increased their levels of per capita consumption. The Third World, on the other hand, which in 1952 averaged only 5 to 6 percent of U.S. per capita consumption, had fallen to about 4 percent of U.S. per capita levels twenty years later. By the mid-1980s, energy consumption of most Western capitalist and industrial communist nations had closed the gap with the United States even more, and the Third World had just barely closed the gap to little beyond the level of the early 1950s. Thus, the inequality worldwide in petroleum use has remained huge over the postwar years, while in Western and industrial communist nations consumption has reached levels that could exhaust petroleum reserves within our lifetime.

Since the OPEC-instituted oil price rise in 1973, U.S. and Western consumption of Third World oil has increased rather than decreased at the same time that Western technology is feverishly pursuing nuclear, solar, fusion, geothermal, and other alternative energy sources. Mesarovic and Pestel, in the second Club of Rome report, point out the tragic irony of this situation for the underdeveloped countries: "The industrialized world is thus granted the time to develop alternative energy sources only by using nearly the entire world oil reserves and by that action preempting the supply of the most efficient and convenient energy source precisely when the developing nations need it most" (1974:68-69).

It could well be that Western technology will succeed in developing alternative energy sources at the same time that Western oil consumption is sucking dry the oil fields of the Middle East, Venezuela, Nigeria, and Indonesia, depriving these nations of oil resources as a crucial input to their own development. It has been argued that the new technologies, especially nuclear power, could provide alternative energy sources for development of all Third World nations, not just those with oil or gas reserves. Leaving aside the many problems now facing the nuclear energy industry (plant safety, adequate uranium supplies, waste disposal and reprocessing, nuclear weapons proliferation, dangers of terrorism/sabotage), nuclear energy for the

268 INTRODUCTION TO COMPARATIVE POLITICS

Third World is an almost perfect example of technological dependence on the West. Nuclear energy as the basis for development in the Third World would mean that the West could in effect turn off energy supplies to "uppity" or "radical" Third World governments by stopping nuclear fuel deliveries, replacement parts, or by recalling operators and maintenance personnel.

Table 14.2 Ratios of Per Capita Energy Consumption, 1952 to 1984
(United States = 100)

Country/Region	*1952*	*1972*	*1984*
United States	100	100	100
Canada	76	93	125
Britain	59	46	47
West Germany	41	46	58
France	30	36	48
Japan	11	28	43
USSR	26	41	63
Communist East Europe	21	39	57
Third World	5-6	4	7-8

SOURCES: Adapted from D. Chirot, *Social Change in the Twentieth Century* (New York: Harcourt Brace Jovanovich, 1977), pp. 160-61; World Bank, *World Development Report,* 1986.

Oil is a leading illustration of resource overconsumption by the developed nations at the possible risk of resource exhaustion and resulting damage to even the potential of the less developed countries (LDCs) for growth. But petroleum is not the only resource whose transnational inequality of consumption poses this danger. Geological Survey figures for a list of major industrial minerals indicate that at current rates of growth in consumption, reserves will be depleted in the next several decades. William Ophuls (1978), in his thoughtful study of the emerging global politics of scarcity, presents a pessimistic but perhaps realistic overview:

> ALAS, the emergence of ecological scarcity appears to have sounded the death knell for the aspirations of the LDCs. . . . In short, the current model of development, which assumes that all countries will eventually become heavily industrialized mass-consumption societies, is doomed to failure. Naturally, this conclusion is totally unacceptable to the modernizing elites of the Third World; their political power is generally founded on the promise of development. Even more important, simply halting growth would freeze the current pattern of inequality, leaving the "have nots" as the peasants of the world community in perpetuity. Thus an end of growth and development would be acceptable to the Third World only in combination with a radical redistribution of the world's wealth and a total restructuring of the world's economy to guarantee the maintenance of economic justice. Yet it

seems absolutely clear that the rich have not the slightest intention of alleviating the plight of the poor if it entails the sacrifice of their own living standards. Ecological scarcity thus greatly increases the probability of naked confrontation between rich and poor. (P. 211)

Table 14.3 Resource Depletion Estimates: Years until Exhaustion

	Minimum	*Maximum*
Aluminim	33	49
Chromium	115	137
Cobalt	90	132
Copper	27	46
Iron	154	—
Lead	28	119
Manganese	106	123
Mercury	19	44
Nickel	50	75
Platinum	41	49
Tin	62	92
Tungsten	27	—
Zinc	76	115
Petroleum	23	43
Coal	118	132

SOURCE: Ophuls, 1978: 66-67, 88.

If Third World governments are in fact (as well as in rhetoric) interested in economic justice, they must in the near future bring this resource drain under control, their own control, for the first time since the imposition of Western colonial dominance. However, it is questionable that ruling elites in many if not most Third World systems are committed to economic justice, either globally or within their own countries. Comprador (collaborator) middle classes in the Third World, in business, government, and the military, are not interested as long as they continue to live on a tiny island of luxury amidst the sea of poverty. It cannot be assumed that any government will act in favor of, or fight for, economic justice. A class-based analysis must ask: (1) Who controls the government? and (2) What are the economic interests of the dominant classes? Only then can we assess the likelihood that a Third World regime will struggle against dependency and imperialism for economic justice.

TRANSNATIONAL INEQUALITY—CAPITAL DRAIN

It is sometimes assumed that because Western-owned corporations are expanding investments in mining, manufacturing, or commercial agriculture in the Third World, or because foreign aid is given by Western governments, there is a net flow of capital funds from the developed West to "aid" development in the poor nations. This would be true if the amounts of Western capital and foreign aid transferred annually to the Third World economies were not exceeded by the amounts of profit being "repatriated," i.e., taken out of the Third World for stockholders in the West. In fact, the amount of profits taken out of the Third World each year by Western MNCs greatly exceeds the amount of Western capital invested to build up productive facilities. According to the U.S. Department of Commerce, between 1950 and 1965 new U.S. investments in the underdeveloped nations totaled some $9 billion, while repatriated profits (and other returns, such as Third World debt repayment, royalties for patents, licenses, and payments for technical services) took $25.6 billion out of the underdeveloped world. Hungarian economist Tamas Szentes (1973: 198-99) has summarized official data from a variety of sources on the extent of capital drain from the Third World. For French and British investment in former colonies in Western Africa, for British investment in India, for American, British, French, and Dutch oil investments in the Middle East, and for total Western investment in Latin America, the story is the same. It is clear that at least up to the mid-1970s the Third World as a whole was sending development capital to the rich nations of the West, mainly through the activity of Western-owned MNCs. The effects of the OPEC oil price actions since 1973 may have changed this picture for some OPEC member states, although this is difficult to determine, since whenever the Shah invested Iran's oil revenues in the West (i.e., in Krupp industries) or whenever the Saudis invest in U.S. properties or simply deposit their funds in Western banks, this also returns capital funds to the West. Szentes (1973:199) has estimated the official capital drain from the Third World at between $3.5 billion and $4 billion annually. This is probably an underestimate, since it excludes indirect capital drains through the entire inequitable structure of exchange rates. To put the matter another way, for every dollar of U.S. investment in the Third World between 1946 and 1959, about 2.5 dollars of profit were drained from the Third World. Dos Santos (1971:232) has calculated that for every U.S. dollar invested in Latin America between 1946 and 1967, 2.73 dollars left Latin America as repatriated profits (see also Chaliand, 1976:12).

Another, perhaps even more serious source of capital drain from the Third World to the rich Western nations is "capital flight," the transfer, whether legal or illegal, of massive amounts of wealth by the rich elites of Third World societies to banks and investments in North America and Western Europe. Some spectacular cases that have come to light include the stashing of stolen public funds and ill-gotten riches in Swiss bank accounts and Miami bank accounts and the purchase of real estate in Europe and the United States by the Shah's family in Iran, the Marcos family in the Philippines, the Duvalier family in Haiti, and the Somoza family in Nicaragua. But these cases are just the best-publicized tip of the iceberg. Capital flight by the rich is a daily large-scale drain on the investment resources of most Third World societies. It indicates a lack of confidence, ability, or loyalty by the Third World economic elite in the future of their own nations and a failure to invest their fortunes in their own societies' development. It has been estimated that $180 billion has been drained from Latin America by the rich elite of that region, which would be about half of that region's foreign debt (Magdoff, 1986). In just the three years from 1980 to 1982, Third World elites transferred an estimated $71 billion from seven of the largest debtor nations (Mexico, Argentina, Venezuela, Indonesia, Egypt, the Philippines, and Nigeria) at the same time that their nations' foreign debt was rising by some $102 billion (Payer, 1985). It is common practice for wealthy families in developing nations to keep a good portion of their assets in the rich developed nations, to do much of their luxury item shopping in the West, and to make arrangements for transferring additional wealth in case of domestic unrest or political upheaval. But this practice, while understandable from the perspective of protecting elite family wealth, is a critical failure in terms of maintaining and utilizing these resources for national development. Instead, these resources are turned over to Western banks and corporations for their use as productive investment capital.

Foreign aid to the Third World, which might seem an example of unblemished Western generosity, in fact adds almost nothing in the way of transferred investment funds. Between 75 and 90 percent of development aid is tied, either by law or by practice, to purchases of goods and services from the donor nation. That is, U.S. aid to poor nations requires them in large measure to spend that money on products made by U.S. corporations. It is no paradox that the U.S. corporate community is one of the firm backers of U.S. development aid, since it means increased sales to Third World nations of their products and services. This then forms a new dependency on U.S. firms for resupply, repair, and related services, while providing little or no new investment in productive facilities in the recipient nation (see Bairoch, 1975; Sachs, 1978; Sutcliffe, 1971, for more extensive commentary).

TRANSNATIONAL INEQUALITY—THE BRAIN DRAIN

Certainly one of the most disheartening aspects of transnational inequality is the strong incentive for the highly skilled and educated to migrate from the Third World to the rich, developed nations of the West. The reasons are not difficult to understand, and at the individual level, they make perfectly good sense. Third World doctors, engineers, and scientists find more stable and secure careers and consumer life-styles in the West than in their homelands. Social unrest, violence directed against the well-to-do, and the danger that

Table 14.4 The Brain Drain from Developing Countries to the United States, Canada, and the United Kingdom, 1962-1972

	Scientists and Engineers			Physicians and Surgeons			Teachers			Total		
	United States 1962-72[a]	Canada 1963-72	United Kingdom 1964-72	United States 1962-72[a]	Canada[b] 1963-72	United Kingdom[c] 1964-72	United States 1962-72[a]	Canada 1963-72	United Kingdom 1964-72	United States 1962-72[a]	Canada 1963-72	United Kingdom 1964-72
Asia	35,708	6,132	3,239	16,239	8,792	11,628	NA	5,055	8,818	51,947	19,979	23,685
Africa	2,334	523	1,035	912	302	3,845	NA	501	5,296	3,246	1,326	10,176
Latin America	6,974	207	1,402	5,704	199	495	NA	159	496	12,678	565	2,393
All Other Developing Countries	3,226	3,784	2,708	2,187	6,622	13,499	NA	5,377	7,967	5,413	15,783	24,174
Total, Developing Countries	48,242	10,646	8,384	25,042	15,915	29,467	NA	11,092	22,577	73,284	37,653	60,428

NA = not available.
a. Excluding 1970
b. Includes dentists, graduate nurses, medical and dental technicians
c. Doctors, dentists, and nurses

Source: Adapted from ILO, 1976: 130.

one's property and wealth may be confiscated either by an arbitrary regime or by a social revolution all predispose well-educated Third Worlders to migrate to the West. Additionally, nations like the United States and Australia give immigration preference to the highly educated professionals, assuring them of relatively easy entry. These professionals, however, have the skills necessary and perhaps most vital to the development of their homelands, and their loss hampers development prospects. As already mentioned in the previous chapter, the Third World has scarce resources in highly trained professionals; because of the dependent underdevelopment of many Third World economies, opportunities for those who are highly educated lie not so much within their home country as in the developed Western nations.

The extent of the Third World brain drain has apparently been increasing over the postwar period. Between 1947 and 1961, some forty-three thousand engineers emigrated from all over the world to the United States, and of this number, 60 percent came from the Third World (Castro, in Fann and Hodges, 1971:194). Between 1951 and 1963, over five thousand qualified engineers emigrated from Argentina alone to the United States. In a more recent study of this brain drain, the ILO reported that from 1962 to 1972 over one hundred seventy thousand scientists, engineers, doctors, and teachers emigrated from the underdeveloped nations to the United States, Great Britain, and Canada. The estimate rises to two hundred fifty thousand if immigration to other rich nations of the West is also included.

India alone lost thirteen thousand scientists and engineers to the United States. The Philippines lost eleven thousand scientists, engineers, and doctors to the United States. In 1970, emigration of physicians, surgeons, and dentists from the Philippines amounted to more than half of new graduations of doctors (ILO, 1976:129). Asia, and especially India and Pakistan, where health care is lacking for the average citizen, lost thirty-six thousand doctors to the United States, Canada, and Great Britain. Africa, where highly educated personnel are most scarce among the regions of the Third World, lost nearly fifteen thousand professionals to these three rich nations in just ten years. The overdeveloped consumer societies of the West are therefore draining off the intellectual as well as the material resources of the less-developed nations.

INTERNAL INEQUALITY—INCOME DISTRIBUTION AND DEVELOPMENT

In addition to the growing gap between the rich and poor nations over the past one hundred fifty years, there is increasing evidence that the dependent capitalist development of the Third World nations since World War II is associated with a growing gap between the rich and poor within the underdeveloped nations as well. In the early 1950s, Harvard economist Simon Kuznets, on the basis of some studies of Western capitalist development, put forward the theory that income distribution becomes more unequal in the early stages of industrialization and only later decreases at more advanced levels of modernization. This thesis has been partially refuted by evidence from several communist nations (China, North Korea, parts of Eastern Europe) where economic development has gone hand in hand with stable or lower levels of income inequality (see Cromwell, 1977:291-308). But for Third World nations, it appears that the pattern of dependent development is indeed increasing internal income inequality. Conventional (i.e., diffusionist) wisdom in development economics of the 1950s asserted that the benefits of growth, while going initially and heavily to the wealthy strata of businessmen and landowners, would then be plowed back into the economy as new investment. By raising the rate of savings and investment, new productive facilities would be built, creating new jobs and raising total production levels. Through new employment opportunities and greater productivity of the economy, benefits would "trickle down" to the lower classes. Careful work by Paul Baran, Irma Adelman, Cynthia Taft Morris, and Roger Hansen, among others, has shown that the "trickle down" strategy has produced few benefits for the lower classes, and in fact has led to a deterioration of conditions for large proportions of the population, what Hansen has called the "forgotten 40 percent." In Brazil, the percentage of income received by the poorest 40 percent of the population fell from 10 percent of national income in 1960 to only 8 percent in 1970; the share going to the richest 5 percent grew from 29 percent to 38 percent over the same period. And during these years Brazil's GNP per capita was growing by a healthy-looking 2.5 percent annually (Adelman and Morris, 1973:1). Henry Bienen reports that in Nigeria economic growth, in particular the rapid growth of the oil industry as a mainstay of Nigerian growth, has produced a sharp increase in income inequality, with the Gini index rising from around 0.5 in 1960 to around 0.6 in 1979 (Bienen and Diejomaoh, 1981:7). In Mexico, the poorest 40 percent of the population received 14.3 percent of national income in 1950, but only 11 percent in 1963; the share going to the richest 20 percent went from 59.8 percent to 59 percent (Hansen, 1974:75). Mexico, during this period, averaged a per capita GNP gain of nearly 3 percent annually. Similarly, a study of the Philippines between 1971 and 1975 shows that the percentage of income going to the top 20 percent increased in just those four years from 53.9 to 55.5 percent, while the income of the poorest 40 percent of the population declined from 11.9 to 11.2 percent (Third World Studies Staff, 1982). Adelman and Morris have correlated wide-ranging cross-national data on the relationship between development and income inequality (in the noncommunist nations) and have related the increase in income inequality to penetration of the Third World economy by foreign (in their terms, "expatriate") corporations:

WHEN economic growth begins in a subsistence agrarian economy through the expansion of a narrow modern sector, inequality in the distribution of income typically increases greatly, particularly where expatriate exploitation of rich natural resources provides the motivating force for growth. The income share of the poorest 60 percent declines significantly, as does that of the middle 20 percent, and the income share of the top 5 percent increases strikingly. (1973:178)

Table 14.5 Income Distribution in the Third World

| | Gini Ratio | Percentage of National Income Going To: | | |
		Top 10%	Bottom 40%	Year
Mexico	.53 (1963)	40.6	9.9	1977
Brazil	.54 (1960)	50.6	7.0	1972
Nigeria	ca. .60 (1979)	—	—	
Kenya	—	45.8	8.9	1976
Tunisia	.53 (1971)	—	—	
India	—	33.6	16.2	1976
Colombia	.62 (1964)	44.4	10.0	1970
South Korea	.26 (1966)	27.5	16.9	1976
Indonesia	—	34.0	14.4	1976
Egypt	—	33.2	16.5	1976
For comparison:				
United States	.34 (1971)	23.3	17.2	1980
Hungary	.27 (1969)	20.5	20.5	1982

SOURCES: Howe, *United States and World Development*, 1975; World Bank, *World Development Report*, 1986; *World Handbook*, 1983.

Economist Gary Fields, from a wide-ranging evaluation of evidence on inequality and growth rates, questions whether there is any clear relationship between the two, but concludes that: "In the absence of a firm commitment to developing for the poor and the courage to act on that commitment, it seems only natural that economic systems will perpetuate the flow of resources to the haves with at best some trickle-down to the have-nots" (1980:242).

The reasons for the failure of the "trickle down" approach are now fairly clear. First of all, it is now apparent that in most Third World nations the fruits of growth are monopolized to an extraordinary degree by a small class of wealthy landowners and businessmen, and those few well-paid workers in the "modern" sector of the economy increasingly in collaboration with Western MNCs. This coalition is backed by the power, both military and economic, of the rich Western democracies. Any attempt to shift income distribution in favor of the lower classes must figure on resistance from this internal-external coalition of vested interests. Thus, when the democratically elected socialist government of Salvador Allende introduced reforms that began to shift income distribution, it was overthrown by the rightwing coalition of military, landowning, and business elites, with the aid of several U.S.-owned MNCs, the Western-dominated international finance banks, and the CIA.

Second, the fruits of growth do not necessarily go into new savings or new investment that would aid overall economic development. The upper classes of the Third World have developed consumer desires no less opulent than those of the upper classes in the developed West. Therefore, much of the excessive income of Third World elites is not saved or invested in new productive facilities, but spent lavishly on Western-style overconsumption. French political scientist Gerard Chaliand (1976:30) has calculated that for fourteen African nations, nearly twice as much was spent on imports of liquor, private cars, gasoline for cars, and various cosmetics as for machinery and equipment necessary for raising production. The parasitic nature of the Third World bourgeoisie has been most vividly described by authors Frantz Fanon for Africa, in *The Wretched of the Earth,* and Eduardo Galeano for Latin America, in *The Open Veins of Latin America.* It is naive to expect such a bourgeoisie to emulate the frugality and efficiency in production of the nineteenth-century Western entrepreneur, even if it possessed the technical skills and inventiveness, which it generally does not (see Chaliand, 1976; Sutcliffe, 1971). Chaliand argues that the main goal of the Third World bourgeoisie has become control of government as the means to sharing in the fruits of dependent development in collaboration with the much more powerful Western MNCs.

Third, as mentioned in the previous chapter, the use of Western labor-saving technology in the modern industrial and commercial agricultural sectors has created little new employment, which means that for both urban and rural poor, unemployment and underemployment have grown. A deterioration of conditions for the poorest strata is the result of such dependent development, even when impressive gains in GNP growth are recorded for individual nations:

REGIONAL income inequality typically increases as the concentration of rapidly growing, technologically advanced enterprises in cities widens the gap between rural and urban per capita income. Income inequality also intensifies in the urban sector with the accumulation of assets in the hands of a relatively small number of owners (usually expatriate) of modern enterprises. The concentration is accelerated by the spread of capital-intensive industrial technology through at least three factors—the ease with which owners of modern enterprises obtain capital abroad, the inability of small-scale enterprises to obtain financing, and a growing preference of medium and large entrepreneurs for advanced modern technologies. This labor-saving bias of technological advance, the rapidity of urban population growth, the migration to the cities of unemployed rural workers, and lack of social mobility all tend to swell the numbers of urban impoverished and to decrease the income share of the poorest segments of the urban population. (Adelman and Morris, 1973:182)

The basic point of this section should be emphasized once again. Growing social inequality is not an accident, nor a misunderstanding, and not the result of simple mistakes in applying the conventional wisdom of capitalist (diffusionist) development economics. It is an integral part of dependent development in the Third World. What Western economists point to as evidence of GNP growth in the Third World is not helping, but hurting, the great majority of Third World people:

THE frightening implication of the present work is that hundreds of millions of desperately poor people throughout the world have been hurt rather than helped by economic development. Unless their destinies become a major and explicit focus of development policy in the 1970's and 1980's, economic development may serve merely to promote social injustice. (Adelman and Morris, 1973:192)

Moreover, Adelman and Morris (1973:201) found no lessening of income inequality associated with liberal democracy in the Third World, which indicates that Western political institutions are not the cure for a growing inequality and a growing awareness of social injustice. Only a revolutionary shift in political power is likely to produce a significant redistribution in favor of the poor, as in Cuba and China, and such a revolutionary shift is not likely to be produced by liberal democratic institutions or to produce liberal democratic institutions.

A few Third World nations, such as Taiwan and South Korea, with an enterprising business class, a highly disciplined and hardworking labor force, special access to Western (especially U.S.) consumer markets, and high levels of U.S. aid, have developed export industries at a rapid pace without increasing income inequality. So there are also capitalist exceptions to the rule of growing inequality. The governments of Chiang Kai-shek and Chiang Ching-kuo in Taiwan or Park Chung Hee and Chun Doo Hwan in South Korea have hardly been examples of democracy, so that even in these "showpieces" of Western-aided and export-oriented development there has been no connection between democratic politics and greater income equality. Since United States and most other Western development aid has been declining for some time and shows no signs of reversal, it is unlikely that the West will be able to sponsor more examples like Taiwan or South Korea. Nor is there any evidence from recent North-South conferences that the West is willing to substantially improve the terms of trade for the Third World as a whole. And finally, the ethnic homogeneity and relative mobilization found in Taiwan and South Korea at the end of World War II and the Korean War are simply not duplicated generally in the Third World.

INTERNAL INEQUALITY—GROWTH OF THE COMPRADOR MIDDLE CLASS

In terms of social elites, dependent development has shifted power as well as wealth to new elements of the Third World bourgeoisie, whose current interests and future prospects rest on collaboration with Western MNCs and Western finance institutions. Within the Third World we can identify several groups of elites. These are found in differing proportions in individual nations: (1) traditional elites, (2) landowning elites, (3) national bourgeoisie, (4) comprador bourgeoisie, (5) government bourgeoisie, and (6) military elites.

Traditional elites played major roles in many Third World societies during the colonial period. In many colonies, Western authorities would exercise their rule through tribal or religious leaders, village elders, or local notables, who agreed to collaborate in return for official recognition by the colonial power of their status and sometimes for material payoffs for themselves and their following (or clientele). Robert Gamer (1976) has described this earlier penetration of Third World societies as the development of a system of patron-client relationships wherein the client, in return for recognition of and obedience to the patron, receives some recognition and/or reward. Patron-client relationships, of course, were common to Third World societies before the advent of Western colonial-imperial dominance and were often quite complex networks just at the local level. Western penetration added several new elements to the system, which gradually transformed the basic nature of social evolution and continues to shape that evolution today. First, the chain of patron-client relations was stretched beyond the traditional village or small town or region, beyond the boundaries of the native society. The top patrons were now Western elites who had no family, kinship, or cultural ties to local society. Top patrons were now foreign (in nearly every sense of the word) to local Third World society. Second, the former traditional elites, by collaborating with the colonial authorities, lost much of their independence and responsibility for the well-being and development of local society. Traditional elites and their peoples who resisted collaboration, like the Herrero in German South West Africa, the Filipinos in the American seizure of the Philippines in 1899, Marathas, Gurkhas, and others in the British domination in India, the Dervishes in the British Sudan, and the many Indian groups in the United States itself, were brutally crushed, often to the point of racial genocide. Third, the new and more complex patron-client chain meant that more goods from the local economy were being siphoned off for Western elites as well as for traditional elites, leaving generally less for those at the bottom of the ladder. In some cases, colonial authorities favored certain ethnic or religious minorities, who acted as native policemen for the Western power, as with the South Moluccans in the Dutch East Indies (Indonesia). This meant better payoffs for these minorities, but also later hostility from nationalist independence movements.

In several postindependence political systems, especially in neocolonial states like Rhodesia and South Africa but also in more conservative regimes like those in Liberia, the Ivory Coast, and Kenya, traditional elites continued to serve important intermediary roles. In general, however, the influence of these traditional elites has declined with the continuing decline in traditional rural society, with the privatization of land ownership, the migration to the cities, the growth of a money-based economy, and the rise of other, stronger elites.

One elite with considerable power in many Third World nations is the large landowning class (hacendados, latifundistas, zamindaris). Latin America and large parts of South Asia and the Middle East have a longer tradition of private ownership of land than most of Africa. Often a tiny minority of aristocratic families control not only most of the agricultural land but the best farmlands as well. In the early 1950s this landowning elite was a formidable force in both the economy and the political system. In Chile, for example, the richest 4.4 percent of landowners owned over 80 percent of total farmland. In Peru, a mere 1.5 percent of big landlords controlled 63 percent of the land; 189 rich families owned 60 percent of agricultural lands, and the 920 largest latifundia took in about 80 percent of total land. In Iran, a few families owned about 70 percent of fertile farmlands. In Egypt, 6 percent of landlords owned 65 percent of arable land (Gamer, 1976:ch. 7). The Gini index for inequality in land tenure, which ranges from 0 at perfect equality to 1.0 at maximum possible inequality, stands at .87 for Argentina, .85 for Brazil, .87 for Colombia, .95 for Peru, .94 for Venezuela, .61 for Turkey, .61 for India, .61 for Pakistan, .58 for the Philippines, and .62 for Iran (World Bank Group, 1975). By comparison, in communist Poland and Yugoslavia, which carried out a redistribution of land without creating a collective agriculture, the Gini indices of land tenure inequality are .47 and .44 respectively. In a few Third World nations, notably Taiwan and South Korea, with Gini indices of .46 and .39, thoroughgoing land reform significantly reduced the power of large landowning elites. In other nations, such as Iran, Egypt, Mexico, and more recently Peru and Ethiopia, land reforms have also reduced the power of landowners as an economic and political elite, to a greater (Ethiopia) or lesser (Mexico) extent. In many cases, however, land reforms have either been a farce or so minimal as to make no great impact on landholding inequality and the power of the big landowners. What has made an impact on the power of the landowning elite in many nations has been the expansion of commercial agriculture for export and the rising power of urban bourgeois elements, both native and foreign. On the whole, the power of the landowners, insofar as this class has not itself turned to commercial export agriculture or investment in industry, has been on the decline, but is still a force, often nationalistic or fascist in orientation, to be reckoned with in the politics of many Third World systems.

The national bourgeoisie corresponds to the entrepreneurial class, which was instrumental in the industrialization of the West in the previous century. Very weak and embryonic in most of black Africa, strongest in some of the Latin American nations with the longest history of national independence (Argentina, Chile, Brazil, Mexico), the national bourgeoisie is the class of investors and business leaders who would have to lead capitalist development if the previous history of the West were to be repeated. André Gunder Frank (1970) has studied the attempts of the national bourgeoisie in Latin America to foster a self-sustaining capitalist development since independence and finds that the most promising periods of industrial progress were achieved during World War I, the Great Depression, and World War II, when the great Western powers were either embroiled in major war efforts or crippled by economic disaster, so that their dominance over the path of economic development in Latin America was temporarily disrupted or diminished. Certainly nations like Argentina, Uruguay, and Chile, by the end of World War II, were close to joining the community of advanced capitalist systems. And yet the performance in the postwar era of these systems has been one of stagnation and growing dependence of the national bourgeoisie on foreign capital, foreign technology, foreign markets, and Western intervention in suppressing revolutionary forces. Cockcroft, Frank, and Johnson conclude that, after the disruptions of two world wars and a major depression, Latin America has been reassimilated into the international capitalist system as a periphery region dominated by the core capitalist powers and their MNC extensions:

> THE Latin American middle classes, strengthened by industrialization at one time, played vaguely nationalist and progressive roles as classes in ascendance. Now they engage in what Claudio Veliz terms "the politics of conformity" and have developed a close ideological affinity with the precepts of the political and social thought promoted by established interests within the international system and national oligarchies (1972:105-6)

In only a few Third World nations does the national bourgeoisie still entertain thoughts (perhaps illusions) of competing with Western investors and leading the industrialization of the national economy. Only in a few exceptional cases, again particularly Taiwan and South Korea in East Asia, has the national business class clearly been able to take such a leading role. Peter Evans (1979) makes a good case for the existence of a still-important national bourgeoisie in Brazil, which is part of a triple alliance of MNCs, state-owned industry, and top private industrialists that controls the Brazilian economy. While Evans admits the inability of the national bourgeoisie to develop the economy or a political system on its own, he argues that the top national industrialists have more bargaining power within the top elite than some dependency theories assume. But Brazil is an exceptional case within the entire spectrum of Third World nations. There are few other nations where this triple alliance includes a national industrialist class of comparable stature. On the other hand, the national bourgeoisie, within the context of its own nation, still acts as an important political elite, trying for control of the government.

A fourth elite element, and a growing one in the Third World since World War II, is the comprador middle class, the relatively pure and straightforward product of the economic dependence of these societies on the core capitalist systems. The main role of the comprador middle class is that of the intermediary for foreign interests, the supplier of local services and minor products to foreign-owned corporations and their Western personnel. In some Third World regions, especially in Africa, where the national bourgeoisie is weakest, the comprador middle class has grown up as an integral part of the postindependence era. In Latin America, where the national bourgeoisie is stronger, the inability to compete with Western capital progressively transforms an existing nationally oriented entrepreneurial class into a comprador middleman for foreign capital. The division of power between national and comprador bourgeoisie, between a bourgeoisie with some autonomy and independence and one with only a dependent relationship to Western investments, generally shifts to the latter as dependent development progresses.

The governmental middle class consists of the higher civil service and the top staffs of government ministries. In almost all Third World nations, the size of the government bureaucracy has grown considerably as governments have taken on greater responsibility for economic growth. Chaliand (1976) notes that in Africa especially, given the weakness of other bourgeoisie elements (except for white settler minorities in certain states), control of government by an administrative middle class has become the basic means of accumulating wealth. That is to say, governmental corruption has become a basic feature, not an aberration, in those regimes where the main service of the local bourgeoisie is to provide and safeguard the avenues of foreign exploitation through maintenance of government power. Suzanne Bodenheimer, with reference to Latin America, has summarized the position and function of this elite:

THE state bureaucracy and other sectors of the middle class—for example, the technical, managerial, professional or intellectual elites—become clientele when their interests, actions, and privileged positions are derived from their ties to foreign interests. Particularly with the expanded role of the state in the national economy, the state bureaucracy (including the military in many countries) has been viewed by some as the key to national autonomy. Nevertheless, when the primary function of the state is to stimulate private enterprise, when the private sector is largely controlled by foreign interests, and when the state bureaucracy itself relies on material and ideological support from abroad (as in Brazil today), the "autonomy" of the state bureaucracy must be illusory. (Cited in Fann and Hodges, 1971:163)

The Third World military leadership is clearly one of the main contenders for power, since it is usually the best-organized and increasingly the heaviest armed force in the society. Often the officer corps may be recruited from one of the other elites, such as the landowners or traditional elites, in which case it may be tied to these interests. In systems with long-term military regimes, on the other hand, military men may blend in with the administrative bourgeoisie. Most military elites in the Third World are dependent on foreign sources for weapons, without which their ability to provide ultimate safeguards for private property, both national and foreign-owned, would be endangered. Several Third World military elites have been able to switch their main sources of military hardware (and thus their dependence) from the West to the Soviet Union (Egypt in the latter 1950s, later Syria and Iraq, and most recently Ethiopia). It may be that military elites are somewhat more independent by virtue of having at least some choice in sources of armaments and can exercise this choice without necessarily leading a social revolution (Egypt, Syria, Iraq).

Politics in Third World nations, except for the still-rare occurrence of an authentic social revolution (as in China, Vietnam, and Cuba in the last thirty years), are characterized by shifting coalitions and conflicts within these elite groupings. Each elite grouping has its own clients, or followers, who benefit when their patrons are able to increase their utility to the dominant Western interests. The great majority of the population, and perhaps a growing majority at that, does not belong to any patron-client network and are thus outside the "normal" (nonrevolutionary) politics of the nation. They are also outside the reward systems that make up the political system. Gamer has likened Third World political systems to the systematic looting of the society by a pirate ship anchored offshore:

> IT is as though governance of these nations took place from ships moored off the shore. On these ships are government leaders, all those involved with major financial transactions, the bureaucracy, and the military. Contact is kept with those needed to extract resources for export and intercept profits from the internal distribution of goods and with those needed to enforce coercive measures. These shore dwellers are paid for their services, but their percentage of the populace is small. When these individuals do not perform their jobs well, or spies report they are engaged in malfeasance, they can be replaced with others. . . .
>
> Basic political activities take place aboard ship. The military are capable of

terrorizing the ship, but do not know how to keep it supplied with consumer goods, or how to build the roads, electrical power, and other basic services on which they depend when they occasionally go ashore to quell civil disturbances. The bureaucracy plays a key role in keeping those services (which also create profits) flowing, and hence cannot be ignored. The businessmen are the only ones capable of generating the profits that keep the ship prosperous. (1976:166-67)

The institutional or symbolic format of government may change, and quite rapidly, with shifting coalitions and power struggles among the elite groupings. Whether the government is a military junta, a one-party system, a multiparty democracy, or some sort of monarchy at the moment is less important to understanding Third World politics than is understanding the system of dependency. The power struggles among elites matter a great deal in terms of the division of spoils among these patron-client minorities. But for the masses of the population, these changes are basically cosmetic and matter very little, for they do not alter the basic system that is draining resources from the society and maintaining the gross inequalities of dependent development.

THE HUMAN TOLL OF STRUCTURAL VIOLENCE

The cost of social inequality is borne in many ways by those at the bottom of the society in all political systems, including the shortening of life for those with insufficient food, shelter, and health care. A group of scholars, including Johan Galtung, Gernot Köhler, Norman Alcock, and Tord Hoivik, have calculated the loss of potential lifespan from persistent deprivation associated with social inequality. This loss is termed "structural violence," since it is associated with the regular functioning of the current world order. Structural violence is contrasted with the loss of human life from international warfare or from domestic homicide. Norwegian political scientist Tord Hoivik (1979), using 1970 data, has calculated the annual number of lives lost as a result of structural violence on a global scale. Hoivik's figures indicate that over 18 million human lives are lost each year through systematic inequality of access to basic diet, housing and health needs. This loss of life exceeds the number of deaths per year from even the largest military conflicts, World War I and World War II. The point is not, however, to minimize the human tragedy of war, but to illustrate the enormity of the human death toll that is produced through social inequality, both within nations and between nations. Deaths from structural violence occur in well-to-do nations of Europe (90,000), North America (90,000), Japan (20,000), and the Soviet Union (100,000), but the overwhelming majority of such human loss is located in the Third World areas of Asia (14 million), Africa (3 million), and Latin America (800,000).

Chapter 15

Liberty, Imperialism, and Dependency

THE PERFORMANCE OF THIRD WORLD SYSTEMS in the area of personal liberty is not generally encouraging, and the reasons for this are often misunderstood in the West. Whether a Third World regime is, at any given moment, a military dictatorship, a one-party system, a personal dictatorship, or a multi-party elected civilian government may make little difference for most of the citizens of that society in terms of personal liberty. At the most local level, even in democratic Brazil in the latter 1980s, for example, the local landlords can and do hire gunslingers to intimidate and, if necessary, kill campesino organizers or those who support them, including teachers and priests. In the Philippines, after the overthrow of the Marcos dictatorship and the return to democracy under President Aquino, vigilante groups financed by local plantation owners continue to attack Catholic clergy who side with the peasants in their grievances (Mydans, 1987). The protection of personal liberty, even in those Third World nations which have elected civilian governments, may be pitifully weak in practice for people at the local level. On the other hand, for the minority with some resources, financial and organizational, and with some links to the elite patron-client networks that participate in the dependency system of benefits, the state of personal liberty may vary considerably and quite suddenly with changes in the nature of the regime. But even for this minority, as for the majority, the penetration of strong outside forces, predominantly from the rich Western nations but also from the Soviet Union, into these dependent systems places limitations, explicit and implicit, on the exercise of political and civil freedoms, even where the local political system permits it or attempts to permit it. The realization of personal liberty in the Third World, as with other performance areas, is tied to both transnational and domestic factors. Those liberties which are most frequently permitted are the rights of emigration and property ownership, which support the continuation of the dependency syndrome. Those most often suppressed, under a variety of regimes, are the rights of free trade unions, leftist political organizations, leftist free speech and press, and peasant activist movements, which are most likely to challenge both local power structures and international dependency relations.

285

WESTERN IMPERIALISM AND LIBERTY

When the exercise of political liberty has gotten "out of hand" in an individual Third World nation, Western interests (i.e., governmental, corporate, and international finance) have attempted to reimpose "acceptable" limits or, if necessary, to suppress political liberty generally. Empirical investigations of what is acceptable and what is unacceptable to Western interests reveal that almost any government is minimally acceptable so long as it does not threaten either (1) the freedom of Western-owned MNCs to invest and repatriate profits or (2) the social existence of the local bourgeoisie. Dictatorships such as those of General Park in South Korea, Suharto in Indonesia, Kitikachorn in Thailand, the Shah in Iran, Selassie in Ethiopia, Pinochet in Chile, Somoza in Nicaragua, Duvalier in Haiti, and the white apartheid regime in South Africa are acceptable. They will receive trade, investment financing, and military aid from Western sources. The list of undemocratic regimes supported by the West or installed by the West could be extended considerably.

Third World nations that accept economic and/or military aid from the Soviet Union are also minimally acceptable (though not welcomed, naturally) as long as they are not engaged in socialist revolutions in their own countries. Thus, while the West did not appreciate Nasser's acceptance of aid from the USSR for the Aswan high dam and of large-scale military aid as well, it did not generally fear a socialist transformation of Egypt as a result (though Sir Anthony Eden, who ordered the 1956 British-French invasion of Egypt, apparently did). Much the same can be said for the West's attitude toward Soviet economic and military aid to India, Algeria, Guinea, Iraq, Syria, and Afghanistan (until the 1978 takeover by the Afghan Communist party, at least). To be sure, there are some uncertain areas, such as the extensive Soviet ties to Ethiopia after 1975 and South Yemen in the 1970s and 1980s, where it is not yet clear whether these regimes are leading socialist transformations of their own nations. In Nicaragua, the Sandinista revolution was initially judged minimally acceptable by the Carter administration, but totally unacceptable by the Reagan administration, which has sought to overthrow the regime.

Third World governments that nationalize Western assets with compensation agreeable to the corporation are also minimally acceptable, though also not encouraged generally. Only when nationalization of MNC holdings is not, in the view of the corporation, sufficiently compensated does this behavior signify an unacceptable regime. There is a ladder of escalation in the forms of Western intervention utilized to remove "unacceptable" political choices from the Third World, even when, and perhaps especially when, these governments represent the popular choice of the society.

TACTICS OF WESTERN INTERVENTION

The most blatant form of Western intervention is, of course, direct military invasion. Because it is so blatant a limitation on political freedom, direct military action is generally used only after other more favored tactics are judged to be ineffective or insufficient. Especially in the era of formal decolonization, the adverse reaction to direct armed intervention in the Third World has probably made this option even less palatable for the 1980s. Still, the United States has used direct military intervention on occasion, as in the Dominican Republic in 1965 and in Vietnam, Laos, and Cambodia. The French and Belgian rescues of the Mobutu regime in Zaire in 1977 indicate that direct military action is not completely ruled out by other Western powers.

Covert intervention, which does not involve the open and direct introduction of regular Western armed forces into Third World politics, covers a broad array of tactics. The American CIA was successful, through the use of paid mob actions and economic sabotage, in overthrowing the nationalist Mossadegh government in Iran in 1953 and restoring the Shah to his throne. The CIA arranged for hired mercenaries to oust the agrarian reform Arbenz regime in Guatemala in 1954 after it had expropriated some (unused) United Fruit Company landholdings. It arranged for the coup that toppled neutralist Prince Souvanna Phouma in Laos in 1960 and replaced his regime with the pro-Western regime of Prince Boun Oum. The CIA was active in "destabilizing" the elected Marxist regime of Salvador Allende in Chile between 1970 and 1973. Of course, the CIA failed in its Bay of Pigs invasion of Cuba in 1961 and in its many attempted assassinations of Fidel Castro. It failed in its support for the FNLA of Holden Roberto in the 1975 Angola civil war. The CIA has attempted for many years to engineer the overthrow of the Sandinista regime in Nicaragua through the contra forces, which were organized, financed, trained, and armed by the CIA. In general, the CIA has found it increasingly difficult to repeat its successes of the 1950s and 1960s (Ranelagh, 1986).

The CIA is not as powerful as it is sometimes portrayed in conspiracy theories of world politics, but it has considerable resources. The CIA budget, while secret, was estimated at several billion dollars annually in the mid-1970s, and it openly employed some fifteen thousand personnel in the 1960s (Wolfe, 1973:193). The CIA has at times been responsible for running mercenary armies, such as General Vung Pao's Meo tribesmen in Laos and the Cuban exiles in the Bay of Pigs operation. The CIA set up "dummy" companies as a channel for supplying heavy weapons and bombers to the Portuguese dictatorship of Antonio Salazar for its war against national liberation movements in Mozambique, Angola, and Guinea-Bissau, when it was deemed inappropriate for the U.S. government to aid the Salazar dictatorship openly. The CIA was, along with the Israelis, responsible for setting up and training the Shah's SAVAK (secret police) in Iran. On a regular basis, the CIA offers its expertise and assistance to military and police forces for suppression of dissent and insurgencies in the Third World. The CIA, according to revelations by a former CIA regional director, Philip Agee, also infiltrates labor unions, student organizations, and U.S. AID programs in the Third World. And when the occasion has called for it, the CIA has arranged for the assassinations of unwanted political figures, sometimes in large numbers, as with the infamous Operation Phoenix, which may have killed twenty thousand Vietnamese suspected of aiding the Vietcong (Prados, 1986:309), but who were often the victims of family feuds and racketeering in Vietnamese society.

One of the ways in which Western imperialism limits political freedom in the Third World is through the training and arming of military and police forces in nondemocratic systems or for use in suppressing democracy, as in Chile. One instrument for United States training of police forces in the Third World was the Office of Public Safety (OPS), a division of AID concerned with carrying out "aid" missions to the underdeveloped world. Third World police were trained both in the United States and in the home countries. In the United States, police training is carried out at the International Police Academy (IPA) in Washington, D.C. As of 1970, IPA had graduated some thirty-five hundred police officers (NACLA, in Leggett, 1973:380–81). Other Third World police have received training at American universities, at the John F. Kennedy Special Warfare Center at Fort Bragg, and in special schools for counterinsurgency in the Panama Canal Zone and in Puerto Rico. In the home countries, U.S. OPS agents known as "public safety advisors" trained police and provided expertise for local operations. Many of these advisors have been FBI and CIA personnel. OPS advisors were especially active in the Dominican Republic after the U.S. invasion of 1965, reorganizing police forces and working to suppress leftist political support for popular leader Juan Bosch. In Uruguay, OPS agent Dan Mitrione, who had earlier been an advisor to the Brazilian police, was special advisor on torture techniques used in the suppression of the Tupamaro urban guerrilla movement (for a particularly unpleasant account of the Mitrione story, in terms of what American democracy does to support repression, see Langguth [1979]). Mitrione was eventually kidnapped and executed by the Tupamaros, and several other OPS agents have been killed in the line of duty (see also Klare, in Leggett, 1973; Tobis, 1971). OPS developed an elaborate national identification (ID) system in South Vietnam, with fingerprints, political and biographical data, and photos on 12 million people for a computer data bank to be used for more efficient police control of the Vietnamese population. This system is now being introduced into various Latin American police systems.

It is clear that protection of U.S. interests, through suppression of dissent, is a major goal of police aid to repressive regimes. General Maxwell Taylor, speaking at the 1965 graduation ceremony of the International Police Academy, admitted this goal openly:

> THE outstanding lesson [of Vietnam] is that we should never let another Vietnam-type situation arise again. We were too late in recognizing the extent of the subversive threat. We appreciate now that every young, emerging country must be constantly on the alert, watching for those symptoms, which, if allowed to develop unrestrained, may eventually grow into a disastrous situation such as that in South Vietnam. We have learned the need for a strong police force and strong police intelligence organization to assist in identifying early the symptoms of an incipient subversive situation. (Quoted in Leggett, 1973:380)

As Alan Wolfe has pointed out in his study of repressive tactics used in U.S. policy, much of U.S. foreign aid is spent in a systematic and global effort to "police" the Third World against political developments perceived as harmful to U.S. investment or other economic and strategic interests, regardless of the interference in the internal politics of these nations:

> AID funds seem to have been used to repress anti-government riots in South Korea, help anti-communists win elections in Colombia and the Dominican Republic, supply Venezuelan police with up-to-date police equipment, suppress labor agitation at Goodyear and Gulf and Western plantations in the Dominican Republic, and pay for the training of Firestone Rubber's security police in Liberia. Here is the internationalization of police repression in its most blatant form. When it is supplemented by the presence of American soldiers around the globe—in at least sixty-four countries in the early 1970s—the result is a most extensive apparatus for violent repression. (Wolfe, 1973:202)

It must be pointed out that this police aid to Third World nations is symptomatic of the dependency of these regimes on the advanced Western democracies. The power relationship is clearly one of domination, not equal partnership. United States policy is openly charged with responsibility for keeping these nations within the Western camp, and it is common in U.S. domestic politics for aspiring candidates to charge that certain administrations were responsible for "losing" Cuba or China or Angola, Mozambique, Vietnam, Iran, or Nicaragua, as though these nations were "owned" in some sense by the United States prior to the overthrow of a certain regime. It should also be noted that the West reserves the option to drop previous allies in the Third World when they seem to become liabilities in the protection of Western interests. The United States arranged for the assassination of South Vietnamese President Diem in 1963 after it was clear that his government was losing the struggle against the NLF. The assassination of Dominican dictator Trujillo in 1961 and the French-planned and aided overthrow of "emperor" Jean Bokassa of the Central African Republic in 1979 are other examples of right-wing regimes toppled by Western covert action in order to install more effective pro-Western regimes.

Economic sanctions and threats of economic reprisals are common weapons used to affect the politics of Third World nations. Certainly any regime that embarks on a socialist transformation of the economy must reckon with a cutoff of Western aid (except perhaps for Sweden), a closing off of international finance sources for development, and an economic embargo on trade with the West and its allies. Thus, in 1961, when it dawned on the United States that the Castro government was serious about social revolution in Cuba and intended to expropriate U.S. holdings, the United States declared an economic blockade against trade with Cuba and pressured other Western and Latin American governments to break all ties with Cuba as well. The idea was to strangle the Cuban economy, which was dependent on the U.S. sugar market for selling its largest export commodity. Most Cuban transport and industrial equipment and in general all technology of the modern sector of the economy was dependent on Western corporations for service and spare parts. A CIA-managed campaign of economic sabotage aimed at further crippling Cuban sugar production, machinery, and transportation facilities (Kwitny, 1984: 242-51). The reliance on Western technology by Third World nations can always be used by the West to blackmail Third World systems, as is now patently clear. In the case of Cuba, the Soviet Union agreed to buy up the sugar crop for an extended period at prices above the world market average, and the Soviet Union and other industrialized East European communist states have provided technological and financial aid to partially offset the Western economic blockade. But the costs of the transition have been high, and only a strongly motivated regime with firm and organized popular support could attempt to defy a complete cutoff from its traditional sources of trade, finance, and technology.

The major international finance banks, including the International Monetary Fund (IMF), the World Bank, the Inter-American Development Bank, and the United States Export-Import Bank, are also useful for disciplining Third World governments that get out of line (see chapter 14). While these banking agencies are either private or multinational, their capital for financing Third World development projects and programs comes from Western sources and is therefore more or less aligned with Western interests. In the latter 1970s, some OPEC funds for Third World development were just beginning to become available, and Western news media were quick to point out how this money was used to buy political influence for the Arab point of view vis-à-vis the Palestinian issue. It should come as no surprise, although it is not well covered in the Western press, that Western finance capital has been used for generations to peddle Western influence in the Third World and to shape Third World politics to meet Western interests. Most (non-OPEC) Third World nations are debtor states (i.e., in debt to foreign and international banks and governments), and must repay interest and principal on these debts annually (called debt "servicing"). They must often come to these sources of financing for further loans and credits in order to pay for imports for both consumption and production. If they cannot secure further credits, they will not have the hard currency necessary to pay for imported food, machinery, and fuels. Decreased food imports will mean higher prices for available foodstuffs, and decreased fuel and production equipment supplies will mean slowdowns in industry and agriculture. It is extremely difficult to quickly break these ties of financial dependence and embark on an independent course of internally directed and self-sustained development. Therefore, even progressive governments, such as Michael Manley's democratic socialism in Jamaica or Juan Velasco's radical military regime in Peru had to compromise their policies, even scrap whole reform programs, to meet conditions for "stabilization" (enforced austerity) set down by the IMF. There is no pretense about the IMF dictating political conditions for the continued extension of credits, and there is little doubt that the IMF, even if it wanted to support social reform in the Third World, could not long oppose the interests of its major capital contributors (although see below for the relative neutrality of the IMF, compared to other banking agencies, in the Chilean case).

THE EXAMPLE OF CHILE

The tactics used by Western imperialism to limit political liberty in the Third World when that liberty begins to threaten Western interests are illustrated by the events in Chile in the early 1970s. In the postwar period, and in the twentieth century generally, Chile had had the best record for constitutional government and free elections anywhere in Latin America. In many ways, Chilean society was closer to some of the societies of Western Europe in its social, cultural, and political traditions than it was to many of the less stable and less developed nations of Latin America. In 1970, a Popular Unity coalition of leftist parties led by socialist Salvador Allende won the presidency in a three-way race. Allende received 36 percent of the vote, the Christian Democratic candidate Tomic got 28 percent, and the National party candidate Allesandri got 35 percent. The United States and several U.S. MNCs had pinned their hopes and several hundred thousand dollars of campaign contributions on the right-wing Allesandri. Nevertheless, Allende received a plurality and was confirmed by the Chilean Congress as the new president. U.S. Ambassador Edward Korry, in a secret statement to outgoing President Eduardo Frei, promised that "once Allende comes to power we shall do all within our power to condemn Chile and the Chileans to utmost deprivation and poverty" (revealed in *U.S. Senate Report on CIA Assassination Plots* in November 1975 and quoted in Roxborough, O'Brien, and Roddick, 1977:277).

The Popular Unity government was then attacked along two fronts: first, an informal economic blockade was established by the United States to strangle the Chilean economy and punish the Chilean people, as Ambassador Korry had promised; second, aid and encouragement were given to internal opponents of Allende and increasingly to those groups intent upon a military overthrow of the government. Like most Third World economies, Chile's was open to attack from the United States for several reasons. Even before Allende took office, Chile was in debt to Western banks and governments to the tune of $2.6 billion, a very high debt for a nation of only 8 million people. Chile's ability to pay off its debts and to continue paying for imports from the West was closely tied to its ability to export copper, its most abundant natural resource, to the West. Additionally, Western and mainly U.S. interests in Chile were extensive across the economy, so that many production, transport, and communications facilities were dependent on the West (the United States in particular) for replacement and spare parts.

The economic blockade against Chile tightened by steps as it became clear that Allende was serious about nationalizing, by legal statute, U.S. corporate holdings in Chile, including those of Kennecott Copper, Anaconda Copper, Cerro Copper, and ITT, on terms that these MNCs deemed "unacceptable." Almost immediately, U.S. aid projects were halted and loan money granted through signed agreements with the previous Christian Democratic Frei government was withheld. Private U.S. bank credit dried up quickly, declining from a level of about $220 million annually to only $35 million in 1972. Under U.S. pressure, the multilateral Inter-American Development Bank and Robert McNamara's World Bank stopped their loans. The United States Export-Import Bank, which had given a $25 million loan to the state-owned Chilean Steel Corporation in 1969 for expansion, refused to disburse the final $13 million after Allende took office. Only the IMF, despite obvious pressure from the United States, took a relatively neutral position and granted some credits ($148 million) in the first year of Allende's government. Additionally, $90 million in aid and credits were given by the communist nations, $32 million came from Brazil, and $100 million from Argentina. Even so, these were not sufficient to keep Chile's international debt situation from deteriorating markedly between 1970 and 1973.

In the transport sector, the denial of spare parts had a debilitating effect on the Chilean economy. By 1972, some 30 percent of privately owned microbuses, 21 percent of taxibuses, and 33 percent of public buses were inoperative because of lack of spare parts and tires. Similar effects were visible in the trucking industry. United States multinationals also added their weight to the economic blockade. Kennecott Copper, expropriated from its huge El Teniente mining complex, took legal action to block payments to Chile for exports of copper to other nations. By 1973, Chile's copper sales, its main source of export earnings, were falling, and its foreign customers were being scared off by threats of court suits if they continued to do business with Chile.

The second broad avenue of attack was through support for Chile's internal enemies. While economic aid and financing was being cut off, military aid to the Chilean armed forces was continued, clearly to maintain support for the United States among the Chilean military. In 1971, $5 million in credits were granted for military purchases and $10 million in 1972, despite the fact that U.S. policy is, by law, to cut off aid to governments that nationalize U.S. corporate properties without satisfactory compensation (Petras and Morley, 1975:127). In May of 1973, five months before the military coup, President Nixon, through presidential waiver power, approved the sale of F-5E fighter aircraft to the Chilean air force, with the rationale that this was "important to the national security of the United States" (Petras and Morley, 1975:128). Clearly the Chilean military, many of whose officers had received training in the United States, was the trump card of U.S. strategy and was afforded favored treatment in preparation for the coup of September 11, 1973. Additional aid went to nonmilitary opponents of the Allende government. The Inter-American Development Bank made two exceptions to its blockade policy, a $7 million loan to Catholic University and a $4.6 million loan to Austral Unviersity, both conservative strongholds. And in 1972–1973, when Chilean truck owners organized a strike in an attempt to paralyze the economy, the CIA funnelled tens of millions of dollars to aid the truck owners' action to compensate for lost business and income.

After the September military coup, which killed Allende and overthrew Chilean democracy, the economic blockade was immediately lifted and the Pinochet dictatorship was extended financial aid. In the first month of military rule, U.S. banks offered nearly $200 million in new credits. The Inter-American Development Bank approved $8.5 million for the junta before its own project study was even complete. The World Bank added $13.5 million, and in February 1974, the IMF approved $95 million in "standby" credits, which was later increased to $158 million. In just the first six months after the military seizure of power and the suppression of democracy in Chile, some $468 million in financial aid was given to the military regime (Petras and Morley, 1975:144). For its part, the Pinochet dictatorship agreed to pay $253 million to Anaconda Copper and $68 million to Kennecott Copper for their nationalized property.

The Chilean military, in overthrowing Allende's government, also destroyed the liberties upon which Western democracies are built. All political parties, including the Christian Democrats and the Nationalists as well as the Socialists and Communists, were suppressed. Freedom of the press and free speech were destroyed. Leftist political and union leaders were hunted down by the new secret police, the DINA, which appeared quickly on the scene as a major element of the military rule. Political dissidents by the thousands were dragged off in the night to unknown fates (several unmarked mass graves were publicly reported in the Western media). Thus United States policy, which verbally supports human rights throughout the world, actively and vigorously promoted and encouraged the brutal suppression of personal liberty in one of the few successful democracies in Latin America.

> THE United States long ago gave up the idea that a parliamentary facade is a necessary accompaniment of capitalist development in Latin America. The incapacity of parliamentary regimes to offer guarantees against radicalism and nationalism and their inability to create favorable conditions for foreign investment have for some time provoked U.S. policy-makers and economic influentials into rethinking the "best" political formula to serve their interests in Latin America. (Petras and Morley, 1975:157)

Allende's Popular Unity program would certainly have run into fierce internal opposition even without U.S. intervention, but it is useless to try to separate out internal and external components. The ties between the Chilean bourgeoisie and U.S. corporate interests were so strong that Popular Unity was inevitably struggling to maintain a democratic system against an internal/external coalition. In the view of many observers, the national bourgeoisie will utilize Western external aid against the domestic left to save capitalism, even if this means sacrificing its own democratic liberty. Roxborough, O'Brien, and Roddick (1977:114), in their sympathetic yet critical analysis of Popular Unity in Chile, conclude that the middle class in the Third World is now "profoundly reactionary." A progressive government, however democratically elected, must reckon with a political onslaught by the bourgeoisie that utilizes tactics both legal and illegal and both peaceful and violent, an onslaught that can draw on Western resources for tipping the balance of power in its favor. The extent of democratic liberty in the Third World is not an internal matter alone and must be placed in the largest context of Western economic interests. In the 1960s, the United States promoted democracy as part of its Alliance for Progress in Latin America; by the 1970s, it had decided that the Brazilian military junta was a more appropriate model for Chile to follow. If, in the 1980s, U.S. foreign policy again has emphasized its support for Latin American democracy, this renewed commitment must be viewed skeptically by any Latin American government, no matter how democratic, committed to major social reforms.

LIBERTY IN THE THIRD WORLD

Democracy remains a possibility in Third World nations, and even without effective parliamentary democracy, certain civil liberties are not inconsistent with dependency and Western interests. Indeed, there are occasions when the United States and its allies have used their influence to try to "humanize" or "liberalize" certain Third World governments. This often occurs when the U.S. government perceives that excessive regime violence is leading to a truly revolutionary situation, one that might endanger not only the present government but the entire social order and its ties to international capital. The United States in 1977 did put some pressure on the Somoza regime in Nicaragua to liberalize its practices in the hope of preventing a Sandinista guerilla victory (which occurred anyway). The United States encouraged a moderation of the vicious Thai military junta in 1977 when it appeared that widespread attacks on students and intellectuals were forcing them into an underground alliance with the communist insurgents in the northeast provinces. The British began to put pressure on the white minority regime in Rhodesia to include blacks when the ZAPU and ZANU (Patriotic Front) insurgency began to have some success in its armed struggle. Other Western efforts to promote liberalization as a means of forestalling revolution were undertaken in Iran in 1978 and El Salvador in 1979. Western pressure on South Africa to end apartheid and to bring blacks, colored and Indians into political participation will in all probability materialize only after an armed black nationalist insurgency has taken root there.

It is also possible that certain liberties may be tolerated within the dependency system, so long as they are either (1) limited to members of the ruling elite grouping or (2) not effectively used by nonelites to demand greater social equity or economic benefits. In the first case, a degree of liberty among elites helps to keep the elite coalition together and may be institutionalized as part of the bargaining process over economic policy. Thus, for example, even while the Somoza family ruled in Nicaragua for over forty years, it did permit some competition to its Liberal party base from the Conservative party, and moderate opposition newspapers were permitted to publish. It was only in the 1970s, and especially after the 1972 earthquake that destroyed Managua, the capital city, that the middle class began to oppose Somoza's rulership more vigorously. This was a result of Somoza's land speculation in the rebuilding of the city of Managua. Somoza forced the rebuilding of the city on Somoza-owned land and reaped huge windfall profits, while denying similar opportunities to other bourgeois groups. In other words, he hogged the whole thing for himself and in the process alienated much middle-class support. With the assassination of Conservative party leader and newspaper publisher Joaquin Chamorro in 1978, presumably by Somoza henchmen, the split between Somoza's Liberal party and the moderate middle-class opposition forced the abandonment of the interelite tolerance and relative liberty for bourgeois groups that had characterized much of the forty-year period of the Somoza dynasty.

Another example of the coexistence of liberty and coercion is the Mexican political system, one of the most stable in Latin America (and the Third World generally) since the 1930s. Formally, Mexico has a federal structure, with a multiparty system of competing parties at local, state, and federal levels. However, the system has been dominated for sixty years by one party, the Institutional Revolutionary party (PRI), which manipulates the nominal opposition parties, the more conservative PAN and the moderate left PSP. On occasion, when the PRI has lost a local election that it wanted to win, the counting of the votes is simply rigged, or the election may be annulled by a higher authority (R. Hansen, 1974:122). The PRI is organized into three sectors, representing agrarian, popular, and labor groups affiliated with the party. These sectors act as patron-client networks and include campesino, civil service, and trade union organizations that have agreed to work within the PRI framework and abide by its rules. These groups are then granted some rewards; in turn they help to maintain the social peace, the "peace of the PRI," by not making militant demands on the government on behalf of peasants and workers. Of course, new and more militant groups arise under the conditions of extreme inequality, landlessness, and poverty that afflict great numbers of Mexican citizens who do not benefit from its economic growth.

Bo Anderson and James Cockcroft (in Cockcroft, Frank, and Johnson, 1972:219–69), Roger Hansen (1974: especially ch. 5), and Pablo Gonzalez Casanova (1970) have described the PRI's methods for dealing with independent political groups that fall outside its definition of acceptable behavior. If possible, the PRI leadership attempts to coopt the leaders of independent unions, student groups, and campesino organizations. Offers of money or political office are common, as are threats of violence if cooptation is refused. If the PRI can coopt militant leaders, it can defuse the demands of their followers. This is a common tactic, of course, and one not peculiar to the Mexican system, except that it is so highly refined and so institutionalized in that system. For those groups whose leaders refuse cooptation, the PRI has not been hesitant to employ assassination squads, to arrest or deport militant leaders, and to employ government troops to shoot strikers and rebellious students. The goal of this dual strategy of cooptation and coercion is to exclude the great majority of the populace from making any effective demand on the political system. The PRI system attempts to maintain the majority of the citizenry in an unorganized, politically passive condition. It is the opposite of a mobilization system in that it sets up threats and punishments against noncoopted groups that want to exercise political liberties; on the other hand, it does not seek to mobilize these groups of lower-class citizens itself. In the late 1970s and 1980s, with the growing debt crisis and the collapse of the Mexican economy, the PRI regime turned more often to violence and corruption to reinforce its political hegemony (Hellman, 1983). In the 1988 elections, the PRI was faced with a strong challenge from PAN candidate Manuel Clouthier on the right and from a coalition of leftist-populist groups united behind the candidacy of Cuauhtémoc Cárdenas, a popular former PRI leader and son of Lázáro Cárdenas, the populist president of Mexico from 1934 to 1940. The PRI candidate, Carlos Salinas de Gortari, a colorless Harvard-educated economist, officially won with 50 percent of the vote (Cárdenas 31 percent, Clouthier 17 percent), but only through massive vote fraud and intimidation by the PRI political machinery. Even his official vote percentage is the lowest in the history of PRI domination and thus may signal the end of PRI hegemony in Mexican politics.

Hansen (1974:120–21) has identified "manifest" and "latent" aspects of Mexican politics. At the manifest (official) level, the PRI provides representation of popular needs and grievances arising from the workers and peasants. At the latent (practical) level, the PRI sectors serve to repress and demobilize, through cooptation and coercion, popular demands for social reform. (In this respect, it is appropriate that the U.S. attempt to break the Vietnamese peasantry's support for the NLF was called a "pacification" program, aimed at demobilizing peasant demands for land reform, honest government, and attention to local health and education needs.)

Mexico and Nicaragua are only two examples and differ from many other Third World systems in that the PRI and the Somoza family provided a "stable" political order for over forty years in each nation. In many Third World nations, of course, the ruling elites have not been able to provide an enduring organizational structure for government. The Mexican PRI is exemplary in that it has maintained an effective elite consensus and a passive populace without serious interelite clashes and without a military coup for over half a century. Most Third World elites have not been able to accomplish this nearly as well and have invited military intervention into the political arena. According to Theodore Sumberg (1975:28–29) there were some 264 military coups (not all successful) in the Third World between 1946 and 1970, including 18 in Bolivia and Venezuela, 16 in Argentina, 14 in Syria, 12 in El Salvador, 11 in Iraq, 9 each in Brazil, Guatemala, Laos, Peru, and South Vietnam, 8 in Paraguay and in Thailand, and 7 in Haiti and in the Sudan. If the figures for the 1970s are added, African nations began to appear more frequently on this list, since most African states achieved independence around 1960.

Robert Gamer (1976) has provided a description of common techniques used to limit the practical expression of liberty while at the same time retaining the facade of a constitutional or parliamentary order. These include:

1. Limitations on potentially challenging groups such as unions, teachers' organizations, and the press. Techniques such as antistrike laws, security or loyalty clearances for teachers and students, purges of suspect educators, restrictions on importation of newsprint, and government ownership or secret sponsorship of certain news media are common.
2. Limitations on independent political groups. Techniques here include police permission for political gatherings, outlawing of selected parties or ideologies, cooptation or coercion of opposition candidates, and rigged vote counting.
3. Intimidation of selected politically active individuals. Methods often employed are loss of employment, threats to family members, arbitrary harassment, arrest, torture, and deportation.
4. Extraordinary extension of government powers, presumably of limited duration. Measures include temporary suspension of part or all of the constitution, declaration of a state of emergency or martial law, and postponement of certain elections.

While these measures can be found in various mixtures at different times in most Third World systems, some greater attention should be placed on the use of torture and death squads, particularly against radical leaders of political, student, peasant, and worker groups. These terrorist squads, similar in function to the earlier Ku Klux Klan in the United States political system, are a basic deterrent to the effective organization of lower-class interests that would threaten the major networks of dependency relations. Death squads are closely affiliated with official police and military forces, although the government in power disowns their activities and pleads ignorance. A brief Third World survey of more prominent death squads would include: the Argentine Anticommunist Alliance (AAA) in Argentina; *Orden* (Order) and the White Warriors Union in El Salvador; *Mano Blanco* (White Hand) and *Ojo por Ojo* (An Eye for an Eye) in Guatemala; the *Red Gaurs* in Thailand; the infamous Tontons Macoute in Haiti; the "death squad" in Brazil; the House of Israel in Guyana; the so-called Lost Command and, at an earlier period, the *Ilagas* (now officially recognized as the Civilian Home Defense Forces) in the Philippines; and *la Banda* in the Dominican Republic. The continued formation and functioning of these thinly disguised, government-sanctioned death squads, even in situations where there is widespread international criticism of this aspect of the regime (as in the case of El Salvador), is an indication of the important need, periodic but systemic, for the regime to prevent at all costs the emergence of organized peasant, labor, or leftist political interests. If other tactics (cooptation, bribery, and so on) should fail, application of officially disowned terror is the systemic pattern of regime response to demobilize various groups in the population.

Still, democracy and personal liberty have uses in Third World systems, since they give the impression of free choice and participation. We may expect that liberalizations and humanizations will continue to appear in the Third World in attempts to restore or build up legitimacy for governing elites; but we may also expect that these liberalizations will disappear whenever the actual use of liberty threatens major patron-client networks of the dependency system.

Theodore Sumberg, writing for the conservative Center for Strategic and International Studies at Georgetown University, concludes in his survey of freedom in the Third World that the lack of personal liberty is related to some natural incapacities for self-rule:

> ORIGINATING in Europe, freedom has also settled among peoples of unequal capacity for self-government. We must be careful here because contemporary xenophobia does not like raising a question about the political capacity of different peoples. It is perhaps our bad conscience on racial matters that shuts off such a discussion. So we will merely state without emphasis that the political arts seem to be no more universal than the arts of dance or sculpture, and that the first in particular seem to be sparse in most areas of the world for hundreds, even thousands, of years, and are not to be acquired on the quick. The political incapacity of some peoples will naturally show up soon after they are free to govern themselves. (1975:65–66)

Sumberg's argument is that the lack of freedom in the Third World, its decline since decolonization, and its dim future are a result of the gradual recession of Western influence. According to Sumberg, the West took the ideas of liberty and democracy to the Third World during the colonial period, but the inherent native incapacity of Third World peoples for self-government is now apparent. (It should be remembered that Freedom House, whose definitions of freedom Sumberg relies on, recognizes the *Transkei bantustan* set up by the racist South African regime as not only an independent nation, but a "partly free" one as well.) This argumentation runs counter to the logic of dependency represented here, which sees freedom or lack of freedom as not purely a local matter, but rather in some measure a function of an international system of dependency in which Western interests and collaborating local elites may find liberty sometimes of use to the dependency system, sometimes threatening.

TWO SPECIAL FREEDOMS AND UNDERDEVELOPMENT

Two freedoms most often found in the Third World are the right to emigrate and the right to private property. Even brutally repressive regimes permit citizens to leave the country, at least before antigovernment activities make them "jail bait." Most regimes maintain the rights of private property intact, although some minorities may have their holdings seized, as with the Indian minority in Uganda under Idi Amin. In fact, suppression of democratic rights is often undertaken, as in Chile after 1973, for the explicit purpose of preserving property rights. We have argued in the previous two chapters that the right of emigration is associated with a "brain drain" of needed skills and talents from the Third World. The rights of private property are utilized by an internal-external coalition of local elites and Western MNCs to produce a type of economic development which serves their interests, with little regard for the social welfare of the majority. If this is the case, then there is a conflict between "healthy development" (in Gamer's terminology) and these two freedoms. There is a contradiction between social justice and self-sustained economic development, on the one hand, and these two freedoms, on the other. If the freedom of Western MNCs and collaborating local elites to choose the pattern of economic investment is not severely restricted (made less free), the syndrome of dependency will continue. If the Third World nations do not restrict the freedom of their talented and highly educated to immigrate to Western societies, a self-sustained development with independent control over technology and resources will be extremely difficult. It is not accidental that the two freedoms most in evidence in the Third World are those functional to the international capitalist market and to the dependency relationship between the developed core powers and the Third World.

INDIAN DEMOCRACY AND PERSONAL LIBERTY

Much of the future of democracy in the Third World will be determined by its ability or inability to survive in India. Along with Sri Lanka and Costa Rica, India has maintained a democratic system with the greatest tenacity in the Third World since independence in 1947 and has maintained broad personal liberty in an environment seemingly hostile to democracy. India is a huge multilingual, multiethnic society, divided also along religious (mainly Hindu and Moslem) and caste lines. India is a desperately poor nation that, in some forty years of independence, has made only slow progress in raising the standard of living and building a modern economy. Despite expensive government programs for family planning, India's population growth has continued to nullify much of the economic growth that has been achieved. India was born in a spasm of rioting and communal violence centered on the issue of the border that separated Pakistan from India, and India has fought several border wars with Pakistan and one with China since 1947. India has been beset by secessionist movements in Kashmir, Assam, Punjab, and Gurkaland; by continued communal violence between Hindus and Moslems and Hindus and Sikhs; and by violence among castes and between language, ethnic, and social class groups. Between 1948 and 1967, there were 558 large-scale riots in India (second only to the United States with 683) and over seventeen hundred armed attacks by political groups on either the government or other organized groups in India (Taylor and Hudson, 1972:94,102).

In the early 1950s, many Western observers looked to India as a democratic Western-oriented model for development that competed with the communist model being applied then in China. Few would now put India forward as a model for other Third World nations to emulate or to claim it as a "test case" of successful Western-style development. A. H. Hansen and Janet Douglas, in an assessment of Indian democracy in the early 1970s, reflect the increasing pessimism over India's failure to combine economic development and social justice with parliamentary democracy:

> THAT India's experiment in combining political democracy with economic development may conceivably be running into the sands is a tragedy, on any showing. It is not only sad for the Indian people, who have had more than their measure of sadness, but of deep concern for the Third World as a whole, and particularly for the Asiatic part of it. There was a time, hardly more than ten years ago, when India was the hope of the well-informed and progressive people throughout the world. It seemed that, contrary to ideas that had gained wide currency, there was at least one underdeveloped country—and a very large and important one—that was making a go of social-democracy. This was the period when India was identified with Nehru, and when Nehru himself was making a bid for Third World leadership, based not on military power but on moral persuasion and practical example. That period came to an end with the Chinese border conflict, Indian rearmament, and the virtual collapse of the Third Five Year Plan. Today India looks much more like a sick man than a pioneer; and, in the manner of sick men directs attention inwards rather than outwards. (1972:216–17)

How, then, has democracy managed to survive in India despite low performance in economic development and social justice? In many ways this is one of the great surprises, but perhaps some factors can be noted. At the time of independence, the new Indian state possessed a competent and coherent civil service system, which was able to provide a basis for both governing and uniting the multitude of Indian groups. The Indian Civil Service already had a long organizational integrity absent in many other Third World nations. Additionally, the independence movement was headed by the Congress party, an umbrella organization founded in 1885.

The Congress party was much more than a political party through its history, and by the time of independence it had enormous political authority and prestige, which were lacking in so many other new nations. The Congress party had built up an elite consensus going far beyond the borders of the party itself; even members of the major opposition parties often got their start in political life through the Congress party and still considered it the legitimate leader of the new nation. In many other new nations, the political organizations of even strong leaders like Nkrumah in Ghana, Nasser in

Egypt, or Sukarno in Indonesia crumbled after the death or overthrow of the top personality. In India, the Congress party could withstand the assassination of Gandhi, even in its early years of self-government, because the Congress organization was not tied to the charisma or fortune of any one personality. The Congress party, however, dominated the Indian system while getting only about 45 percent of the vote in national elections through the 1950s and 1960s. This was largely because the opposition was greatly divided among a panorama of parties of the left and of the right, and regional and local parties, with whom Congress often made temporary or localized coalitions. On the right were the traditionalist Jana Sangh and the pro-business Swatantra; on the left the moderate Socialists, the pro-Moscow Communist party of India (CPI), later also the more militant CPI-Marxist (CPI-M) and the pro-Peking CPI-Marxist-Leninist (CPI-ML). Thus, while the Congress party was not able to mobilize overwhelming popular support for its policies, the extremely divided nature of Indian society and the anti-Congress opposition made stable government possible until the early 1970s. This stability in government, backed by a loyal army and coherent civil service, was sufficient to ward off localized and sporadic uprisings without the necessity of suppressing oppositional activity across the board. Finally, the very failure of the government in promoting development meant that large segments of Indian society remained rooted in traditional village life, immobile, nonparticipant, and passive toward central government authority. As long as local society remained largely intact for tens of millions of Indians, it was difficult for antisystem groups to organize on a broad basis for political revolution, although this was certainly attempted, most notably by the pro-Peking Naxalites in the later 1960s and early 1970s. In these ways, Indian democracy has survived not only in spite of, but also because of its low economic and equity performance. Just as the Congress party required a very long period to build up its authority as an all-India national movement, so it will probably take any serious opposition force a long time to put together a nationwide antisystem movement. Indeed, it may be questioned whether any alternative basis exists for a nationwide political opposition to the Congress party.

Even so, Indian democracy in the 1970s began to show serious strains. The Congress party had been split several times and was probably irreparably torn into competing factions. The first split came in the late 1960s, when Indira Gandhi challenged the most conservative old-guard elite, producing a New Congress around Mrs. Gandhi and a rump Old Congress, which did poorly in the 1971 elections. In June of 1975, under mounting pressure from opposition parties and the press to resign, Prime Minister Gandhi declared Emergency Rule, under which press freedom was curtailed and many opposition party and union leaders were jailed. The "Indira dictatorship," as the twenty-one month Emergency is sometimes called, was the most serious breach of parliamentary democracy since independence. The Emergency Rule period signalled the end of the elite consensus against throwing political opponents into jail for nonviolent dissent. Nevertheless, in a surprise move in January of 1977, Mrs. Gandhi called for new elections, in which free political debate was again permitted. Various opposition groups, including the traditionalist Jana Sangh, the Old Congress, the pro-business Swatantra, and the moderate Socialist party formed a new coalition party, the Janata, specifically for the purpose of defeating Mrs. Gandhi. In mid-campaign, Jagjivan Ram, a prominent leader of the untouchables, broke away from Mrs. Gandhi's New Congress and founded the Congress for Democracy, which supported the Janata party in the elections. For the first time since 1947, a non-Congress majority was elected to the Indian parliament (the Lok Sabha), with Janata getting about 43 percent of the vote and Mrs. Gandhi's New Congress falling to 34 percent of the national vote. In a style uncharacteristic of most Third World authoritarian leaders, Mrs. Gandhi accepted the defeat and resigned her office. Press, party, and union freedoms were quickly restored. Indian democracy had made a strong comeback.

This resurgence of democracy was hailed at the time as an historic event and even as the beginning of a more stable two-party system (Janata and Congress) within India (see Weiner, 1978:95–97; Park and Bueno de Mesquita, 1979:172–74). Yet, even the enthusiastic appraisals of the 1977 elections and of Janata, insofar as they were not simply partisan rhetoric, contained some reservations as to the solidity of the Janata coalition and skepticism of its ability to govern effectively (Weiner, 1978:106–110).

In less than two years, the Janata party had broken up into its original component parts, its coherence as a majority government all but collapsed, and Mrs. Gandhi was triumphantly returned to power in national elections. However, the Congress party in the 1980s has continued to lose its legitimacy as a national governing party and has appeared more as the extension of patronage and corruption controlled at the top by the Gandhi family, under Indira Gandhi until her assassination in 1984, and then under the leadership of her son, Rajiv Gandhi, prime minister since 1984. In 1987, after a period of great popularity for Rajiv Gandhi, who introduced bold initiatives in the Punjab and Sri Lankan crises, and who seemed to steer the Indian economy towards a more unregulated market-oriented path of development, a series of scandals, expulsions of dissident leaders, and splits in the Congress party again threatened its legitimacy and governing capability. No opposition party has developed as yet to challenge Congress on a national basis.

Thus, on the national level, the Indian government has continued to be dominated by the Congress party with the Gandhi family at the top, while at the state level, regional, ideological, ethnic, and caste-based parties have done quite well. Personal liberty in the area of political choice, freedom of press, assembly, and speech survives because of the lack of capacity by

Congress, as demonstrated in 1975–77, to effectively suppress its opponents. Yet the Congress party is able, due to the fragmented nature of the opposition, to dominate national politics.

At the local level, Indian citizens are subject to a series of unofficial but pervasive restraints which limit their personal liberty. Caste restrictions, while formally abolished, remain in force through caste-based violence, in which poor lower castes, sometimes organized into peasant guerrilla bands, are pitted against armed vigilantes hired by higher castes. Communal violence between Hindus and Moslems, between Hindus and Sikhs, between Gurkhas and Bengalis, between Assamese and Bangladesh immigrants also limits personal freedoms, including freedom of travel, job opportunities, education, interest group organization, and even marriage and personal friendship. The organized violence used to restrict these personal freedoms is no less real because of its unofficial or traditional social basis. Nevertheless, the future of Indian democracy is of tremendous importance for the viability of political democracy and its proven *potential* for expanding personal liberty.

LIBERTY AND DEPENDENT DEVELOPMENT

In a major way, the extent of personal liberty in the Third World is related to elite interests in the same way as in the Western capitalist and East European communist societies. At the point where the Western bourgeoisie feared that democracy might lead to socialism in the 1920s and 1930s, it supported fascism and Nazism and the suppression of personal liberty, including its own. At the point where the Soviet Union feared that democracy under the liberal communism of the Prague Spring in 1968 might lead to a restoration of capitalism or a pullout from the Warsaw Pact, it intervened militarily to suppress the Dubcek regime. But the Western consumer societies of the post-World War II era are relatively successful systems, providing for basic needs of the great majorities of citizens and then some. There is little likelihood that masses of workers and employees will demand radical socialist changes under these circumstances. These systems can afford a wide spectrum of personal liberty, and indeed personal liberty has expanded as affluence has reached new and unprecedented heights. Communist systems are also, on a world scale, relatively successful systems, providing for the basic needs of their citizens with greater social equality and some advantages in quality of life (in crime and drug fighting and provisions for full employment). Communist systems mobilize the populace to achieve these goals by suppressing personal liberty, however, and to a certain extent their very success has been so far tied to a relatively low priority given to personal liberty and democratic practices. Most Third World systems are unsuccessful in providing for the basic needs of their people. (The most successful, like Taiwan or South

Korea, have not been democracies.) The dependency syndrome does not call for mobilization of workers and peasants; it requires their political passivity. If workers and peasants organize to make demands on the system to meet basic needs, their organizations threaten the system and must be suppressed and their leaders killed or coopted.

Peter Evans, in an extensive study of dependent development in Brazil, has concluded that in the most successful growth economies in the Third World, which are in his terms part of the "semi-periphery," a basic aim of the state must be political exclusion of workers and peasants:

> In the context of dependent development, the need for repression is great while the need for democracy is small. One of the functions of parliamentary regimes is to provide a forum for the resolution of differences among the bourgeoisie. During the original industrial revolution a degree of political consensus among the members of the owning classes was essential to carrying out their "class project" of capital accumulation. But when accumulation depends on the triple alliance of multinationals, state enterprises, and their local private allies, parliamentary means of achieving consensus are inappropriate. . . .
>
> When repression of the urban working class, effective bargaining with the multinationals, and entrepreneurial initiatives on the part of the state bourgeoisie are the critical components of capital accumulation, then imperative control, not consensus building within the bourgeoisie, is the response. (1979:48–49)

On the other hand, freedoms to hold private property and to emigrate are tolerable, since they are consistent with the interests of Western MNCs and local elites. If dependent development in the Third World cannot fulfill basic material needs, then militant worker-peasant demands will continue to arise, and democratic liberty must remain fleeting and fragile. The unsuccessful Third World systems cannot afford the postwar Western luxury of steadfast support for political liberty, nor can they in most cases justify its suppression as a necessary trade-off for the fulfillment of basic material needs. This is, of course, the dilemma of liberty in the Third World, a basic feature of dependency.

Chapter 16

Quality of Life—Reactions to Dependency and Imperialism

THIS CHAPTER PRESENTS THIRD WORLD quality of life performance as a pattern of reactions to the domination that is expressed not only through economic, political, and military penetration, but also through the mass media, consumer styles, language, and educational institutions in the Third World itself. These factors, taken together, are sometimes described as "Westernization," the growing dominance of Western capitalist values over local values. Westernization in this sense is sometimes taken as identical with "modernization," which does not imply any pattern of exploitation of the Third World by Western interests or the loss of autonomy by Third World peoples over their destiny. We will use the term Westernization with the understanding from previous chapters that this form of "modernization," known as dependent capitalist development, is in fact connected to Western economic interests and loss of Third World control over the process of development.

CULTURAL IMPERIALISM—"WESTERNIZATION"

Cultural imperialism involves so many factors that we will be able to concentrate on only a selected number for purposes of illustration. In the colonial period, cultural imperialism was expressed through the spread of Western languages as *the* languages of government, science, the professions—of higher education in general (or even middle-level education). English in India, the Philippines, Nigeria, Malaysia; French in Indochina, Senegal, Algeria, Madagascar, Djibouti; Dutch and English in South Africa; and Belgian-French in the Congo became the languages of rulership. This penetration of Western languages did not evaporate with the end of colonialism, and in the postcolonial period the West has continued to heavily influence the mass media of Third World nations. Aside from the continued use of the languages of the former colonial powers by educated elites, Third World newspapers, magazines, and radio and television are dependent on the developed nations for news of international events, since they lack their own organization of reporters and news "stringers" stationed around the world. From the developed West, UPI (United Press International), AP (Associated

Press), Reuters, and Agence-France Presse are the major sources of events coverage; from the communist world TASS is the major source. These are the interpreters of important happenings for the Third World media, and they are organized from the perspective of the liberal democracies and the industrialized communist nations. Moreover, "most of the news that circulates in the world is news about rich countries distributed to the people of rich countries. Apart from local news, the media in poor countries are filled with news from rich countries, hardly at all with news from other poor countries" (Goldthorpe, 1975:205–6). Even when the local language of communication is used, the information, values, and orientation of Third World media may be thoroughly "Westernized."

Some examples drawn from Mexico, relatively advanced in GNP/capita and industrialization, may be useful. Magazines with the largest circulation are *Life en Español* (the Spanish edition of *Life*) and *Selecciones* (the Spanish edition of *Reader's Digest*). The three largest U.S. magazines published in Spanish and sold in Mexico had a total circulation (546,000 in 1964) greater than that of the largest ten Mexican magazines (338,000). In terms of international news coverage by the major newspapers (*Excelsior, El Universal, Novedades, El Sol de Puebla*), from 60 to 80 percent was provided by the two U.S. news agencies, UPI and AP. Some additional stories were drawn from APF and Reuters; only an occasional international report came from sources beyond these four. Along with the predominance of Western (and mainly United States) news agencies as sources of international news information, there was also a predominance of stories about the rich Western nations. Newspaper space devoted to news about the United States in *Novedades* and *Excelsior*, two large Mexican dailies, in one single month was as great as the space devoted by the *New York Times* to all foreign countries (Gonzalez Casanova, 1970:59–64, 216). Films are another avenue for both entertainment and communication, particularly through the "demonstration effect"—showing what consumer life-styles look like in other nations or cultures. Between 1950 and 1964, fully 52 percent of films shown in Mexico were American made. Among the Third World nations, only India has a well-established and vigorous motion picture industry, able to compete with United States, British, Soviet, French, and Japanese films.

Mexico might seem to be a special case because of its geographic proximity to the United States and the extensive economic and tourist trade between the two nations. But, in fact, this pattern exists for other Third World nations as well. Wilbur Schramm (1964), in a study of mass media and development, reports that for three large daily newspapers in Pakistan, 33 percent of all foreign news was about the United States, 17 percent about Great Britain, 16 percent about France, 13 percent about the Soviet Union, and only 13 percent about India, Pakistan's immediate neighbor and adversary. In the case of Argentina, only 6 percent of international coverage was about Brazil, while 43 percent was about the United States, an additional 15 percent about France, 11 percent about Great Britain, and 12 percent about the Soviet Union.

In the colonial period, Western standards of education were introduced into Third World societies, displacing or competing with traditional and local religious educational practices. The language of middle and higher education was generally that of the colonial power, the language of success, material affluence, Western domination, and of the white man. The double connection between Western science and "modernization" and between native ways and impoverished ignorance created and continues to create feelings of alienation for Third World peoples in their own countries, perhaps most acutely for those interested in progress and development for their nations. Frantz Fanon, the black Algerian psychiatric analyst, has probably described these feelings in their full fury in his *Wretched of the Earth*. More recently, novelists like Naipaul and N'gugi have described from other perspectives these feelings of alienation from society and from self. Political scientist Elbaki Hermasi has observed that "against what they consider cultural imperialism . . . Third World writers try to take national culture in its authenticity as a reference point and to express in the realm of culture the ongoing political and social struggles of emancipation from imperialism" (1980:147).

The economic, political, and military successes of Western values over native ways on the one hand lead to feelings of insecurity and inferiority, reinforced by colonial authorities and by the pattern of dependent development beyond the colonial period. On the other hand, those who assimilate Western ideas, including language, dress, science, and life-style, become isolated from the great mass of their own people; they become "Westernized," even though their goal may be to free their nations from the domination of Western interests. "Modern" education and "modern" science, in part because it is Western and foreign, unadapted to local environment and social history, contains within it both the hope for development (personal and societal) and a continuing demonstration of the "backwardness" of the local culture:

AMONG the critical shortages in educational development in poor countries is often that of textbooks and other educational materials related to the local environment. There are many "horror stories" about the importation of unsuitable material and inappropriate methods into the schools of the Third World—of African pupils being taught about the coalfields of England or the dissolution of the monasteries, of Algerian Muslim children taught to refer to "nos ancetres les Galles," of the 300-acre demonstration farms attached to agricultural colleges in countries where the average peasant holding is less than 10 acres, and of the teaching of science by means of the bunsen burner in countries with no indigenous source of gas. Many such stories are told about the colonial period, and are cited as examples of "cultural imperialism," the foisting of an alien culture on a subject people. But not all the "horrors" came at once to an end with political independence, and there were reasons for them more substantial than the cultural arrogance of white missionaries and colonial officials. (Goldthorpe, 1975:202–3)

Cultural imperialism, combined with the widespread penetration of Western interests into Third World societies, raises a major question: What types of reaction are generated by the systematic and largely successful challenge to local control of social values? With the failures of these systems to provide for basic economic needs, social equity, and political liberty, why haven't there been more social revolutions in the Third World? While revolutionary movements have had their greatest success in the less-developed nations (tzarist Russia, China, Yugoslavia, Cuba, Vietnam) during this century, these are still a minority of nations. There are clearly other responses to the dependency syndrome besides revolution. These responses may be at various levels: individual, small group, or mass. They may be peaceful or violent, but only rarely do they threaten to overthrow the entire social order. These reactions to the system of dependent development may be characterized generally as: (1) elite corruption, (2) personal resignation, (3) deflected rebellion, and (4) counterorganization and revolution.

CORRUPTION IN THIRD WORLD SYSTEMS

The thesis of this segment is that high levels of corruption and crime are characteristic of dependent political systems. Widespread political corruption is a typical feature of the systems we have been describing and as such can be seen as an integral part of the dependency syndrome. It follows that corruption will in all probability not significantly and permanently diminish unless and until the dependency syndrome is broken.

First, let it be clear that we are *not* analyzing corruption from a moralist point of view. We are not interested in condemning corrupt practices because they violate some ethical code. We are interested rather in trying to identify the various types of corruption and to estimate the extent of such behavior in the underdeveloped world. Along the way, we will compare corruption in the Third World with corruption in both the liberal democracies and the communist systems, since each system-type has its own "typical" mixture.

Definitions of corruption can be problematic, especially so in comparative analysis (see Scott, 1972:ch. 1). James Scott, in a thoughtful study of comparative political corruption, opts for a basically legalistic working definition that defines corruption as behavior that violates formal legal norms set down for public officials, regardless of whether such behavior is widely practiced or publicly accepted or in the public interest.

Although there is by nature a general lack of comprehensive and accurate data as to the extent of corruption in any political system, most observers agree that corruption is far more prevalent in the Third World than in either the liberal democracies or the communist systems. Individual visitors to Indonesia, Brazil, Nigeria, or India can document the extensive demands for bribes by lower-level bureaucrats for various services (getting a ticket on a plane flight, getting on the flight, getting baggage through customs, getting money changed in a bank). For the Third World citizen, gifts and bribes for officials to overlook tax evasion or to grant a business permit, government license, or health service are commonplace, though not universal to all systems at all times. The variety of such practices across cultures defies short description. Some are related to long traditions of gifts to social or caste superiors or to kinship relations (nepotism), and in that sense are not necessarily new or locally perceived as corrupt. British sociologist J. E. Goldthorpe warns, however:

> CULTURAL relativity on this topic can be exaggerated, however. New situations arising as a result of modern economic activity create new opportunities for and new forms of, corruption, in ways for which there may be little or no traditional sanction, such as bribing a tax inspector to accept a low return of one's income, or an airport official to overlook excess baggage. It is simply not the case that corruption is condemned only by the codes of modern western democracies. On the contrary, it is condemned everywhere. Indeed, whenever there is a military coup in one of the new states of Asia or Africa, one of the justifications that are invariably advanced is the corruption of the former regime. (1975:105)

Other evidence of Third World corruption comes from high-level scandals, sometimes in the wake of a military coup or revolution or from revelations about the behavior of MNCs in these nations. After the Sandinista victory in Nicaragua, the extent of the Somoza family's looting of that country became officially documented. After the Iranian revolution, at least some of the corrupt elite enrichment under the Shah made international news in the West. After the rebellion in Shaba province in Zaire, the media noted that President Mobutu became a billionaire through straightforward pilfering of government funds. The military coup in Ghana by Flight Captain Jerry Rawlings revealed the blatant self-enrichment of General Akufo and General Acheampong, leaders of earlier military regimes. The fall of the American puppet regime in South Vietnam brought to light some details of high-level corruption by President Thieu and other top aides. The overthrow in 1986 of the Marcos dictatorship in the Philippines revealed that Ferdinand and Imelda Marcos had amassed over $10 billion in personal wealth, much of it stashed abroad in New York real estate and Swiss bank accounts. Similarly, the ouster of President Jean-Claude (Baby Doc) Duvalier in Haiti brought media attention to the personal wealth built by the Duvalier family at the expense of one of the world's poorest peoples. Rare is the case of a Third World dictator who has not used control of government to enrich himself, but in recent years the amounts of corrupt wealth have reached new heights. The personal gain of Marcos accounts alone for nearly half the foreign debt of the Philippines, the fortune of Zaire's Mobutu for most of that nation's foreign obligations. This is just the tip of the iceberg—the most egregious cases that were already widely suspected by competent observers of these systems. In many Third World systems, the practices of corruption are as unstable as the government and change rapidly with shifts in elite coalitions. In Mexico, the ruling PRI has institutionalized a pattern of elite corruption. Frank Brandenburg, in his description of graft in the upper levels of the Mexican system, reports in the early 1960s:

> THE precise amount a cabinet minister or state-industry manager finally accumulated . . . largely depends on himself, although when grafting becomes excessive and injurious to his rule, the President of Mexico may step in and close some sources of a subordinate's income. The average minister or director finishes his term with two or three houses, a good library, two or three automobiles, a ranch, and $100,000 cash; about 25 directors and ministers hold posts from which they can leave office with fifty times that amount in cash. (1964:162)

In India there is some information from official investigations (the Kripilani Report, the Santhanam Committee Report) on the relatively stable patterns of corruption at lower levels of the government civil service. John Monteiro (in Heidenheimer, 1970:223) cites one documented example of corruption in the administration of government contracts:

> ONE sub-contractor on the Railways was candid enough to admit that the Railway contractors (including himself) made regular payments to the engineering officials on a percentage basis. The following percentage breakdown on the amount of their bills was indicated by him:

Executive Engineer	5%
Assistant Engineer	5
PWD Supervisor	5
Accounts section	2
District pay clerk	$\frac{1}{4}$
Head clerk in XEN	1
Ministry/work-in-charge	1
Miscellaneous	$\frac{3}{4}$
Total	20%

> It may not be so meticulously systematic as represented here, but the fact of the percentages was mentioned by many witnesses, and is popularly known.

Another well-documented case is the famous "cement racket" in Nigeria. In 1975–1976, the Nigerian government ordered approximately ten times the amount of cement it needed for its development plans from foreign suppliers at approximately twice the international market price. Roughly $2 billion of Nigeria's oil earnings were siphoned off through this scheme, which represented a pure loss for Nigerian development, but a windfall profit for top-level Nigerian officials and the Western MNCs who supplied the cement (see Evans, 1979:313). Further accounts of political corruption in the Third World are provided by Scott (1972), Heidenheimer (1970), Goldthorpe (1975), and Chaliand (1978); despite the great cultural diversity, the underlying patterns become clear. Political corruption has, of course, been denounced within the Third World by nearly every government upon taking power. Yet even military coups that initially were dedicated to the suppression of corruption have fallen into much the same routine of behavior. Thus the record of the Nasser regime, which ousted the corrupt King Farouk in Egypt, or the Suharto regime, which replaced the graft-ridden regime of President Sukarno, or the Mexican PRI, successor to the classic corrupt machine politics of Porfirio Diaz, demonstrates the extreme difficulty of combating corruption without a thorough social revolution.

It is often forgotten that some Third World dictators, like Ferdinand Marcos and François (Papa Doc) Duvalier, achieved national leadership with the reputation of reformers or populists. Marcos was first elected president in the Philippines in 1964 with a program of honesty in government and was re-elected in 1968 before declaring martial law in 1972 and ruling as a dictator thereafter. François Duvalier was elected president of Haiti in 1957 in perhaps the only free election modern-day Haiti has ever seen. He was seen as a populist representative of poor blacks running against the interests of the mulatto elite of the island. This might suggest that these leaders, whose reform credentials once seemed so strong, at some point turned cynical about the prospects for improving their nations' fortunes and opted instead for changing their personal fortunes through the use of political power. The frustrations of progressive reform are high and the possibilities of financial corruption so tempting that it takes a truly remarkable leader to keep faith and resist the offers to sell out ideals.

Some amount of this elite corruption is clearly linked to the activities of the Western MNCs. In the 1970s, the era of Watergate revelations, a number of bribery payoffs by MNCs to high government officials were revealed. While some payoffs went to high-level officials of nations like Italy and Japan, many others were made to Third World government leaders. The common excuses given by the MNCs are: (1) such corruption is standard operating procedure and (2) any MNC not paying bribe money would lose out to competing MNCs who do make payoffs. Recently the U.S. Justice Department reported that McDonnell Douglas, producer of the DC-10 aircraft, was involved in payoffs to business and government leaders in

Pakistan, the Philippines, South Korea, Venezuela, and Zaire. In the case of Pakistan, McDonnell Douglas is also charged with defrauding Pakistan International Airlines of a total of $1.6 million on the sale of four DC-10 aircraft, a sum that was pocketed by the McDonnell Douglas sales team. The U.S.-based firm is charged with paying $3.3 million to two owners of Korean Airlines, $2.1 million to three businessmen for sales to the government-owned Venezuelan airline, $625,000 to Zaire's minister of transportation and the governor of Zaire's National Bank, and $400,000 to two officials of Philippine Airlines (*Guardian,* December 19, 1979:2).

Scholarly analysis of political corruption in Third World systems has gone through a number of changing emphases since the early 1950s. Sociologist Daniel Bell, in a 1953 article entitled "Crime as an American Way of Life," denounces the moral indignation of affluent Americans and academics over behavior that was, in America's own history, part of its economic development and immigration socialization:

> THE pioneers of American capitalism were not graduated from Harvard's School of Business Administration. The early settlers and founding fathers, as well as those who "won the west" and built up the cattle, mining and other fortunes, often did so by shady speculations and a not inconsiderable amount of violence. They ignored, circumvented or stretched the law when it stood in the way of America's destiny, and their own—or, were themselves the law when it served their purposes. This has not prevented them and their descendants from feeling proper moral outrage when under the changed circumstances of the crowded urban environments later comers pursued equally ruthless tactics. (Bell, in Heidenheimer, 1970:164–65)

Bell's analysis, while limited to the American experience, related corruption and organized crime to the process of economic development and the widening of economic opportunity to newer immigrant groups within American society. Bell concludes that organized crime and political corruption played positive roles in making room within the system for "latecomer" ethnic groups. He asserts that both organized crime and political corruption will decline after these latecomers have achieved higher economic status, so that economic success can be had through legitimate business activities and when respectability and social status become more pressing goals. Crime and corruption, in other words, were useful vehicles for some ethnics to achieve the good life, but the very success of that behavior leads to its later decline, since it becomes both unnecessary and counterproductive to other goals.

Following on this general train of thought, which was less ethnocentric and less moralizing than much of the earlier commentary on corruption, a number of observers began to perceive positive functions of corruption in the development process of Third World "latecomers" (Ley, Leff, Veloso Abueva, and Greenstone, in Heidenheimer, 1970). Two dominant themes were that Western moralizing was both inappropriate, given the role of political corruption in Western development of an earlier period, and wrong, given the positive functions of corruption. These studies, while not trying to justify all forms of corruption as useful to development, nevertheless assert that political corruption served in many cases to: (1) aid in capital formation through the building of individual fortunes, which could then be invested in the economy; (2) sustain and promote entrepreneurial activity, especially among certain minority groups, who are ethnic "pariahs" or socially marginal within the dominant culture (Chinese in Indonesia, Lebanese in West Africa and Brazil, Indians in East Africa); (3) avoid delays and inefficiencies associated with government bureaucracy and avoid public disclosures that, in view of public hostility to the wealthy business class, could retard investment; and (4) promote nation building through the ability of different groups, using money-power to buy influence, to achieve benefits within the system. It was also stressed, especially by American political scientist Samuel Huntington (1968), that corruption in the Third World was a major mechanism for preventing basic social reform and avoiding social revolution. In political systems with weak legitimacy and low levels of institutionalization, Huntington sees corruption as a conservative force for stability:

> LIKE machine politics or clientalistic politics in general, corruption provides immediate, specific, and concrete benefits to groups which might otherwise be thoroughly alienated from society. Corruption may thus be functional to the maintenance of a political system in the same way that reform is. Corruption itself may be a substitute for reform, and both corruption and reform may be substitutes for revolution. (1968:61)

For Huntington, "he who corrupts a system's police officers is more likely to identify with the system than he who storms the system's police stations" (1968:61). Huntington's analysis was one of the most supportive of political corruption's positive role in the Third World, but with the primarily negative goal of avoiding revolution, rather than promoting development. Huntington believes that social revolution, and particularly communist revolution, may be the main alternative to corruption and that only a revolutionary upheaval could change the dependency syndrome, which needs political corruption to maintain itself.

A turning point in the debate over the effects of corruption in the Third World came in the latter 1960s, when observers began to argue that the human costs outweigh any benefits that might arise from the widespread corruption in Third World systems. Myrdal's *Asian Drama* (1968) points out the extensive delegitimization of the government through graft and pocket lining by officials, generating a tendency toward military coups and political cynicism. Myrdal further asserts that bureaucracies riddled by corruption are likely to become even more inefficient and ineffective to keep the price of bribery high. They may even, in parasitic behavior, grow in response to the money-making potential from graft and bribery. Myrdal also mentions the extensive role of Western MNCs:

> AMONG the Western nations, French, American, and especially West German companies are usually said to have the least inhibitions about bribing their way through. Japanese firms are said to be even more willing to pay up. On the other hand, the writer has never heard it alleged that bribes are offered or paid by the commercial agencies of Communist countries. (Cited in Heidenheimer, 1970:236)

Although investment capital may be accumulated through corruption, wealth is often deposited in Swiss or American banks (as Haile Selassie and the Shah of Iran did) or in Miami real estate (as Somoza of Nicaragua did), in which case it constitutes an absolute drain of the resources of the Third World nation. Further, much of the wealth of the corrupt elite may be spent on luxury consumption or invested in luxury goods, import businesses, or speculative real estate, which does little to foster development to meet basic human needs for the poor and jobless. To a lesser degree, corruption may also waste valuable government skills and provoke social unrest and military takeovers. James Scott concludes from his studies of political corruption that it is less likely to hinder economic growth when:

1. National rulers are either uninterested or hostile to economic growth.
2. The government lacks the skills, capacity, or resources to effectively promote economic growth.
3. Corruption is "market" corruption where all the "buyers" of influence have equal access to bureaucrats and politicians. (The assumption here is that if parochial considerations are weak, only the ability to pay will count and efficient producers will have more of an advantage.)
4. Corruption benefits groups with a high marginal propensity to save (e.g., wealthy elites) more than groups with a low marginal propensity to save (voters).
   —this situation is, in turn, more likely in a noncompetitive political system than in a competitive one where votes can be traded for influence.
5. The cost of a unit of influence is not so high as to discourage many otherwise profitable undertakings.
   —this situation is more likely when there is price competition among the bureaucrats who sell influence.
6. There is greater certainty as to the price of a unit of influence and a high probability of receiving the paid-for "decision." This is more likely when:
   a. The political and bureaucratic elites are strong and cohesive.
   b. Corruption has become "regularized"—even institutionalized after a fashion—by long practice.
7. Corruption serves to increase competition in the private sector rather than to secure a special advantage or monopolistic position for any one competitor. (Scott, 1972:90–91)

Even if these conditions were met, it is uncertain whether economic growth within the dependency syndrome would bring significant benefits to any but the well-connected members of the dominant patron-client groupings. As we have argued, the meeting of the conditions might actually lead to deterioration in the position of the bottom 40 to 60 percent of the population. Scott's discussion of corruption's impact on economic growth is weakened by a lack of discussion on the nature of growth in dependent Third World systems. But it is clear to Scott, in any case, that most of these conditions are not fulfilled, in part because of pervasive political corruption itself. Most citizens do not have equal access to government officials nor do they have equal resources with which to buy influence. The benefits of corruption are heavily weighted in favor of the wealthy, the top bureaucratic bourgeoisie with control over government purchases, franchises, and operations, and the large corporations (both locally and Western owned). Corruption tends not to increase competition but to solidify and increase inequality and monopoly. A laissez-faire model of corruption leading to greater market competition and production efficiency may be valid at the local level, in certain countries, but at the national level it is probably as much of a fairy tale as the notion of price competition and market efficiency is in the advanced capitalist economies.

The Third World nations of today are simply not the Western nations of the past century. Their bureaucratic and national bourgeoisies are not the captains of industry, the "robber barons," of England, the United States, or Germany. Most important, for the nineteenth-century West there was no external coalition of much more powerful governments and MNCs capable of systematically dominating development.

The discrepancy between official rhetoric of concern for public welfare and actual performance in Third World systems is also the basis for an extensive system of political corruption through which a minority with ties to ruling patron-client networks may enrich themselves in defiance of official regulations or goals. Yet, both the officially stated goals (justice, meeting basic needs, growth) and widespread political corruption are inherent components of the system. A decrease in this discrepancy between rhetoric and reality could lead to a decline in corruption, but that would require breaking the dependency syndrome.

RESIGNATION: FATALISM, ALCOHOLISM, MACHISMO, VIOLENCE

For the great majority of Third World citizens, there is little opportunity to participate in the networks of political rewards (legal and illegal). Yet, despite widespread disaffection and discontent among those outside the major patron-client networks, organization for social revolution is still an unusual response to the political system. Given the riskiness of open political dissent and the ability of ruling elites to coopt or coerce leaders of potentially challenging groups, it should not be surprising that many people are deterred from any organized political challenge to the system.

One type of response to great social inequality, poverty, joblessness, disease, and oppression is fatalistic resignation. Fatalism reflects a feeling of powerlessness to struggle for change and a passive, even passionate, acceptance of the status quo. Social fatalism may be found in traditional village society where the forces of nature (monsoon, drought, disease) are still viewed (worshipped) as more powerful than human effort—as beyond human control. This is the fatalist coexistence with nature that existed before the rise of modern science and industry, the spread of education, and increasing human mobility. But social fatalism clearly persists even in the most modern urban environments. In many areas, organized religion preaches passive acceptance of the social order and opposes social revolution. Although there is now a small Catholic socialist grouping within the Latin American clergy, the Catholic church as an institution has historically acted as a powerful force for acceptance of the existing system in exchange for consolation and hope for eternal salvation. In a rather more decentralized fashion, Hinduism in India and Buddhism in much of Southeast Asia tend toward acceptance of the social order (or caste system) and downplay the need to organize and struggle for social change. The role of Islam in the Middle East, Africa, and South Asia is more difficult to characterize. Certainly the mullahs in Iran and Afghanistan provided a rallying point for popular uprisings, in the one case against the American-supported Shah and in the other against the Soviet-supported Afghan Marxist regime, although not with the goal of revolutionizing the social order, but rather in the spirit of national independence from the great powers.

These are, of course, broad generalizations that neglect the local and periodic shifts in the social orientation of organized religion. At one point in the struggle against Somoza, for example, the Catholic church in Nicaragua issued a statement supporting a non-Marxist socialism for that country. On the other hand, despite variations and internal tensions within organized religion, the weight of the institution itself has been to reconcile the individual to his/her fate within society. The church has called on the individual to rebel primarily when the institutional interests of the church itself were threatened, usually by socialist revolutions that would affect its landholdings or its dominance in education.

Fatalism may be expressed in pervasive gambling or playing the numbers or the lottery; here the individual hopes to escape from poverty, through luck or fortune or some magical charm. Alcoholism and drug addiction are forms of individual-level escapism, attempts to drown out problems of daily life, to achieve, temporarily, a state of euphoria. These expressions of social fatalism are found in the developed industrial nations, and it should not be surprising that many people in the Third World also turn to drink and drugs rather than social or political organizing for solutions to social problems. In some cases, dominant elites may utilize alcoholism as a social weapon to try to defuse or sidetrack worker and peasant anger. In the Republic of South Africa, the apartheid regime supplies cheap "bantu beer" to black industrial workers, even though white Afrikaner society is fairly puritanical in its attitude toward drinking. In the huge black township of Soweto outside white Johannesburg, Saturday night is an occasion for widespread drinking, gambling, and individual-level violence among the local population. This sort of catharsis, or release of pent-up emotion, can be seen in local sporting events; for example, soccer matches in some Latin American countries, where heavy drinking, gambling, fist- and knife-fighting often explode into full-blown riots, costing the lives of scores of people. Within the family setting, urban working-class males are able to vent their frustrations on wives and children. Oscar Lewis (1959) and Wayne Cornelius (1975) have noted the high frequency of physical force in arguments, of wife- and child-beating, and of alcoholism among the urban poor in Latin America. While the "machismo complex" of male domination within the family is also found in more traditional rural society, the greater mobility, diversity, and anonymity of urban society weaken the force of local opinion and traditions in restraining family violence. Robert Gamer (1976), Eric Wolf and Edward Hansen (1972), and Oscar Lewis (1959) have described the great variety of means for cathartic release that does not challenge the social or political system, yet provides temporary outlets for feelings of alienation. There is no doubt that feelings of alienation (of not being able to cope, of powerlessness, of physical and social insecurity) are widespread in Third World societies. Gamer in particular emphasizes that repression of organized protest, combined with opportunities for deflecting hostility from the social and political spheres onto localized objects, may be a significant stabilizing force for the dominant elites. Gamer (1976:187–88) explores the possibility that through the effective use, or simply the availability, of liquor, gambling, fighting, sports, and other distractions from class-based grievances, Third World systems may avoid revolutionary challenges indefinitely.

DEFLECTION FROM REVOLUTION: EMIGRATION, ETHNIC AND GENERATIONAL CONFLICT, CRIMINALITY

Even when individuals are bitterly dissatisfied with their government or desperate for greater economic opportunities to hold themselves and their families together, it does not follow that they will organize to challenge the current regime or to join a movement for economic and political change. At the individual and family level, the course of wisdom and highest probability for success is emigration—leaving the social and political system which has failed them and migrating to a country with greater opportunities. This has always been preferable to facing repression by the police and military or struggling for years in a seemingly hopeless union, peasant, populist, or socialist effort to change the basic social and political system. Emigration is not a fatalistic alternative; it has a high success ratio for those with the enterprise and possibility to attempt it. So, while there were in 1987 perhaps 6,000 to 8,000 guerrillas fighting to overthrow the regime in El Salvador, it is estimated that between 250,000 and 300,000 Salvadorans had migrated to the United States, some legally but most illegally, rather than fight on either side in the Salvadoran civil war. More than 200,000 Nicaraguans have left that country for the United States since the overthrow of Somoza, most of them hostile to the Sandinista regime, but less than 20,000 are fighting with the contras to overthrow the Managua government. Literally millions of Mexicans, lesser numbers of Filipinos, Koreans, Taiwanese, Haitians, Guatemalans, and Guyanese have migrated to the United States in search of a better life, rather than organize to try to change the political or social order in their own country. It is not necessary that the nation to which one migrates be a free or democratic society, as long as it provides opportunities (or even just physical safety) unavailable in one's home country. More than a million Ghanaians migrated to find work in oil-rich Nigeria in the 1970s (before being expelled in large part when oil revenues shrank); hundreds of thousands of Egyptians, Koreans, and Pakistanis have found work in the oil-rich Gulf states of the Arabian peninsula despite severe restrictions on personal and political liberty there. In Europe, Turks, Yugoslavs, North Africans, Pakistanis, Indians, Caribbean blacks, and in most recent times Tamil refugees from Sri Lanka, boat people from Southeast Asia, and Sikhs from India have made their way to lands where better opportunities and physical safety are available.

Several additional factors may deflect lower-class alienation away from social revolution. One is the cultural diversity of many Third World societies that makes organization of a broad revolutionary movement difficult and offers ruling elites opportunities to play off ethnic, religious, racial, caste, or regional groups against each other. In some cases, popular anger may be shifted from the regime or the economic system onto "outcast" minorities. Overseas Chinese minorities, concentrated in the cities and prominent in trade and commerce, are often the subjects of racial distrust and open hostility (as in Malaysia, Indonesia, Vietnam, and Thailand). Lebanese communities in Ghana, Nigeria, and Brazil, Indians and Pakistanis in Uganda and elsewhere in East Africa, Jews in Iran and Argentina occupy similar positions.

In other cases, ethnic hostility among major population groupings may produce competition for political power, but along ethnic lines rather than class lines. Shifts in regimes may signal changes in fortune for ethnic patron-client networks, but do not challenge the basic dependency system, since cross-ethnic organization of workers and peasants is so difficult. In Guyana, there is political competition between Cheddi Jagan's PPP (People's Progressive party) representing the East Indian population and Forbes Burnham's PNC (People's National Congress) representing the black population. In Nigeria, divisions among the major (Hausa-Fulani, Yoruba, and Ibo) and minor tribal groupings have contributed to political instability and several military coups. But they have also contributed to the failure of radical or revolutionary counterelites to build a national movement based on lower class interests, regardless of tribal affiliation. Much the same could be said for Malaysia, where Malay, Chinese, and Indian patron-client networks have built a three-sector coalition party, the Alliance party, which attempts to maintain an ethnic balance over patronage and at the same time maintains an ethnic "division of labor" within the economy. Demands of the lower class find little opportunity for expression and the lower class lacks the strength to challenge the system in this environment.

Many examples of cultural cleavages overriding and hindering the expression of worker-peasant demands can be cited: Moslems and Christians in the Philippines; Indians and Europeans and mestizos and blacks, in varying mixtures, in Latin America; Persians, Azerbaijanis, Arabs, Baluchis, and Kurds in Iran; a welter of ethnic, linguistic, caste, and religious groups in India. In most circumstances, ethnic politics, even when racial, caste, or religious rioting and bloodshed result, may lend support to the maintenance of the dependency syndrome by deflecting class issues and making multiethnic worker-peasant movements unlikely. Ultimately, ethnic conflict tends to support existing patron-client networks and facilitates control of the system by dominant elites.

An exception to this notion may be found in societies where the ethnic dividing lines are also the social class divisions. In the white settler regimes in Rhodesia and South Africa, for example, the white European minority was both an ethnic group and the dominant bourgeoisie, while the black population, divided along tribal lines, was almost totally excluded from bourgeois status. Cynthia Enloe (1973), in a study of ethnic conflict in the Third World, suggests that, in this situation, an ethnic confrontation with the dominant group might also be a revolutionary challenge to the entire social order. Some Caribbean societies like Jamaica may also fall into this category; the Cuban revolution and the revolutionary overthrow of the Portuguese colonial regimes in Mozambique and Angola may offer partial support for this thesis.

Another hindrance to broad-based class organization is the generational cleavage that is often found among the poor, especially within the urban working class. Wayne Cornelius (1975) has shown that, among the urban poor in Latin America, first-generation migrants from the countryside are less likely to engage in political protest or rebellion. Continuing links of kinship to the countryside, seasonal or occasional migration back to the village, general lack of urban social and political skills, and optimism about future prospects in the city all tend to diminish the likelihood that the first generational wave of urban migrants will revolt in any organized and sustained fashion against the system. Stuart Sinclair (1978) has also noted the optimism that pervades certain squatter developments on the edges of large Third World cities, and Lisa Redfield Peattie (1968) has described the pride in material progress that characterized one Venezuelan working-class barrio.

The theory of political generations developed by Ryder, Lambert, and Keniston (see Nagle, 1977) posits that basic political orientations are shaped and crystallized during early maturity (ages seventeen to twenty-five) by major social and political events. Once basic orientations are solidified for an individual, it becomes less likely that changing social and political circumstances in later years will cause significant shifts in orientation. Beyond early adulthood, most people "settle into" a cluster of political beliefs and stick with them, trying to adapt new circumstances to an existing framework. For first-generation urban migrants, the basic orientation may be one of optimism and general support for an urban environment of apparent broad opportunities, particularly compared with the rural village. Mounting disappointments and frustrations of the first urban migrant generation may not change this basic orientation, at least not enough to produce a radical rejection of the entire system. Rejection of the system as a whole is far more likely within succeeding urban generations born and raised in the barrios, favelas, Sowetos, and bidonvilles of the Third World, who are wise in the ways and skills needed in the big city, are less likely to be naively optimistic about chances for personal success, and perhaps most important, do not compare their life-styles with an even poorer village life, but with the Western-style affluence of the urban elite, within sight but beyond reach. The urban poor in the Third World are constantly in generational flux, and the generational perspectives may not agree on the necessity for social revolution. Generational perspectives of the urban working class as a whole will tend to lag behind real circumstances, delaying or retarding opportunities for broad, class-based opposition to the structures of dependent development. Just as it is often difficult to bridge political differences across generations in the United States, for example, between the Depression-era and Vietnam-era generations, so it is often difficult to reconcile or unite generational cleavages in the Third World.

One more outlet that may deflect mass alienation from revolutionary activity is criminal behavior. Crime in many societies, not only in the Third World, represents a mixed rejection and acceptance of the existing system. It represents personal rejection of formal legality, since for a variety of reasons the criminal seeks to attain goals through illegal means. Yet, this is a low-level rejection of the system's formalities, and even at the level of large-scale looting, well-organized rural banditry, or urban crime syndicates, criminality does not threaten basic social and political structures. No social system has ever been overthrown by massive criminality. Occasionally rural bandits like Pancho Villa in Mexico and more recently bandit insurgents in Colombia and India have become politicized, but these are the exceptions. It is the armed politicization, not the banditry, that represents a challenge (which is still ineffective). At both high and low levels of illegality, professional crime may connect to and support the political system through routine corruption of government officials. Government corruption is therefore a component of drug trafficking, smuggling, piracy, large-scale prostitution, and slave trade in various parts of the Third World. Mass prostitution for Western tourists was once one of the main attractions and a source of hard Western currency in prerevolutionary Havana. It is now a major tourist attraction in Manila, Bangkok, Nairobi, and Rio de Janeiro. It is estimated that drugs have replaced coffee beans as Colombia's leading export to the United States. These activities, although formally illegal and occasionally risky for the individuals involved, are a normal part of economic activity within the dependency syndrome, and therefore do not represent a challenge to, or a deviation from, the pattern of dependent development.

At the local and most decentralized level, criminality may represent an acceptance of the system. Given the levels of unemployment and underemployment, criminality may represent a job placement decision to try to achieve a better material life through the use of personal skills and available opportunities. As in the developed nations, poverty in the Third World does not itself cause criminal behavior. Indeed, although there is a general rise of rural crime (rustling, smuggling) in many Third World areas, the great growth in crime has been in the urban areas, which are economically better off than the villages. As in Sweden, West Germany, and the United States, economic growth in Brazil, Mexico, and Nigeria has not reduced crime, but is associated with large increases in crime. Criminologists Marshall Clinard and David Abbott (1973), in a wide-ranging account of crime in the Third World, point to the raised expectations and wider opportunities for criminal behavior in the cities as reasons for the dramatic growth of crime. Urban areas, with their glittering array of consumer goods, which raise the living standard and change the ideas of what is "needed," offer greater anonymity, social disorganization, and heterogeneity. The political system is both corrupt and institutionally less interested in fighting crime than in policing radical dissent and potential rebellion.

If it is correct that social revolution is one alternative (perhaps the major one) to widespread crime and political corruption, as we have argued, then it is probable that widespread crime will continue to characterize the growing urban environments of the Third World. One of the basic features of fighting crime and corruption in communist systems (see chapter 11) is thorough mobilization and coherent organization of the population, combined with effective limitations on the ability to accumulate great wealth and enjoy an affluent life-style. Dependent political systems, we have further argued, are not only uninterested in organizing and mobilizing the population, but are actively trying to prevent lower-class organizations from emerging. They attempt to disarm or repress efforts by workers and peasants to politicize their needs. Third World systems with few exceptions are characterized by the lack of any effective limitations on accumulation of wealth or its conspicuous enjoyment.

Table 16.1 Percentage of the Labor Force Unemployed and Underemployed in the Third World, 1975

	1975 Total	1975 Urban Only
Africa	45.0	35.9
Asia	40.3	30.1
Latin America	34.0	29.3
Third World	40.4	31.3

SOURCES: Adapted from UN *Handbook of the Social Situation*, 1979, and Sewell, 1977.

REBELLION, COUNTERORGANIZATION, AND REVOLUTION

Despite all barriers to an organized challenge, there are opportunities and possibilities for organized resistance to imperialism and dependency. The Japanese nationalist response to Western encroachments in the mid-nineteenth century and the Russian, Chinese, Vietnamese, and Cuban revolutions in the current century indicate that such challenges are difficult to defeat once they become organized and are capable of restoring local control over economic and social development.

The purpose of this chapter has been to outline the wide range of reactions and to put into perspective the struggle against imperialism and dependency. In one fashion or another, this struggle has been going on for some time, going back centuries in certain regions (India, South Africa, China). We noted in chapter 12 that the division of the underdeveloped world into colonies and semicolonies during the latter part of the nineteenth century was not unopposed. The Filipino uprisings against American occupation, the Chinese Boxer Rebellion against all Western influences, the national liberation movement of Augusto Sandino in Nicaragua in the 1930s, and the

MauMau movement in Kenya in the 1950s show that organized struggle for national independence and freedom from external domination has been constant though not continuous. Many of these earlier challenges have been forgotten or relatively undocumented by Western historians. The unsuccessful challenges tend to be relegated to historical oblivion, just as Indian and black slave revolts tended to be written out of American history. The rewriting of history by Third World historians (as heretical as this sounds) is still a major task, important for an understanding of the evolution of current struggles.

Three types of organized response to imperialism and dependency outlined here are: (1) traditionalism/fundamentalism; (2) nationalist counterorganization; and (3) socialist revolution. All three elements may be present, may form partial coalitions, may be synthesized within single organizations, or may compete for leadership of the anti-imperialist struggle, so that different orientations of the struggle may emerge in a single society.

Cultural or religious fundamentalism attacks the secularism and materialism of Westernization, the loss of ethical norms, and the intrusion of foreign life-styles by advocating a return to traditional ways, even to a rural peasant society. A recent example of the fundamentalist struggle is the Islamic movement in Iran, led by the organized mullahs and the Ayatollah Khomeini against the Shah and the American influence in Iranian society. The Ayatollah Khomeini regarded virtually all forms of modernization as signs of erosion in ethical values and of elements of foreign (mostly American) dominance within Iran, a dominance symbolized by the monarchy of the Pahlevi family. The overthrow of the pro-American Shah after several months of bloody confrontations between largely unarmed masses and the Shah's well-equipped army gives testimony to the potential strength of this reaction, at least in some areas. Within the Moslem world, religious fundamentalism as a challenge to imperialism and dependency has played a role in the Libyan regime of Colonel Quadaffi, combined there with elements of Arab socialism and pan-Arabism. In Egypt, the militant Moslem Brotherhood played a role in the opposition to former President Sadat's "opening to the West," though without the success of the Ayatollah. In Afghanistan, local mullahs and village chiefs have been leading an Islamic resistance movement to both the Marxist government in Kabul and the Soviet military occupation. In this Islamic resurgence, Soviet hegemonism as well as Western imperialism are regarded as dangers, since both represent expansionist secular (atheist) and materialist conceptions of human society.

Outside the Moslem world, however, the strength of the traditionalist challenge to dependency seems to be in decline. The feudal Ethiopian monarchy has crumbled, the Latin Catholic nationalist landowning oligarchies are fading, and even in India, the Hindu revivalism of the RSS or the Jan Sangh party has played a minor and not increasing role. At the local village level, traditionalism is now simply no match for the forces of development, whether dependent capitalist or state-planned communist. Barring another worldwide depression, which would halt the expansion of the world market system, even the most remote regions will probably be reached by the money-based market economy, by literacy and mass communications, and by some central government by the end of the century.

A second response to dependency is Third World counterorganization for defense of its interests against the core capitalist powers. A counterorganizational approach seeks to generate a self-sustained economic development through more effective bargaining between periphery and core capitalist nations (the communist world is still relatively marginal to this strategy). The staff of the U.N. Economic Commission on Latin America (ECLA) and the thinking of Raul Prebisch was one center of this counterorganizational strategy and the inspiration for the birth of UNCTAD (see chapter 12), a forum for the North-South dialogue. One school of Latin American dependency theory hopes to foster nationalist and state-supported efforts to change the terms of trade between the periphery and core nations. This could be the result of more nationalist government orientations toward development by individual states, which would encourage the growth and support demands of a modern national business class able eventually to compete and bargain as equals with Western MNCs. It could also include formation of Third World bargaining coalitions or cartels with increased leverage in bargaining with Western consumer nations or Western MNCs. Finally, counterorganization might involve a conscious and government-enforced effort to "delink" the local economy from Western markets, not to improve the terms of trade, but rather to re-establish autonomous and internally directed development, with reliance on local skills, materials, and technology.

The first variety of counterorganizational response is best represented by some of the nationalist regimes in Latin America, including the military government in Brazil, the Perón regime in Argentina, and certain aspects of Mexicanization under the PRI in Mexico. Part of this strategy involved and still involves "import substitution," the gradual replacement of Western manufactured imports with domestically produced manufactures, sponsored and protected by the government through tariff barriers, quotas, or direct and indirect subsidies. Through this process, the national bourgeoisie will grow in strength and industrial competence and will eventually take the lead in a self-sustaining development. This strategy had much more appeal in the 1950s than it has today. Brazil, with its large population and extensive natural resources, may be the only possibility for this approach in the near future, and even there it is doubtful that the pattern of dependency has been overthrown (see esp. Evans, 1979).

A second type of counterorganization is illustrated by OPEC (Organization of Petroleum Exporting Countries). Although OPEC became widely known in the 1970s, it was originally founded in 1960 by Venezuela, Iran, Iraq, Kuwait, and Saudi Arabia for the purpose of checking the decline in oil prices, which were then set unilaterally by the Western oil multinationals. The price of crude oil had fallen from $2.17 per barrel in 1948 to only $1.80 per barrel in 1960. It was not until 1971 that OPEC succeeded in restoring oil prices to their 1940 level (Singh, 1977: 4,6–7). Over this period from 1960 to 1971, however, OPEC was able to wrest basic control over price setting from the MNCs, and the Arab oil-producing nations were able, during the 1973 Yom Kippur War between Israel and Egypt, to institute an oil embargo against selected Western consumer nations and to immediately quadruple the price of OPEC-produced oil. OPEC is the leading example of what a coalition of Third World nations, encompassing the major producers of a key commodity required by Western consumer nations, can achieve in shifting the terms of trade in favor of the developing nations.

OPEC now includes a variety of nations from Latin America (Venezuela, Ecuador), black Africa (Nigeria, Gabon), and Asia (Indonesia, Iran), as well as the Arab world. Some OPEC governments are considered radical (Algeria, Libya), some moderate (Venezuela, Nigeria), and some quite conservative (Saudi Arabia, Kuwait, Arab Emirates). Western analysts and commentators have vacillated between hopes that OPEC would quickly disintegrate (from internal divisions, from Western covert or overt intervention, or from Western consumer cartelization) and fears that OPEC would become a model for Third World producer cartels (able to blackmail the West not only on prices of other commodities, but also on political issues such as the Palestinian cause). Neither fondest hopes nor darkest fears have proved accurate. OPEC is now a relatively stable organization with three decades of experience, in which time it has effectively removed Western corporate control from the pricing system for crude oil. Oil, however, is a "special" commodity, vital in the short run to the economies of the West and unable to be replaced quickly by other energy sources or by conservation. Some efforts have been made to repeat the OPEC counterorganization formula for bauxite (source for aluminum), with Jamaica's government taking the lead. Some possibilities exist for copper and tin; just four Third World nations account for at least half of all exports (52 percent in copper, 75 percent in tin) (Fishlow et al., 1978:35-36). But in these areas, alternative sources, both proven and potential, including recycling of scrap and greater possibilities for substitution of other metals, decrease the prospects for OPEC-like success, although not for some lesser gains in terms of trade.

The OPEC counterorganization was advanced initially as a defensive strategy to reverse declining terms of trade in oil; it remains doubtful whether the OPEC nations can use their new-found petrodollar wealth to generate a self-sustaining development process at home. When the oil begins to run out or when the West develops new sources of energy, both of which will probably occur within a generation and perhaps sooner, a political system capable~~of~~ promoting effective and independently managed development must be in place. In a sense, OPEC's use of its oil-pricing power in the 1970s has started the clock running; those OPEC nations with oil as their only main natural resource now have a limited time to use their petrodollars to replace the dependency syndrome not only in one area, but across an entire spectrum. Just how this can be done in technology, in investment strategies for growth, in military self-reliance, and especially in political institution-building remains a problem to which OPEC itself is not the answer.

Nevertheless, OPEC has certainly been far more successful than the broader counterorganizaitons, such as the Group of 77 working through UNCTAD and the fifty-eight Third World nations that negotiated the LOME I and LOME II trade agreements with the European Community. Even if OPEC were the only case of Third World counterorganization leading to a decisive break with dependency, it would still be an important strategy for a sizeable group of nations.

A third type of counterorganizational response is represented by the Tanzanian system, which has attempted to selectively "delink" itself from the world market system. President Julius Nyerere and the TANU party have sponsored a development program, outlined in the Arusha Declaration, of both abstention from expensive consumer imports and local village self-development (Ujamaa). Here the state acts to restrict dependency on Western technology and manufactures and to promote development of an adapted, self-controlled technology appropriate for overall development at the village level. The Tanzanian program has reduced social inequalities between city and village, and TANU has allowed within its one-party system for considerable local feedback through multicandidate competition in parliamentary elections. Yet, by most accounts economic progress has been slight, and it is not at all clear that the system has yet achieved a capacity for self-reliant development. The "delinking" strategy has been tried, to some extent, by the Burmese regime of General Ne Win and his Burmese Socialist Program party (BSPP); evaluations of the Burmese experience are generally less favorable than those of the Tanzanian. It is doubtful that small and poor Third World nations can develop in isolation, even self-selected isolation, since they lack material resource riches, a large labor pool, and a sizeable internal market for domestic products.

The final type of response to imperialism and dependency is socialist revolution. The aim is the overthrow of capitalism, which includes the overthrow of the local bourgeoisie's political and economic power and the power of the Western multinationals. This requires, in some fashion, armed struggle against the bourgeoisie, the military, Western suppliers and advisors, and potentially against the soldiers of the Western powers. The tactics, intensity, and duration of armed struggle may vary considerably. In China, huge peasant-based forces of the People's Liberation Army (PLA) fought a bitter civil war (with some pause) against Chiang Kai-shek's Nationalist armies (backed by the United States) for two decades before final victory in 1949. In Cuba, on the other hand, Castro's Rebel Army of at most three thousand was able, in a few years of hit-and-run raids, to demoralize Batista's military and to convince Batista and his army associates to flee the country, leaving the rebels victorious largely by default. In Vietnam, the Vietminh of Ho Chi Minh fought against the Japanese occupation in World War II, against the French attempt to recolonize the country from 1945 to 1954, and against the American intervention in the 1960s and 1970s. Some of this epic struggle took the form of guerrilla warfare, some was a more conventional battlefield campaign. The main adversary of the Vietnamese communist (Lao Dong) party was the foreign occupier of the country, and once the Japanese, or the French, or the Americans withdrew, the outcome of the internal struggle was fairly clear.

The strategies for development followed by victorious socialist revolutions have differed considerably, as described in the section on communist systems; they can best be classified as noncapitalist paths of development. It is probable that further socialist revolutions, perhaps like the more recent ones in Mozambique, Angola, or Nicaragua, will evolve new variants, but speculation on their specific innovations is not the focus of this section. Rather, we wish to note the spread of socialist revolution in the Third World as a response to imperialism and dependency, despite the many hindrances to political organization of workers and peasants and the many distractions from class-based and revolutionary opposition to the existing system. There is no presumption that all or even most of these movements will be successful. Indeed, the Tupamaros in Uruguay and the Montoneros and Trotskyite ERP in Argentina were defeated by campaigns of military and police repression, and Fretilin in East Timor has been all but starved to death by the Indonesian army. However, socialist (that is, Marxist-based) revolution has now established roots and is proving relevant to radical organizers and radicalized masses in all major Third World regions. The claims made often in the 1950s that Marxism is simply alien to Latin American "corporativist" cultures, that it is inappropriate to a naturally "classless" African society, and that it can make no headway against a vibrant Islamic religion are eroding. Moreover, there is a psychological "domino effect" in the increasing number of socialist revolutions in the Third World. This domino effect may be more important than any military spillover of revolution to neighboring nations; it encourages people and organizations to become more active, more willing to sacrifice, more daring, because victory seems possible. This is particularly important for lower-class workers and peasants, those less likely than businessmen, intellectuals, or government and military officials to feel socially confident and politically assertive. The success of Fidel Castro's Rebel Army encouraged similar strategies in a number of Latin American countries for a decade, even though Castro's success was never duplicated. The Vietnamese victory was followed by greater activity by the Communist party of Thailand and the New People's Army in the Philippines, even if these movements are not closely allied with the Vietnamese. The Sandinista triumph in Nicaragua was closely followed by revolutionary upsurges in El Salvador and Guatemala. And in Africa, the examples of FRELIMO in Mozambique and the MPLA in Angola, victorious over white settler forces, gave confidence to blacks in Rhodesia, Namibia, and South Africa (as well as considerable sanctuary space from which to operate).

The spread of socialist revolution throughout the Third World nations is neither automatic nor inevitable. The resonance of a Cuban revolution, or an Angolan revolution, or a Vietnamese revolution depends first on the similarity of social conditions in other countries; if there were not similar conditions of dependency and imperialism in so many Third World societies, there would be little or no domino effect. Thus the Vietnamese revolution does not produce a similar armed resistance movement in France or Czechoslovakia. Socialist revolution has required, up to now, at least, a combination of objective conditions of dependency and imperialist domination and the subjective consciousness of the need and capacity to overthrow the social order in favor of a noncapitalist path of development. If the great majority of workers and peasants actually benefit from dependent development, or if they can be convinced that efforts to achieve a radically different social order are hopeless, then socialist revolution will find little support and will wither as an alternative. The first requires that dependency radically change its "normal" distribution of benefits, which would imply a very different world order; the second requires that the MNCs, the local bourgeoisie, and the core capitalist powers continue to oppose, by a variety of means, any occurrence of social revolution.

In Angola, Cambodia, Afghanistan, and Ethiopia, there are active guerrilla insurgencies opposing Soviet-supported socialist regimes. UNITA, one of the defeated contenders for power in the 1975–1976 civil war in Angola, is still contesting for control of southern Angola against the Soviet and Cuban backed MPLA government in Luanda, with considerable tribal, United States, and South African support. In Cambodia, a sizeable remnant of the bloody Pol Pot regime, ousted from Phnom Penh by the Vietnamese intervention in late 1978, is leading a coalition resistance movement supported by the Chinese against the Heng Samrin government. In Ethiopia, the socialist EPLF is fighting for Eritrean independence from the Soviet and Cuban backed Marxist regime in Addis Ababa. The Soviet-supported regime of Najibullah and the Afghan communist party are faced with an uprising of a variety of ethnic groupings, representing generally the traditions of Islamic feudalism.

The insurgent groups are widely divergent in their ideological orientations. UNITA is a fairly straightforward pro-Western advocate of capitalist development for Angola; Pol Pot's Khmer Rouge sponsored, in its four years in power, an ultra-"left" primitive communism, which apparently destroyed the nation's schools, factories, and cities and killed as many of the educated as it could find; the EPLF, in the areas it controls, has emphasized education for all, women's emancipation, and popular participation in local planning; the Moslem insurgents in Afghanistan are religious fundamentalists, opposed to modern education, women's emancipation, and generally to any central government programs in the provinces. A unifying point, which adds a significant amount of nationalist support for these movements, is opposition to a regime that is militarily and politically dependent on the Soviet Union, or Cuba, or Vietnam. A direct parallel between the Soviet Union's role in these nations with the U.S. role in Vietnam is probably more misleading than enlightening, since it fails to analyze the popular support that the MPLA in Angola, the Heng Samrin regime in Phnom Penh, the DERG in Ethiopia, and the Afghan communist party possess on their own, and this varies considerably from case to case. Nevertheless, to the extent that the Soviet Union, Cuba, and Vietnam attempt to impose a particular government or particular policies on other nations (not only in the Third World but also in Eastern Europe), one response, but again not by any means automatically or mechanistically, may be armed resistance, though of quite varied character. To the extent that Soviet-allied regimes, as in Cuba or Vietnam, independently determine their own policies and pursue their own paths of noncapitalist development, their alliance with the Soviet Union is not a sign of Soviet hegemonism and does not carry the same stigma. There is no substitute for concrete analysis of the circumstances of each case, the organization and support for contending sides, before any parallels between Soviet hegemonism and United States imperialism are made.

References

CHAPTER 2. LIBERAL DEMOCRACY—THEORY AND HISTORY

Adams, John Clarke. *The Quest for Democratic Law.* New York: Thomas Crowell, 1970.

Bracher, Karl-Dietrich. *The German Dictatorship.* New York: Praeger, 1970.

Brogan, D. W., and Douglas Verney. *Political Patterns in Today's World.* New York: Harcourt, Brace and World, 1968.

Fromm, Erich. *Escape from Freedom.* New York: Farrar and Rinehart, 1941.

Giddens, Anthony. *The Class Structure of the Advanced Societies.* New York: Barnes and Noble, 1973.

Hancock, M. Donald. *Sweden: The Politics of Post-Industrial Change.* Hinsdale, Ill.: Dryden Press, 1972.

Heidenheimer, Arnold. *The Governments of Germany.* New York: Thomas Crowell, 1971.

Herlitz, Nils. *Sweden: A Modern Democracy on Ancient Foundations.* Minneapolis: University of Minnesota Press, 1939.

Hobbes, Thomas. *Leviathan.* New York: Collier Books, 1962. Originally published 1651.

Knauerhase, Ramon. *An Introduction to National Socialism 1920–1939.* Columbus, Ohio: Merrill, 1972.

Krieger, Leonard. *The German Idea of Freedom.* Chicago: University of Chicago Press, 1972.

Lipset, S. Martin. *Political Man.* New York: Doubleday, 1963.

Locke, John. *The Second Treatise of Government.* New York: Bobbs-Merrill, 1952. Originally published 1690.

Mann, Golo. *History of Germany Since 1789.* London: Chatte and Windus, 1968.

Marx, Karl. "The Eighteenth Brumaire of Louis Bonaparte." In Robert Tucker, ed., *Marx-Engels Reader.* New York: Norton, 1972.

Nagle, John. *The National Democratic Party: Right Radicalism in the Federal Republic of Germany.* Berkeley: University of California Press, 1970.

Neumann, Franz. *Behemoth.* New York: Harper and Row, 1942.

Nolte, Ernest. *Three Faces of Fascism.* New York: Mentor, 1966.

Rustow, Dankwart. *The Politics of Compromise.* Princeton, N.J.: Princeton University Press, 1955.

Schweitzer, Arthur. *Big Business in the Third Reich.* Bloomington: University of Indiana Press, 1964.

Smith, Adam. *An Inquiry into the Nature and Causes of the Wealth of Nations*. New York: Modern Library, 1939.

Sweezy, Paul. *Theory of Capitalist Development*. New York: Monthly Review Press, 1942.

Tucker, Robert, ed. *Marx-Engels Reader*. New York: Norton, 1972.

Vermeil, Edmond. *Germany's Three Reichs*. New York: H. Fertig, 1969.

Verney, Douglas. *Parliamentary Reform in Sweden, 1866–1921*. Oxford: Clarendon Press, 1957.

CHAPTER 3. ECONOMIC DEVELOPMENT—AFFLUENT CONSUMERISM

Anderson, Odin. *Health Care: Can There Be Equity?* New York: Wiley, 1972.

Ashton, T. S. *The Industrial Revolution 1760–1830*. London: Oxford University Press, 1948.

Groth, Alexander. *Comparative Politics: A Distributive Approach*. New York: Macmillan, 1971.

Heidenheimer, Arnold, Hugh Heclo, and Carolyn Adams. *Comparative Public Policy*. New York: St. Martin's Press, 1975.

Jackman, Robert. *Politics and Social Equality: A Comparative Analysis*. New York: Wiley, 1975.

Parkin, Frank. *Class Inequality and Political Order*. New York: Praeger, 1971.

Pryor, Frederic. *Public Expenditures in Communist and Capitalist Nations*. London: Allen and Unwin, 1968.

Rosenstein-Rodan, Paul N. "The Haves and Have-Nots Around the Year 2000." In J. N. Bhagwati, ed., *Economics and World Order*. London: Macmillan, 1972.

Tomasson, Richard F. "From Elitism to Egalitarianism in Swedish Education." *Sociology of Education* (Spring 1965).

Tucker, Robert, ed. *Marx-Engels Reader*. New York: Norton, 1972.

Wilensky, Harold. *The Welfare State and Equality*. Berkeley: University of California Press, 1975.

CHAPTER 4. SOCIAL EQUALITY—OPPORTUNITY VERSUS RESULTS

Bacon, John, and J. B. Mays. *Crime and Its Treatment*. London: Longman, 1970.

Bell, Daniel. "Meritocracy and Equality." *Public Interest* (Fall 1972).

Bell, Daniel. *The Coming of Post-Industrial Society*. New York: Basic Books, 1974.

Bernard, Jesse. *Women and the Public Interest*. Chicago: Aldine, 1971.

Blondel, Jean. *Comparative Legislatures*. Englewood Cliffs, N.J.: Prentice-Hall, 1973.

Bottomore, Thomas B. *Elites and Society*. London: Penguin, 1966.

Clinard, Marshall, and Peter Yeager. *Corporate Crime*. New York: Free Press, 1980.

Cohen, David. "Does IQ Matter?" *Commentary* (April 1972).

Coleman, James, et al. *Equality of Educational Opportunities*. Washington, D.C.: U.S. Government Printing Office, 1966.

Coons, John, et al. *Private Wealth and Public Education*. Çambridge, Mass.: Belknap Press, 1970.

Cressey, Donald. *Delinquency, Crime, and Differential Association*. The Hague: M. Nijhoff, 1974.

Cromwell, Jerry. "The Size Distribution of Income." In *Review of Income and Wealth*. New Haven, Conn.: International Association for Research in Income and Wealth, 1977.

Geis, Gilbert. "White Collar Crime." In M. Clinard and R. Quinney, eds., *Criminal Behavior Systems*. New York: Holt, Rinehart and Winston, 1967.

Giddens, Anthony. *Class Structure of the Advanced Societies*. New York: Barnes and Noble, 1973.

Giele, Janet. *Women: Roles and Status in Eight Countries*. New York: Wiley, 1977.

Gordon, David. "Class and the Economics of Crime." In D. Gordon, ed., *Problems in Political Economy*, 2d ed. Lexington, Mass.: D. C. Heath, 1977.

Gurr, Theodore, Peter Grabosky, and Richard Hula. *Politics of Crime and Conflict*. Beverly Hills, Calif.: Sage, 1977.

Harrington, Michael. *The Twilight of Capitalism*. New York: Simon and Schuster, 1976.

Heidenheimer, Arnold, Hugh Heclo, and Carolyn T. Adams. *Comparative Public Policy*. New York: St. Martin's Press, 1975.

Henle, Peter. "Exploring the Distribution of National Income." *Monthly Labor Review* (Dec. 1972), 95 (12).

Hewlett, Sylvia. *A Lesser Life: The Myth of Women's Liberation in America*. New York: Morrow, 1986.

Howe, James. *United States and World Development: Agenda for Action 1975*. New York: Praeger, 1975.

Iglitzin, Lynn, and R. Ross. *Women in the World*. Santa Barbara, Calif.: CLIO Books, 1976.

Jencks, Christopher. *Inequality*. New York: Basic Books, 1972.

Kloby, Jerry. "The Growing Divide: Class Polarization in the 1980's." *Monthly Review* (Sept. 1987), 39(4).

Kolko, Gabriel. *Wealth and Power in America*. New York: Praeger, 1962.

Kubota, Akira. *Higher Civil Servants in Postwar Japan*. Princeton, N.J.: Princeton University Press, 1969.

Lampman, Robert. *Changes in the Share of Wealth*. New York: National Bureau of Economic Research, 1960.

Little, Alan, and John Westergaard. "The Trend of Class Differentials." *British Journal of Sociology* (1964), 15.

Mandel, William. *Soviet Women*. Garden City, N.Y.: Anchor, 1975.

Matthews, Donald. *The Social Background of Political Decision-Makers*. New York: Random House, 1954.

Mayer, Lawrence. *Politics in Industrial Societies*. New York: Wiley, 1977.

Meade, James. *Efficiency, Equality and the Ownership of Property*. London: Allen and Unwin, 1964.

Means, Ingunn N. "Scandinavian Women." In L. Iglitzin and R. Ross, eds., *Women in the World*. Santa Barbara, Calif.: CLIO Books, 1976.

Miliband, Ralph. *The State in Capitalist Society*. New York: Basic Books, 1969.

Miller, S. M. "Comparative Social Mobility." *Current Sociology* (1969), 1.

Mills, C. Wright. *The Power Elite*. New York: Oxford University Press, 1956.

Musgrove, Richard. *Fiscal Systems*. New Haven, Conn.: Yale University Press, 1969.

Nagle, John. *System and Succession*. Austin: University of Texas Press, 1977.

Parkin, Frank. *Class Inequality and Political Order*. New York: Praeger, 1971.

Peters, Guy. *The Politics of Bureaucracy*. New York: Longman, 1978.

Putnam, Robert. *Comparative Study of Political Elites*. Englewood Cliffs, N.J.: Prentice-Hall, 1976.

Quinney, Richard. *Social Reality of Crime*. Boston, Mass.: Little, Brown, 1970.

Rimlinger, Gaston. *Welfare Policy and Industrialization in Europe*. New York: Wiley, 1971.

Schafer, Stephen, ed. *Readings in Contemporary Criminology*. Reston, Va.: Reston Pub., 1976.

Schnitzer, Martin. *Income Distribution*. New York: Praeger, 1974.

Stern, Philip. *The Rape of the Taxpayer*. New York: Random House, 1973.

Sullerot, E. *Women, Society, and Change*. New York: McGraw-Hill, 1971.

Sutherland, Edwin. *Criminology*, 9th ed. Philadelphia, Pa.: Lippincott, 1974.

Tanzi, Vito. *Individual Income Tax and Economic Growth*. Baltimore, Md.: Johns Hopkins University Press, 1969.

Westergaard, John. "The Withering Away of Class: A Contemporary Myth." In P. Anderson and R. Blackburn, eds., *Towards Socialism*. Ithaca, N.Y.: Cornell University Press, 1965.

Wilensky, Harold. *The Welfare State and Equality*. Berkeley: University of California Press, 1975.

Williamson, Jeffrey, and Peter Lindert. "Three Centuries of American Inequality." In P. Uselding, ed., *Research in Economic History*. Greenwich, Conn.: JAI Press, 1976.

CHAPTER 5. LIBERTY—HIGH-WATER MARK OF INDIVIDUALISM

Gans, Herbert. *More Equality*. New York: Pantheon, 1973.

Gastil, Raymond. "Survey." *Freedom at Issue* (Jan.-Feb. 1976).

Gastil, Raymond. *Freedom in the World: Political Rights and Civil Liberties 1978*. New York: Freedom House, 1978.

Jones, Mary. *The Autobiography of Mother Jones*. Chicago, Ill.: C. H. Kerr, 1925.

Nagle, John. *The National Democratic Party: Right Radicalism in the Federal Republic of Germany*. Berkeley: University of California Press, 1970.

Parenti, Michael. *Democracy for the Few*. New York: St. Martin's Press, 1974.

Stouffer, Samuel. *Communism, Conformity and Civil Liberties*. Garden City, N.Y.: Doubleday, 1954.

Wolfe, Alan. *The Seamy Side of Democracy*. New York: McKay, 1973.

CHAPTER 6. QUALITY OF LIFE—THE DARK SIDE OF MODERNISM

Bakalar, James, and Lester Grinspoon. *Drug Control in a Free Society*. New York: Cambridge University Press, 1984.

Bejerot, Nils. *Addiction and Society.* Springfield, Ill.: Charles C. Thomas, 1970.

Bell, Daniel. "Crime as a Way of Life." *Antioch Review* (Summer 1953), 13:2.

Bell, Daniel. *The Cultural Crisis of Capitalism.* New York: Basic Books, 1976.

Bohm, Peter, and Allan Kneese, eds. *The Economics of Environment.* London: Macmillan, 1971.

Cantril, Hadley. *The Pattern of Human Concern.* New Brunswick, N.J.: Rutgers University Press, 1965.

Commoner, Barry. "The Environment." *New Yorker,* June 15, 1987.

Enloe, Cynthia. *The Politics of Pollution in a Comparative Perspective.* New York: McKay, 1975.

Fromm, Erich. *The Sane Society.* New York: Holt, Rinehart and Winston, 1955.

Goodwin, Richard. *The American Condition.* Garden City, N.Y.: Doubleday, 1974.

Gordon, David, ed. *Problems in Political Economy,* 2d ed. Lexington, Mass.: D.C. Heath, 1977.

Gurr, Theodore R., Peter Grabosky, and Richard Hula. *The Politics of Crime and Conflict.* Beverly Hills, Calif.: Sage, 1977.

Holahan, John F. "The Economics of Heroin." In P. Wald and P. Hutt, eds., *Dealing with Drug Abuse.* New York: Praeger, 1972.

Lewis, Paul. "For the World Economy, Even the Best Signs are None Too Good." *New York Times* Briefing Papers for Public Affairs, 1978.

Loraine, John A. *The Death of Tomorrow.* Philadelphia, Penn.: Lippincott, 1972.

Marcuse, Herbert. *One Dimensional Man.* Boston, Mass.: Beacon Press, 1967.

May, Edgar. "Narcotics Addition and Control in Great Britain." In P. Wald and P. Hutt, eds., *Dealing with Drug Abuse.* New York: Praeger, 1972.

Nettler, Groyan. *Explaining Crime.* New York: McGraw-Hill, 1974.

Quinney, Richard. *The Social Reality of Crime.* Boston, Mass.: Little, Brown, 1969.

Quinney, Richard. *Class, State and Crime.* New York: McKay, 1977.

Reisman, David, Nathan Glazer, and Reuel Denny. *The Lonely Crowd.* Garden City, N.Y.: Doubleday, 1950.

Rhinestein, Max. *Marriage Stability, Divorce, and the Law.* Chicago, Ill.: University of Chicago Press, 1972.

Schnitzer, Martin. *The Economy of Sweden.* New York: Praeger, 1970.

Sussman, Marvin. "Family, Kinship and Bureaucracy." In A. Campbell and P. Converse, eds., *The Human Meaning of Social Change.* New York: Russell Sage, 1972.

Wald, Patricia, and Peter Hutt. *Dealing with Drug Abuse.* New York: Praeger, 1972.

Ward, Barbara. *The Home of Man.* New York: Norton, 1976.

Warren, Roland. *The Community in America,* 2d ed. Chicago, Ill.: Rand McNally, 1972.

CHAPTER 7. COMMUNISM—THEORY AND ORIGINS

Bernstein, Eduard. *Evolutionary Socialism.* New York: Schocken, 1975.

Bertsch, Gary, and Thomas Ganschow, eds. *Comparative Communism: The Soviet, Chinese, and Yugoslav Models.* San Francisco, Calif.: W. H. Freeman, 1976.

Harcave, Sidney. *Russia: A History.* Chicago, Ill.: Lippincott, 1959.

Moore, Barrington. *Terror and Progress*. New York: Harper and Row, 1966.

Tucker, Robert, ed. *Marx-Engels Reader*. New York: Norton, 1972.

Tucker, Robert, ed. *The Lenin Anthology*. New York: Norton, 1975.

CHAPTER 8. ECONOMIC DEVELOPMENT—NON-CAPITALIST ROADS TO MODERNIZATION

Abouchar, Alan. *Economic Evaluation of Soviet Socialism*. New York: Pergamon Press, 1979.

Bush, Keith. "Soviet Living Standards: Some Salient Data." In *Economic Aspects of Life in the USSR*. Brussels: NATO Directorate of Economic Affairs, 1975.

Feldmesser, Robert. "Social Status and Access to Higher Education." *Harvard Educational Review* (1957), 27 (2).

Gaaster, Michael. *China's Struggle to Modernize*. New York: Knopf, 1972.

Gripp, Richard C. *The Political System of Communism*. New York: Dodd, Mead, 1973.

Groth, Alexander. *Comparative Politics: A Distributional Approach*. New York: Macmillan, 1971.

Hinton, William H. "China's New Family Concept." *Monthly Review* (Nov. 1983), 35 (6):1–28.

Horvat, Branko. *An Essay on Yugoslav Society*. White Plains, N.Y.: International Arts and Sciences Press, 1969.

Jacobs, Everett. "Urban Housing in the Soviet Union." In *Economic Aspects of Life in the USSR*. Brussels: NATO Directorate of Economic Affairs, 1975.

Lane, David. *The End of Inequality?* Middlesex, England: Penguin, 1971.

Mayer, Lawrence. *Politics in Industrial Societies*. New York: Wiley, 1977.

Milenkovitch, Deborah. *Planning and Market in Yugoslav Economic Thought*. New Haven, Conn.: Yale University Press, 1971.

Oksenberg, Michael. *China's Developmental Experience*. New York: Praeger, 1973.

Osborn, Robert. *Soviet Social Policies: Welfare, Equality and Community*. Homewood, Ill.: Dorsey Press, 1970.

Pryor, Frederic. *Public Expenditures in Communist and Capitalist Naitons*. London: Allen and Unwin, 1968.

Schell, Orville. "A Reporter at Large (China)." *New Yorker*, Jan. 23, 1984, pp. 43–85.

Sewell, James. *United States and World Development: Agenda for Action 1977*. New York: Praeger, 1977.

Sherman, Howard. *The Soviet Economy*. Boston: Little, Brown, 1969.

Wilensky, Harold. *The Welfare State and Equality*. Berkeley: University of California Press, 1975.

CHAPTER 9. SOCIAL EQUALITY—ACHIEVEMENTS IN SOCIAL JUSTICE

Aspaturian, V. V. "The Non-Russian Nationalities." In A. Kassof, ed., *Prospects for Soviet Society*. London: Pall Mall Press, 1968.

Chapman, Janet. "Are Earnings More Equal Under Socialism?" In John Moroney, ed., *Income Inequality*. Lexington, Mass.: Lexington Books, 1979.

Cromwell, Jerry. "The Size Distribution of Income: An International Comparison." *Review of Income and Wealth* (Sept. 1977), 23 (3): 291–308.

Djilas, Milovan. *The New Class*. New York: Holt, Rinehart and Winston, 1957.

Dodge, Norton. "Women in the Professions." In D. Atkinson, A. Dallin, and G. Lapidus, eds., *Women in Russia*. Stanford, Calif.: Stanford University Press, 1977.

Echols, John M. "Does Socialism Mean Greater Equality?" *American Journal of Political Science* (Feb. 1981), 25 (1).

Giddens, Anthony. *Class Structure in the Advanced Societies*. New York: Harper, 1973.

Gordon, Leonid, and E. Klopov. *Man after Work*. Moscow: Progress Pub., 1975.

Hancock, M. Donald. "The Bundeswehr and the National People's Army: A Comparative Study of German Civil-Military Polity." Monograph Series in World Affairs, 10:2. Denver, Colo.: University of Denver, 1973.

Howe, James. *United States and World Development: Agenda for Action 1975*. New York: Praeger, 1975.

Huntington, Samuel, and Zbigniew Brzezinski. *Political Power: USA/USSR*. New York: Viking, 1973.

Kirschen, E. S. *Economic Policies Compared*. Amsterdam: North Holland-Elsevier, 1974.

Lane, David. *Politics and Society in the USSR*. New York: Random House, 1971. (a)

Lane, David. *The End of Inequality?* Manchester: Penguin, 1971. (b)

Lenski, Gerhard. *Power and Privilege: A Theory of Social Stratification*. New York: McGraw-Hill, 1966.

Lyall, Harold. "Some Problems in Making International Comparisons in Inequality." In John Moroney, ed., *Income Inequality*. Lexington, Mass.: Lexington Books, 1979.

Mandel, William. *Soviet Women*. New York: Anchor, 1975.

Matthews, Mervyn. "Top Incomes in the USSR." In *Economic Aspects of Life in the USSR*. Brussels: NATO Directorate of Economic Affairs, 1975.

Moses, Joel. "The Soviet Union in the Women's Decade 1975-1985." In L. Iglitzin and R. Ross, eds., *Women in the World*. Santa Barbara, Calif.: Clio Press, 1986.

Nagle, John. *System and Succession: The Social Bases of Political Elite Recruitment*. Austin: University of Texas Press, 1977.

Parkin, Frank. *Class Inequality and Political Order*. New York: Praeger, 1971.

Sacks, Michael P. "Women in the Industrial Labor Force." In *Women in Russia*. Stanford, Calif.: Stanford University Press, 1977.

Scott, Hilda. *Does Socialism Liberate Women?* Boston, Mass.: Beacon, 1974.

Szczepanski, Jan. *Empirical Sociology in Poland*. Warsaw: Polish Scientific Pub., 1966.

Szczepanski, Jan. *Systems of Higher Education: Poland*. New York: International Council for Educational Development, 1978.

Vinocur, Aaron, and Gur Ofer. "Inequality of Earnings, Household Income, and Wealth in the Soviet Union in the 1970s." In James Millar, ed., *Politics, Work, and Daily Life in the USSR*. New York: Cambridge University Press, 1987.

Wiles, Peter. "Recent Data on Soviet Income Distribution." In *Economic Aspects of Life in the USSR*. Brussels: NATO Directorate of Economic Affairs, 1975.

CHAPTER 10. LIBERTY—FAILURES IN PERSONAL FREEDOM

Barry, Donald, and Carol Barner-Barry. *Contemporary Soviet Politics.* Englewood Cliffs, N.J.: Prentice-Hall, 1978. Especially ch. 11.

Brown, Archie, and Jack Gray, eds. *Political Culture and Political Change in Communist Systems.* New York: Holmes and Meier, 1977.

Conquest, Robert. *The Great Terror.* New York: Macmillan, 1968.

Denitch, Bogdan. "The Relevance of Yugoslav Self-Management." In G. Bertsch and T. Ganschow, eds., *Comparative Communism.* San Francisco, Calif.: W. H. Freeman, 1976.

Fainsod, Merle. *How Russia Is Ruled.* Cambidge, Mass.: Harvard University Press, 1963. Especially ch. 13.

Hough, Jerry. *The Soviet Union and Social Science Theory.* Cambridge, Mass.: Harvard University Press, 1977.

Khrushchev, Nikita. *Report to the Twentieth Congress of the CPSU.* New York: Columbia University Press, 1956.

Lane, David. *Politics and Society in the USSR.* New York: Random House, 1971. Especially ch. 8.

Marx, Karl, and Friedrich Engels. "The Manifesto of the Communist Party." In Robert Tucker, ed., *Marx-Engels Reader.* New York: Norton, 1972.

Medish, Vadim. *The Soviet Union.* Englewood Cliffs, N.J.: Prentice-Hall, 1987.

Medvedev, Roy. *On Socialist Democracy.* New York: Knopf, 1975.

Medvedev, Zhores. *The Rise and Fall of T. D. Lysenko.* New York: Columbia University Press, 1969.

Oksenberg, Michael. "Occupational Groups and the Chinese Cultural Revolution." In Bertsch and Ganschow, eds., *Comparative Communism.* San Francisco, Calif.: W. H. Freeman, 1976.

Skilling, Gordon, and Franklyn Griffiths, eds. *Interest Groups in Soviet Politics.* Princeton, N.J.: Princeton University Press, 1971.

Szelenyi, Ivan. "Socialist Opposition in Eastern Europe." In Rudolf Tökes, ed. *Opposition in Eastern Europe.* Baltimore, Md.: Johns Hopkins University Press, 1979.

Tatu, Michel. *Power in the Kremlin: From Khrushchev to Kosygin.* New York: Viking, 1969.

Tokes, Rudolf, ed. *Dissent in the USSR.* Baltimore, Md.: Johns Hopkins University Press, 1975.

CHAPTER 11. QUALITY OF LIFE—SECURITY AND ALIENATION

Abouchar, Alan. *Economic Evaluation of Soviet Socialism.* New York: Pergamon Press, 1979.

Barry, Donald, and Carole Barner-Barry. *Contemporary Soviet Politics.* Englewood Cliffs, N.J.: Prentice-Hall, 1978.

Blyakman, L., and O. Shkaratan. *Man at Work.* Moscow: Progress, 1977.

Bush, Keith. "Soviet Living Standards: Some Salient Data." In *Economic Aspects of Life in the USSR.* Brussels: NATO Directorate of Economic Affairs, 1975.

Chalidze, Valery. *Criminal Russia: Essays on Crime in the Soviet Union.* New York: Random House, 1977.

Connor, Walter. *Deviance in Soviet Society.* New York: Columbia University Press, 1972.

Enloe, Cynthia. *The Politics of Pollution in a Comparative Perspective.* New York: McKay, 1975.

Goldman, Marshal. *The Spoils of Progress.* Cambridge, Mass.: MIT Press, 1972.

Groth, Alexander. *Comparative Politics: A Distributional Approach.* New York: Macmillan, 1971.

Hinton, William H. "China's New Family Concept." *Monthly Review* (Nov. 1983) 35 *(6)*:1–28.

Huntington, Samuel. *Political Order in Changing Societies.* New Haven, Conn.: Yale University Press, 1968.

Juvilier, Peter. "Crime and Its Study." In H. Morton and R. Tokes, eds., *Soviet Society in the 1970s.* New York: Free Press, 1974.

Kelley, Donald, Kenneth Stunkel, and Richard Wescott. *The Economic Superpowers and the Environment: The United States, the Soviet Union, and Japan.* San Francisco, Calif.: Freeman, 1976.

Kollontai, Alexandra. "The New Morality and the Working Classes." In Lane, *Politics and Society in the USSR.* New York: Random House, 1971. Pp. 374–77.

Lane, David. *Politics and Society in the USSR.* New York: Random House, 1971.

Mandel, William. *Soviet Women.* Garden City, N.Y.: Anchor, 1975.

Manevich, Efim. *USSR: Full Employment?* Moscow: Novosti, 1968.

Moses, Joel. "The Soviet Union in the Women's Decade." In L. Iglitzin and R. Ross, eds., *Women in the World.* Santa Barbara, Calif.: Clio Press, 1986.

Ophuls, William. *Ecology and the Politics of Scarcity.* San Francisco, Calif.: Freeman, 1977.

Parkin, Frank. *Class Inequality and Political Order.* New York: Praeger, 1971.

Salas, Luis. *Social Control and Deviance in Cuba.* New York: Praeger, 1979.

Schell, Orville. "A Reporter at Large (China)." *New Yorker,* Jan. 23, 1984, pp. 43–85.

Scott, James. *Comparative Political Corruption.* Englewood Cliffs, N.J.: Prentice-Hall, 1972.

Zdravomyslov, A. G., and V. A. Yadov. "Effect of Vocational Distinctions on the Attitude to Work." In G. V. Osipov, ed., *Industry and Labour in the USSR.* London: Tavistock, 1966.

Zeitlin, Maurice. *Revolutionary Politics and the Cuban Working Class.* Princeton, N.J.: Princeton University Press, 1970.

Chapter 12. The Third World, Imperialism, and Dependency

Baran, Paul, and Paul Sweezy. "Notes on the Theory of Imperialism." In K. T. Fann and Donald Hodges, eds., *Readings In U.S. Imperialism.* Boston, Mass.: Porter Sargent, 1971.

Bodenheimer, Suzanne. "Dependency and Imperialism: The Roots of Latin American Underdevelopment." In K. T. Fann and D. Hodges, eds., *Readings in U.S. Imperialism.* Boston, Mass.: Porter Sargent, 1971.

Chilcote, Ronald, and Joel Edelstein, eds. *Latin America: The Struggle with Dependency and Beyond.* Cambridge, Mass.: Schenckman, 1974.

Cockcroft, James, Andre Gunder Frank, and Dale Johnson. *Dependence and Underdevelopment.* Garden City, N.Y.: Anchor, 1972.

Dos Santos, Theotonio. "The Structure of Dependence." In K. T. Fann and D. Hodges, *Readings,* 1971.

Erb, Guy, and Valerian Kallab. *Beyond Dependency: The Developing World Speaks Out.* New York: Praeger, 1975.

Fanon, Frantz. "The Pitfalls of National Consciousness—Africa." In K. T. Fann and D. Hodges, eds., *Readings in U.S. Imperialism.* Boston, Mass.: Porter Sargent, 1971.

Fishlow, Albert, et al. *Rich and Poor Nations in the World Economy.* New York: McGraw-Hill, 1978.

Gamer, Robert. *The Developing Nations: A Comparative Perspective.* Boston, Mass.: Allyn and Bacon, 1976.

Johnson, Harry. *Trade Strategy for Rich and Poor Nations.* Toronto: University of Toronto Press, 1971.

Lenin, V. I. *Imperialism: The Highest Stage of Capitalism.* New York: International Pub., 1969. Originally published in 1916.

Magdoff, Harry, and Paul Sweezy. "Notes on the Multinational Corporation." In K. T. Fann and D. Hodges, eds., *Readings in U.S. Imperialism.* Boston, Mass.: Porter Sargent, 1971.

O'Connor, James. "The Meaning of U.S. Imperialism." In K. T. Fann and D. Hodges, eds., *Readings in U.S. Imperialism.* Boston, Mass.: Porter Sargent, 1971.

Oxaal, Ivar, Tony Barnett, and David Booth, eds. *Beyond the Sociology of Development.* London: Routledge and Kegan Paul, 1975.

Payer, Cheryl. *The Debt Trap: The IMF and the Third World.* New York: Monthly Review Press, 1976.

Singh, Jyoti Shankar. *A New International Economic Order: Toward a Fair Redistribution of the World's Resources.* New York: Praeger, 1977.

Wriggens, W. Howard, and Gunnar Adler-Karlsson. *Reducing Global Inequalities.* New York: McGraw-Hill, 1978.

Chapter 13. Economic Development—Growth and the Widening Gap

Apter, David, and D. Goodman. *The MNC and Social Change.* New York: Praeger, 1976.

Bairoch, Paul. *Economic Development in the Third World Since 1900.* Berkeley: University of California Press, 1975.

Brown, Lester. *Seeds of Change: The Green Revolution and International Development in the 1970s.* New York: Praeger, 1973.

Calder, Nigel. *Technopolis: Social Control of the Uses of Science.* New York: Simon and Schuster, 1970.

Chaliand, Gerard. *Revolution in the Third World.* New York: Viking, 1978.

Chirot, Daniel. *Social Change in the Twentieth Century.* New York: Harcourt Brace Jovanovich, 1977.

Cockcroft, James. A. G. Frank, and Dale Johnson. *Dependence and Underdevelopment.* Garden City, N.Y.: Anchor, 1972.

Erb, Guy, and Valerian Kallab. *Beyond Dependency: The Developing World Speaks Out.* New York: Praeger, 1975.

Gamer, Robert. *The Developing Nations.* Boston, Mass.: Allyn and Bacon, 1976.

Goldthorpe, J. E. *Sociology of the Third World.* Cambridge: Cambridge University Press, 1975.

Hansen, Roger. *The Politics of Mexican Development.* Baltimore, Md.: Johns Hopkins Press, 1974.

Hansen, Roger, ed. *The United States and World Development: Agenda for Action 1976.* New York: Praeger, 1976.

Howe, James, ed. *The United States and World Development: Agenda for Action 1975.* New York: Praeger, 1975.

International Labor Office (ILO). *Cost of Social Security (1967–1971).* Geneva: ILO, 1976.

International Labor Office (ILO). *Employment, Growth and Basic Needs.* Geneva: ILO, 1976.

Myrdal, Gunnar. *Asian Drama.* New York: Twentieth Century Fund, 1968.

Payer, Cheryl, *The Debt Trap.* New York: Monthly Review, 1974.

Payer, Cheryl. *The World Bank: A Critical Analysis.* New York: Monthly Review, 1982.

Payer, Cheryl. "Repudiating the Past." *NACLA Report* (March/April 1985), 19(2).

Rhodes, Robert I. *Imperialism and Underdevelopment.* New York: Monthly Review Press, 1970.

Rollins, Charles. "Mineral Development and Economic Growth." In Robert Rhodes, ed., *Imperialism and Underdevelopment.* New York: Monthly Review Press, 1970.

Sachs, Ignacy. *Discovery of the Third World.* Cambridge, Mass.: MIT Press, 1978.

Sewell, James, ed. *The United States and World Development: Agenda for Action 1977.* New York: Praeger, 1977.

Sinclair, Stuart. *Urbanization and Labor Markets in Developing Countries.* New York: St. Martin's Press, 1978.

Singh, Jyoti Shankar. *A New International Economic Order: Toward a Fair Redistribution of the World's Resources.* New York: Praeger, 1977.

Sutcliffe, Robert. *Industrialization and Underdevelopment.* Reading, Mass.: Addison-Wesley, 1971.

Tanzer, Michael. *The Race for Resources.* New York: Monthly Review, 1980.

"Two Faces of Third World Debt." *Monthly Review* (Jan. 1984), 35(8).

Uri, Pierre. *Development without Dependency.* New York: Praeger, 1976.

Ward, Barbara. *The Home of Man.* New York: Norton, 1976.

Ward, Barbara, J. D. Runnels, and Lenore D'Anjou, eds. *The Widening Gap: Development in the 1970s.* New York: Columbia University Press, 1971.

Weiskopf, Thomas, C. Edwards, and M. Reich, eds. *The Capitalist System.* Englewood Cliffs, N.J.: Prentice-Hall, 1972.

Weitz, Raanon, ed. *Urbanization and the Developing Countries*. New York: Praeger, 1973.

Wilbur, Charles, ed. *The Political Economy of Development and Underdevelopment*. New York: Random House, 1973.

CHAPTER 14. INEQUALITY—FAILURES IN SOCIAL JUSTICE

Adelman, Irma, and Cynthia T. Morris. *Economic Growth and Social Equity in Developing Countries*. Stanford, Calif.: Stanford University Press, 1973.

Bairoch, Paul. *The Economic Development of the Third World since 1900*. Berkeley: University of California Press, 1975.

Baran, Paul. *Political Economy of Growth*. New York: Monthly Review Press, 1957.

Barnett, Richard, and Ronald Muller. *Global Reach*. New York: Simon and Schuster, 1974.

Bhagwati, Jagdish, ed. *Economics and World Order from the 1970s to the 1990s*. London: Macmillan, 1972.

Bienen, Henry, and V. P. Diejomaoh, eds. *The Political Economy of Income Distribution in Nigeria*. New York: Holmes and Meier, 1981.

Bodenheimer, Suzanne. "Dependency and Imperialism." In K. T. Fann and D. Hodges, eds., *Readings in U.S. Imperialism*. Boston, Mass.: Porter Sargent, 1971.

Brown, Lester. *World without Borders*. New York: Random House, 1972.

Castro, Fidel. *The World Economic and Social Crisis*. Havana: Council of State Publishing Office, 1983.

Chaliand, Gerard. *Revolution in the Third World*. New York: Viking, 1976.

Clifford, Juliet, and Gavin Osmond. *World Development Handbook*. London: Charles Knight, 1971.

Cockcroft, James, A. G. Frank, and Dale Johnson. *Dependency and Underdevelopment*. Garden City, N.Y.: Anchor, 1972.

Cromwell, Jerry. "The Size Distribution of Income." In *Review of Income and Wealth*. New Haven, Conn.: International Association for Research in Income and Wealth, 1977.

Dos Santos, Theotonio. "The Structure of Dependency." In K. T. Fann and D. Hodges, eds., *Readings in U.S. Imperialism*. Boston, Mass.: Porter Sargent, 1971.

Evans, Peter. *Dependent Development: The Alliance of Multinational, State, and Local Capital in Brazil*. Princeton, N.J.: Princeton University Press, 1979.

Fann, K. T., and Donald Hodges, eds. *Readings in U.S. Imperialism*. Boston, Mass.: Porter Sargent, 1971.

Fanon, Frantz. *The Wretched of the Earth*. New York: Grove Press, 1968.

Fields, Gary S. *Poverty, Inequality and Development*. Cambridge: Cambridge University Press, 1980.

Frank, André Gunder. *Latin America: Underdevelopment or Revolution?* New York: Monthly Review Press, 1970.

Galeano, Eduardo. *Open Veins of Latin America*. New York: Monthly Review Press, 1973.

Gamer, Robert. *The Developing Nations.* Boston, Mass.: Allyn and Bacon, 1976.

Hansen, Roger. *The Politics of Mexican Development.* Baltimore, Md.: Johns Hopkins University Press, 1974.

Hansen, Roger. "The Emerging Challenge: Global Distribution of Income and Economic Opportunity." In J. Howe, ed., *The United States and World Development.* New York: Praeger, 1975.

Hoivik, Tord. "The Demography of Structural Violence." Unpublished manuscript.

International Labor Office. *Employment, Growth, and Basic Needs.* Geneva: International Labor Office, 1976.

Langguth, A. J. *Hidden Terrors: The Truth about U.S. Police Operations in Latin America.* New York: Pantheon, 1979.

LeMoyne, James. "Honduran Army Linked to Death of 200 Leftists." *New York Times,* May 2, 1987.

Magdoff, Harry. "Third World Debt" *Monthly Review* (Feb. 1986), 37 (9).

Meadows, Dennis, et al. *Dynamics of Growth in a Finite World.* Cambridge, Mass.: Wright-Allen, 1974.

Meadows, Dennis, et al. *The Limits of Growth.* New York: Universe, 1972.

Mesarovic, Mihailo, and Eduard Pestel. *Mankind at the Turning Point.* New York: Dutton, 1974.

Ophuls, William. *Ecology and the Politics of Scarcity.* San Francisco, Calif.: W. H. Freeman, 1978.

Payer, Cheryl. "Repudiating the Past." *NACLA Report* (March/April 1985), 19(2).

Sachs, Ignacy. *Discovery of the Third World.* Cambridge, Mass.: MIT Press, 1978.

Sivard, Ruth L. *World Military and Social Expenditures 1986.* Washington, D.C.: World Priorities, 1986.

Sutcliffe, Robert. *Industrialization and Underdevelopment.* Reading, Mass.: Addison-Wesley, 1971.

Szentes, Tamas. *The Political Economy of Underdevelopment.* Budapest:Akamemiai Kiado, 1973.

Third World Studies Staff. "The Philippines: Growth of Poverty." Unpublished paper, University of the Philippines, 1982.

World Bank Group. *Assault on World Poverty.* Baltimore, Md.: Johns Hopkins University Press, 1975.

Zimmerman, L. J. *Poor Lands, Rich Lands.* New York: Random House, 1965.

CHAPTER 15. LIBERTY, IMPERIALISM, AND DEPENDENCY

Agee, Philip. *Inside the Company: CIA Diary.* New York: Stonehill, 1975.

Birns, Lawrence, ed. *The End of Chilean Democracy.* New York: Seabury Press, 1974.

Cockcroft, James, A. G. Frank, and Dale Johnson. *Dependence and Underdevelopment.* Garden City, N.Y.: Anchor, 1972.

Evans, Peter. *Dependent Development: The Alliance of Multinational, State and Local Capital in Brazil.* Princeton, N.J.: Princeton University Press, 1979.

Gamer, Robert. *The Developing Nations.* Boston, Mass.: Allyn and Bacon, 1976.

Gonzalez Casanova, Pablo. *Democracy in Mexico*. London: Oxford University Press, 1970.

Hansen, Albert H., and Janet Douglas. *India's Democracy*. New York: Norton, 1972.

Hansen, Roger. *The Politics of Mexican Democracy*. Baltimore, Md.: Johns Hopkins University Press, 1974.

Hellman, Judith. *Mexico in Crisis*. New York: Holmes and Meier, 1983.

Klare, Michael. "The Military Research Network." In J. Leggett, ed., *Taking State Power*. New York: Harper and Row, 1973.

Kwitny, Jonathan. *Endless Enemies*. New York: Congdon and Weed, 1984.

Langguth, A. J. *Hidden Terrors: The Truth about U.S. Police Operations in Latin America*. New York: Pantheon, 1979.

Leggett, John, ed. *Taking State Power*. New York: Harper and Row, 1973.

Mydans, Seth. "Grenades and Shrapnel for the Priests Who Dare." *New York Times*, May 23, 1987.

Park, Richard, and Bruce Bueno de Mesquita. *India's Political System*. Englewood Cliffs, N.J.: Prentice-Hall, 1979.

Petras, James, and Morris Morley. *The United States and Chile*. New York: Monthly Review Press, 1975.

Prados, John. *Presidents' Secret Wars*. New York: Morrow, 1986.

Ranelagh, John. *The Agency: The Rise and Decline of the CIA*. New York: Simon and Schuster, 1986.

Roxborough, Ian, Philip O'Brien, and Jackie Roddick. *Chile: The State and Revolution*. New York: Holmes and Meier, 1977.

Sethi, J. D. *India in Crisis*. Delhi: Vikas Publishing House, 1974.

Sumberg, Theodore. "Freedom in the World." Monograph. Washington, D.C.: Center for Strategic and International Studies, 1975.

Taylor, Charles L., and Michael Hudson. *World Handbook of Political and Social Indicators*. 2d ed. New Haven, Conn.: Yale University Press, 1972.

Tobis, David. "Foreign Aid: The Case of Guatemala." In K. T. Fann and D. Hodges, eds., *Readings in U.S. Imperialism*. Boston, Mass.: Porter Sargent, 1971.

Weiner, Myron. *India at the Polls*. Washington, D.C.: American Enterprise Institute, 1978.

Wolfe, Alan. *The Seamy Side of Democracy*. New York: McKay, 1973.

Chapter 16. Quality of Life—Reactions to Dependency and Imperialism

Achebe, Chinua. *Things Fall Apart*. London: Heinemann, 1958.

Achebe, Chinua. *Morning Yet on Creation Day*. London: Heinemann, 1975.

Bell, Daniel. "Crime as an American Way of Life." *Antioch Review* (Summer 1953), 13:2.

Brandenburg, Frank. *The Making of Modern Mexico*. Englewood Cliffs, N.J.: Prentice-Hall, 1964.

Chaliand, Gerard. *Revolution in the Third World*. New York: Viking Press, 1978.

Clinard, Marshall, and David Abbott. *Crime in the Developing Countries*. New York: Wiley-Interscience, 1973.

Cornelius, Wayne. *Politics and the Migrant Poor in Mexico City*. Stanford, Calif.: Stanford University Press, 1975.

Enloe, Cynthia. *Ethnic Conflict and Political Development*. Boston, Mass.: Little Brown, 1973.

Evans, Peter. *Dependent Development: The Alliance of Multinational, State and Local Capital*. Princeton, N.J.: Princeton University Press, 1979.

Fanon, Frantz. *The Wretched of the Earth*. New York: Grove Press, 1968.

Fishlow, Albert, et al. *Rich and Poor Nations in the World Economy*. New York: McGraw-Hill, 1978.

Gamer, Robert. *The Developing Nations*. Boston, Mass.: Allyn and Bacon, 1976.

Goldthorpe, J. E. *Sociology of the Third World*. Cambridge: Cambridge University Press, 1975.

Gonzalez Casanova, Pablo. *Democracy in Mexico*. New York: Oxford University Press, 1970.

Heidenheimer, Arnold, ed. *Political Corruption*. New York: Holt, Rinehart and Winston, 1970.

Hermasi, Elbaki. *The Third World Reconsidered*. Berkeley: University of California Press, 1980.

Huntington, Samuel. *Political Order in Changing Societies*. New Haven, Conn.: Yale University Press, 1968.

Lewis, Oscar. *Five Families: Mexican Case Studies in the Culture of Poverty*. New York: Basic Books, 1959.

Myrdal, Gunnar. *Asian Drama*. New York: Twentieth Century Fund, 1968.

Nagle, John. *System and Succession: The Social Bases of Political Elite Recruitment*. Austin: University of Texas Press, 1977.

Naipaul, Vidiadhar S. *A Bend in the River*. New York: Knopf, 1979.

N'gugi Wa Thiog'o. *Petals of Blood*. London: Heinemann, 1977.

Peattie, Lisa R. *View from the Barrio*. Ann Arbor: University of Michigan Press, 1968.

Schramm, Wilbur. *Mass Media and National Development*. Stanford, Calif.: Stanford University Press, 1964.

Scott, James. *Comparative Political Corruption*. Englewood Cliffs, N.J.: Prentice-Hall, 1972.

Sewell, James. *The United States and World Development: Agenda for Action 1977*. New York: Praeger, 1977.

Sinclair, Stuart. *Urbanization and Labor Markets in Developing Countries*. New York: St. Martins Press, 1978.

Singh, Jyoti Shankar. *A New International Economic Order*. New York: Praeger, 1977.

Wolf, Eric, and Edward Hansen. *The Human Condition in Latin America*. New York: Oxford University Press, 1972.

Index

Abbott, David, 323
Abouchar, Alan, 144, 198
Adams, John, 19, 20
Adelman, Irma, 274, 277
Afghanistan, 286; Islamic rebellion in, 318, 325, 330, 331
Agee, Philip, 288
Allende, Salvador, 36, 227, 276, 287, 291–94
Amin, Idi, 227
Anderson, Bo, 296
Anderson, Odin, 51
Angola: civil war in, 287, 330, 331; MPLA victory; 134, 135, 141
Arendt, Hannah, 215
Argentina, 206, 207, 273
Ashton, T.S., 52, 53
Aspaturian, Vernon, 167, 168

Bacon, John, 81
Bairoch, Paul, 235, 236, 239, 242, 243, 246, 251, 252, 253
Bakunin, Mikhail, 121–22
Baran, Paul, 223, 274
Barner-Barry, Carole, 192–93, 202
Barnett, Richard, 262
Barry, Donald, 192–93, 202
Bejerot, Nils, 116–17
Bell, Daniel, 70, 101, 105, 106, 171, 314
Bernard, Jesse, 83
Bernstein, Eduard, 125, 128. *See also* Communism; Socialism
Bhagwati, Jagdish, 261, 262
Bienen, Henry, 274
Bismarck, Otto von, 26–27, 55–56
Blyakman, L., 203
Bodenheimer, Suzanne, 281
Borlaug, Norman, 237
Bottomore, T.B., 78
Bourgiba, Habib, 207
Bracher, Karl Dietrich, 29
Brandenburg, Frank, 312
Brazil, 249, 254, 259, 285; economy of, 280, 281, 326; housing in, 257-

58; income distribution in, 274
Brogan, D.W., 21
Brown, Lester, 237, 238, 265
Brezhnev, Leonid, 181–83
Brzezinski, Zbigniew, 168
Burma, 328
Bush, Keith, 199

Calcutta, 257
Calder, Nigel, 251
Cambodia, 134, 140, 230, 330, 331
Cantril, Hadley, 106
Castro, Fidel, 287, 330
Chaliand, Gerard, 276, 281, 313
Chalidze, Valery, 195
Chapman, Janet, 164
Chile: and Allende government, 291–94; CIA and, 276, 287; demise of democracy in, 36, 221, 300
China, People's Republic of: at Bandung, 210, 211; crime in, 192, 193; education in, 152–53; elite recruitment in, 170–71; health care in, 156; housing in, 158; income distribution in, 164; and Maoist program, 135, 137, 147–48; personal liberty in, 185–87; post-Mao economy of, 148–49, 150, 199; and split with USSR, 135; unemployment in, 199
CIA (Central Intelligence Agency), 276, 287–88, 290, 292
Civil rights movement (U.S.), 91–93
Clinard, Marshall, 81, 323
Club of Rome, 266–67
Cockcroft, James, 225, 280, 296
Cohen, David, 73
Commoner, Barry, 115
Communism: and alienation, 202–4; in comparative studies, 2–3, 6; and crime, 191–96; and economic growth, 143–49; and education, 152–54, 165–68; and elite recruitment, 168–71; employment under, 198–99; and family life,

349